SACRED TEXTS

THE
CONFESSIONS OF
ST. AUGUSTINE

Spiritual Meditations
and Divine Insights

Translated by E.B. Pusey

Introduction to this edition by
Revd Canon Dr Philip D. Noble

WATKINS PUBLISHING
LONDON

This translation of *The Confessions of St. Augustine*
was first published in 1904

This edition produced in 2006 for Sacred Texts,
an imprint of Watkins Publishing
Sixth Floor, Castle House, 75–76 Wells Street,
London W1T 3QH

1 3 5 7 9 10 8 6 4 2

Designed in Great Britain by Jerry Goldie
Typeset in Great Britain by Dorchester Typesetting Group
Printed and bound in Thailand by Imago

British Library Cataloguing-in-Publication data available

ISBN-10: 1-84293-199-7
ISBN-13: 9-781842-931998

www.watkinspublishing.com

CONTENTS

BOOK IV

BOOK V

BOOK VIII

BOOK IX

BOOK X

BOOK XI

BOOK XII

always beholding His countenance; "earth," the formless matter whereof the corporeal creation was afterwards formed. He does not reject, however, other interpretations, which he adduces, but rather confesses that such is the depth of Holy Scripture, that manifold senses may and ought to be extracted from it, and that whatever truth can be obtained from its words, does, in fact, lie concealed in them

INTRODUCTION

Augustine, one of the great Latin Fathers of the Church, was born in 354 in Tagaste, North Africa. Highly intelligent, he was brought up as a Christian under the influence of his devout mother, Monica, who is recognized as a saint in her own right. He lost his faith at an early age, however, and led a wild life, full of false beliefs. Augustine moved to the city of Carthage, "a cauldron of unholy loves", as he puts it, to become a teacher of rhetoric. While there he came upon Cicero's book *Hortensius*, which urged the reader not to be satisfied with one particular version of truth but, rather, to seek absolute wisdom. This became Augustine's quest.

Augustine attempted to read the scriptures but, due to the combination of a poor Latin translation and personal arrogance, he dismissed them as worthless in his pursuit of wisdom. During this period he took a Carthaginian woman, whom he never names, as his concubine and remained faithful to her for fifteen years, having a son by her. In this relationship Augustine painfully experienced the difference between the marriage covenant and lustful love.

After investigating and experimenting with several philosophies, Augustine became a Manichaean, a member of the religious sect founded by Mani, a Persian painter, who declared himself to be the other Comforter promised by Jesus Christ. Manichaeism was based on a dualistic view of nature, regarding God as good but not omnipotent. This view is prevalent in much of today's popular culture. The original *Star Wars* trilogy, for example, is decidedly Manichaean in its presentation.

Disturbed by the unruly behaviour of the students in Carthage, Augustine decided to move to Rome where the students were reputedly better behaved. While this proved to be true, these same students had the bad habit of not paying their teachers, which distressed him greatly. During his time in Rome, Augustine once again became disillusioned with his "panting after honours", as he called it, and turned to the philosophy of Platonism. This, however, he found to be an unsatisfying answer to his quest.

By this time Augustine was gradually being drawn towards the Christian faith, but conversion was no simple process for him. On moving to Milan, he met Ambrose, then bishop of that city, and was impressed by his kind demeanour and rhetorical skills. Although Augustine's mind became convinced by Ambrose's preaching, his passions remained untamed.

His conversion eventually took place in 387, under a fig tree in the spacious garden attached to his lodging house. Augustine had been weeping profusely out of desperation when he heard a voice say, "Take up and read." On opening the Bible, his eyes fell on verses 13 and 14 from chapter 13 of Paul's letter to the Romans:

Not in rioting and drunkenness, not in
chambering and wantonness,
not in strife and envying; but put ye on the Lord
Jesus Christ.

Before he had finished reading, the darkness of doubt
had vanished; soon after he was baptized by Bishop
Ambrose. Augustine was ordained priest at Hippo in
North Africa in 391 and was made bishop four years later.

Augustine's *Confessions* were written between 397 and
400 in the form of thirteen short books, and have spoken
powerfully to many generations for over sixteen centuries.
His stated intention in writing them was to make a
confession of both God's goodness and his own weakness.
The first ten books form an autobiography up to the time
of his conversion, while the last three contain an allegor-
ical explanation of the Mosaic account of Creation.

This edition of the *Confessions* has value on three
levels. Firstly, it is an accurate record of the text of one
of the most highly revered of all the Christian classics.
Secondly, it is brimful of fascinating detail relating to
family life, relationships, travel, education and the
workings of the state. It reveals many sociological
parallels to the present day, such as the problem of evil,
the need for self-discipline, the role of the family and
the valuing of form over content. Thirdly, this particular
translation by Edward Bouverie Pusey (1800–82) is a
groundbreaking book in its own right. At the time of
publication, Pusey, a brilliant scholar and linguist, was

one of the most influential figures in the Anglican Church. He was a friend of John Henry Newman and a leader in the Oxford Movement, which strove to reform the Church in England through, among other things, a study of the ancient Christian tradition. Published in 1838, Augustine's *Confessions* was the very first of the 48 works of the Church fathers to be translated.

In his preface Pusey explains why he has attempted to present the text in an unmodified form:

> The additional pains which might be requisite to understand [the text] would be rewarded by the greater insight into the author's uncommented meaning . . . and let St. Augustine speak . . . the truths which he wrapped up in the words for those who wished to find them.

Pusey's use of the word "speak" is significant, for Augustine is in essence an orator rather than a writer, and his *Confessions* are best regarded as a prayerful conversation with God rather than a theological treatise. Whereas today reading tends to be a silent pursuit, for many centuries Augustine's *Confessions* would have been *heard* rather than read.

The narrative that follows is, in essence, a complex and compelling love story. It is a story of the love of self, the love of others – both sensual and sexual – and the love of God. Such a story can be read with profit over and over again in any age.

Revd Canon Dr Philip D. Noble

Confessions of the greatness and unsearchableness of God, of God's mercies in infancy and boyhood, and human wilfulness; of his own sins of idleness, abuse of his studies, and of God's gifts up to his fifteenth year.

[I] 1 *Great art Thou, O Lord, and greatly to be praised; great is Thy power, and Thy wisdom infinite.* And Thee would man praise; man, but a particle of Thy creation; man, that bears about him his mortality, the witness of his sin, the witness, that *Thou resistest the proud:* yet would man praise Thee; he, but a particle of Thy creation. Thou awakest us to delight in Thy praise; for Thou madest us for Thyself, and our heart is restless, until it repose in Thee. Grant me, Lord, to know and understand which is first, to call on Thee or to praise Thee? and, again, to know Thee or to call on Thee? For who can call on Thee, not knowing Thee? For he that knoweth Thee not, may call on Thee as other than Thou art. Or, is it rather, that we call on Thee that we may know Thee? But *how shall they call on Him in whom they have not believed? or how shall they believe without a preacher?* And *they that seek the Lord shall praise Him.* For *they that seek shall find Him,* and they that find shall praise Him. I will seek Thee, Lord, by calling on Thee; and will call on Thee, believing in Thee; for to us hast Thou been preached. My faith, Lord, shall call on Thee, which Thou hast given me, wherewith Thou hast inspired me, through the Incarnation of Thy Son, through the ministry of the Preacher.[1]

[II] 2 And how shall I call upon my God, my God and Lord, since, when I call for Him, I shall be calling Him to myself? and what room is there within me, whither my God can come into me? Whither can God come into me, God who made heaven and earth? Is there, indeed, O Lord my God, aught in me that can contain Thee? Do then heaven and earth, which Thou hast made, and wherein Thou hast made me, contain Thee? or, because nothing which exists could exist without Thee, doth therefore whatever exists contain Thee? Since, then, I too exist, why do I seek that Thou shouldest enter into me, who were not, wert Thou not in me? Why? Because I am not gone down in hell, and yet Thou art there also. For *if I go down into hell, Thou art there*. I could not be then, O my God, could not be at all, wert Thou not in me; or, rather, unless I were in Thee, *of whom are all things, by whom are all things, in whom are all things?* Even so, Lord, even so. Whither do I call Thee, since I am in Thee? or whence canst Thou enter into me? For whither can I go beyond heaven and earth, that thence my God should come into me, who hath said, *I fill the heaven and the earth?*

[III] 3 Do[2] the heaven and earth then contain Thee, since Thou fillest them? or dost Thou fill them and yet overflow, since they do not contain Thee? And whither, when the heaven and the earth are filled, pourest Thou forth the remainder of Thyself? Or hast Thou no need that aught contain Thee, who containest all things, since what Thou fillest Thou fillest by containing it? For the vessels which Thou fillest uphold Thee not, since, though they were broken, Thou wert not poured out. And when Thou art *poured out* on us, Thou art not cast down, but Thou upliftest us; Thou art not dissipated, but Thou gatherest us. But Thou who fillest all things, fillest Thou them with Thy whole self? or, since all things cannot contain Thee wholly, do they contain part of Thee? and all at once the same part? or each its own part, the greater more, the smaller less? And is, then, one part of Thee greater, another less? or, art Thou wholly every where, while nothing contains Thee wholly?

[IV] 4 What art Thou then, my God? What, but the Lord God? *For who is Lord but the Lord? or who is God save our God?* Most highest, most good, most potent, most omnipotent; most merciful, yet most just; most hidden, yet most present; most beautiful, yet most strong; stable, yet incomprehensible; unchangeable, yet all-changing; never new, never old; all-renewing, and *bringing age upon the proud, and they know it not*; ever working, ever at rest; still gathering, yet nothing lacking; supporting, filling, and over-spreading; creating, nourishing, and maturing; seeking, yet having all things. Thou lovest, without passion; art jealous, without anxiety; repentest, yet grievest not; art angry, yet serene; changest Thy works, Thy purpose unchanged; receivest again what Thou findest, yet didst never lose; never in need, yet rejoicing in gains; never covetous, yet exacting usury. Thou receivest over and above, that Thou mayest owe; and who hath aught that is not Thine? Thou payest debts, owing nothing; remittest debts, losing nothing. And what have I now said, my God, my life, my holy joy? or what saith any man when he speaks of Thee? Yet woe to him that speaketh not, since mute are even the most eloquent.

[V] 5 Oh! that I might repose on Thee! Oh! that Thou wouldest enter into my heart, and inebriate it, that I may forget my ills, and embrace Thee, my sole good? What art Thou to me? In Thy pity, teach me to utter it. Or what am I to Thee that Thou demandest my love, and, if I give it not, are wroth with me, and threatenest me with grievous woes? Is it then a slight woe to love Thee not? Oh! for Thy mercies' sake, tell me, O Lord my God, what Thou art unto me. *Say unto my soul, I am thy salvation.* So speak, that I may hear. Behold, Lord, my heart is before Thee; open Thou the ears thereof, and *say unto my soul, I am thy salvation.* After this voice let me haste, and take hold on Thee. Hide not Thy face from me. Let me die[3]—lest I die—only let me see Thy face.

6 Narrow is the mansion of my soul; enlarge Thou it, that Thou mayest enter in. It is ruinous; repair Thou it. It has that within which must offend Thine eyes; I confess and know it. But who shall cleanse it? or to whom should I cry, save Thee? *Lord, cleanse me from my secret faults, and spare Thy servant from the power of the enemy.*[4] I believe, and therefore do I speak. Lord, Thou knowest. *Have I not*

confessed against myself my transgressions unto Thee, and Thou, my God, hast forgiven the iniquity of my heart? I *contend not in judgment with Thee*, who art the truth; I fear to deceive myself; *lest mine iniquity lie unto itself.* Therefore I contend not in judgment with Thee; *for if Thou, Lord, shouldest mark iniquities, O Lord, who shall abide it?*

[VI] 7 Yet suffer me to speak unto Thy mercy, me, *dust and ashes*. Yet suffer me to speak, since I speak to Thy mercy, and not to scornful man. Thou too, perhaps, despisest me, yet wilt Thou *return and have compassion* upon me. For what would I say, O Lord my God, but that I know not whence I came into this dying life (shall I call it?) or living death. Then immediately did the comforts of Thy compassion take me up, as I heard (for I remember it not) from the parents of my flesh, out of whose substance Thou didst sometime fashion me. Thus there received me the comforts of woman's milk. For neither my mother nor my nurses stored their own breasts for me; but Thou didst bestow the food of my infancy through them, according to Thine ordinance, whereby Thou distributest Thy riches through the hidden springs of all things. Thou also gavest me to desire no more than Thou gavest; and to my nurses willingly to give me what Thou gavest them. For they, with an heaven-taught affection, willingly gave me, what they abounded with from Thee. For this my good from them, was good for them. Nor, indeed, from them was it, but through them; for from Thee, O God, are all good things, and *from my God is all my health*. This I since learned, Thou, through these Thy gifts, within me and without, proclaiming Thyself unto me. For then I knew but to suck; to repose in what pleased, and cry at what offended my flesh; nothing more.

8 Afterwards I began to smile; first in sleep, then waking: for so it was told me of myself, and I believed it; for we see the like in other infants, though of myself I remember it not. Thus, little by little, I became conscious where I was; and to have a wish to express my wishes to those who could content them, and I could not; for the wishes were within me, and they without; nor could they by any sense of theirs enter within my spirit. So I flung about at random limbs and voice, making the few signs I could, and such as I could, like, though in truth very little like, what I wished. And when I was not presently obeyed, (my wishes being hurtful or unintelligible,) then I was indignant with my elders for not submitting to me, with those owing me no service, for not serving me; and avenged myself on them by tears. Such have I learnt infants to be from observing them; and, that I was myself such, they, all unconscious, have shewn me better than my nurses who knew it.

9 And, lo! my infancy died long since, and I live. But Thou, Lord, who for ever livest, and in whom nothing dies: for before the foundation of the worlds, and before all that can be called "before," Thou art, and art God and Lord of all which Thou hast created: in Thee abide, fixed for ever, the first causes of all things unabiding; and of all things changeable, the springs abide in Thee

unchangeable: and in Thee live the eternal reasons of all things unreasoning and temporal. Say, Lord, to me, Thy suppliant; say, all-pitying, to me, Thy pitiable one; say, did my infancy succeed another age of mine that died before it? Was it that which I spent within my mother's womb? for of that I have heard somewhat, and have myself seen women with child? and what before that life again, O God my joy, was I any where or any body? For this have I none to tell me, neither father nor mother, nor experience of others, nor mine own memory. Dost Thou mock me for asking this, and bid me praise Thee and acknowledge Thee, for that I do know?

10 I acknowledge Thee, Lord of heaven and earth, and praise Thee for my first rudiments of being, and my infancy, whereof I remember nothing; for Thou hast appointed that man should from others guess much as to himself; and believe much on the strength of weak females. Even then I had being and life, and (at my infancy's close) I could seek for signs, whereby to make known to others my sensations. Whence could such a being be, save from Thee, Lord? Shall any be his own artificer? Or can there elsewhere be derived any vein, which may stream essence and life into us, save from Thee, O Lord, in whom essence and life are one? for Thou Thyself art supremely Essence and Life. *For Thou art most high, and art not changed*, neither in Thee doth To-day come to a close; yet in Thee doth it come to a close; because all such things also are in Thee. For they had no way to pass away, unless Thou up-heldest them. And since *Thy years fail not*, Thy years are one To-day. How many

of ours and our fathers' years have flowed away through Thy "to-day," and from it received the measure and the mould of such being as they had; and still others shall flow away, and so receive the mould of their degree of being. But *Thou art still the same*, and all things of to-morrow, and all beyond, and all of yesterday, and all behind it, Thou hast done to-day. What is it to me, though any comprehend not this? Let him also rejoice and say, *What thing is this?* Let him rejoice even thus; and be content rather by not discovering to discover Thee, than by discovering not to discover Thee.

[VII] 11 Hear, O God. Alas, for man's sin! So saith man, and Thou pitiest him; for Thou madest him, but sin in him Thou madest not. Who remindeth me of the sins of my infancy? *for in Thy sight none is pure from sin, not even the infant whose life is but a day upon the earth.* Who remindeth me? Doth not each little infant, in whom I see what of myself I remember not? What then was my sin? Was it that I hung upon the breast and cried? For should I now so do for food suitable to my age, justly should I be laughed at and reproved. What I then did was worthy reproof; but since I could not understand reproof, custom and reason forbade me to be reproved. For those habits, when grown, we root out and cast away. Now no man, though he prunes, wittingly casts away what is good. Or was it then good, even for a while, to cry for what, if given, would hurt? bitterly to resent, that persons free, and its own elders, yea, the very authors of its birth, served it not? that many besides, wiser than it, obeyed not the nod of its good pleasure? to do its best to strike and hurt, because commands were not obeyed, which had been obeyed to its hurt? The weakness then of infant limbs, not its will, is its innocence. Myself have seen and known even a baby envious; it could not speak, yet it turned pale and looked bitterly on its foster-brother. Who knows not this? Mothers and nurses tell you, that they allay these things by I know not what remedies. Is that too innocence, when the fountain of milk is flowing in rich abundance, not to endure one to share it, though in extremest need, and whose very life as yet depends thereon? We bear gently with all this, not as being no or slight evils, but because they will disappear as years increase; for, though tolerated now, the very same tempers are utterly intolerable when found in riper years.

12 Thou, then, O Lord my God, who gavest life to this my infancy, furnishing thus with senses (as we see) the frame Thou gavest, compacting its limbs, ornamenting its proportions, and, for its general good and safety, implanting in it all vital functions, Thou commandest me to praise Thee in these things, *to confess unto Thee, and sing unto Thy name, Thou most Highest*. For Thou art God, Almighty and Good, even hadst Thou done nought but only this, which none could do but Thou: whose Unity is the mould of all things; who out of Thy own fairness makest all things fair; and orderest all things by Thy law. This age then, Lord, whereof I have no remembrance, which I take on others' word, and guess from other infants that I have passed, true though the guess be, I am yet loth to count in this life of mine which I live in this world. For no less than that which I spent in my mother's

womb, is it hid from me in the shadows of forgetfulness. But if *I was shapen in iniquity, and in sin did my mother conceive me,* where, I beseech Thee, O my God, where, Lord, or when, was I Thy servant guiltless? But, lo! that period I pass by; and what have I now to do with that, of which I can recal no vestige?

[VIII] 13 Passing hence from infancy, I came to boyhood, or rather it came to me, displacing infancy. Nor did that depart,—(for whither went it?)—and yet it was no more. For I was no longer a speechless infant, but a speaking boy. This I remember; and have since observed how I learned to speak. It was not that my elders taught me words (as, soon after, other learning) in any set method; but I, longing by cries and broken accents and various motions of my limbs to express my thoughts, that so I might have my will, and yet unable to express all I willed, or to whom I willed, did myself, by the understanding which Thou, my God, gavest me, practise the sounds in my memory. When they named any thing, and as they spoke turned towards it, I saw and remembered that they called what they would point out, by the name they uttered. And that they meant this thing and no other, was plain from the motion of their body, the natural language, as it were, of all nations, expressed by the coun-tenance, glances of the eye, gestures of the limbs, and tones of the voice, indicating the affections of the mind, as it pursues, possesses, rejects, or shuns. And thus by constantly hearing words, as they occurred in various sentences, I collected gradually for what they stood; and having broken in my mouth to these signs, I thereby gave utterance to my will. Thus I exchanged with those about me these current signs of our wills, and so launched deeper into the stormy intercourse of human life, yet depending on parental authority and the beck of elders.

[IX] 14 O God my God, what miseries and mockeries did I now experience, when obedience to my teachers was proposed to me, as proper in a boy, in order that in this world I might prosper, and excel in tongue-science, which should serve to the "praise of men," and to deceitful riches. Next I was put to school to get learning, in which I (poor wretch) knew not what use there was; and yet, if idle in learning, I was beaten. For this was judged right by our forefathers; and many, passing the same course before us, framed for us weary paths, through which we were fain to pass; multiplying toil and grief upon the sons of Adam. But, Lord, we found that men called upon Thee, and we learnt from them to think of Thee (according to our powers) as of some great One, who, though hidden from our senses, couldst hear and help us. For so I began, as a boy, to pray to Thee, my aid and refuge; and broke the fetters of my tongue to call on Thee, praying Thee, though small, yet with no small earnestness, that I might not be beaten at school. And when Thou heardest me not, (*not thereby giving me over to folly,*[3]) my elders, yea, my very parents, who yet wished me no ill, mocked my stripes, my then great and grievous ill.

15 Is there, Lord, any of soul so great, and cleaving to Thee with so intense affection, (for a sort of stupidity will in a way do it); but is there any one, who, from cleaving

devoutly to Thee, is endued with so great a spirit, that he can think as lightly of the racks and hooks and other torments, (against which, throughout all lands, men call on Thee with extreme dread,) mocking at those by whom they are feared most bitterly, as our parents mocked the torments which we suffered in boyhood from our masters? For we feared not our torments less; nor prayed we less to Thee to escape them. And yet we sinned, in writing or reading or studying less than was exacted of us. For we wanted not, O Lord, memory or capacity, whereof Thy will gave enough for our age; but our sole delight was play; and for this we were punished by those who yet themselves were doing the like. But elder folks' idleness is called "business"; that of boys, being really the same, is punished by those elders; and none commiserates either boys or men. For will any of sound discretion approve of my being beaten as a boy, because, by playing at ball, I made less progress in studies which I was to learn, only that, as a man, I might play more unbeseem-ingly? And what else did he, who beat me? who, if worsted in some trifling discussion with his fellow-tutor, was more embittered and jealous than I, when beaten at ball by a play-fellow?

[X] 16 And yet, I sinned herein, O Lord God, the Creator and Disposer of all things in nature, of sin the Disposer only, O Lord my God, I sinned in transgressing the commands of my parents and those of my masters. For what they, with whatever motive, would have me learn, I might afterward have put to good use. For I disobeyed, not from a better choice, but from love of play, loving the pride of victory in my contests, and to have my ears tickled with lying fables, that they might itch the more; the same curiosity flashing from my eyes more and more, for the shows and games of my elders. Yet those who give these shows are in such esteem, that almost all wish the same for their children, and yet are very willing that they should be beaten, if those very games detain them from the studies, whereby they would have them attain to be the givers of them. Look with pity, Lord, on these things, and deliver us who call upon Thee now; deliver those too who call not on Thee yet, that they may call on Thee, and Thou mayest deliver them.

[XI] 17 As a boy, then, I had already heard of an eternal life, promised us through the humility of the Lord our God stooping to our pride; and even from the womb of my mother, who greatly hoped in Thee, I was sealed with the mark of His cross and salted with His salt.[6] Thou sawest, Lord, how while yet a boy, being seized on a time with sudden oppression of the stomach, and like near to death—Thou sawest, my God, (for Thou wert my keeper), with what eagerness and what faith I sought, from the pious care of my mother and Thy Church, the mother of us all, the baptism of Thy Christ my God and Lord. Whereupon the mother of my flesh, being much troubled, (since, with a heart pure in Thy faith, she even more lovingly *travailed in birth* of my salvation,) would in eager haste have provided for my consecration and cleansing by the healthgiving sacraments, confessing Thee, Lord Jesus, for the remission of sins, unless I had suddenly recovered. And so, as if I must needs be again polluted should I live, my cleansing was deferred, because the defilements of sin would, after that washing, bring greater and more perilous guilt. I then already believed; and my mother, and the whole household, except my father: yet did not he prevail over the power of my mother's piety in me, that as he did not yet believe, so neither should I. For it was her earnest care, that Thou my God, rather than he, shouldest be my father; and in this Thou didst aid her to prevail over her husband, whom she, the better, obeyed, therein also obeying Thee, who hast so commanded.

18 I beseech Thee, my God, I would fain know, if so Thou willest, for what purpose my baptism was then deferred? Was it for my good that the rein was laid loose, as it were, upon me, for me to sin? or was it not laid loose? If not, why does it still echo in our ears on all sides, "Let him alone, let him do as he will, for he is not yet baptized?" but as to bodily health, no one says, "Let him be worse wounded, for he is not yet healed." How much better then, had I been at once healed; and then, by my friends' diligence and my own, my soul's recovered health had been kept safe in Thy keeping who gavest it. Better truly. But how many and great waves of temptation seemed to hang over me after my boyhood! These my mother foresaw; and preferred to expose to them the clay whence I might afterwards be moulded, than the very cast, when made.[7]

[XII] 19 In boyhood itself, however, (so much less dreaded for me than youth,) I loved not study, and hated to be forced to it. Yet I was forced; and this was well done towards me, but I did not well; for, unless forced, I had not learnt. But no one doth well against his will, even though what he doth, be well. Yet neither did they well who forced me, but what was well came to me from Thee, my God. For they were regardless how I should employ what they forced me to learn, except to satiate the insatiate desires of a wealthy beggary, and a shameful glory. But Thou, *by whom the very hairs of our head are numbered*, didst use for my good the error of all who urged me to learn; and my own, who would not learn, Thou didst use for my punishment—a fit penalty for one, so small a boy and so great a sinner. So by those who did not well, Thou didst well for me; and by my own sin Thou didst justly punish me. For Thou hast commanded, and so it is, that every inordinate affection should be its own punishment.

[XIII] 20 But why did I so much hate the Greek, which I studied as a boy? I do not yet fully know. For the Latin I loved; not what my first masters, but what the so-called grammarians taught me. For those first lessons, reading, writing, and arithmetic, I thought as great a burden and penalty as any Greek. And yet whence was this too, but from the sin and vanity of this life, because *I was flesh, and a breath that passeth away and cometh not again*? For those first lessons were better certainly, because more certain; by them I obtained, and still retain, the power of reading what I find written, and myself writing what I will; whereas in the others, I was forced to learn the wanderings of one Æneas, forgetful of my own, and to weep for dead Dido, because she killed herself for love; the while, with dry eyes, I endured my miserable self dying among these things, far from Thee, O God my life.

21 For what more miserable than a miserable being who commiserates not himself; weeping the death of Dido for love to Æneas, but weeping not his own death for want of love to Thee, O God. Thou light of my heart, Thou bread of my inmost soul, Thou Power who givest vigour to my mind, who quickenest my thoughts, I loved Thee not. I committed fornication against Thee, and all around me thus fornicating there echoed "Well done! well done!" *for the friendship of this world is fornication against Thee;* and "Well done! well done!" echoes on till one is ashamed not to be thus a man. And all this I wept not, I who wept for Dido slain, and "seeking by the sword a stroke and wound extreme," myself seeking the while a worse extreme, the extremest and lowest of Thy creatures, having forsaken Thee, earth passing into the earth. And if forbid to read all this, I was grieved that I might not read what grieved me. Madness like this is thought a higher and a richer learning, than that by which I learned to read and write.

22 But now, my God, cry Thou aloud in my soul; and let Thy truth tell me, "Not so, not so. Far better was that first study." For, lo, I would readily forget the wanderings of Æneas and all the rest, rather than how to read and write. But over the entrance of the Grammar School is a vail[8] drawn! true; yet is this not so much an emblem of aught recondite, as a cloke of error. Let not those, whom I no longer fear, cry out against me, while I confess to Thee, my God, whatever my soul will, and acquiesce in the con-

demnation of my evil ways, that I may love Thy good ways.
Let not either buyers or sellers of grammar-learning cry out
against me. For if I question them whether it be true, that
Æneas came on a time to Carthage, as the Poet tells, the less
learned will reply that they know not, the more learned
that he never did. But should I ask with what letters the
name "Æneas" is written, every one who has learnt this
will answer me aright, as to the signs which men have con-
ventionally settled. If, again, I should ask, which might be
forgotten with least detriment to the concerns of life,
reading and writing or these poetic fictions? who does not
foresee, what all must answer who have not wholly
forgotten themselves? I sinned, then, when as a boy I
preferred those empty to those more profitable studies, or
rather loved the one and hated the other. "One and one,
two;" "two and two, four;" this was to me a hateful sing-
song: "the wooden horse lined with armed men," and "the
burning of Troy," and "Creusa's shade and sad similitude,"
were the choice spectacle of my vanity.

[XIV] 23 Why then did I hate the Greek classics, which
have the like tales? For Homer also curiously wove the like
fictions, and is most sweetly-vain, yet was he bitter to my
boyish taste. And so I suppose would Virgil be to Grecian
children, when forced to learn him as I was Homer.
Difficulty, in truth, the difficulty of a foreign tongue,
dashed, as it were, with gall all the sweetness of Grecian
fable. For not one word of it did I understand, and to
make me understand I was urged vehemently with cruel
threats and punishments. Time was also, (as an infant,) I
knew no Latin; but this I learned without fear of

suffering, by mere observation, amid the caresses of my nursery and jests of friends, smiling and sportively encouraging me. This I learned without any pressure of punishment to urge me on, for my heart urged me to give birth to its conceptions, which I could only do by learning words not of those who taught, but of those who talked with me; in whose ears also I gave birth to the thoughts, whatever I conceived. No doubt then, that a free curiosity has more force in our learning these things, than a frightful enforcement. Only this enforcement restrains the rovings of that freedom, through Thy laws, O my God, Thy laws, from the master's cane to the martyr's trials, being able to temper for us a wholesome bitter, recalling us to Thyself from that deadly pleasure which lures us from Thee.

[XV] 24 Hear, Lord, my prayer; let not my soul faint under Thy discipline, nor let me faint in confessing unto Thee all Thy mercies, whereby Thou hast drawn me out of all my most evil ways, that Thou mightest become a delight to me above all the allurements which I once pursued; that I may most entirely love Thee, and clasp Thy hand with all my affections, and Thou mayest yet rescue me from every temptation, even unto the end. For, lo, O Lord, my King and my God, for Thy service be whatever useful thing my childhood learned; for Thy service, that I speak—write—read—reckon. For Thou didst grant me Thy discipline, while I was learning vanities; and my sin of delighting in those vanities Thou hast forgiven. In them, indeed, I learnt many a useful word, but these may as well be learned in things not vain; and that is the safe path for the steps of youth.

[XVI] 25 But woe is thee, thou torrent of human custom! Who shall stand against thee? How long shalt thou not be dried up? How long roll the sons of Eve into that huge and hideous ocean, which even they scarcely overpass who climb the cross? Did not I read in thee of Jove the thunderer and the adulterer? Both, doubtless, he could not be; but so the feigned thunder might countenance and pander to real adultery. And now which of our gowned masters, lends a sober ear to one[9] who from their own school cries out, "These were Homer's fictions, transferring things human to the gods; would he had brought down things divine to us!" Yet more truly had he said, "These are indeed his fictions; but attributing a divine nature to wicked men, that crimes might be no longer crimes, and whoso commits them might seem to imitate not abandoned men, but the celestial gods."

26 And yet, thou hellish torrent, into thee are cast the sons of men with rich rewards, for compassing such learning; and a great solemnity is made of it, when this is going on in the forum, within sight of laws appointing a salary beside the scholar's payments; and thou lashest thy rocks and roarest, "Hence words are learnt; hence eloquence; most necessary to gain your ends, or maintain opinions." As if we should have never known such words as "golden shower," "lap," "beguile," "temples of the heavens," or others in that passage, unless Terence had brought a lewd youth upon the stage, setting up Jupiter as his example of seduction.[10]

> *Viewing a picture, where the tale was drawn,*
>
> *Of Jove's descending in a golden shower*
>
> *To Danae's lap, a woman to beguile.*

And then mark how he excites himself to lust as by celestial authority;

> *And what God? Great Jove,*
>
> *Who shakes heav'n's highest temples with his thunder,*
>
> *And I, poor mortal man, not do the same!*
>
> *I did it, and with all my heart I did it.*

Not one whit more easily are the words learnt for all this vileness; but by their means the vileness is committed with less shame. Not that I blame the words, being, as it were, choice and precious vessels; but that wine of error which is drunk to us in them by intoxicated teachers; and if we, too, drink not, we are beaten, and have no sober judge to whom we may appeal. Yet, O my God, (in whose presence I now without hurt may remember this,) all this unhappily I learnt willingly with great delight, and for this was pronounced a hopeful boy.

[XVII] 27 Bear with me, my God, while I say somewhat of my wit, Thy gift, and on what dotages I wasted it. For a task was set me, troublesome enough to my soul, upon terms of praise or shame, and fear of stripes, to speak the words of Juno, as she raged and mourned that she could not

This Trojan prince from Ladum turn.

Which words I had heard that Juno never uttered; but we were forced to go astray in the footsteps of these poetic fictions, and to say in prose much what he expressed in verse. And his speaking was most applauded, in whom the passions of rage and grief were most pre-eminent, and clothed in the most fitting language, maintaining the dignity of the character. What is it to me, O my true life, my God, that my declamation was applauded above so many of my own age and class? Is not all this smoke and wind? And was there nothing else whereon to exercise my wit and tongue? Thy praises, Lord, Thy praises might have stayed the yet tender shoot of my heart by the prop of Thy Scriptures; so had it not trailed away amid these empty trifles, a defiled prey for the fowls of the air. For in more ways than one do men sacrifice to the rebellious angels.

[XVIII] 28 But what marvel that I was thus carried away to vanities, and went out from Thy presence, O my God, when men were set before me as models, who, if in relating some action of theirs, in itself not ill, they committed some barbarism or solecism, being censured, were abashed; but when in rich and adorned and well-ordered discourse they related their own disordered life, being bepraised, they gloried? These things Thou seest, Lord, and holdest Thy peace; *long-suffering, and plenteous in mercy and truth*. Wilt Thou hold Thy peace for ever? And even now Thou drawest out of this horrible gulf the soul that seeketh Thee, that thirsteth for Thy pleasures, *whose heart saith unto Thee, I have sought Thy face; Thy face, Lord, will I seek*. For *darkened* affections is removal from Thee. For it is not by our feet, or change of place, that men leave Thee, or return unto Thee. Or did that Thy younger son look out for horses or chariots, or ships, fly with visible wings, or journey by the motion of his limbs, that he might in a far country waste in riotous living all Thou gavest at his departure? A loving Father, when Thou gavest, and more loving unto him, when he returned empty. So then in lustful, that is, in darkened affections, is the true distance from Thy face.

29 Behold, O Lord God, yea, behold patiently as Thou art wont, how carefully the sons of men observe the covenanted rules of letters and syllables received from those who spake before them, neglecting the eternal covenant of everlasting salvation received from Thee. Insomuch, that a teacher or learner of the hereditary laws of pronunciation will more offend men, by speaking without the aspirate, of a "*uman* being," in despite of the laws of grammar, than if he, a "human being," hate a "human being" in despite of Thine. As if any enemy could be more hurtful than the hatred with which he is incensed against him; or could wound more deeply him whom he persecutes, than he wounds his own soul by his enmity. Assuredly no science of letters can be so innate as the record of conscience, "that he is doing to another what from another he would be loth to suffer." How deep are Thy ways, O God, Thou only great, *that sittest* silent *on high* and by an unwearied law dispensing penal blindness to lawless desires. In quest of the fame of eloquence, a man standing before a human judge,

surrounded by a human throng, declaiming against his enemy with fiercest hatred, will take heed most watchfully, lest, by an error of the tongue, he murder the word "human-being;" but takes no heed, lest, through the fury of his spirit, he murder the real human being."

30 This was the world at whose gate unhappy I lay in my boyhood; this the stage, where I had feared more to commit a barbarism, than having committed one, to envy those who had not. These things I speak and confess to Thee, my God; for which I had praise from them, whom I then thought it all virtue to please. For I saw not the abyss of vileness, wherein *I was cast away from Thine eyes*. Before them what more foul than I was already, dis-pleasing even such as myself? with innumerable lies deceiving my tutor, my masters, my parents, from love of play, eagerness to see vain shows, and restlessness to imitate them! Thefts also I committed, from my parents' cellar and table, enslaved by greediness, or that I might have to give to boys, who sold me their play, which all the while they liked no less than I. In this play, too, I often sought unfair conquests, conquered myself meanwhile by vain desire of pre-eminence. And what could I so ill endure, or, when I detected it, upbraided I so fiercely, as that I was doing to others? and for which if, detected, I was upbraided, I chose rather to quarrel, than to yield. And is this the innocence of boyhood? Not so, Lord, not so; I cry Thy mercy, O my God. For these very sins, as riper years succeed, these very sins are transferred from tutors and masters, from nuts and balls and sparrows, to magistrates and kings, to gold and manors and slaves, just

as severer punishments displace the cane. It was the low stature then of childhood, which Thou our King didst commend as an emblem of lowliness, when Thou saidst, *Of such is the kingdom of heaven.*

31 Yet, Lord, to Thee, the Creator and Governor of the universe, most excellent and most good, thanks were due to Thee our God, even hadst Thou destined for me boyhood only. For even then I was, I lived, and felt; and had an implanted providence over my own well-being,—a trace of that mysterious Unity,[12] whence I was derived;—I guarded by the inward sense the entireness of my senses, and in these minute pursuits, and in my thoughts on things minute, I learnt to delight in truth, I hated to be deceived, had a vigorous memory, was gifted with speech, was soothed by friendship, avoided pain, baseness, ignorance. In so small a creature, what was not wonderful, not admirable? But all are gifts of my God; it was not I, who gave them me; and good these are, and these together are myself. Good, then, is He that made me, and He is my good; and before Him will I exult for every good which of a boy I had. For it was sin, that not in Him, but in His creatures— myself and others—I sought for pleasures, sublimities, truths, and so fell headlong into sorrows, confusions, errors. Thanks be to Thee, my joy and my glory and my confidence, my God, thanks be to Thee for Thy gifts; but do Thou preserve them to me. For so wilt Thou preserve me, and those things shall be enlarged and perfected, which Thou hast given me, and I myself shall be with Thee, since even to be Thou hast given me.

BOOK II

O bject of these Confessions. Further ills of idleness developed in his sixteenth year. Evils of ill society, which betrayed him into theft.

[II] 1 I will now call to mind my past foulness, and the carnal corruptions of my soul: not because I love them, but that I may love Thee, O my God. For love of Thy love I do it; reviewing my most wicked ways in the very bitterness of my remembrance, that Thou mayest grow sweet unto me; (Thou sweetness never failing, Thou blissful and assured sweetness;) and gathering me again out of that my dissipation, wherein I was torn piecemeal, while turned from Thee, the One Good, I lost myself among a multiplicity of things. For I even burnt in my youth heretofore, to be satiated in things below; and I dared to grow wild again, with these various and shadowy loves: *my beauty consumed away*, and I stank in Thine eyes; pleasing myself, and desirous to please in the eyes of men.

[II] 2 And what was it that I delighted in, but to love, and be beloved? but I kept not the measure of love, of mind to mind, friendship's bright boundary; but out of the muddy concupiscence of the flesh, and the bubblings of youth, mists fumed up which beclouded and overcast my heart, that I could not discern the clear brightness of love, from the fog of lustfulness. Both did confusedly boil in me, and hurried my unstayed youth over the precipice of unholy desires, and sunk me in a gulf of flagitiousnesses. Thy wrath had gathered over me, and I knew it not. I was grown deaf by the clanking of the chain of my mortality, the punishment of the pride of my soul, and I strayed further from Thee, and Thou lettest me alone, and I was tossed about, and wasted, and dissipated, and I boiled over in my fornications, and Thou heldest Thy peace, O Thou my tardy joy! Thou then heldest Thy peace, and I wandered further and further from Thee, into more and more fruitless seed-plots of sorrows, with a proud dejectedness, and a restless weariness.

3 Oh! that some one had then attempered my disorder, and turned to account the fleeting beauties of these, the extreme points of Thy creation! had put a bound to their pleasurableness, that so the tides of my youth might have cast themselves upon the marriage shore, if they could not be calmed, and kept within the object of a family, as Thy law prescribes, O Lord: who this way formest the offspring of this our death, being able with a gentle hand to blunt the thorns, which were excluded from Thy paradise? For Thy omnipotency is not far from us, even when we be far from Thee. Else ought I more watchfully to have heeded the voice from the clouds; *Nevertheless such shall have trouble in the flesh, but I spare you.* And, *it is good for a man not to touch a woman.* And, *he that is unmarried thinketh of the things of*

the Lord, how he may please the Lord; but he that is married careth for the things of this world, how he may please his wife.

4 To these words I should have listened more attentively, and being severed *for the kingdom of heaven's sake*, had more happily awaited Thy embraces; but I, poor wretch, foamed like a troubled sea, following the rushing of my own tide, forsaking Thee, and exceeded all Thy limits; yet I escaped not Thy scourges. For what mortal can? For Thou wert ever with me mercifully rigorous, and besprinkling with most bitter alloy all my unlawful pleasures; that I might seek pleasures without alloy. But where to find such, I could not discover, save in Thee, O Lord, who *teachest by sorrow*,[1] and woundest us, to heal; and killest us, lest we die from Thee. Where was I, and how far was I exiled from the delights of Thy house, in that sixteenth year of the age of my flesh, when the madness of lust (to which human shamelessness giveth free license, though unlicensed by Thy laws) took the rule over me, and I resigned myself wholly to it? My friends meanwhile took no care by marriage to save my fall; their only care was that I should learn to speak excellently, and be a persuasive orator.

[III] 5 For that year were my studies intermitted: whilst after my return from Madaura,[2] (a neighbour city, whither I had journeyed to learn grammar and rhetoric,) the expenses for a further journey to Carthage were being provided for me; and that, rather by the resolution than the means of my father, who was but a poor freeman of

Thagaste. To whom tell I this? not to Thee, my God; but before Thee to mine own kind, even to that small portion of mankind as may light upon these writings of mine. And to what purpose? that whosoever reads this, may think *out of what depths we are to cry unto Thee*. For what is nearer to Thine ears than a confessing heart, and a life of faith? Who did not extol my father, for that beyond the ability of his means, he would furnish his son with all necessaries for a far journey for his studies' sake? For many far abler citizens did no such thing for their children. But yet this same father had no concern, how I grew towards Thee, or how chaste I were; so that I were but copious in speech, however barren I were to Thy culture, O God, who art the only true and good Lord of Thy field, my heart.

6 But while in that my sixteenth year I lived with my parents, leaving all school for a while, (a season of idleness being interposed through the narrowness of my parents' fortunes,) the briers of unclean desires grew rank over my head, and there was no hand to root them out. When that my father saw me at the baths, now growing toward manhood, and endued with a restless youthfulness, he, as already hence anticipating his descendants, gladly told it to my mother; rejoicing in that tumult of the senses wherein the world forgetteth Thee its Creator, and becometh enamoured of Thy creature, instead of Thyself, through the fumes of that invisible wine of its self-will, turning aside and bowing down to the very basest things. But in my mother's breast Thou hadst already begun Thy temple, and the foundation of Thy holy habitation,

whereas my father was as yet but a catechumen, and that but recently. She then was startled with an holy fear and trembling; and though I was not as yet baptized, feared for me those crooked ways, in which they walk, who *turn their back to Thee, and not their face.*

7 Woe is me! and dare I say that Thou heldest Thy peace, O my God, while I wandered further from Thee? Didst Thou then indeed hold Thy peace to me? And whose but Thine were these words which by my mother, Thy faithful one, Thou sangest in my ears? Nothing whereof sunk into my heart, so as to do it. For she wished, and I remember in private with great anxiety warned me, "not to commit fornication; but especially never to defile another's wife." These seemed to me womanish advices, which I should blush to obey. But they were Thine, and I knew it not: and I thought Thou wert silent, and that it was she who spake; by whom Thou wert not silent unto me; and in her wast despised by me, her son, *the son of Thy handmaid, Thy servant.* But I knew it not; and ran headlong with such blindness, that amongst my equals I was ashamed of a less shamelessness, when I heard them boast of their flagitiousness, yea, and the more boasting, the more they were degraded: and I took pleasure, not only in the pleasure of the deed, but in the praise. What is worthy of dispraise but Vice? But I made myself worse than I was, that I might not be dispraised; and when in any thing I had not sinned as the abandoned ones, I would say that I had done what I had not done, that I might not seem contemptible in proportion as I was innocent; or of less account, the more chaste.

8 Behold with what companions I walked the streets of Babylon, and wallowed in the mire thereof, as if in a bed of spices, and precious ointments. And that I might cleave the faster to its very centre, the invisible enemy trod me down, and seduced me, for that I was easy to be seduced. Neither did the mother of my flesh, (who had now *fled out of the centre of Babylon*, yet went more slowly in the skirts thereof,) as she advised me to chastity, so heed what she had heard of me from her husband, as to restrain within the bounds of conjugal affection, (if it could not be pared away to the quick,) what she felt to be pestilent at present, and for the future dangerous. She heeded not this, for she feared, lest a wife should prove a clog and hindrance to my hopes. Not those hopes of the world to come, which my mother reposed in Thee; but the hope of learning, which both my parents were too desirous I should attain; my father, because he had next to no thought of Thee, and of me but vain conceits; my mother, because she accounted that those usual courses of learning would not only be no hindrance, but even some furtherance towards attaining Thee. For this I conjecture, recalling, as well as I may, the disposition of my parents. The reins, mean time, were slackened to me, beyond all temper of due severity, to spend my time in sport, yea, even unto dissoluteness in whatsoever I affected. And in all was a mist, intercepting from me, O my God, the brightness of Thy truth; and *mine iniquity burst out as from very fatness.*

[IV] 9 Theft is punished by Thy law, O Lord, and the law written in the hearts of men, which iniquity itself effaces not. For what thief will abide a thief? not even a rich thief, one stealing through want. Yet I lusted to thieve, and did it, compelled by no hunger, nor poverty, but through a cloyedness of welldoing, and a pamperedness of iniquity. For I stole that, of which I had enough, and much better. Nor cared I to enjoy what I stole, but joyed in the theft and sin itself. A pear tree there was near our vineyard, laden with fruit, tempting neither for colour nor taste. To shake and rob this, some lewd young fellows of us went, late one night, (having according to our pestilent custom prolonged our sports in the streets till then,) and took huge loads, not for our eating, but to fling to the very hogs, having only tasted them. And this, but to do, what we liked only, because it was misliked. Behold my heart, O God, behold my heart, which Thou hadst pity upon in the bottom of the bottomless pit. Now, behold let my heart tell Thee, what it sought there, that I should be gratuitously evil, having no temptation to ill, but the ill itself. It was foul, and I loved it; I loved to perish, I loved mine own fault, not that for which I was faulty, but my fault itself. Foul soul, falling from Thy firmament to utter destruction; not seeking aught through the shame, but the shame itself!

[V] 10 For there is an attractiveness in beautiful bodies, in gold and silver, and all things; and in bodily touch, sympathy hath much influence, and each other sense hath his proper object answerably tempered. Worldly honour hath also its grace, and the power of overcoming, and of mastery; whence springs also the thirst of revenge. But yet, to obtain all these, we may not depart from Thee, O Lord, nor decline from Thy law. The life also which here we live hath its own enchantment, through a certain proportion of its own, and a correspondence with all things beautiful here below. Human friendship also is endeared with a sweet tie, by reason of the unity formed of many souls. Upon occasion of all these, and the like, is sin committed, while through an immoderate inclination towards these goods of the lowest order, the better and higher are forsaken,—Thou, our Lord God, Thy truth, and Thy law. For these lower things have their delights, but not like my God, who made all things; for *in Him doth the righteous delight, and He is the joy of the upright in heart.*

11 When, then, we ask why a crime was done, we believe it not, unless it appear that there might have been some desire of obtaining some of those which we called lower goods, or a fear of losing them. For they are beautiful and comely; although compared with those higher and beatific goods, they be abject and low. A man hath murdered another; why? he loved his wife or his estate; or would rob for his own livelihood; or feared to lose some such thing by him; or, wronged, was on fire to be revenged. Would any commit murder upon no cause, delighted simply in murdering? Who would believe it? For as for that furious and savage man, of whom it is said that he was gratuitously evil and cruel, yet is the cause assigned;[3] "lest" (saith he) "through idleness hand or heart should grow inactive." And to what end? That,

through that practice of guilt, he might, having taken the city, attain to honours, empire, riches, and be freed from fear of the laws, and his embarrassments from domestic needs, and consciousness of villanies. So then, not even Catiline himself loved his own villanies, but something else, for whose sake he did them.

[VI] 12 What then did wretched I so love in thee, thou theft of mine, thou deed of darkness, in that sixteenth year of my age? Lovely thou wert not, because thou wert theft. But art thou any thing, that thus I speak to thee? Fair were the pears we stole, because they were Thy creation, Thou fairest of all, Creator of all, Thou good God; God, the sovereign good and my true good. Fair were those pears, but not them did my wretched soul desire; for I had store of better, and those I gathered, only that I might steal. For, when gathered, I flung them away, my only feast therein being my own sin, which I was pleased to enjoy. For if aught of those pears came within my mouth, what sweetened it was the sin. And now, O Lord my God, I enquire what in that theft delighted me; and behold it hath no loveliness; I mean not such loveliness as in justice and wisdom; nor such as is in the mind and memory, and senses, and animal life of man; nor yet as the stars are glorious and beautiful in their orbs; or the earth, or sea, full of embryo-life, replacing by its birth that which decayeth; nay, nor even that false and shadowy beauty, which belongeth to deceiving vices.

13 For so doth pride imitate exaltedness; whereas Thou Alone art God exalted over all. Ambition, what seeks it, but honours and glory? whereas Thou Alone art to be honoured above all, and glorious for evermore. The cruelty of the great would fain be feared; but who is to be feared but God alone, out of whose power what can be wrested or withdrawn? when, or where, or whither, or by whom? The tendernesses of the wanton would fain be counted love: yet is nothing more tender than Thy charity; nor is aught loved more healthfully than Thy truth, bright and beautiful above all. Curiosity makes semblance of a desire of knowledge; whereas Thou supremely knowest all. Yea, ignorance and foolishness itself is cloked under the name of simplicity and uninjuriousness; because nothing is found more single than Thee: and what less injurious, since they are his own works, which injure the sinner?⁴ Yea, sloth would fain be at rest; but what stable rest besides the Lord? Luxury affects to be called plenty and abundance; but Thou art the fulness and never-failing plenteousness of incorruptible pleasures. Prodigality presents a shadow of liberality: but Thou art the most overflowing Giver of all good. Covetousness would possess many things: and Thou possessest all things. Envy disputes for excellency: what more excellent than Thou? Anger seeks revenge: who revenges more justly than Thou? Fear startles at things unwonted and sudden, which endanger things beloved, and takes fore-thought for their safety; but to Thee what unwonted or sudden, or who separateth from Thee what Thou lovest? Or where but with Thee is unshaken safety? Grief pines

away for things lost, the delight of its desires; because it would have nothing taken from it, as nothing can from Thee.

14 Thus doth the soul commit fornication, when she turns from Thee, seeking without Thee, what she findeth not pure and untainted, till she returns to Thee. Thus all pervertedly imitate Thee, who remove far from Thee, and lift themselves up against Thee. But even by thus imitating Thee, they imply Thee to be the Creator of all nature; whence there is no place whither altogether to retire from Thee. What then did I love in that theft? and wherein did I even corruptly and pervertedly imitate my Lord? Did I wish even by stealth to do contrary to Thy law, because by power I could not, so that being a prisoner, I might mimic a maimed liberty by doing with impunity things unpermitted me, a darkened likeness of Thy Omnipotency?[5] Behold, Thy servant, fleeing from his Lord, and obtaining a shadow. O rottenness, O monstrousness of life, and depth of death! could I like what I might not, only because I might not?

[VII] 15 *What shall I render unto the Lord*, that, whilst my memory recalls these things, my soul is not affrighted at them? *I will love Thee, O Lord, and thank Thee, and confess unto Thy name;* because Thou hast forgiven me these so great and heinous deeds of mine. To Thy grace I ascribe it, and to Thy mercy, that Thou hast melted away my sins as it were ice. To Thy grace I ascribe also whatsoever I have not done of evil; for what might I not have done, who even loved a sin for its own sake? Yea, all I confess to have been forgiven me; both what evils I committed by my own wilfulness, and what by Thy guidance I committed not. What man is he, who, weighing his own infirmity, dares to ascribe his purity and innocency to his own strength; that so he should love Thee the less, as if he had less needed Thy mercy, whereby Thou remittest sins to those that turn to Thee? For whosoever, called by Thee, followed Thy voice, and avoided those things which he reads me recalling and confessing of myself, let him not scorn me, who being sick, was cured by that Physician, through Whose aid it was that he was not, or rather was less, sick: and for this let him love Thee as much, yea and more; since by Whom he sees me to have been recovered from such deep consumption of sin, by Him he sees himself to have been from the like consumption of sin preserved.

[VIII] 16 *What fruit had I then* (wretched man!) *in those things, of the remembrance whereof I am now ashamed?* Especially, in that theft which I loved for the theft's sake; and it too was nothing,[6] and therefore the more miserable I, who loved it. Yet alone I had not done it: such was I then, I remember, alone I had never done it. I loved then in it also the company of the accomplices, with whom I did it? I did not then love nothing else but the theft, yea rather I did love nothing else; for that circumstance of the company was also nothing. What is, in truth? who can teach me, save He that enlighteneth my heart, and discovereth its dark corners? What is it which hath come into my mind to enquire, and discuss, and consider? For had I then loved the pears I stole, and wished to enjoy them, I might have done it alone, had the bare commission of the theft sufficed to attain my pleasure; nor needed I have inflamed the itching of my desires, by the excitement of accomplices. But since my pleasure was not in those pears, it was in the offence itself, which the company of fellow-sinners occasioned.

[IX] 17 What then was this feeling? For of a truth it was too foul: and woe was me, who had it. But yet what was it? *Who can understand his errors?* It was the sport, which, as it were, tickled our hearts, that we beguiled, those who little thought what we were doing, and much misliked it. Why then was my delight of such sort, that I did it not alone? Because none doth ordinarily laugh alone? ordinarily no one; yet laughter sometimes masters men alone and singly when no one whatever is with them, if any thing very ludicrous presents itself to their senses or mind. Yet I had not done this alone; alone I had never never done it. Behold my God, before Thee, the vivid remembrance of my soul; alone, I had never committed that theft, wherein what I stole pleased me not, but that I stole; nor had it alone liked me to do it, nor had I done it. O friendship too unfriendly! thou incomprehensible inveigler of the soul, thou greediness to do mischief out of mirth and wantonness, thou thirst of others' loss, without lust of my own gain or revenge: but when it is said, "Let's go, let's do it," we are ashamed not to be shameless.

[X] 18 Who can disentangle that twisted and intricate knottiness? Foul is it: I hate to think on it, to look on it. But Thee I long for, O Righteousness and Innocency, beautiful and comely to all pure eyes, and of a satisfaction unsating. With Thee is rest entire, and life imperturbable. Whoso enters into Thee, *enters into the joy of his Lord:* and shall not fear, and shall do excellently in the All-Excellent. I sank away from Thee, and I wandered, O my God, too much astray from Thee my stay, in these days of my youth, and I became to myself a barren land.

BOOK III

His residence at Carthage from his seventeenth to his nineteenth year. Source of his disorders. Love of shows. Advance in studies, and love of wisdom. Distaste for Scripture. Led astray to the Manichæans. Refutation of some of their tenets. Grief of his mother Monnica at his heresy, and prayers for his conversion. Her vision from God, and answer through a Bishop.

[I] 1 To Carthage I came, where there sang all around me in my ears a cauldron of unholy loves. I loved not yet, yet I loved to love, and out of a deepseated want, I hated myself for wanting not. I sought what I might love, in love with loving, and safety I hated, and a way without snares. For within me was a famine of that inward food, Thyself, my God; yet, through that famine I was not hungered; but was without all longing for incorruptible sustenance, not because filled therewith, but the more empty, the more I loathed it. For this cause my soul was sickly and full of sores, it miserably cast itself forth, desiring to be scraped by the touch of objects of sense. Yet if these had not a soul, they would not be objects of love. To love then, and to be beloved, was sweet to me; but more, when I obtained to enjoy the person I loved. I defiled, therefore, the spring of friendship with the filth of concupiscence, and I beclouded its brightness with the hell of lustfulness; and thus foul and unseemly, I would fain, through exceeding vanity, be fine and courtly. I fell headlong then into the love, wherein I longed to be ensnared. My God, my Mercy, with how much gall didst thou out of thy great goodness besprinkle for me that sweetness? For I was both beloved, and secretly arrived at the bond of enjoying; and was with joy fettered with sorrow-bringing bonds, that I might be scourged with the iron burning rods of jealousy, and suspicions, and fears, and angers, and quarrels.

[II] 2 Stage-plays also carried me away, full of images of my miseries, and of fuel to my fire. Why is it, that man desires to be made sad, beholding doleful and tragical things, which yet himself would by no means suffer? yet he desires as a spectator to feel sorrow at them, and this very sorrow is his pleasure. What is this but a miserable madness? for a man is the more affected with these actions, the less free he is from such affections. Howsoever, when he suffers in his own person, it uses to be styled misery: when he compassionates others, then it is mercy. But what sort of compassion is this for feigned and scenical passions? for the auditor is not called on to relieve, but only to grieve: and he applauds the actor of these fictions the more, the more he grieves. And if the calamities of those persons (whether of old times, or mere fiction) be so acted, that the spectator is not moved to tears, he goes away disgusted and criticising; but if he be moved to passion, he stays intent, and weeps for joy.

3 Are griefs then too loved? Verily all desire joy. Or whereas no man likes to be miserable, is he yet pleased to be merciful? which because it cannot be without passion, for this reason alone are passions loved? This also springs from that vein of friendship. But whither goes that vein? whither flows it? wherefore runs it into that¹ torrent of pitch bubbling forth those monstrous tides of foul lustfulness, into which it is wilfully changed and transformed, being of its own will precipitated and corrupted from its heavenly clearness? Shall compassion then be put away? by no means. Be griefs then sometimes loved. But beware of uncleanness, O my soul, under the guardianship of my God, the *God of our fathers, who is to be praised and exalted above all for ever*, beware of uncleanness. For I have not now ceased to pity; but then in the theatres I rejoiced with lovers, when they wickedly enjoyed one another, although this was imaginary only in the play. And when they lost one another, as if very compassionate, I sorrowed with them, yet had my delight in both. But now I much more pity him that rejoiceth in his wickedness, than him who is thought to suffer hardship, by missing some pernicious pleasure, and the loss of some miserable felicity. This certainly is the truer mercy, but in it, grief delights not. For though he that grieves for the miserable, be commended for his office of charity; yet had he, who is genuinely compassionate, rather there were nothing for him to grieve for. For if good will be ill willed, (which can never be,) then may he, who truly and sincerely commiserates, wish there might be some miserable, that he might commiserate. Some sorrow may then be allowed, none loved. For thus dost Thou,

O Lord God, who lovest souls far more purely than we, and hast more incorruptibly pity on them, yet are wounded with no sorrowfulness. *And who is sufficient for these things?*

4 But I, miserable, then loved to grieve, and sought out what to grieve at, when in another's and that feigned and personated misery, that acting best pleased me, and attracted me the most vehemently, which drew tears from me. What marvel that an unhappy sheep, straying from Thy flock, and impatient of Thy keeping, I became infected with a foul disease? And hence the love of griefs; not such as should sink deep into me; for I loved not to suffer, what I loved to look on; but such as upon hearing their fictions should lightly scratch the surface; upon which as on envenomed nails, followed inflamed swelling, impostumes, and a putrified sore. My life being such, was it life, O my God?

[III] 5 And Thy faithful mercy hovered over me afar. Upon how grievous iniquities consumed I myself, pursuing a sacrilegious curiosity, that having forsaken Thee, it might bring me to the treacherous abyss, and the beguiling service of devils, to whom I sacrificed my evil actions, and in all these things thou didst scourge me! I dared even, while Thy solemnities were celebrated within the walls of Thy Church, to desire, and to compass a business, deserving death for its fruits, for which Thou scourgedst me with grievous punishments, though nothing to my fault, O Thou my exceeding mercy, my God, my refuge from those terrible destroyers, among whom I wandered with a stiff neck, withdrawing further from Thee, loving mine own ways, and not Thine; loving a vagrant liberty.

6 Those studies also, which were accounted commendable, had a view to excelling in the courts of litigation; the more bepraised, the craftier. Such is men's blindness, glorying even in their blindness. And now I was chief in the rhetoric school, whereat I joyed proudly, and I swelled with arrogancy, though (Lord, Thou knowest) far quieter and altogether removed from the subvertings of those "Subverters"[2] (for this ill-omened and devilish name, was the very badge of gallantry) among whom I lived, with a shameless shame that I was not even as they. With them I lived, and was sometimes delighted with their friendship, whose doings I ever did abhor, i.e. their "subvertings," wherewith they wantonly persecuted the modesty of strangers, which they disturbed by a gratuitous jeering feeding thereon their malicious mirth. Nothing can be liker the very actions of devils than these. What then could they be more truly called than "subverters?" themselves subverted and altogether perverted first, the deceiving spirits secretly deriding and seducing them, wherein themselves delight to jeer at, and deceive others.

[IV] 7 Among such as these, in that unsettled age of mine, learned I books of eloquence, wherein I desired to be eminent, out of a damnable and vain glorious end, a joy in human vanity. In the ordinary course of study, I fell upon a certain book of Cicero, whose speech almost all admire, not so his heart. This book of his contains an exhortation to philosophy, and is called "*Hortensius*." But this book altered my affections, and turned my prayers to Thyself, O Lord; and made me have other purposes and desires. Every vain hope at once became worthless to me; and I longed with an incredibly burning desire for an immortality of wisdom, and began now to arise, that I might return to Thee. For not to sharpen my tongue, (which thing I seemed to be purchasing with my mother's allowances, in that my nineteenth year, my father being dead two years before,) not to sharpen my tongue did I employ that book; nor did it infuse into me its style, but its matter.

8 How did I burn then, my God, how did I burn to re-mount from earthly things to Thee, nor knew I what Thou wouldest do with me? For with Thee is wisdom. But the love of wisdom is in Greek called "philosophy," with which that book inflamed me. Some there be that seduce through philosophy, under a great, and smooth, and honourable name colouring and disguising their own errors: and almost all who in that and former ages were such, are in that book censured and set forth: there also is made plain that wholesome advice of Thy Spirit, by Thy good and devout servant; *Beware lest any man spoil you through philosophy and vain deceit, after the tradition of men, after the rudiments of the world, and not after Christ. For in Him dwelleth all the fulness of the Godhead bodily*. And since at that time (Thou, O light of my heart, knowest) Apostolic Scripture was not known to me, I was delighted with that exhortation, so far only, that I was

thereby strongly roused, and kindled, and inflamed to love, and seek, and obtain, and hold, and embrace not this or that sect, but wisdom itself whatever it were; and this alone checked me thus enkindled, that the name of Christ was not in it. For this name, according to Thy mercy, O Lord, this name of my Saviour Thy Son, had my tender heart, even with my mother's milk, devoutly drunk in, and deeply treasured; and whatsoever was without that name, though never so learned, polished, or true, took not entire hold of me.

[V] 9 I resolved then to bend my mind to the holy Scriptures, that I might see what they were. But behold, I see a thing not understood by the proud, nor laid open to children, lowly in access, in its recesses lofty, and veiled with mysteries; and I was not such as could enter into it, or stoop my neck to follow its steps. For not as I now speak, did I feel when I turned to those Scriptures; but they seemed to me unworthy to be compared to the stateliness of Tully: for my swelling pride shrunk from their lowliness, nor could my sharp wit pierce the interior thereof. Yet were they such as would grow up in a little one. But I disdained to be a little one; and, swoln with pride, took myself to be a great one.

[VI] 10 Therefore I fell among men[3] proudly doting, exceeding carnal and prating, in whose mouths were the snares of the Devil, lined with the mixture of the syllables of Thy name, and of our Lord Jesus Christ, and of the Holy Ghost, the Paraclete, our Comforter. These names departed not out of their mouth, but so far forth, as the sound only and the noise of the tongue, for the heart was void of truth. Yet they cried out "Truth, Truth," and spake much thereof to me, yet *it was not in them*: but they spake falsehood, not of Thee only, (who truly art Truth,) but even of those elements of this world, Thy creatures. And I indeed ought to have passed by even philosophers who spake truth concerning them, for love of Thee, my Father, supremely good, Beauty of all things beautiful. O Truth, Truth, how inwardly did even then the marrow of my soul pant after Thee, when they often and diversly, and in many and huge books, echoed of Thee to me, though it was but an echo? And these were the dishes wherein to me, hungering after Thee, they, instead of Thee, served up the Sun and Moon, beautiful works of Thine, but yet Thy works, not Thyself, no nor Thy first works. For Thy spiritual works are before these corporeal, works, celestial though they be, and shining. But I hungered and thirsted not even after those first works of Thine, but after Thee Thyself, the Truth, *in whom is no variableness, neither shadow of turning*: yet they still set before me in those dishes, glittering fantasies, than which better were it to love this very sun, (which is real to our sight at least,) than those fantasies which by our eyes deceive our mind. Yet because I thought them to be Thee, I fed thereon; not eagerly,[4] for Thou didst not in them taste to me as Thou art; for Thou wast not these emptinesses, nor was I nourished by them, but exhausted rather. Food in sleep shews very like our food awake; yet are not those asleep nourished by it, for they are asleep. But those were not even any way like to Thee, as Thou hast now spoken to me; for those were corporeal fantasies, false bodies, than which these true bodies, celestial or terrestrial, which with our fleshly sight we behold, are far more certain: these things the beasts and birds discern as well as we, and they are more certain than when we fancy them. And again, we do with more certainty fancy them, than by them conjecture other vaster and infinite bodies which have no being. Such empty husks was I then fed on; and was not fed. But Thou, my soul's Love, *in looking for whom I fail*, that I may become strong, art neither those bodies which we see, though in heaven; nor those which we see not there; for Thou hast created them, nor dost Thou account them among the chiefest of Thy works. How far then art Thou from those fantasies of mine, fantasies of bodies which altogether are not, than which the images of those bodies, which are, are far more certain, and more certain still the bodies themselves, which yet Thou art not; no, nor yet the soul, which is the life of the bodies. So then, better and more certain is the life of the bodies, than the bodies. But Thou art the life of souls, the life of lives, having life in Thyself; and changest not, life of my soul.

11 Where then wert Thou then to me, and how far from me? Far verily was I straying from Thee, barred from the very husks of the swine, whom with husks I fed. For how much better are the fables of poets and grammarians, than these snares? For verses, and poems, and "Medea flying," are more profitable truly, than these men's five elements, variously disguised, answering to five dens of darkness, which have no being, yet slay the believer. For verses and poems I can turn to⁵ true food,

and "Medea flying," though I did sing, I maintained not; though I heard it sung, I believed not: but those things I did believe. Woe, woe, by what steps was I brought down to *the depths of hell!* toiling and turmoiling through want of Truth, since I sought after Thee, my God, (to Thee I confess it, who hadst mercy on me, not as yet confessing,) not according to the understanding of the mind, wherein Thou willedst that I should excel the beasts, but according to the sense of the flesh. But Thou wert more inward to me, than my most inward part; and higher than my highest. I lighted upon that bold woman, *simple and knoweth nothing,* shadowed out in Solomon, *sitting at the door, and saying, Eat ye bread of secrecies willingly, and drink ye stolen waters which are sweet:* she seduced me, because she found my soul dwelling abroad in the eye of my flesh, and ruminating on such food, as through it I had devoured.

[VII] 12 For other than this, that which really is I knew not; and was, as it were through sharpness of wit, persuaded to assent to foolish deceivers, when they asked me, "whence is evil?"[6] "is God bounded by a bodily shape, and has hairs and nails?" "are they to be esteemed righteous, who had many wives at once, and did kill men, and sacrificed living creatures?" At which I, in my ignorance, was much troubled, and departing from the truth, seemed to myself to be making towards it; because as yet I knew not that evil was nothing but a privation of good, until at last a thing ceases altogether to be; which how should I see, the sight of whose eyes reached only to bodies, and of my mind to a phantasm? And I knew not

God to be a Spirit, not One who hath parts extended in length and breadth, or whose being was bulk; for every bulk is less in a part, than in the whole: and if it be infinite, it must be less in such part as is defined by a certain space, than in its infinitude; and so is not wholly every where, as Spirit, as God. And what that should be in us, by which we were like to God, and might in Scripture be rightly said to be *after the Image of God*, I was altogether ignorant.

13 Nor knew I that true inward righteousness, which judgeth not according to custom, but out of the most rightful law of God Almighty, whereby the ways of places and times were disposed, according to those times and places; itself meantime being the same always and every where, not one thing in one place, and another in another; according to which Abraham, and Isaac, and Jacob, and Moses, and David, were righteous, and all those commended by the mouth of God; but were judged unrighteous by silly men, *judging out of man's judgment*, and measuring by their own petty habits, the moral habits of the whole human race. As if in an armory, one ignorant what were adapted to each part, should cover his head with greaves, or seek to be shod with a helmet, and complain that they fitted not; or as if on a day, when business is publicly stopped in the afternoon, one were angered at not being allowed to keep open shop, because he had been in the forenoon; or when in one house he observeth some servant take a thing in his hand, which the butler is not suffered to meddle with; or something permitted out of doors, which is forbidden in the dining-

room; and should be angry, that in one house, and one family, the same thing is not allotted every where, and to all. Even such are they, who are fretted to hear something to have been lawful for righteous men formerly, which now is not; or that God, for certain temporal respects, commanded them one thing, and these another, obeying both the same righteousness: whereas they see, in one man, and one day, and one house, different things to be fit for different members, and a thing formerly lawful, after a certain time not so; in one corner permitted or commanded, but in another rightly forbidden and punished. Is justice therefore various or mutable? No, but the times, over which it presides, flow not evenly, because they are times. But men, whose *days are few upon the earth*, for that by their senses[7] they cannot harmonize the causes of things in former ages and other nations, which they had no experience of, with these which they have experience of, whereas in one and the same body, day, or family, they easily see what is fitting for each member, and season, part, and person; to the one they take exceptions, to the other they submit.

14 These things I then knew not, nor observed; they struck my sight on all sides, and I saw them not. I indited verses, in which I might not place every foot every where, but differently in different metres; nor even in any one metre the self-same foot in all places. Yet the art itself, by which I indited, had not different principles for these different cases, but comprised all in one. Still I saw not how that righteousness, which good and holy men obeyed, did far more excellently and sublimely contain in

one all those things which God commanded, and in no part varied; although in varying times it prescribed not every thing at once, but apportioned and enjoined what was fit for each. And I, in my blindness, censured the holy Fathers, not only wherein they made use of things present as God commanded and inspired them, but also wherein they were foretelling things to come, as God was revealing in them.[8]

[VIII] 15 Can it at any time or place be unjust *to love God with all his heart, with all his soul, and with all his mind; and his neighbour as himself?* Therefore are those foul offences which be against nature, to be every where and at all times detested and punished; such as were those of the men of Sodom: which should all nations commit, they should all stand guilty of the same crime, by the law of God, which hath not so made men, that they should so abuse one another. For even that intercourse which should be between God and us is violated, when that same nature, of which He is Author, is polluted by the perversity of lust. But those actions which are offences against the customs of men, are to be avoided according to the customs severally prevailing; so that a thing agreed upon, and confirmed, by custom or law of any city or nation, may not be violated at the lawless pleasure of any, whether native or foreigner. For any part, which harmonizeth not with its whole, is offensive. But when God commands a thing to be done, against the customs or compact of any people, though it were never by them done heretofore, it is to be done; and if intermitted, it is to be restored; and if never ordained, is now to be ordained. For lawful if it be for a king, in the state which he reigns over, to command that, which no one before him, nor he himself heretofore, had commanded, and to obey him cannot be against the common weal of the state; (nay, it were against it if he were not obeyed, for to obey princes is a general compact of human society;) how much more unhesitatingly ought we to obey God, in all which He commands, the Ruler of all His creatures! For as among the powers in man's society, the greater authority is obeyed in preference to the lesser, so must God above all.

16 So in acts of violence, where there is a wish to hurt, whether by reproach or injury; and these either for revenge, as one enemy against another; or for some profit belonging to another, as the robber to the traveller; or to avoid some evil, as towards one who is feared; or through envy, as one less fortunate to one more so, or one well thriven in any thing, to him whose being on a par with himself he fears, or grieves at, or for the mere pleasure at another's pain, as spectators of gladiators, or deriders and mockers of others. These be the heads of iniquity, which spring from the lust of the flesh, of the eye, or of rule, either singly, or two combined, or all together; and so do men live ill against the three, and seven,[9] that psaltery *of ten strings*, Thy Ten Commandments, O God, most high, and most sweet. But what foul offences can there be against Thee, who canst not be defiled? or what acts of violence against Thee, who canst not be harmed? But Thou avengest what men commit against themselves, seeing also when they sin against Thee, they do wickedly against their own souls, and *iniquity gives itself the lie*, by

corrupting and perverting their nature, which Thou hast created and ordained, or by an immoderate use of things allowed, or in *burning* in things unallowed, *to that use which is against nature*; or are found guilty, raging with heart and tongue against Thee, *kicking against the pricks*; or when, bursting the pale of human society, they boldly joy in self-willed combinations or divisions, according as they have any object to gain or subject of offence. And these things are done when Thou art forsaken, O Fountain of Life, who art the only and true Creator and Governor of the Universe, and by a self-willed pride, any one false thing is selected therefrom and loved.[10] So then by a humble devoutness we return to Thee; and Thou cleansest us from our evil habits, and art merciful to their sins who confess, and *hearest the groaning of the prisoner*, and loosest us from the chains which we made for ourselves, if we lift not up against Thee the horns of an unreal liberty, suffering the loss of all, through covetousness of more, by loving more our own private good, than Thee, the Good of all.

[IX] 17 Amidst these offences of foulness and violence, and so many iniquities, are sins of men, who are on the whole making proficiency; which by those that judge rightly, are, after the rule of perfection, discommended, yet the persons commended, upon hope of future fruit, as in the green blade of growing corn. And there are some, resembling offences of foulness or violence, which yet are no sins; because they offend neither Thee, our Lord God, nor human society; when, namely, things fitting for a given period are obtained for the service of life, and we know not whether out of a lust of having; or when things are, for the sake of correction, by constituted authority punished, and we know not whether out of a lust of hurting. Many an action then which in men's sight is disapproved, is by Thy testimony approved; and many, by men praised, are (Thou being witness) condemned: because the shew of the action, and the mind of the doer, and the unknown exigency of the period, severally vary. But when Thou on a sudden commandest an unwonted and unthought-of thing, yea, although Thou hast sometime forbidden it, and still for the time hidest the reason of Thy command, and it be against the ordinance of some society of men, who doubts but it is to be done,[11] seeing that society of men is just which serves Thee? But blessed are they who know Thy commands! For all things were done by Thy servants;[12] either to shew forth something needful for the present, or to foreshew things to come.

[X] 18 These things I being ignorant of, scoffed at those Thy holy servants and prophets. And what gained I by scoffing at them, but to be scoffed at by Thee, being insensibly and step by step drawn on to those follies, as to believe that a fig-tree wept when it was plucked, and the tree, its mother, shed milky tears? Which fig notwithstanding (plucked by some other's, not his own, guilt) had some (Manichæan) saint eaten, and mingled with his bowels, he should breathe out of it angels, yea, there shall burst forth particles of divinity, at every moan or groan in his prayer, which particles of the most high and true God had remained bound in that fig, unless they had been set at liberty by the teeth or belly of some "Elect" saint! And I, miserable, believed that more mercy was to be shewn to the fruits of the earth, than men, for whom they were created. For if any one an hungered, not a Manichæan, should ask for any, that morsel would seem as it were condemned to capital punishment, which should be given him.

[XI] 19 And Thou *sentest Thine hand from above*, and drewest my soul out of that profound darkness, my mother, Thy faithful one, weeping to Thee for me, more than mothers weep the bodily deaths of their children. For she, by that faith and spirit which she had from Thee, discerned the death wherein I lay, and Thou heardest her, O Lord; Thou heardest her, and despisedst not her tears, when streaming down, they watered the ground[13] under her eyes in every place where she prayed; yea Thou heardest her. For whence was that dream whereby Thou comfortedst her; so that she allowed me to live with her, and to eat at the same table in the house, which she had begun to shrink from, abhorring and detesting the blasphemies of my error? For she saw herself standing on a certain wooden rule, and a shining youth coming towards her, cheerful and smiling upon her, herself grieving, and overwhelmed with grief. But he having (in order to instruct, as is their wont, not to be instructed) enquired of her the causes of her grief and daily tears, and she answering that she was bewailing my perdition, he bade her rest contented, and told her to look and observe, "That where she was, there was I also." And when she looked, she saw me standing by her in the same rule.

Whence was this, but that Thine ears were towards her heart? O Thou Good omnipotent, who so carest for every one of us, as if Thou caredst for him only; and so for all, as if they were but one!

20 Whence was this also, that when she had told me this vision, and I would fain bend it to mean, "That she rather should not despair of being one day what I was;" she presently, without any hesitation, replies; "No; for it was not told me that, 'where he, there thou also;' but 'where thou, there he also?'" I confess to Thee, O Lord, that to the best of my remembrance, (and I have oft spoken of this,) that Thy answer, through my waking mother,—that she was not perplexed by the plausibility of my false interpretation, and so quickly saw what was to be seen, and which I certainly had not perceived, before she spake,—even then moved me more than the dream itself, by which a joy to the holy woman, to be fulfilled so long after, was, for the consolation of her present anguish, so long before foresignified. For almost nine years passed, in which I wallowed in the mire of that deep pit, and the darkness of falsehood, often assaying to rise, but dashed down the more grievously. All which time that chaste, godly, and sober widow, (such as Thou lovest,) now more cheered with hope, yet no whit relaxing in her weeping and mourning, ceased not at all hours of her devotions to bewail my case unto Thee. And her *prayers entered into Thy presence*; and yet Thou sufferest me to be yet involved and reinvolved in that darkness.

[XII] 21 Thou gavest her meantime another answer, which I call to mind; for much I pass by, hasting to those things which more press me to confess unto Thee, and much I do not remember. Thou gavest her then another answer, by a Priest of Thine, a certain Bishop brought up in Thy Church, and well studied in Thy books. Whom when this woman had entreated to vouchsafe to converse with me, refute my errors, unteach me ill things, and teach me good things, (for this he was wont to do, when he found persons fitted to receive it,) he refused, wisely, as I afterwards perceived. For he answered, that I was yet unteachable, being puffed up with the novelty of that heresy, and had already perplexed divers unskilful persons with captious questions,[14] as she had told him: "but let him alone a while," (saith he,) "only pray God for him, he will of himself by reading find what that error is, and how great its impiety." At the same time he told her, how himself, when a little one, had by his seduced mother been consigned over to the Manichees, and had not only read, but frequently copied out almost all, their books, and had (without any argument or proof from any one) seen how much that sect was to be avoided; and had avoided it. Which when he had said, and she would not be satisfied, but urged him more, with intreaties and many tears, that he would see me, and discourse with me; he, a little displeased at her importunity, saith, "Go thy ways, and God bless Thee, for it is not possible that the son of these tears should perish." Which answer she took (as she often mentioned in her conversations with me) as if it had sounded from heaven.

BOOK IV

Aug.'s life from nineteen to eight and twenty;
himself a Manichæan, and seducing others to
the same heresy; partial obedience amidst vanity and
sin, consulting astrologers, only partially shaken
herein; loss of an early friend, who is converted by
being baptized when in a swoon; reflections on grief,
on real and unreal friendship, and love of fame; writes
on "the fair and fit," yet cannot rightly, though God
had given him great talents, since he entertained
wrong notions of God; and so even his knowledge he
applied ill.

[I] 1 For this space of nine years then (from my
nineteenth year, to my eight and twentieth) we lived
seduced and seducing, deceived and deceiving, in divers
lusts; openly, by sciences which they call liberal; secretly,
with a false named religion; here proud, there superstitious, every where vain! Here, hunting after the
emptiness of popular praise, down even to theatrical
applauses, and poetic prizes, and strifes for grassy
garlands, and the follies of shows, and the intemperance
of desires. There, desiring to be cleansed from these
defilements, by carrying food to those who were called
"elect" and "holy," out of which, in the workhouse of
their stomachs, they should forge for us Angels and Gods,

by whom we might be cleansed. These things did I follow, and practise with my friends, deceived by me, and with me. Let the arrogant mock me, and such as have not been, to their soul's health, stricken and cast down by Thee, O my God; but I would still confess to Thee mine own shame in Thy praise. Suffer me, I beseech Thee, and give me grace to go over in my present remembrance the wanderings of my forepassed time, and *to offer unto Thee the sacrifice of thanksgiving.* For what am I to myself without Thee, but a guide to mine own downfall?[1] or what am I even at the best, but an infant sucking the milk Thou givest, and feeding upon Thee, *the food that perisheth not?* But what sort of man is any man, seeing he is but a man? Let now the strong and the mighty laugh at us, but let us *poor and needy* confess unto Thee.

[II] 2 In those years I taught rhetoric, and, overcome by cupidity, made sale of a loquacity to overcome by. Yet I preferred (Lord, Thou knowest) honest scholars, (as they are accounted,) and these I, without artifice, taught artifices, not to be practised against the life of the guiltless, though sometimes for the life of the guilty. And Thou, O God, from afar perceivedst me stumbling in that slippery course, and amid much smoke sending out some sparks of faithfulness, which I shewed in that my guidance of *such as loved vanity,* and *sought after leasing,* myself their companion. In those years I had one,—not in that which is called lawful marriage, but whom I had found out in a wayward passion, void of understanding; yet but one, remaining faithful even to her; in whom I in my own case experienced, what difference there is betwixt the self-restraint of the marriage-convenant, for the sake of issue, and the bargain of a lustful love, where children are born against their parents' will, although, once born, they constrain love.

3 I remember also, that when I had settled to enter the lists for a theatrical prize, some wizard asked me what I would give him to win: but I, detesting and abhorring such foul mysteries, answered, "Though the garland were of imperishable gold, I would not suffer a fly to be killed to gain me it." For he was to kill some living creatures in his sacrifices, and by those honours to invite the devils to favour me. But this ill also I rejected, not out of a pure love[2] for Thee, O God of my heart; for I knew not how to love Thee, who knew not how to conceive aught beyond a material brightness. And doth not a soul, sighing after such fictions, commit fornication against Thee, trust in things unreal,[3] and *feed the wind*? Still I would not forsooth have sacrifices offered to devils for me, to whom I was sacrificing myself by that superstition. For, what else is it *to feed the wind*, but to feed them, that is, by going astray to become their pleasure and derision?

[III] 4 Those impostors then, whom they style Mathematicians, I consulted without scruple; because they seemed to use no sacrifice, nor to pray to any spirit for their divinations: which art, however, Christian and true piety consistently rejects and condemns. For, *it is a good thing to confess unto Thee*, and to say, *Have mercy upon me, heal my soul, for I have sinned against Thee*; and not to abuse Thy mercy for a license to sin, but to remember the Lord's words, *Behold, thou art made whole, sin no more, lest a worse thing come unto thee*. All which wholesome advice they labour to destroy, saying, "The cause of thy sin is inevitably determined in heaven;" and "This did Venus, or Saturn, or Mars:" that man, forsooth, flesh and blood, and proud corruption, might be blameless; while the Creator and Ordainer of heaven and the stars is to bear the blame. And who is He but our God? the very sweetness and well-spring of righteousness, who *renderest to every man according to his works:* and *a broken and contrite heart wilt Thou not despise*.

5 There was in those days a wise man,[4] very skilful in physic, and renowned therein, who had with his own proconsular hand put the Agonistic garland upon my distempered head, but not as a physician: for this disease Thou only curest, *who resistest the proud, and givest grace to the humble*. But didst Thou fail me even by that old man, or forbear to heal my soul? For having become more acquainted with him, and hanging assiduously and fixedly on his speech, (for though in simple terms, it was vivid, lively, and earnest,) when he had gathered by my discourse, that I was given to the books of nativity-casters, he kindly and fatherly advised me to cast them away, and not fruitlessly bestow a care and diligence, necessary for useful things, upon these vanities; saying, that he had in his earliest years studied that art, so as to make it the profession whereby he should live, and that, understanding Hippocrates, he could soon have understood such a study as this; and yet he had given it over, and taken to physic, for no other reason, but that he found it utterly

false; and he, a grave man would not get his living by deluding people. "But thou," saith he, "hast rhetoric to maintain thyself by, so that thou followest this of free choice, not of necessity: the more then oughtest Thou to give me credit herein, who laboured to acquire it so perfectly, as to get my living by it alone." Of whom when I had demanded, how then could many true things be foretold by it, he answered me (as he could) "that the force of chance, diffused throughout the whole order of things, brought this about. For if when a man by hap-hazard opens the pages of some poet, who sang and thought of something wholly different, a verse oftentimes fell out, wondrously agreeable to the present business: it were not to be wondered at, if out of the soul of man, unconscious what takes place in it, by some higher instinct an answer should be given, by hap, not by art, corresponding to the business and actions of the demander."

6 And thus much, either from or through him, Thou conveyedst to me, and tracedst in my memory, what I might hereafter examine for myself. But at that time neither he, nor my dearest Nebridius, a youth singularly good and of a holy fear,[5] who derided the whole body of divination, could persuade me to cast it aside, the authority of the authors swaying me yet more, and as yet I had found no certain proof (such as I sought) whereby it might without all doubt appear, that what had been truly foretold by those consulted was the result of hap-hazard, not of the art of the star-gazers.

[IV] 7 In those years when I first began to teach rhetoric in my native town, I had made one my friend, but too dear to me, from a community of pursuits, of mine own age, and, as myself, in the first opening flower of youth. He had grown up of a child with me, and we had been both school-fellows, and play-fellows. But he was not yet my friend as afterwards, nor even then, as true friendship is; for true it cannot be, unless in such as Thou cementest together, cleaving unto Thee, by that *love which is shed abroad in our hearts by the Holy Ghost, which is given unto us.* Yet was it but too sweet, ripened by the warmth of kindred studies: for, from the true faith (which he as a youth had not soundly and thoroughly imbibed,) I had warped him also to those superstitious and pernicious fables, for which my mother bewailed me. With me he now erred in mind, nor could my soul be without him. But behold Thou wert close on the steps of Thy fugitives, at once *God of vengeance*, and Fountain of mercies, turning us to Thyself by wonderful means; Thou tookest that man out of this life, when he had scarce filled up one whole year of my friendship, sweet to me above all sweetness of that my life.

8 *Who can recount all Thy praises*, which he hath felt in his one self? What diddest Thou then, my God, and how unsearchable is the *abyss of Thy judgments*? For long, sore sick of a fever, he lay senseless in a death-sweat; and his recovery being despaired of, he was baptized, unknowing; myself meanwhile little regarding, and presuming that his soul would retain rather what it had received of me, not what was wrought on his unconscious

body. But it proved far otherwise: for he was refreshed, and restored. Forthwith, as soon as I could speak with him, (and I could, so soon as he was able, for I never left him, and we hung but too much upon each other,) I essayed to jest⁶ with him, as though he would jest with me at that baptism which he had received, when utterly absent in mind and feeling, but had now understood that he had received. But he so shrunk from me, as from an enemy; and with a wonderful and sudden freedom bade me, as I would continue his friend, forbear such language to him. I, all astonished and amazed, suppressed all my emotions till he should grow well, and his health were strong enough for me to deal with him, as I would. But he was taken away from my phrensy, that with Thee he might be preserved for my comfort; a few days after, in my absence, he was attacked again by the fever, and so departed.

9 At this grief my heart was utterly darkened; and whatever I beheld was death. My native country was a torment to me, and my father's house a strange unhappiness; and whatever I had shared with him, wanting him, became a distracting torture. Mine eyes sought him every where, but he was not granted them; and I hated all places, for that they had not him; nor could they now tell me, "he is coming," as when he was alive and absent. I became a great riddle to myself, and I asked my soul, *why she was so sad, and why she disquieted me sorely:* but she knew not what to answer me. And if I said, *Trust in God,* she very rightly obeyed me not; because that most dear friend, whom she had lost, was, being man, both truer

and better, than that phantasm she was bid to trust in. Only tears were sweet to me, for they succeeded my friend, in the dearest of my affections.

[V] 10 And now, Lord, these things are passed by, and time hath assuaged my wound. May I learn from Thee, who art Truth, and approach the ear of my heart unto Thy mouth, that Thou mayest tell me why weeping is sweet to the miserable? Hast Thou, although present every where, cast away our misery far from Thee? And Thou abidest in Thyself, but we are tossed about in divers trials. And yet unless we mourned in Thine ears, we should have no hope left. Whence then is sweet fruit gathered from the bitterness of life, from groaning, tears, sighs, and complaints? Doth this sweeten it, that we hope Thou hearest? This is true of prayer, for therein is a longing to approach unto Thee. But is it also in grief for a thing lost, and the sorrow wherewith I was then overwhelmed? For I neither hoped he should return to life, nor did I desire this with my tears; but I wept only and grieved. For I was miserable, and had lost my joy. Or is weeping indeed a bitter thing, and for very loathing of the things, which we before enjoyed, does it then, when we shrink from them, please us?

[VI] 11 But what speak I of these things? for now is no time to question, but to confess unto Thee. Wretched I was; and wretched is every soul bound by the friendship of perishable things; he is torn asunder when he loses them, and then he feels the wretchedness, which he had, ere yet he lost them. So was it then with me; I wept most bitterly, and found my repose in bitterness. Thus was I wretched, and that wretched life I held dearer than my friend.[7] For though I would willingly have changed it, yet was I more unwilling to part with it, than with him; yea, I know not whether I would have parted with it even for him, as is related (if not feigned) of Pylades and Orestes, that they would gladly have died for each other or together, not to live together being to them worse than death. But in me there had arisen some unexplained feeling, too contrary to this, for at once I loathed exceedingly to live, and feared to die. I suppose, the more I loved him, the more did I hate, and fear (as a most cruel enemy) death, which had bereaved me of him: and I imagined it would speedily make an end of all men, since it had power over him. Thus was it with me, I remember. Behold my heart, O my God, behold and see into me; for well I remember it, O my Hope, who cleansest me from the impurity of such affections, directing *mine eyes towards Thee*, and *plucking my feet out of the snare*. For I wondered at others, subject to death, did live, since he whom I loved, as if he should never die, was dead: and I wondered yet more that myself, who was to him a second self, could live, he being dead. Well said one[8] of his friend, "Thou half of my soul:" for I felt that my soul and his soul were "one soul in two bodies:"[9] and therefore was my life a horror to me, because I would not live halved. And therefore perchance[10] I feared to die, lest he whom I had much loved, should die wholly.

[VII] 12 O madness, which knowest not how to love men, like men! O foolish man that I then was, enduring impatiently the lot of man! I fretted then, sighed, wept, was distracted; had neither rest nor counsel. For I bore about a shattered and bleeding soul, impatient of being borne by me, yet where to repose it, I found not. Not in calm groves, not in games and music, nor in fragrant spots, nor in curious banquettings, nor in the pleasures of the bed and the couch; nor (finally) in books or poesy, found it repose. All things looked ghastly, yea, the very light; whatsoever was not what he was, was revolting and hateful, except groaning and tears. For in those alone found I a little refreshment. But when my soul was withdrawn from them, a huge load of misery weighed me down. To Thee, O Lord, it ought to have been raised, for Thee to lighten; I knew it; but neither could nor would; the more, since, when I thought of Thee, Thou wert not to me any solid or substantial thing. For Thou wert not Thyself, but a mere phantom, and my error was my God. If I offered to discharge my load thereon, that it might rest, it glided through the void, and came rushing down again on me; and I had remained to myself a hapless spot, where I could neither be, nor be from thence. For whither should my heart flee from my heart? Whither should I flee from myself? Whither not follow myself? And yet I fled out of my country; for so should mine eyes less look for him, where they were not wont to see him. And thus from Thagaste, I came to Carthage.

[VIII] 13 Times lose no time; nor do they roll idly by; through our senses they work strange operations on the mind. Behold, they went and came day by day, and by coming and going, introduced into my mind other imaginations, and other remembrances; and little by little patched me up again with my old kind of delights, unto which that my sorrow gave way. And yet there succeeded, not indeed other griefs, yet the causes of other griefs. For whence had that former grief so easily reached my very inmost soul, but that I had poured out my soul upon the dust, in loving one that must die, as if he would never die? For what restored and refreshed me chiefly, was the solaces of other friends, with whom I did love, what instead of Thee I loved: and this was a great fable, and protracted lie, by whose adulterous stimulus, our soul, which lay itching in our ears, was being defiled. But that fable would not die to me, so oft as any of my friends died. There were other things which in them did more take my mind; to talk and jest together, to do kind offices by turns; to read together honied books; to play the fool or be earnest together; to dissent at times without discontent, as a man might with his own self; and even with the seldomness of these dissentings, to season our more frequent consentings; sometimes to teach, and sometimes learn; long for the absent with impatience; and welcome the coming with joy. These and the like expressions, proceeding out of the hearts of those that loved and were loved again, by the countenance, the tongue, the eyes, and a thousand pleasing gestures, were so much fuel to melt our souls together, and out of many make but one.

[IX] 14 This is it that is loved in friends; and so loved, that a man's conscience condemns itself, if he love not him that loves him again, or love not again him that loves him, looking for nothing from his person, but indications of his love. Hence that mourning, if one die, and darkenings of sorrows, that steeping of the heart in tears, all sweetness turned to bitterness; and upon the loss of life of the dying, the death of the living. Blessed whoso loveth Thee, and his friend in Thee, and his enemy for Thee. For he alone loses none dear to him, to whom all are dear in Him Who cannot be lost. And who is this but our God, the *God that made heaven and earth*, and *filleth them*, because by filling them He created them?[11] Thee none loseth, but who leaveth. And who leaveth Thee, whither goeth or whither fleeth he, but from Thee well-pleased, to Thee displeased? For where doth he not find Thy law in his own punishment? *And Thy law is truth*, and truth Thou.

[X] 15 *Turn, us O God of Hosts, shew us Thy countenance, and we shall be whole.* For whithersoever the soul of man turns itself, unless towards Thee, it is rivetted upon sorrows,[12] yea though it is rivetted on things beautiful. And yet they, out of Thee, and out of the soul, were not, unless they were from Thee. They rise, and set; and by rising, they begin as it were to be; they grow, that they may be perfected; and perfected, they wax old and wither; and all grow not old, but all wither. So then when they rise and tend to be, the more quickly they grow that they may be, so much the more they haste not to be. This is the law of them. Thus much hast Thou allotted them, because they are portions of things, which exist not all at once, but by passing away and succeeding, they together complete that universe, whereof they are portions. And even thus is our speech completed by signs giving forth a sound: but this again is not perfected unless one word pass away when it hath sounded its part, that another may succeed. Out of all these things let my soul praise Thee, O God, Creator of all; yet let not my soul be rivetted unto these things with the glue of love, through the senses of the body. For they go whither they were to go, that they might not be; and they rend her with pestilent longings, because she longs to be, yet loves to repose in what she loves.[13] But in these things is no place of repose; they abide not, they flee; and who can follow them with the senses of the flesh? yea, who can grasp them, when they are hard by? For the sense of the flesh is slow, because it is the sense of the flesh; and thereby is it bounded. It sufficeth for that it was made for; but it sufficeth not to stay things running their course from their appointed starting place to the end appointed. For in Thy Word, by which they are created, they hear their decree, "hence and hitherto."

[XI] 16 Be not foolish, O my soul, nor become deaf in the ear of thine heart with the tumult of thy folly. Hearken thou too. The Word Itself calleth thee to return: and there is the place of rest imperturbable, where love is not forsaken, if itself forsaketh not. Behold, these things pass away, that others may replace them, and so this lower universe be completed by all his parts. But do I depart any whither? saith the Word of God. There fix thy dwelling, trust there whatsoever thou hast thence, O my soul, at least now thou art tired out with vanities. Entrust Truth, whatsoever thou hast from the Truth, and thou shalt lose nothing; and thy decay shall bloom again, and *all thy diseases be healed*, and thy mortal parts be re-formed and renewed, and bound around thee: nor shall they lay thee whither themselves descend; but they shall stand fast with thee, and abide for ever before God, *who abideth* and standeth fast *for ever*.

17 Why then be perverted and follow thy flesh? Be it converted and follow thee. Whatever by her thou hast sense of, is in part; and the whole, whereof these are parts, thou knowest not; and yet they delight thee. But had the sense of thy flesh a capacity for comprehending the whole, and not itself also, for thy punishment, been justly restricted to a part of the whole, thou wouldest, that whatsoever existeth at this present, should pass away, that so the whole might better please thee. For what we speak also, by the same sense of the flesh thou hearest; yet wouldest not thou have the syllables stay, but fly away, that others may come, and thou hear the whole.[14] And so ever, when any one thing is made up of many, all of which do not exist together, all collectively would please more than they do severally, could all be perceived collectively. But far better than these, is He who made all; and He is our God, nor doth He pass away, for neither doth aught succeed Him.

[XII] 18 If bodies please thee, praise God on occasion of them, and turn back thy love upon their Maker;[15] lest in these things which please thee, thou displease. If souls please thee, be they loved in God: for they too are mutable, but in Him are they firmly stablished; else would they pass, and pass away. In Him then be they beloved; and carry unto Him along with thee what souls thou canst, and say to them, "Him let us love, Him let us love: He made these, nor is He far off. For He did not make them, and so depart, but they are of Him, and in Him.[16] See there He is, where truth is loved. He is within the very heart, yet hath the heart strayed from Him. *Go back into your heart,*[17] *ye transgressors*, and cleave fast to Him that made you. Stand with Him, and ye shall stand fast. Rest in Him, and ye shall be at rest. Whither go ye in rough ways? Whither go ye? The good that you love is from Him;[18] but it is good and pleasant[19] through reference to Him, and justly shall it be embittered,[20] because unjustly is any thing loved which is from Him, if He be forsaken for it. To what end then would ye still and still walk these difficult and toilsome ways? There is no rest, where ye seek it. Seek what ye seek; but it is not there where ye seek. Ye seek a blessed life in the land of death; it is not there. For how should there be a blessed life, where life itself is not?"

19 "But our true Life came down hither, and bore our death, and slew him, out of the abundance of His own life: and He thundered, calling aloud to us to return hence to Him into that secret place, whence He came forth to us, first into the Virgin's womb, wherein He espoused the

human creation, our mortal flesh, that it might not be for ever mortal, and thence *like a bridegroom coming out of his chamber, rejoicing as a giant to run his course.* For He lingered not, but ran, calling aloud by words, deeds, death, life, descent, ascension; crying aloud to us to return unto Him. And He departed from our eyes, that we might return into our heart, and there find Him. For He departed, and lo, He is here. He would not be long with us, yet left us not; for He departed thither, whence He never parted, *because the world was made by Him.* And *in this world He was, and into this world He came to save sinners,* unto whom my soul confesseth, *and He healeth it, for it hath sinned against Him. O ye sons of men, how long so slow of heart?* Even now, after the descent of Life to you, will ye not ascend and live? But whither ascend ye, when ye are on high, and *set your mouth against the heavens?* Descend, that ye may ascend,[21] and ascend to God. For ye have fallen, by ascending against Him."[22] Tell them this, that they may weep *in the valley of tears,* and so carry them up with thee unto God; because out of His Spirit thou speakest thus unto them, if thou speakest, burning with the fire of charity.

[XIII] 20 These things I then knew not, and I loved these lower beauties, and I was sinking to the very depths, and to my friends I said, "do we love any thing but the beautiful? What then is the beautiful? and what is beauty? What is it that attracts and wins us to the things we love? for unless there were in them a grace and beauty, they could by no means draw us unto them." And I marked and perceived that in bodies themselves, there was a beauty, from their forming a sort of whole, and again, another from apt and mutual correspondence, as of a part of the body with its whole, or a shoe with a foot, and the like. And this consideration sprang up in my mind, out of my inmost heart, and I wrote "on the fair and fit," I think, two or three books. Thou knowest, O Lord, for it is gone from me; for I have them not, but they are strayed from me, I know not how.

[XIV] 21 But what moved me, O Lord my God, to dedicate these books unto Hierius, an orator of Rome, whom I knew not by face, but loved for the fame of his learning which was eminent in him, and some words of his I had heard, which pleased me? But more did he please me, for that he pleased others, who highly extolled him, amazed that out of a Syrian, first instructed in Greek eloquence, should afterwards be formed a wonderful Latin orator, and one most learned in things pertaining unto philosophy. One is commended, and, unseen, he is loved: doth this love enter the heart of the hearer from the mouth of the commender? Not so. But by one who loveth is another kindled. For hence he is loved, who is commended, when the commender is believed to extol him with an unfeigned heart; that is, when one that loves him, praises him.

22 For so did I then love men, upon the judgment of men, not thine, O my God, in Whom no man is deceived. But yet why not for qualities, like those of a famous charioteer, or fighter with beasts in the theatre, known far and wide by a vulgar popularity, but far otherwise,

and earnestly, and so as I would be myself commended? For I would not be commended or loved, as actors are, (though I myself did commend and love them,) but had rather be unknown, than so known; and even hated, than so loved. Where now are the impulses to such various and divers kinds of loves laid up in one soul? Why, since we are equally men, do I love in another what, if I did not hate, I should not spurn and cast from myself? For it holds not, that as a good horse is loved by him, who would not, though he might, be that horse, therefore the same may be said of an actor, who shares our nature. Do I then love in a man, what I hate to be, who am a man? Man himself is a great deep, whose very *hairs Thou numberest*, O Lord, *and they fall not to the ground without Thee*. And yet are the hairs of his head easier to be numbered, than are his feelings, and the beatings of his heart.

23 But that orator was of that sort whom I loved, as wishing to be myself such; and I erred through a swelling pride, and *was tossed about with every wind*, but yet was steered by Thee, though very secretly. And whence do I know, and whence do I confidently confess unto Thee, that I had loved him more for the love of his commenders, than for the very things for which he was commended? Because, had he been unpraised, and these selfsame men had dispraised him, and with dispraise and contempt told the very same things of him, I had never been so kindled and excited to love him. And yet the things had not been other, nor he himself other; but only the feelings of the relators. See where the impotent soul lies along, that is not yet stayed up by the solidity of truth! Just as the gales of

tongues blow from the breast of the opinionative, so is it carried this way and that, driven forward and backward, and the light is overclouded to it, and the truth unseen. And lo, it is before us. And it was to me a great matter, that my discourse and labours should be known to that man: which should he approve, I were the more kindled; but if he disapproved, my empty heart, void of Thy solidity, had been wounded. And yet the "fair and fit," whereon I wrote to him, I dwelt on with pleasure, and surveyed it, and admired it, though none joined therein.

[XV] 24 But I saw not yet, whereon this weighty matter turned in Thy wisdom, O Thou Omnipotent, *who only doest wonders*; and my mind ranged through corporeal forms; and "fair," I defined and distinguished what is so in itself, and "fit," whose beauty is in correspondence to some other thing: and this I supported by corporeal examples. And I turned to the nature of the mind, but the false notion which I had of spiritual things, let me not see the truth. Yet the force of truth did of itself flash into mine eyes, and I turned away my panting soul from incorporeal substance to lineaments, and colours, and bulky magnitudes. And not being able to see these in the mind, I thought I could not see my mind. And whereas in virtue I loved peace, and in viciousness I abhorred discord; in the first I observed an unity, but in the other, a sort of division. And in that unity, I conceived the rational soul, and the nature of truth and of the chief good to consist: but in this division I miserably imagined there to be some unknown substance of irrational life, and the nature of the chief evil, which should not only be a substance, but real life also, and yet not derived from Thee, O my God, of whom are all things. And yet that first I called a Monad, as it had been a soul without sex;[23] but the latter a Duad;—anger, in deeds of violence, and in flagitiousness, lust; not knowing whereof I spake. For I had not known or learned, that neither was evil a substance, nor our soul that chief and unchangeable good.

25 For as deeds of violence arise, if that emotion of the soul be corrupted, whence vehement action springs, stirring itself insolently and unrulily; and lusts, when that affection of the soul is ungoverned, whereby carnal pleasures are drunk in, so do errors and false opinions defile the conversation, if the reasonable soul itself be corrupted; as it was then in me, who knew not that it must be enlightened by another light, that it may be partaker of truth, seeing itself is not that nature of truth. *For Thou shalt light my candle, O Lord my God, Thou shalt enlighten my darkness: and of Thy fulness have we all received, for Thou art the true light that lighteth every man that cometh into the world; for in Thee there is no variableness, neither shadow of change.*

26 But I pressed towards Thee, and was thrust from Thee, that I might taste of death: for *thou resistest the proud.* But what prouder, than for me with a strange madness to maintain myself to be that by nature which Thou art? For whereas I was subject to change, (so much being manifest to me, my very desire to become wise, being the wish, of worse to become better;) yet chose I rather to imagine Thee subject to change, than myself not to be that which Thou art. Therefore I was repelled by Thee, and Thou

resistedst my vain stiff-neckedness, and I imagined corporeal forms, and—myself flesh, I accused flesh; and, *a wind that passeth away, I returned not* to Thee, but I passed on and on to things which have no being, neither in Thee, nor in me, nor in the body. Neither were they created for me by Thy truth, but by my vanity devised out of things corporeal. And I was wont to ask Thy faithful little ones, my fellow-citizens, (from whom, unknown to myself, I stood exiled,) I was wont, prating and foolishly, to ask them, "Why then doth the soul err which God created?" But I would not be asked, "Why then doth God err?" And I maintained, that Thy unchangeable substance did err upon constraint, rather than confess that my changeable substance had gone astray voluntarily, and now, in punishment, lay in error.

27 I was then some six or seven and twenty years old when I wrote those volumes; revolving within me corporeal fictions, buzzing in the ears of my heart, which I turned, O sweet truth, to thy inward melody, meditating on the "fair and fit," and longing to stand and hearken to Thee, and *to rejoice greatly at the Bridegroom's voice*, but could not; for by the voices of mine own errors, I was hurried abroad, and through the weight of my own pride, I was sinking into the lowest pit. For Thou didst not *make me to hear joy and gladness*, nor did *the bones exult which were not yet humbled*.

[XVI] 28 And what did it profit me, that scarce twenty years old, a book of Aristotle, which they call the ten Predicaments, falling into my hands, (on whose very name I hung, as on something great and divine, so often as my rhetoric master of Carthage, and others, accounted learned, mouthed it with cheeks bursting with pride,) I read and understood it unaided? And on my conferring with others, who said that they scarcely understood it with very able tutors, not only orally explaining it, but drawing many things in sand, they could tell me no more of it than I had learned, reading it by myself. And the book appeared to me to speak very clearly of substances, such as "man," and of their qualities, as the figure of a man, of what sort it is; and stature, how many feet high; and his relationship, whose brother he is; or where placed; or when born; or whether he stands or sits; or be shod or armed; or does, or suffers any thing; and all the innumerable things which might be ranged under these nine Predicaments,[24] of which I have given some specimens, or under that chief Predicament of Substance.

29 What did all this further me, seeing it even hindered me? when, imagining whatever was, was comprehended under those ten Predicaments, I essayed in such wise to understand, O my God, Thy wonderful and unchangeable Unity also, as if Thou also hadst been subjected to Thine own greatness or beauty; so that (as in bodies) they should exist in Thee, as their subject: whereas Thou Thyself art Thy greatness and beauty; but a body is not great or fair in that it is a body, seeing that, though it were less great or fair, it should notwithstanding be a body. But it was falsehood which of Thee I conceived, not truth; fictions of my misery, not the realities of Thy Blessedness. For Thou hadst commanded, and it was done in me, that

the *earth should bring forth briars and thorns to me*, and that *in the sweat of my brows I should eat my bread*.

30 And what did it profit me, that all the books I could procure of the so-called liberal arts, I the vile slave of vile affections, read by myself, and understood? And I delighted in them, but knew not whence came all, that therein was true or certain. For I had my back to the light, and my face to the things enlightened; whence my face, with which I discerned the things enlightened, itself was not enlightened. Whatever was written, either on rhetoric, or logic, geometry, music, and arithmetic, by myself without much difficulty or any instructor, I understood, Thou knowest, O Lord my God; because both quickness of understanding, and acuteness in discerning, is Thy gift: yet did I not thence sacrifice to Thee. So then it served not to my use, but rather to my perdition, since I went about to get so good a *portion of my substance* into my own keeping; and I *kept not my strength for Thee*, but wandered from Thee *into a far country, to spend it upon harlotries*. For what profited me good abilities, not employed to good uses? For I felt not that those arts were attained with great difficulty, even by the studious and talented, until I attempted to explain them to such; when he most excelled in them, who followed me not altogether slowly.

31 But what did this further me, imagining that Thou, O Lord God, the Truth, wert a vast and bright body, and I a fragment of that body? Perverseness too great! But such was I. Nor do I blush, O my God, to *confess to Thee Thy*

mercies towards me, and to call upon Thee, who blushed not then to profess to men my blasphemies, and to bark against Thee. What profited me then my nimble wit in those sciences and all those most knotty volumes, unravelled by me, without aid from human instruction; seeing I erred so foully, and with such sacrilegious shamefulness, in the doctrine of piety? Or what hindrance was a far slower wit to Thy little ones, since they departed not far from Thee, that in the nest of Thy Church they might securely be fledged, and nourish the wings of charity, by the food of a sound faith. O Lord our God, *under the shadow of Thy wings let us hope*; protect us, and carry us. Thou wilt carry us both when little, and *even to hoar hairs wilt Thou carry us*; for our firmness, when it is Thou, then is it firmness; but when our own, it is infirmity. Our good ever lives with Thee; from which when we turn away, we are turned aside. Let us now, O Lord, return, that we may not be overturned, because with Thee our good lives without any decay, which good art Thou; nor need we fear, lest there be no place whither to return, because we fell from it: for through our absence, our mansion fell not—Thy eternity.

BOOK V

St. Aug.'s twenty-ninth year. Faustus, a snare of Satan to many, made an instrument of deliverance to St. Aug., by shewing the ignorance of the Manichees on those things, wherein they professed to have divine knowledge. Aug. gives up all thought of going further among the Manichees: is guided to Rome and Milan, where he hears St. Ambrose, leaves the Manichees, and becomes again a Catechumen in the Church Catholic.

[I] 1 Accept the sacrifice of my confessions from the ministry of my tongue, which Thou hast formed and stirred up to confess unto Thy name. *Heal Thou all my bones, and let them say, O Lord, who is like unto Thee?* For he who confesses to Thee, doth not teach Thee what takes place within him; seeing a closed heart closes not out Thy eye, nor can man's hard-heartedness thrust back Thy hand: for Thou dissolvest it at Thy will in pity or in vengeance, *and nothing can hide itself from Thy heat*. But let my soul praise Thee, that it may love Thee; and let it confess Thy own mercies to Thee, that it may praise Thee. Thy whole creation ceaseth not, nor is silent in Thy praises; neither the spirit of man with voice directed unto Thee, nor creation animate or inanimate, by the voice of those who meditate thereon: that so our souls may from their weariness arise towards Thee, leaning[1] on those things which Thou hast created, and passing on to Thyself, who madest them wonderfully; and there is refreshment and true strength.

[II] 2 Let the restless, the godless, depart and flee from Thee; yet Thou seest them, and dividest the darkness. And behold, the universe with them is fair, though they are foul.[2] And how have they injured Thee?[3] or how have they disgraced[4] Thy government, which, from the heaven to this lowest earth, is just and perfect? For whither fled they, when they fled from Thy presence? Or where dost not Thou find them? But they fled, that they might not see Thee seeing them, and, blinded, might stumble against Thee; (because *Thou forsakest nothing Thou hast made;*) that the unjust, I say, might stumble upon Thee, and justly be hurt; withdrawing themselves from Thy gentleness, and stumbling at Thy uprightness, and falling upon their own ruggedness. Ignorant, in truth, that Thou art everywhere, Whom no place encompasseth! and Thou alone art near, even to those that *remove far from Thee.* Let them then be turned, and seek Thee; because not as they have forsaken their Creator, hast Thou forsaken Thy creation. Let them be turned and seek Thee; and behold, Thou art there in their heart, in the heart of those that confess to Thee, and cast themselves upon Thee, and weep in Thy bosom, after all their rugged ways. Then dost Thou gently wipe away their tears, and they weep the more, and joy in weeping; even for that Thou, Lord,—not man of flesh and blood, but—Thou, Lord, who madest them, re-makest and comfortest them. But where was I, when I was seeking Thee? And Thou wert before me, but I had gone away from Thee; nor did I find myself, how much less Thee!

[III] 3 I would lay open before my God that nine and twentieth year of mine age. There had then come to Carthage, a certain Bishop of the Manichees, Faustus[5] by name, a great snare of the Devil, and many were entangled by him through that lure of his smooth language: which though I did commend, yet could I separate from the truth of the things which I was earnest to learn: nor did I so much regard the service of oratory, as the science which this Faustus, so praised among them, set before me to feed upon. Fame had before bespoken him most knowing in all valuable learning, and exquisitely skilled in the liberal sciences. And since I had read and well remembered much of the philosophers, I compared some things of theirs with those long fables of the Manichees, and found the former the more probable; even although they *could only prevail so far as to make judgment of this lower world, the Lord of it they could by no means find out. For Thou art great, O Lord, and hast respect unto the humble, but the proud Thou beholdest afar off*. Nor dost thou *draw near*, but to *the contrite in heart*, nor art found by the proud, no, not though by curious skill they could number the stars and the sand, and measure the starry heavens, and track the courses of the planets.

4 For with their understanding and wit, which Thou bestowedst on them, they search out these things; and much have they found out; and foretold, many years before, eclipses of those luminaries, the sun and moon,—what day and hour, and how many digits,—nor did their calculation fail; and it came to pass as they foretold; and they wrote down the rules they had found out, and these are read at this day, and out of them do others foretell in what year, and month of the year, and what day of the month, and what hour of the day, and what part of its light, moon or sun is to be eclipsed, and so it shall be, as it is foreshewed. At these things men, that know not this art, marvel and are astonished, and they that know it, exult, and are puffed up; and by an ungodly pride departing from Thee, and failing of Thy light, they foresee a failure of the sun's light, which shall be, so long before, but see not their own, which is. For they search not religiously whence they have the wit, wherewith they search out this. And finding that Thou madest them, they give not themselves up to Thee, to preserve what Thou madest, nor sacrifice to Thee, what they have made themselves; nor slay their own soaring imaginations, as *fowls of the air*,[6] nor their own diving curiosities, (wherewith, like the *fishes of the sea*, they wander over the unknown paths of the abyss,) nor their own luxuriousness, as *beasts of the field*, that *Thou, Lord, a consuming fire*, mayest burn up those dead cares of theirs, and re-create themselves immortally.

5 But they knew not the way, Thy Word, by Whom Thou madest these things which they number, and themselves who number, and the sense whereby they perceive what they number, and the understanding, out of which they number; or that *of Thy wisdom there is no number*. But the Only Begotten is Himself *made unto us wisdom, and righteousness, and sanctification*, and was numbered among us, and *paid tribute unto Cæsar*. They knew not this Way⁷ whereby to descend to Him from themselves, and by Him ascend unto Him. They knew not this way, and deemed themselves exalted amongst the stars and shining; and behold, they *fell upon the earth, and their foolish heart was darkened*. They discourse many things truly concerning the creature; but Truth, Artificer of the creature, they seek not piously, and therefore find Him not; or if they find Him, *knowing Him to be God, they glorify Him not as God, neither are thankful, but become vain in their imaginations*, and *profess themselves to be wise*, attributing to themselves what is Thine; and thereby with most perverse blindness, study to impute to Thee what is their own, forging lies of Thee who art the Truth, and *changing the glory of the uncorruptible God, into an image made like corruptible man, and to birds, and four-footed beasts, and creeping things, changing Thy truth into a lie, and worshipping and serving the creature more than the Creator.*

6 Yet many truths concerning the creature retained I from these men, and saw the reason thereof from calculations, the succession of times, and the visible testimonies of the stars; and compared them with the saying of Manichæus, which in his phrenzy he had written most largely on these

subjects; but discovered not any account of the solstices, or equinoxes, or the eclipses of the greater lights, nor whatever of this sort I had learned in the books of secular philosophy. But I was commanded to believe; and yet it corresponded not with what had been established by calculations and my own sight, but was quite contrary.

[IV] 7 Doth then, O Lord God of truth, whoso knoweth these things, therefore please Thee? Surely unhappy is he who knoweth all these, and knoweth not Thee: but happy whoso knoweth Thee, though he know not these.[8] And whoso knoweth both Thee and them, is not the happier for them, but for Thee only, if, *knowing Thee, he glorifies Thee as God, and is thankful, and becomes not vain in his imaginations.* For as he is better off, who knows how to possess a tree, and returns thanks to Thee for the use thereof, although he know not how many cubits high it is, or how wide it spreads, than he that can measure it, and count all its boughs, and neither owns it, nor knows or loves its Creator: so a believer, whose all this world of wealth is, and *who having nothing, yet possesseth all things,* by cleaving unto Thee, whom all things serve, though he know not even the circles of the Great Bear, yet is it folly to doubt but he is in a better state than one who can measure the heavens, and number the stars, and poise the elements, yet neglecteth Thee *who hast made all things in number, weight, and measure.*

[V] 8 But yet who bade that Manichæus write on these things also, skill in which was no element of piety? For Thou hast said to man, *Behold, piety and wisdom;* of which he might be ignorant, though he had perfect knowledge of these things; but these things, since, knowing not, he most impudently dared to teach, he plainly could have no knowledge of piety. For it is vanity to make profession of these worldly things even when known; but confession to Thee is piety. Wherefore this wanderer to this end spake much of these things, that convicted by those who had truly learned them, it might be manifest what understanding he had in the other abstruser things. For he would not have himself meanly thought of, but went about to persuade men, "That the Holy Ghost, the Comforter and Enricher of Thy faithful ones, was with plenary authority personally within him." When then he was found out to have taught falsely of the heaven and stars, and of the motions of the sun and moon, (although these things pertain not to the doctrine of religion,) yet his sacrilegious presumption would become evident enough, seeing he delivered things which not only he knew not, but which were falsified, with so mad a vanity of pride, that he sought to ascribe them to himself, as to a divine person.

9 For when I hear any Christian brother ignorant of these things, and mistaken on them, I can patiently behold such a man holding his opinion; nor do I see that any ignorance as to the position or character of the corporeal creation can injure him, so long as he doth not believe any thing unworthy of Thee, O Lord, the Creator of all. But it doth injure him, if he imagine it to pertain to the form of the doctrine of piety, and will yet affirm that too stiffly whereof he is ignorant. And yet is even such an infirmity,

in the infancy of faith, borne by our mother Charity, till the new-born may *grow up unto a perfect man*, so as *not to be carried about with every wind of doctrine*. But in him, who in such wise presumed to be the teacher, source, guide, chief of all whom he could so persuade, that whoso followed him, thought that he followed, not a mere man, but Thy Holy Spirit; who would not judge that so great madness, when once convicted of having taught any thing false, were to be detested and utterly rejected? But I had not as yet clearly ascertained, whether the vicissitudes of longer and shorter days and nights, and of day and night itself, with the eclipses of the greater lights, and whatever else of the kind I had read of in other books, might be explained consistently with his sayings; so that, if they by any means might, it should still remain a question to me, whether it were so or no; but I might, on account of his reputed sanctity, rest my credence upon his authority.

[VI] 10 And for almost all those nine years, wherein with unsettled mind I had been their disciple, I had longed but too intensely for the coming of this Faustus. For the rest of the sect, whom by chance I had lighted upon, when unable to solve my objections about these things, still held out to me the coming of this Faustus, by conference with whom, these and greater difficulties, if I had them, were to be most readily and abundantly cleared. When then he came, I found him a man of pleasing discourse, and who could speak fluently and in better terms, yet still but the self-same things which they were wont to say. But what availed the utmost neatness of the cup-bearer to my thirst for a more precious draught? Mine ears were already cloyed with the like, nor did they seem to me therefore better, because better said; nor therefore true, because eloquent; nor the soul therefore wise, because the face was comely, and the language graceful. But they who held him out to me, were no good judges of things; and therefore to them he appeared understanding and wise, because in words pleasing. I felt however that another sort of people were suspicious even of truth, and refused to assent to it, if delivered in a smooth and copious discourse. But Thou, O my God, hadst already taught me by wonderful and secret ways, and therefore I believe that Thou taughtest me, because it is truth, nor is there besides Thee any teacher of truth, where or whencesoever it may shine upon us.[9] Of Thyself therefore had I now learned, that neither ought any thing to seem to be spoken truly, because eloquently; nor therefore falsely, because the utterance of the lips is inharmonious; nor, again, therefore true, because rudely delivered; nor therefore false, because the language is rich; but that wisdom and folly, are as wholesome and unwholesome food; and adorned or unadorned phrases, as courtly or country vessels; either kind of meats may be served up in either kind of dishes.

11 That greediness then, wherewith I had of so long time expected that man, was delighted verily with his action and feeling when disputing, and his choice and readiness of words to clothe his ideas. I was then delighted, and, with many others and more than they, did I praise and extol him. It troubled me, however, that in the assembly of his auditors, I was not allowed to put in, and communicate[10] those questions that troubled me, in familiar

converse with him. Which when I might, and with my friends began to engage his ears at such times as it was not unbecoming for him to discuss with me, and had brought forward such things as moved me; I found him first utterly ignorant of liberal sciences, save grammar, and that but in an ordinary way. But because he had read some of Tully's Orations, a very few books of Seneca, some things of the poets, and such few volumes of his own sect, as were written in Latin and neatly, and was daily practised in speaking, he acquired a certain eloquence, which proved the more pleasing and seductive, because under the guidance of a good wit, and with a kind of natural gracefulness. Is it not thus, as I recall it, O Lord my God, Thou Judge of my conscience? Before Thee is my heart, and my remembrance, Who didst at that time direct me by the hidden mystery of Thy providence, and didst set those shameful errors of mine before my face, that I might see and hate them.

[VII] 12 For after it was clear, that he was ignorant of those arts in which I thought he excelled, I began to despair of his opening and solving the difficulties which perplexed me; (of which indeed however ignorant, he might have held the truths of piety, had he not been a Manichee.) For their books are fraught with prolix fables, of the heaven, and stars, sun, and moon, and I now no longer thought him able satisfactorily to decide what I much desired, whether, on comparison of these things with the calculations I had elsewhere read, the account given in the books of Manichæus were preferable, or at least as good. Which when I proposed to be considered and discussed, he, so far modestly, shrunk from the burthen. For he knew that he knew not these things, and was not ashamed to confess it. For he was not one of those talking persons, many of whom I had endured, who undertook to teach me these things, and said nothing. But this man had a heart, though not right towards Thee, yet neither altogether treacherous to himself. For he was not altogether ignorant of his own ignorance, nor would he rashly be entangled in a dispute, whence he could neither retreat, nor extricate himself fairly. Even for this I liked him the better. For fairer is the modesty of a candid mind, than the knowledge of those things which I desired;[11] and such I found him, in all the more difficult and subtile questions.

13 My zeal for the writings of Manichæus being thus blunted, and despairing yet more of their other teachers, seeing that in divers things which perplexed me, he, so renowned among them, had so turned out; I began to engage with him in the study of that literature, on which he also was much set, (and which as rhetoric-reader I was at that time teaching young students at Carthage,) and to read with him, either what himself desired to hear, or such as I judged fit for his genius. But all my efforts whereby I had purposed to advance in that sect, upon knowledge of that man, came utterly to an end; not that I detached myself from them altogether, but as one finding nothing better, I had settled to be content meanwhile with what I had in whatever way fallen upon, unless by chance something more eligible should dawn upon me. Thus that Faustus, to so many a snare of death,

had now, neither willing nor witting it, begun to loosen that wherein I was taken. For Thy hands, O my God, in the secret purpose of Thy providence, did not forsake my soul; and out of my mother's heart's blood, through her tears night and day poured out, was a sacrifice offered for me unto Thee; and Thou didst deal with me by wondrous ways. Thou didst it, O my God: for *the steps of a man are ordered by the Lord, and He shall dispose his way.* Or how shall we obtain salvation, but from Thy hand, re-making what It made?

[VIII] 14 Thou didst deal with me, that I should be persuaded to go to Rome, and to teach there rather, what I was teaching at Carthage. And how I was persuaded to this, I will not neglect to confess to Thee: because herein also the deepest recesses of Thy wisdom, and Thy most present mercy to us, must be considered and confessed. I did not wish therefore to go to Rome, because higher gains and higher dignities were warranted me by my friends who persuaded me to this, (though even these things had at that time an influence over my mind,) but my chief and almost only reason was, that I heard that young men studied there more peacefully, and were kept quiet under a restraint of more regular discipline; so that they did not, at their pleasures, petulantly rush into the school of one, whose pupils they were not, nor were even admitted without his permission. Whereas at Carthage, there reigns among the scholars a most disgraceful and unruly licence. They burst in audaciously, and with gestures almost frantic, disturb all order which any one hath established for the good of his scholars. Divers outrages they commit, with a wonderful stolidity, punishable by law, did not custom uphold them; that custom evincing them to be the more miserable, in that they now do as lawful, what by Thy eternal law shall never be lawful; and they think they do it unpunished, whereas they are punished with the very blindness whereby they do it, and suffer incomparably worse than what they do. The manners then which, when a student, I would not make my own,[12] I was fain, as a teacher, to endure in others: and so I was well pleased to go where, all that knew it, assured me that the like was not done. But Thou, *my refuge and my portion in the land of the living*, that I might change my earthly dwelling for the salvation of my soul, at Carthage didst goad me, that I might thereby be torn from it; and at Rome didst proffer me allurements, whereby I might be drawn thither, by men in love with a dying life, the one doing frantic, the other promising vain, things; and, to correct my steps, didst secretly use their and my own perverseness. For both they who disturbed my quiet, were blinded with a disgraceful phrenzy, and they who invited me elsewhere, savoured of earth. And I, who here detested real misery, was there seeking unreal happiness.

15 But why I went hence, and went thither, Thou knewest, O God, yet shewedst it neither to me, nor to my mother, who grievously bewailed my journey, and followed me as far as the sea. But I deceived her, holding me by force, that either she might keep me back, or go with me, and I feigned that I had a friend whom I could not leave, till he had a fair wind to sail. And I lied to my

mother, and such a mother, and escaped: for this also hast Thou mercifully forgiven me, preserving me, thus full of execrable defilements, from the waters of the sea, for the water[13] of Thy Grace; whereby when I was cleansed, the streams of my mother's eyes should be dried, with which for me she daily watered the ground under her face. And yet refusing to return without me, I scarcely persuaded her to stay that night in a place hard by our ship, where was an Oratory[14] in memory of the blessed Cyprian. That night I privily departed, but she was not behind in weeping and prayer. And what, O Lord, was she with so many tears asking of Thee, but that Thou wouldest not suffer me to sail? But Thou, in the depth of Thy counsels and hearing the main point of her desire, regardest not what she then asked, that Thou mightest make me what she ever asked. The wind blew and swelled our sails, and withdrew the shore from our sight; and she on the morrow was there, frantic with sorrow, and with complaints and groans filled Thine ears, who didst then disregard them; whilst through my desires, Thou wert hurrying me to end all desire, and the earthly part of her affection to me was chastened by the allotted scourge of sorrows. For she loved my being with her, as mothers do, but much more than many; and she knew not how great joy Thou wert about to work for her out of my absence. She knew not; therefore did she weep and wail, and by this agony there appeared in her the inheritance of Eve, with sorrow seeking, what in sorrow she had brought forth. And yet, after accusing my treachery and hardheartedness, she betook herself again to intercede to Thee for me, went to her wonted place, and I to Rome.

[IX] 16 And lo, there was I received by the scourge of bodily sickness, and I was going down to hell, carrying all the sins which I had committed, both against Thee, and myself, and others, many and grievous, over and above that bond of original sin, whereby *we all die in Adam*. For Thou hadst not forgiven me any of these things in Christ, nor had He *abolished by His cross*[15] *the enmity* which by my sins I had incurred with Thee. For how should He, by the crucifixion of a phantasm,[16] which I believed Him to be? So true, then, was the death of my soul, as that of His flesh seemed to me false; and how true the death of His body, so false was the life of my soul, which did not believe it. And now the fever heightening, I was parting and departing for ever. For had I then parted hence, whither had I departed, but into fire and torments, such as my misdeeds deserved in the truth of Thy appointment? And this she knew not, yet in absence prayed for me. But Thou, every where present, heardest her where she was, and where I was, hadst compassion upon me; that I should recover the health of my body, though phrenzied as yet in my sacrilegious heart. For I did not in all that danger desire Thy baptism; and I was better as a boy, when I begged it of my mother's piety, as I have before recited and confessed.[17] But I had grown up to my own shame, and I madly scoffed[18] at the prescripts of Thy medicine, who wouldest not suffer me, being such, to die a double death. With which wound had my mother's heart been pierced, it could never be healed. For I cannot express the affection she bare to me, and with how much more vehement anguish she was now in labour of me in the spirit, than at her childbearing in the flesh.

17 I see not then how she should have been healed, had such a death of mine stricken through the bowels of her love. And where would have been those her so strong and unceasing prayers, unintermitting to Thee alone? But wouldest Thou, God of mercies, *despise* the *contrite and humbled heart* of that chaste and sober widow, so frequent in almsdeeds, so full of duty and service to Thy saints, no day intermitting the oblation at Thine altar, twice a day, morning and evening, without any intermission, coming to Thy church, not for idle tattlings and old wives *fables;* but that she might hear Thee in Thy discourses and Thou her, in her prayers. Couldest Thou despise and reject from Thy aid the tears of such an one, wherewith she begged of Thee not gold or silver, nor any mutable or passing good, but the salvation of her son's soul? Thou, by whose gift she was such? Never, Lord. Yea, Thou wert at hand, and wert hearing and doing, in that order wherein Thou hadst determined before, that it should be done. Far be it that Thou shouldest deceive her in Thy visions and answers, some whereof I have,[19] some I have not[20] mentioned, which she laid up in her faithful heart, and ever praying, urged upon Thee, as Thine own hand-writing. For Thou, *because Thy mercy endureth for ever,* vouchsafest to those to whom Thou forgivest all their debts, to become also a debtor by Thy promises.

[X] 18 Thou recoveredst me then of that sickness, and healedst the son of Thy handmaid, for the time in body, that he might live, for Thee to bestow upon him a better and more abiding health. And even then, at Rome, I joined myself to those deceiving and deceived "holy ones;" not with their disciples only, (of which number was he, in whose house I had fallen sick and recovered;) but also with those whom they call "The Elect." For I still thought, "that it was not we that sin, but that I know not what other nature sinned in us;" and it delighted my pride, to be free from blame; and when I had done any evil, not to confess I had done any, *that Thou mightest heal my soul because it had sinned against Thee:* but I loved to excuse it, and to accuse I know not what other thing, which was with me, but which I was not. But in truth it was wholly I, and mine impiety had divided me against myself: and that sin was the more incurable, whereby I did not judge myself a sinner; and execrable iniquity it was, that I had rather have Thee, Thee, O God Almighty, to be overcome in me to my destruction, than myself of Thee to salvation. Not as yet then hadst Thou *set a watch before my mouth, and a door of safe keeping around my lips, that my heart might not turn aside to wicked speeches, to make excuses of sins, with men that work iniquity:* and, therefore, was I still *united with their Elect.*[21]

19 But now despairing to make proficiency in that false doctrine, even those things (with which if I should find no better, I had resolved to rest contented) I now held more laxly and carelessly. For there half arose a thought in me, that those philosophers, whom they call Academics, were wiser than the rest, for that they held, men ought to doubt every thing, and laid down that no truth can be comprehended by man: for so, not then understanding even their meaning, I also was clearly convinced that they thought, as they are commonly[22]

reported. Yet did I freely and openly discourage that host of mine from that over-confidence which I perceived him to have in those fables, which the books of Manichæus are full of. Yet I lived in more familiar friendship with them, than with others who were not of this heresy. Nor did I maintain it with my ancient eagerness; still my intimacy with that sect (Rome secretly harbouring many of them) made me slower[23] to seek any other way: especially since I despaired of finding the truth, from which they had turned me aside, in Thy Church, O Lord of heaven and earth, Creator of all things visible and invisible: and it seemed to me very unseemly to believe Thee to have the shape of human flesh, and to be bounded by the bodily lineaments of our members. And because, when I wished to think on my God, I knew not what to think of, but a mass of bodies, (for what was not such, did not seem to me to be any thing,) this was the greatest, and almost only cause of my inevitable error.

20 For hence I believed Evil also to be some such kind of substance, and to have its own foul, and hideous bulk; whether gross, which they called earth, or thin and subtile, (like the body of the air,) which they imagine to be some malignant mind, creeping through that earth. And because a piety, such as it was, constrained me to believe, that the good God never created any evil nature, I conceived two masses, contrary to one another, both unbounded, but the evil narrower, the good more expansive. And from this pestilent beginning, the other sacrilegious conceits followed on me. For when my mind endeavoured to recur to the Catholic faith, I was driven

back, since that was not the Catholic faith, which I thought to be so. And I seemed to myself more reverential, if I believed of Thee, my God, (to whom Thy mercies confess out of my mouth,) as unbounded, at least on other sides, although on that one where the mass of evil was opposed to Thee, I was constrained to confess Thee bounded; than if on all sides I should imagine Thee to be bounded by the form of a human body. And it seemed to me better to believe Thee to have created no evil, (which to me ignorant seemed not some only, but a bodily, substance, because I could not conceive of mind, unless as a subtile body, and that diffused in definite spaces,) than to believe the nature of evil, such as I conceived it, could come from Thee. Yea, and our Saviour Himself, Thy Only Begotten, I believed to have been reached forth (as it were) for our salvation, out of the mass of Thy most lucid substance, so as to believe nothing of Him, but what I could imagine in my vanity. His Nature then, being such, I thought could not be born of the Virgin Mary, without being mingled with the flesh: and how that which I had so figured to myself, could be mingled, and not defiled, I saw not. I feared therefore to believe Him born in the flesh, lest I should be forced to believe Him defiled by the flesh.[24] Now will Thy spiritual ones mildly and lovingly smile upon me, if they shall read these my confessions. Yet such was I.

[XI] 21 Furthermore, what the Manichees had criticised[25] in Thy Scriptures, I thought could not be defended; yet at times verily I had a wish to confer upon these several points with some one very well skilled in those books,

and to make trial what he thought thereon: for the words
of one Helpidius, as he spoke and disputed face to face
against the said Manichees, had begun to stir me even at
Carthage: in that he had produced things out of the
Scriptures, not easily withstood, the Manichees' answer
whereto seemed to me weak. And this answer they liked
not to give publicly, but only to us in private. It was, that
the Scriptures of the New Testament had been corrupted
by I know not whom, who wished to engraff the law of
the Jews upon the Christian faith: yet themselves
produced not any uncorrupted copies. But I, conceiving
of things corporeal only, was mainly held down,
vehemently oppressed and in a manner suffocated by
those "masses;"[26] panting under which after the breath of
Thy truth, I could not breathe it pure and untainted.

[XII] 22 I began then diligently to practise that for which
I came to Rome, to teach rhetoric; and first, to gather
some to my house, to whom, and through whom, I had
begun to be known; when lo, I found other offences
committed in Rome, to which I was not exposed in Africa.
True, those "subvertings"[27] by profligate young men,
were not here practised, as was told me: but on a sudden,
said they, to avoid paying their master's stipend, a number
of youths plot together, and remove to another;—breakers
of faith, who for love of money hold justice cheap. These
also *my heart hated*, though not *with a perfect hatred*: for
perchance I hated them more because I was to suffer by
them, than because they did things utterly unlawful. Of
a truth such are base persons, and they go a whoring from
Thee, loving these fleeting mockeries of things temporal,

and filthy lucre, which fouls the hand that grasps it; hugging the fleeting world, and despising Thee, who abidest, and recallest, and forgivest the adulteress soul of man, when she returns to Thee. And now I hate such depraved and crooked persons, though I love them if corrigible, so as to prefer to money the learning, which they acquire, and to learning, Thee, O God, the truth and fulness of assured good, and most pure peace. But then I rather for my own sake misliked them evil, than liked and wished them good for Thine.

[XIII] 23 When therefore they of Milan had sent to Rome to the prefect of the city, to furnish them with a rhetoric reader for their city, and send him at the public expense, I made application (through those very persons, intoxicated with Manichæan vanities, to be freed wherefrom I was to go, neither of us however knowing it) that Symmachus, then prefect of the city, would try me by setting me some subject, and so send me. To Milan I came, to Ambrose the Bishop, known to the whole world as among the best of men, Thy devout servant; whose eloquent discourse did then plentifully dispense unto Thy people the flour of Thy wheat, the gladness of Thy oil, and the sober inebriation of Thy wine. To him was I unknowing led by Thee, that by him I might knowingly be led to Thee. That man of God received me as a father, and shewed me an Episcopal kindness on my coming. Thenceforth I began to love him, at first indeed not as a teacher of the truth, (which I utterly despaired of in Thy Church,) but as a person kind towards myself. And I listened diligently to him preaching to the people, not

with that intent I ought, but, as it were, trying his
eloquence, whether it answered the fame thereof, or
flowed fuller or lower than was reported; and I hung on
his words attentively; but of the matter I was as a careless
and scornful looker-on; and I was delighted with the
sweetness of his discourse, more recondite, yet in manner,
less winning and harmonious, than that of Faustus. Of the
matter, however, there was no comparison; for the one
was wandering amid Manichæan delusions, the other
teaching salvation most soundly. But *salvation is far from
sinners*, such as I then stood before him; and yet was I
drawing nearer by little and little, and unconsciously.

[XIV] 24 For though I took no pains to learn what he
spake, but only to hear how he spake; (for that empty care
alone was left me, despairing of a way open for man, to
Thee,) yet together with the words which I would choose,
came also into my mind the things which I would refuse;
for I could not separate them. And while I opened my
heart to admit "how eloquently he spake," there also
entered "how truly he spake;" but this by degrees. For
first, these things also had now begun to appear to me
capable of defence; and the Catholic faith, for which I had
thought nothing could be said against the Manichees'
objections, I now thought might be maintained without
shamelessness; especially after I had heard one or two
places of the Old Testament resolved, and ofttimes *"in a
figure,"* which when I understood literally, I was slain
spiritually. Very many places then of those books having
been explained, I now blamed my despair, in believing,
that no answer could be given to such as hated and

scoffed[28] at the Law and the Prophets. Yet did I not therefore then see, that the Catholic way was to be held, because it also could find learned maintainers, who could at large and with some shew of reason answer objections; nor that what I held was therefore to be condemned, because both sides could be maintained. For the Catholic cause seemed to me in such sort not vanquished, as still not as yet to be victorious.

25 Hereupon I earnestly bent my mind, to see if in any way I could by any certain proof convict the Manichees of falsehood. Could I once have conceived a spiritual substance, all their strong holds had been beaten down, and cast utterly out of my mind; but I could not. Notwithstanding, concerning the frame of this world, and the whole of nature, which the senses of the flesh can reach to, as I more and more considered and compared things, I judged the tenets of most of the philosophers to have been much more probable. So then after the manner of the Academics (as they are supposed[29]) doubting of every thing, and wavering between all, I settled so far, that the Manichees were to be abandoned; judging that, even while doubting, I might not continue in that sect, to which I already preferred some of the philosophers; to which philosophers notwithstanding, for that they were without the saving Name of Christ, I utterly refused to commit the cure of my sick soul. I determined therefore so long to be a Catechumen in the Catholic Church, to which I had been commended by my parents, till something certain should dawn upon me, whither I might steer my course.[30]

BOOK VI

Arrival of Monnica at Milan; her obedience to St. Ambrose, and his value for her; St. Ambrose's habits; Aug.'s gradual abandonment of error; finds that he has blamed the Church Catholic wrongly; desire of absolute certainty, but struck with the contrary analogy of God's natural Providence; how shaken in his worldly pursuits; God's guidance of his friend Alypius; Aug. debates with himself and his friends about their mode of life; his inveterate sins, and dread of judgment.

[I] 1 *O Thou, my hope from my youth*, where wert Thou to me, and whither wert Thou gone? Hadst not Thou created me, and separated me from the beasts of the field, and fowls of the air? Thou hadst made me wiser, yet did I walk in darkness, and in slippery places, and sought Thee abroad[1] out of myself, and found not the God of my heart; and had come into the depths of the sea, and distrusted and despaired of ever finding truth. My mother had now come to me, resolute through piety, following me over sea and land, in all perils confiding in Thee. For in perils of the sea, she comforted the very mariners, (by whom passengers unacquainted with the deep, use rather to be comforted when troubled,) assuring them of a safe arrival, because Thou hadst by a vision assured her thereof. She found me in grievous peril, through despair of ever finding truth. But when I had discovered to her, that I was now no longer a Manichee, though not yet a Catholic Christian, she was not overjoyed, as at something unexpected; although she was now assured concerning that part of my misery, for which she bewailed me as one dead, though to be reawakened by Thee, carrying me forth upon the *bier* of her thoughts, that Thou mightest say to the *son of the widow, Young man, I say unto thee, Arise; and he should revive, and begin to speak, and thou shouldest deliver him to his mother*. Her heart then was shaken with no tumultuous exultation, when she heard that what she daily with tears desired of Thee, was already in so great part realized; in that, though I had not yet attained the truth, I was rescued from falsehood; but, as being assured, that Thou, who hadst promised the whole, wouldest one day give the rest, most calmly, and with an heart full of confidence, she replied to me, "She believed in Christ, that before she departed this life, she should see me a Catholic believer."[2] Thus much to me. But to Thee, Fountain of mercies, poured she forth more copious prayers and tears, that Thou wouldest hasten Thy help, and enlighten my darkness; and she hastened the more eagerly to the Church, and hung upon the lips of Ambrose, praying for *the fountain*[3] of that water, which springeth up unto life everlasting. But that man she loved *as an angel of God*, because she knew that by him I had been brought for the present to that doubtful state of faith I now was in, through which she anticipated most confidently, that I should pass from sickness unto health, after the access, as it were, of a sharper fit, which physicians call "the crisis."

[II] 2 When then my mother had once, as she was wont in Afric, brought to the Churches built in memory of the Saints,[4] certain cakes, and bread and wine, and was forbidden by the door-keeper; so soon as she knew that the Bishop had forbidden this, she so piously and obediently embraced his wishes, that I myself wondered how readily she censured her own practice, rather than discuss his prohibition. For wine-bibbing did not lay siege to her spirit, nor did love of wine provoke her to hatred of the truth, as it doth too many, (both men and women,) who revolt at a lesson of sobriety, as men well-drunk at a draught mingled with water. But she, when she had brought her basket with the accustomed festival-food, to be but tasted by herself, and then given away, never joined therewith more than one small cup of wine, diluted according to her own abstemious habits, which for courtesy she would taste. And if there were many Churches of the departed saints, that were to be honoured in that manner, she still carried round that same one cup, to be used every where; and this, though not only made very watery, but unpleasantly heated with carrying about, she would distribute to those about her by small sips; for she sought their devotion, not pleasure. So soon, then, as she found this custom to be forbidden by that famous preacher, and most pious prelate, even to those that would use it soberly, lest so an occasion of excess might be given to the drunken;[5] and for that these, as it were, anniversary funeral solemnities did much resemble the superstition of the Gentiles, she most willingly forbare it: and for a basket filled with fruits of the earth, she had learned to bring to the Churches of the martyrs, a breast filled with more purified petitions, and to give what she could to the poor; that so the communication[6] of the Lord's Body might be there rightly celebrated, where, after the example of His Passion, the martyrs had been sacrificed and crowned. But yet it seems to me, O Lord my God, and thus thinks my heart of it in Thy sight, that perhaps she would not so readily have yielded to the cutting off of this custom, had it been forbidden by another, whom she loved not as Ambrose, whom, for my salvation, she loved most entirely; and he her again, for her most religious conversation, whereby in good works, so *fervent in spirit*, she was constant at church; so that, when he saw me, he often burst forth into her praises; congratulating me, that I had such a mother; not knowing what a son she had in me, who doubted of all these things, and imagined the way to life could not be found out.

[III] 3 Nor did I yet groan in my prayers, that Thou wouldest help me; but my spirit was wholly intent on learning, and restless to dispute. And Ambrose himself, as the world counts happy, I esteemed a happy man, whom personages so great held in such honour; only his celibacy seemed to me a painful course. But what hope he bore within him, what struggles he had against the temptations which beset his very excellencies, or what comfort in adversities, and what sweet joys Thy Bread had for the hidden mouth of his spirit, when chewing the cud[7]

thereof, I neither could conjecture, nor had experienced.
Nor did he know the tides of my feelings, or the abyss of
my danger. For I could not ask of him, what I would as I
would, being shut out both from his ear and speech by
multitudes of busy people, whose weaknesses he served.
With whom when he was not taken up, (which was but a
little time,) he was either refreshing his body with the
sustenance absolutely necessary, or his mind with reading.
But when he was reading, his eye glided over the pages,
and his heart searched out the sense, but his voice and
tongue were at rest. Oft-times when we had come, (for no
man was forbidden to enter, nor was it his wont that any
who came should be announced to him,) we saw him thus
reading to himself, and never otherwise; and having long
sat silent, (for who durst intrude on one so intent?) we
were fain to depart, conjecturing, that in the small
interval, which he obtained, free from the din of others'
business, for the recruiting of his mind, he was loath to
be taken off; and perchance he dreaded lest if the author
he read should deliver any thing obscurely, some attentive
or perplexed hearer should desire him to expound it, or
to discuss some of the harder questions; so that his time
being thus spent, he could not turn over so many volumes
as he desired; although the preserving of his voice (which
a very little speaking would weaken) might be the truer
reason for his reading to himself. But with what intent
soever he did it, certainly in such a man it was good.

4 I however certainly had no opportunity of enquiring
what I wished, of that so holy oracle of Thine, his breast,
unless the thing might be answered briefly. But those

tides in me, to be poured out to him, required his full leisure, and never found it. I heard him indeed every Lord's day, *rightly expounding the Word of Truth* among the people; and I was more and more convinced, that all the knots of those crafty calumnies, which those our deceivers had knit against the Divine Books, could be unravelled. But when I understood withal, that *"man, created by Thee, after Thine own image,"* was not so understood by Thy spiritual sons, whom of the Catholic Mother Thou hast born again through grace, as though they believed and conceived of Thee as bounded by human shape; (although what a spiritual substance should be I had not even a faint or shadowy notion;) yet, with joy I blushed at having so many years barked not against the Catholic faith, but against the fictions of carnal imaginations. For so rash and impious had I been, that what I ought by enquiring to have learned, I had pronounced on, condemning. For Thou, Most High, and most near; most secret, and most present; Who hast not limbs some larger, some smaller, but art wholly every where, and no where in space, art not of such corporeal shape, yet hast Thou made man after Thine own image; and behold, from head to foot is he contained in space.

[IV] 5 Ignorant then how this Thy image should subsist, I should have knocked and proposed the doubt, how it was to be believed, not insultingly opposed it, as if believed. Doubt, then, what to hold for certain, the more sharply gnawed my heart, the more ashamed I was, that so long deluded and deceived by the promise of certainties, I had with childish error and vehemence, prated of so many uncertainties. For that they were falsehoods, became clear to me later. However I was certain that they were uncertain, and that I had formerly accounted them certain, when with a blind contentiousness, I accused Thy Catholic Church, whom I now discovered, not indeed as yet to teach truly, but at least not to teach that, for which I had grievously censured her. So I was confounded, and converted: and I joyed, O my God, that the One Only Church, the body of Thine Only Son, (wherein the name of Christ had been put upon me as an infant,) had no taste for infantine conceits; nor in her sound doctrine, maintained any tenet which should confine Thee, the Creator of all, in space, however great and large, yet bounded every where by the limits of a human form.

6 I joyed also, that the old Scriptures of the Law and the Prophets, were laid before me, not now to be perused with that eye to which before they seemed absurd, when I reviled Thy holy ones for so thinking, whereas indeed they thought not so: and with joy I heard Ambrose in his sermons to the people, oftentimes most diligently recommend this text for a rule, *The letter killeth, but the Spirit giveth life;* whilst he drew aside the mystic veil, laying open spiritually what according to the letter, seemed to teach something unsound; teaching herein nothing that offended me, though he taught what I knew not as yet, whether it were true. For I kept my heart from assenting to any thing, fearing to fall headlong; but by hanging in suspense I was the worse killed. For I wished to be as assured of the things I saw not, as I was that

seven and three are ten. For I was not so mad, as to think that even this could not be comprehended; but I desired to have other things as clear as this, whether things corporeal, which were not present to my senses, or spiritual, whereof I knew not how to conceive, except corporeally. And by believing might I have been cured, that so the eyesight of my soul being cleared, might in some way be directed to Thy truth, which abideth always, and in no part faileth. But as it happens that one, who has tried a bad physician, fears to trust himself with a good one, so was it with the health of my soul, which could not be healed but by believing, and lest it should believe falsehoods, refused to be cured; resisting Thy hands, who hast prepared the medicines of faith, and hast applied them to the diseases of the whole world, and given unto them so great authority.

[V] 7 Being led, however, from this to prefer the Catholic doctrine, I felt that her proceeding was more unassuming and honest, in that she required to be believed things not demonstrated, (whether it was that they could in themselves be demonstrated but not to certain persons, or could not at all be,) whereas among the Manichees our credulity was mocked by a promise of certain knowledge, and then so many most fabulous and absurd things were imposed to be believed, because they could not be demonstrated. Then Thou, O Lord, little by little with most tender and most merciful hand, touching and composing my heart, didst persuade me—considering what innumerable things I believed, which I saw not, nor was present while they were done, as so many things in secular history, so many reports of places and of cities, which I had not seen; so many of friends, so many of physicians, so many continually of other men, which unless we should believe, we should do nothing at all in this life; lastly, with how unshaken an assurance I believed, of what parents I was born, which I could not know, had I not believed upon hearsay—considering all this, Thou didst persuade me, that not they who believed Thy Books, (which Thou hast established in so great authority among almost all nations,) but they who believed them not, were to be blamed; and that they were not to be heard, who should say to me, "How knowest thou those Scriptures to have been imparted unto mankind by the Spirit of the one true and most true God?" For this very thing was of all most to be believed, since no contentiousness of blasphemous questionings, of all that multitude which I had read in the self-contradicting philosophers, could wring this belief from me, "That Thou art" whatsoever Thou wert, (what I knew not,) and "That the government of human things belongs to Thee."

8 This I believed, sometimes more strongly, more weakly other-whiles; yet I ever believed both that Thou wert, and hadst a care of us; though I was ignorant, both what was to be thought of Thy substance, and what way led or led back to Thee. Since then we were too weak by abstract reasonings to find out truth: and for this very cause needed the authority of Holy Writ; I had now begun to believe, that Thou wouldest never have given such excellency of authority to that Writ in all lands, hadst Thou not willed thereby to be believed in, thereby

sought. For now what things, sounding strangely in the Scripture, were wont to offend me, having heard divers of them expounded satisfactorily, I referred to the depth of the mysteries, and its authority appeared to me the more venerable, and more worthy of religious credence, in that, while it lay open to all to read, it reserved the majesty of its mysteries within its profounder meaning, stooping to all in the great plainness of its words and lowliness of its style, yet calling forth the intensest application of such as are not light of heart; that so it might receive all in its open bosom, and through narrow passages waft over towards Thee some few, yet many more than if it stood not aloft on such a height of authority, nor drew multitudes within its bosom by its holy lowliness. These things I thought on, and Thou wert with me; I sighed, and Thou heardest me; I wavered, and Thou didst guide me; I wandered through the broad way of the world, and Thou didst not forsake me.

[VI] 9 I panted after honours, gains, marriage; and Thou deridedst me. In these desires I underwent most bitter crosses, Thou being the more gracious, the less Thou sufferedst aught to grow sweet to me, which was not Thou. Behold my heart, O Lord, who wouldest I should remember all this, and confess to Thee. Let my soul cleave unto Thee, now that Thou hast freed it from that fast-holding birdlime of death. How wretched was it! and Thou didst irritate the feeling of its wound, that forsaking all else, it might be converted unto Thee, who art above all, and without whom all things would be nothing; be converted, and be healed. How miserable was I then, and how didst Thou deal with me, to make me feel my misery on that day, when I was preparing to recite a panegyric of the Emperor,[8] wherein I was to utter many a lie, and lying, was to be applauded by those who knew I lied, and my heart was panting with these anxieties, and boiling with the feverishness of consuming thoughts. For, passing through one of the streets of Milan, I observed a poor beggar, then, I suppose, with a full belly, joking and joyous: and I sighed, and spoke to the friends around me, of the many sorrows of our phrenzies; for that by all such efforts of ours, as those wherein I then toiled, dragging along, under the goading of desire, the burthen of my own wretchedness, and, by dragging, augmenting it, we yet looked to arrive only at that very joyousness, whither that beggar-man had arrived before us, who should never perchance attain it. For what he had obtained by means of a few begged pence, the same was I plotting for by many a toilsome turning and winding; the joy of a temporary felicity. For he verily had not the true joy; but yet I with those my ambitious designs was seeking one much less true. And certainly he was joyous, I anxious; he void of care, I full of fears. But should any ask me, had I rather be merry or fearful? I would answer, merry. Again, if he asked had I rather be such as he was, or what I then was? I should choose to be myself, though worn with cares and fears; but out of wrong judgment; for, was it the truth? For I ought not to prefer myself to him, because more learned than he, seeing I had no joy therein, but sought to please men by it; and that not to instruct, but simply to please. Wherefore also Thou didst break my bones with the staff of thy correction.

10 Away with those then from my soul, who say to her, "It makes a difference, whence a man's joy is. That beggar-man joyed in drunkenness; Thou desiredst to joy in glory." What glory, Lord? That which is not in Thee. For even as his was no true joy, so was that no true glory: and it overthrew my soul more. He that very night should digest his drunkenness; but I had slept and risen again with mine, and was to sleep again, and again to rise with it, how many days, Thou, God, knowest. But "it doth make a difference whence a man's joy is." I know it, and the joy of a faithful hope lieth incomparably beyond such vanity. Yea, and so was he then beyond me: for he verily was the happier; not only for that he was throughly drenched in mirth, I disembowelled with cares: but he, by fair wishes, had gotten wine; I, by lying was seeking for empty, swelling praise. Much to this purpose said I then to my friends: and I often marked in them how it fared with me; and I found it went ill with me, and grieved, and doubled that very ill; and if any prosperity smiled on me, I was loath to catch at it, for almost before I could grasp it, it flew away.

[VII] 11 These things we, who were living as friends together, bemoaned together, but chiefly and most familiarly did I speak thereof with Alypius and Nebridius, of whom Alypius was born in the same town with me, of persons of chief rank there, but younger than I. For he had studied under me, both when I first lectured in our town, and afterwards at Carthage, and he loved me much, because I seemed to him kind, and learned; and I him, for his great towardliness to virtue, which was eminent enough in one of no greater years. Yet the whirlpool of Carthaginian habits (amongst whom those idle spectacles are hotly followed) had drawn him into the madness of the Circus. But while he was miserably tossed therein, and I, professing rhetoric there, had a public school, as yet he used not my teaching, by reason of some unkindness risen betwixt his father and me. I had found then how deadly he doted upon the Circus, and was deeply grieved that he seemed likely, nay, or had thrown away so great promise: yet had I no means of advising or with a sort of constraint reclaiming him, either by the kindness of a friend, or the authority of a master. For I supposed that he thought of me as did his father; but he was not such; laying aside then his father's mind in that matter, he began to greet me, come sometimes into my lecture-room, hear a little, and be gone.

12 I however had forgotten to deal with him, that he should not, through a blind and headlong desire of vain pastimes, undo so good a wit. But Thou, O Lord, who guidest the course of all Thou hast created, hadst not forgotten him, who was one day to be among Thy children, Priest and Dispenser of Thy Sacrament; and that his amendment might plainly be attributed to Thyself, Thou effectedst it through me, but unknowingly. For as one day I sat in my accustomed place, with my scholars before me, he entered, greeted me, sat down, and applied his mind to what I then handled. I had by chance a passage in hand, which while I was explaining, a likeness from the Circensian races occurred to me, as likely to make what I would convey pleasanter and plainer, seasoned

with biting mockery of those whom that madness had enthralled; God, Thou knowest, that I then thought not of curing Alypius of that infection. But he took it wholly to himself, and thought that I said it simply for his sake. And whence another would have taken occasion of offence with me, that right-minded youth took as a ground of being offended at himself, and loving me more fervently. For Thou hadst said it long ago, and put it into Thy book, *Rebuke a wise man and he will love thee*. But I had not rebuked him, but Thou, who employest all, knowing or not knowing, in that order which Thyself knowest, (and that order is just,) didst of my heart and tongue make burning coals, by which to set on fire the hopeful mind, thus languishing, and so cure it. Let him be silent in Thy praises, who considers not Thy mercies, which confess unto Thee out of my inmost soul. For he upon that speech, burst out of that pit so deep, wherein he was wilfully plunged, and was blinded with its wretched pastimes; and he shook his mind with a strong self-command; whereupon all the filths of the Circensian pastimes flew off from him, nor came he again thither. Upon this, he prevailed with his unwilling father, that he might be my scholar. He gave way, and gave in. And Alypius beginning to be my hearer again, was involved in the same superstition with me, loving in the Manichees that show of continency, which he supposed true and unfeigned. Whereas it was a senseless and seducing continency, ensnaring precious souls, unable as yet to reach the depth of virtue, yet readily beguiled with the surface of what was but a shadowy and counterfeit virtue.

[VIII] 13 He, not forsaking that secular course which his parents had charmed him to pursue, had gone before me to Rome, to study law, and there he was carried away incredibly with an incredible eagerness after the shows of gladiators. For being utterly averse to and detesting such spectacles, he was one day by chance met by divers of his acquaintance and fellow-students coming from dinner, and they with a familiar violence haled him, vehemently refusing and resisting, into the Amphitheatre, during these cruel and deadly shows, he thus protesting; "Though you hale my body to that place, and there set me, can you force me also to turn my mind or my eyes to those shows? I shall then be absent while present, and so shall overcome both you and them." They hearing this, led him on nevertheless, desirous perchance to try that very thing, whether he could do as he said. When they were come thither, and had taken their places as they could, the whole place kindled with that savage pastime. But he, closing the passages of his eyes, forbade his mind to range abroad after such evils; and would he had stopped his ears also! For in the fight, when one fell, a mighty cry of the whole people striking him strongly, overcome by curiosity, and as if prepared to despise and be superior to it whatsoever it were, even when seen, he opened his eyes, and was stricken with a deeper wound in his soul, than the other, whom he desired to behold, was in his body; and he fell more miserably than he, upon whose fall that mighty noise was raised, which entered through his ears, and unlocked his eyes, to make way for the striking and beating down of a soul, bold rather than resolute, and the weaker, in that it had presumed on itself, which ought to have relied on Thee. For so soon as he saw that blood, he therewith drunk down savageness; nor turned away, but fixed his eye, drinking in phrenzy, unawares, and was delighted with that guilty light, and intoxicated with the bloody pastime. Nor was he now the man he came, but one of the throng he came unto, yea, a true associate of theirs that brought him thither. Why say more? He beheld, shouted, kindled, carried thence with him the madness which should goad him to return not only with them who first drew him thither, but also before them, yea and to draw in others. Yet thence didst Thou with a most strong and most merciful hand pluck him, and taughtest him to have confidence not in himself, but in Thee. But this was after.

[IX] 14 But this was already being laid up in his memory to be a medicine hereafter. So was that also, that when he was yet studying under me at Carthage, and was thinking over at mid-day in the market-place what he was to say by heart, (as scholars use to practise,) Thou sufferedst him to be apprehended by the officers of the market-place for a thief. For no other cause, I deem, didst Thou, our God, suffer it, but that he, who was hereafter to prove so great a man, should already begin to learn, that in judging of causes, man was not readily to be condemned by man out of a rash credulity. For as he was walking up and down by himself before the judgment-seat, with his note-book and pen, lo, a young man, a lawyer, the real thief, privily bringing a hatchet, got in, unperceived by Alypius, as far as the leaden gratings, which fence in the silversmiths' shops, and began to cut away the lead. But the noise of the hatchet being heard, the silversmiths beneath began to make a stir, and sent to apprehend whomever they should find. But he hearing their voices, ran away, leaving his hatchet, fearing to be taken with it. Alypius now, who had not seen him enter, was aware of his going, and saw with what speed he made away. And being desirous to know the matter, entered the place; where finding the hatchet, he was standing, wondering and considering it, when behold, those that had been sent, find him alone with the hatchet in his hand, the noise whereof had startled and brought them thither. They seize him, hale him away, and gathering the dwellers in the market-place together, boast of having taken a notorious thief, and so he was being led away to be taken before the judge.

15 But thus far was Alypius to be instructed. For forthwith, O Lord, Thou succouredst his innocency, whereof Thou alone wert witness. For as he was being led either to prison or to punishment, a certain architect met them, who had the chief charge of the public buildings. Glad they were to meet him especially, by whom they were wont to be suspected of stealing the goods lost out of the market-place, as though to shew him at last by whom these thefts were committed. He, however, had divers times seen Alypius at a certain Senator's house, to whom he often went to pay his respects; and recognizing him immediately, took him aside by the hand, and enquiring the occasion of so great a calamity, heard the whole matter, and bade all present, amid much uproar and threats, to go with him. So they came to the house of the young man, who had

done the deed. There, before the door, was a boy so young, as to be likely, not apprehending any harm to his master, to disclose the whole. For he had attended his master to the market-place. Whom so soon as Alypius remembered, he told the architect: and he shewing the hatchet to the boy, asked him "Whose that was?" "Ours," quoth he presently: and being further questioned, he discovered every thing. Thus the crime being transferred to that house, and the multitude ashamed, which had begun to insult over Alypius, he who was to be a dispenser of Thy Word, and an examiner of many causes in Thy Church,[9] went away better experienced and instructed.

[X] 16 Him then I had found at Rome, and he clave to me by a most strong tie, and went with me to Milan, both that he might not leave me, and might practise something of the law he had studied, more to please his parents, than himself. There he had thrice sat as Assessor with an uncorruptness, much wondered at by others, he wondering at others rather, who could prefer gold to honesty. His character was tried besides, not only with the bait of covetousness, but with the goad of fear. At Rome he was Assessor to the Count of the Italian Treasury.[10] There was at that time a very powerful senator, to whose favours many stood indebted, many much feared. He would needs, by his usual power, have a thing allowed him, which by the laws was unallowed. Alypius resisted it: a bribe was promised; with all his heart he scorned it: threats were held out; he trampled upon them: all wondering at so unwonted a spirit, which neither desired the friendship, nor feared the enmity of one so

great and so mightily renowned for innumerable means of
doing good or evil. And the very Judge, whose councillor
Alypius was, although also unwilling it should be, yet did
not openly refuse, but put the matter off upon Alypius,
alleging that he would not allow him to do it: for in truth
had the Judge done it, Alypius would have decided
otherwise.[11] With this one thing in the way of learning
was he well-nigh seduced, that he might have books
copied for him at Prætorian prices,[12] but consulting
justice, he altered his deliberation for the better;
esteeming equity whereby he was hindered more gainful
than the power whereby he were allowed. These are slight
things, but *he that is faithful in little, is faithful also in
much.* Nor can that any how be void, which proceeded out
of the mouth of Thy Truth; *If ye have not been faithful
in the unrighteous Mammon, who will commit to your
trust true riches? And if ye have not been faithful in that
which is another man's, who shall give you that which is
your own?* He, being such, did at that time cleave to me,
and with me wavered in purpose, what course of life was
to be taken.

17 Nebridius also, who having left his native country
near Carthage, yea and Carthage itself, where he had much
lived, leaving his excellent family-estate and house, and
a mother behind, who was not to follow him, had come
to Milan, for no other reason, but that with me he might
live in a most ardent search after truth and wisdom. Like
me he sighed, like me he wavered, an ardent searcher after
true life, and a most acute examiner of the most difficult
questions.[13] Thus were there the mouths of three indigent

persons, sighing out their wants one to another, and *waiting upon Thee that Thou mightest give them their meat in due season*. And in all the bitterness, which by Thy mercy followed our worldly affairs, as we looked towards the end, why we should suffer all this, darkness met us; and we turned away groaning, and saying, *How long shall these things be?* This too we often said; and so saying forsook them not, for as yet there dawned nothing certain, which, these forsaken, we might embrace.

[XI] 18 And I, viewing and reviewing things, most wondered at the length of time from that my nineteenth year, wherein I had begun to kindle with the desire of wisdom, settling when I had found her, to abandon all the empty hopes and lying phrenzies of vain desires. And lo, I was now in my thirtieth year, sticking in the same mire, greedy of enjoying things present, which passed away and wasted my soul; while I said to myself, "To-morrow I shall find it; it will appear manifestly, and I shall grasp it; lo, Faustus the Manichee will come, and clear every thing! O you great men, ye Academicians, it is true then, that no certainty can be attained for the ordering of life! Nay, let us search the more diligently, and despair not. Lo, things in the ecclesiastical books are not absurd to us now, which sometimes seemed absurd, and may be otherwise taken, and in a good sense. I will take my stand, where, as a child, my parents placed me, until the clear truth be found out. But where shall it be sought or when? Ambrose has no leisure; we have no leisure to read; where shall we find even the books? Whence, or when procure them? from whom borrow them? Let set times be

appointed, and certain hours be ordered for the health of
our soul. Great hope has dawned; the Catholic Faith
teaches not what we thought, and vainly accused it of;
her instructed members hold it profane, to believe God to
be bounded by the figure of a human body: and do we
doubt to 'knock,' that the rest 'may be opened?' The
forenoons our scholars take up; what do we during the
rest? Why not this? But when then pay we court to our
great friends, whose favour we need? When compose
what we may sell to scholars? When refresh ourselves,
unbending our minds from this intenseness of care?"

19 "Perish every thing, dismiss we these empty vanities,
and betake ourselves to the one search for truth! Life is
vain, death uncertain; if it steals upon us on a sudden,
in what state shall we depart hence? and where shall we
learn what here we have neglected? and shall we not
rather suffer the punishment of this negligence? What,
if death itself cut off and end all care and feeling? Then
must this be ascertained. But God forbid this! It is no
vain and empty thing, that the excellent dignity of the
authority of the Christian Faith hath overspread the
whole world.[14] Never would such and so great things be
by God wrought for us, if with the death of the body, the
life of the soul came to an end. Wherefore delay then to
abandon worldly hopes, and give ourselves wholly to
seek after God and the blessed life? But wait! Even those
things are pleasant; they have some, and no small
sweetness. We must not lightly abandon them, for it were
a shame to return again to them. See, it is no great matter
now to obtain some station, and then what should we

more wish for? We have store of powerful friends; if nothing else offer, and we be in much haste, at least a president-ship may be given us: and a wife with some money, that she increase not our charges: and this shall be the bound of desire. Many great men, and most worthy of imitation, have given themselves to the study of wisdom in the state of marriage."

20 While I went over these things, and these winds shifted and drove my heart this way and that, time passed on, but I delayed to turn to the Lord; and from day to day deferred to live in Thee, and deferred not daily to die in myself. Loving a happy life, I feared it in its own abode, and sought it, by fleeing from it. I thought I should be too miserable, unless folded in female arms;[15] and of the medicine of Thy mercy to cure that infirmity I thought not, not having tried it. As for continency, I supposed it to be in our own power, (though in myself I did not find that power) being so foolish as not to know what is written, *None can be continent unless Thou give it*; and that Thou wouldest give it, if with inward groanings I did knock at Thine ears, and with a settled faith did cast my care on Thee.

[XII] 21 Alypius indeed kept me from marrying; alleging, that so could we by no means with undistracted leisure live together in the love of wisdom, as we had long desired. For himself was even then most pure in this point, so that it was wonderful; and that the more, since in the outset of his youth he had entered into that course, but had not stuck fast therein; rather had he felt remorse and revolting at it, living thenceforth until now most continently. But I opposed him with the examples of those, who as married men had cherished wisdom, and served God acceptably, and retained their friends, and loved them faithfully. Of whose greatness of spirit I was far short; and bound with the disease of the flesh, and its deadly sweetness, drew along my chain, dreading to be loosed, and as if my wound had been fretted, put back his good persuasions, as it were the hand of one that would unchain me. Moreover, by me did the serpent speak unto Alypius himself, by my tongue weaving and laying in his path pleasurable snares, wherein his virtuous and free feet[16] might be entangled.

22 For when he wondered that I, whom he esteemed not slightly, should stick so fast in the birdlime of that pleasure, as to protest (so oft as we discussed it) that I could never lead a single life; and urged in my defence when I saw him wonder, that there was great difference between his momentary and scarce-remembered knowledge of that life, which so he might easily despise, and my continued acquaintance whereto if but the honourable name of marriage were added, he ought not to wonder why I could not contemn that course; he began also to desire to be married; not as overcome with desire of such pleasure, but out of curiosity. For he would fain know, he said, what that should be, without which my life, to him so pleasing, would to me seem not life but a punishment. For his mind, free from that chain, was amazed at my thraldom; and through that amazement was going on to a desire of trying it, thence to the trial itself, and thence perhaps to sink into that bondage whereat he

wondered, seeing he was willing to *make a covenant with death*; and, *he that loves danger, shall fall into it*. For whatever honour there be in the office of well-ordering a married life, and a family, moved us but slightly. But me for the most part the habit of satisfying an insatiable appetite tormented, while it held me captive; him, an admiring wonder was leading captive. So were we, until Thou, O Most High, not forsaking our dust, commiserating us miserable, didst come to our help, by wondrous and secret ways.

[XIII] 23 Continual effort was made to have me married. I wooed, I was promised, chiefly through my mother's pains, that so once married, the health-giving baptism might cleanse me, towards which she rejoiced that I was being daily fitted, and observed that her prayers, and Thy promises, were being fulfilled in my faith. At which time verily, both at my request and her own longing, with strong cries of heart she daily begged of Thee, that Thou wouldest by a vision discover unto her something concerning my future marriage; Thou never wouldest. She saw indeed certain vain and phantastic things, such as the energy of the human spirit, busied thereon, brought together; and these she told me of, not with that confidence she was wont, when Thou shewedst her anything, but slighting them. For she could, she said, through a certain feeling, which in words she could not express, discern betwixt Thy revelations, and the dreams of her own soul. Yet the matter was pressed on, and a maiden asked in marriage, two years under the fit age; and, as pleasing, was waited for.

[XIV] 24 And many of us friends conferring about, and detesting the turbulent turmoils of human life, had debated and now almost resolved on living apart from business and the bustle of men; and this was to be thus obtained; we were to bring whatever we might severally procure, and make one household of all; so that through the truth of our friendship nothing should belong especially to any; but the whole thus derived from all, should as a whole belong to each, and all to all. We thought there might be some ten persons in this society; some of whom were very rich, especially Romanianus[17] our townsman, from childhood a very familiar friend of mine, whom the grievous perplexities of his affairs had brought up to court; who was the most earnest for this project; and therein was his voice of great weight, because his ample estate far exceeded any of the rest. We had settled also, that two annual officers, as it were, should provide all things necessary, the rest being undisturbed. But when we began to consider whether the wives, which some of us already had, others hoped to have, would allow this, all that plan, which was being so well moulded, fell to pieces in our hands, was utterly dashed and cast aside. Thence we betook us to sighs, and groans, and our steps to follow the *broad and beaten ways* of the world; for many thoughts were in our heart, *but Thy counsel standeth for ever*. Out of which counsel Thou didst deride ours, and preparedst Thine own; purposing to *give us meat in due season, and to open Thy hand, and to fill our souls with blessing*.

[XV] 25 Meanwhile my sins were being multiplied, and my concubine being torn from my side as a hindrance to my marriage, my heart which clave unto her was torn and wounded and bleeding. And she returned to Afric, vowing unto Thee never to know any other man, leaving with me my son by her. But unhappy I, who could not imitate a very woman, impatient of delay, inasmuch as not till after two years was I to obtain her I sought, not being so much a lover of marriage, as a slave to lust, procured another, though no wife, that so by the servitude of an enduring custom, the disease of my soul might be kept up and carried on in its vigor or even augmented, into the dominion of marriage. Nor was that my wound cured, which had been made by the cutting away of the former, but after inflammation and most acute pain, it mortified, and my pains became less acute, but more desperate.[18]

[XVI] 26 To Thee be praise, glory to Thee, Fountain of mercies. I was becoming more miserable, and Thou nearer. Thy right hand was continually ready to pluck me out of the mire, and to wash me throughly, and I knew it not; nor did any thing call me back from a yet deeper gulf of carnal pleasures, but the fear of death, and of Thy judgment to come; which amid all my changes, never departed from my breast. And in my disputes with my friends Alypius and Nebridius, of the nature of good and evil, I held that Epicurus had in my mind won the palm, had I not believed, that after death there remained a life for the soul, and places of requital according to men's deserts, which Epicurus would not believe. And I asked, "were we immortal, and to live in perpetual bodily pleasure, without fear of losing it, why should we not be happy, or what else should we seek?" not knowing that great misery was involved in this very thing, that, being thus sunk and blinded, I could not discern that light of excellence and beauty, to be embraced for its own sake, which the eye of flesh cannot see, and is seen by the inner man. Nor did I, unhappy, consider from what source it sprung, that even on these things, foul as they were, I with pleasure discoursed with my friends, nor could I, even according to the notions I then had of happiness, be happy without friends, amid what abundance soever of carnal pleasures. And yet these friends I loved for themselves only, and I felt that I was beloved of them again for myself only.

27 O crooked paths! Woe to the audacious soul, which hoped, by forsaking Thee, to gain some better thing! Turned it hath, and turned again, upon back, sides, and belly, yet all was painful,[19] and Thou alone rest. And behold, Thou art at hand, and deliverest us from our wretched wanderings, and placest us in Thy way, and dost comfort us, and say, "Run; I will carry you; yea I will bring you through; there also will I carry you."

BOOK VII

Aug's thirty-first year; gradually extricated from his errors, but still with material conceptions of God; much aided by an argument of Nebridius; sees that the cause of sin lies in free-will, rejects the Manichæan heresy, but cannot altogether embrace the doctrine of the Church; recovered from the belief in Astrology, but miserably perplexed about the origin of evil; is led to find in the Platonists the seeds of the doctrine of the Divinity of the WORD, but not of His humiliation; hence he obtains clearer notions of God's majesty, but, not knowing Christ to be the Mediator, remains estranged from Him; all his doubts removed by the study of Holy Scripture, especially St. Paul.

[I] 1 Deceased was now that my evil and abominable youth, and I was passing into early manhood; the more defiled by vain things as I grew in years, who could not imagine any substance, but such as is wont to be seen with these eyes. I thought not of Thee, O God, under the figure of an human body; since I began to hear aught of wisdom, I always avoided this; and rejoiced to have found the same in the faith of our spiritual mother, Thy Catholic Church. But what else to conceive Thee I knew not. And I, a man, and such a man, sought to conceive of Thee the

sovereign, only, true God; and I did in my inmost soul
believe that Thou wert incorruptible, and uninjurable,
and unchangeable; because though not knowing whence
or how, yet I saw plainly and was sure, that that which
may be corrupted, must be inferior to that which cannot;
what could not be injured I preferred unhesitatingly to
what could receive injury; the unchangeable to things
subject to change. My heart passionately cried out against
all my phantoms, and with this one blow I sought to beat
away from the eye of my mind all that unclean troop,
which buzzed around it. And lo, being scarce put off, in
the twinkling of an eye they gathered again thick about
me, flew against my face, and beclouded it; so that though
not under the form of the human body, yet was I constrained to conceive of Thee (that incorruptible,
uninjurable, and unchangeable, which I preferred before
the corruptible, and injurable, and changeable) as being
in space, whether infused into the world, or diffused
infinitely without it. Because whatsoever I conceived,
deprived of this space, seemed to me nothing, yea
altogether nothing, not even a void, as if a body were
taken out of its place, and the place should remain empty
of any body at all, of earth and water, air and heaven, yet
would it remain a void place, as it were a spacious
nothing.

2 I then being thus gross-hearted, nor clear[1] even to
myself, whatsoever was not extended over certain spaces,
nor diffused, nor condensed, nor swelled out, or did not
or could not receive some of these dimensions, I thought
to be altogether nothing. For over such forms as my eyes

are wont to range, did my heart then range: nor yet did I see that this same notion of the mind, whereby I formed those very images, was not of this sort, and yet it could not have formed them, had not itself been some great thing. So also did I endeavour to conceive of Thee, Life of my life, as vast, through infinite spaces, on every side penetrating the whole mass of the universe, and beyond it, every way, through unmeasurable boundless spaces; so that the earth should have Thee, the heaven have Thee, all things have Thee, and they be bounded in Thee, and Thou bounded no where. For that as the body of this air which is above the earth, hindereth not the light of the sun from passing through it, penetrating it, not by bursting or by cutting, but by filling it wholly: so I thought the body not of heaven, air, and sea only, but of the earth too, pervious to Thee, so that in all its parts, the greatest as the smallest, it should admit Thy presence, by a secret inspiration, within and without, directing all things which Thou hast created. So I guessed, only as unable to conceive aught else, for it was false. For thus should a greater part of the earth contain a greater portion of Thee, and a less, a lesser: and all things should in such sort be full of Thee, that the body of an elephant should contain more of Thee than that of a sparrow, by how much larger it is, and takes up more room; and thus shouldest Thou make the several portions of Thyself present unto the several portions of the world, in fragments, large to the large, petty to the petty. But such art not Thou. But not as yet hadst Thou enlightened my darkness.

[II] 3 It was enough for me, Lord, to oppose to those deceived deceivers, and dumb praters, since Thy word sounded not out of them;—that was enough which long ago, while we were yet at Carthage, Nebridius used to propound, at which all we that heard it, were staggered; "That said² nation of darkness, which the Manichees are wont to set as an opposing mass, over against Thee, what could it have done unto Thee, hadst Thou refused to fight with it? For, if they answered, 'it would have done Thee some hurt,' then shouldest Thou be subject to injury and corruption: but if 'it could do Thee no hurt,' then was no reason brought for Thy fighting with it; and fighting in such wise, as that a certain portion or member of Thee, or offspring of Thy very Substance, should be mingled with opposed powers, and natures not created by Thee, and be by them so far corrupted and changed to the worse, as to be turned from happiness into misery, and need assistance, whereby it might be extricated and purified; and that this offspring of Thy Substance was the soul, which being enthralled, defiled, corrupted, Thy Word, free, pure, and whole, might relieve; that Word Itself being still corruptible, because It was of one and the same Substance. So then, should they affirm Thee, whatsoever Thou art, that is, Thy Substance whereby Thou art, to be incorruptible, then were all these sayings false and execrable; but if corruptible, the very statement shewed it to be false, and revolting." This argument then of Nebridius sufficed against those, who deserved wholly to be vomited out of the overcharged stomach; for they had no escape, without horrible blasphemy of heart and tongue, thus thinking and speaking of Thee.

[III] 4 But I also as yet, although I held and was firmly persuaded, that Thou our Lord the true God, who madest not only our souls, but our bodies, and not only our souls and bodies, but all beings, and all things, wert undefilable and unalterable, and in no degree mutable; yet understood I not, clearly and without difficulty, the cause of evil. And yet whatever it were, I perceived it was in such wise to be sought out, as should not constrain me to believe the immutable God to be mutable, lest I should become that evil I was seeking out. I sought it out then, thus far free from anxiety, certain of the untruth of what these held, from whom I shrunk with my whole heart: for I saw, that through enquiring the origin of evil, they were filled with evil, in that they preferred to think that Thy substance did suffer ill than their own did commit it.

5 And I strained to perceive what I now heard, that freewill was the cause of our doing ill, and Thy just judgment, of our suffering ill.[3] But I was not able clearly to discern it. So then endeavouring to draw my soul's vision out of that deep pit, I was again plunged therein, and endeavouring often, I was plunged back as often. But this raised me a little into Thy light, that I knew as well that I had a will, as that I lived: when then I did will or nill any thing, I was most sure, that no other than myself did will and nill: and I all but saw that there was the cause of my sin. But what I did against my will, I saw that I suffered rather than did, and I judged not to be my fault, but my punishment; whereby however, holding thee to be just, I speedily confessed myself to be not unjustly punished. But again I said, Who made me? Did not my

God, who is not only good, but goodness itself? Whence then came I to will evil and nill good, so that I am thus justly punished? who set this in me, and ingrafted into me this plant of bitterness, seeing I was wholly formed by my most sweet God? If the devil were the author, whence is that same devil? And if he also by his own perverse will, of a good angel became a devil, whence, again, came in him that evil will, whereby he became a devil, seeing the whole nature of angels was made by that most good Creator? By these thoughts I was again sunk down and choked; yet not brought down to that hell of error, (where no man confesseth unto Thee,) to think rather that Thou dost suffer ill, than that man doth it.

[IV] 6 For I was in such wise striving to find out the rest, as one who had already found, that the incorruptible must needs be better than the corruptible: and Thee therefore, whatsoever Thou wert, I confessed to be incorruptible. For never soul was, nor shall be, able to conceive any thing which may be better than Thou, who art the sovereign and the best good. But since most truly and certainly, the incorruptible is preferable to the corruptible, (as I did now prefer it,) then, wert Thou not incorruptible, I could in thought have arrived at something better than my God. Where then I saw the incorruptible to be preferable to the corruptible, there ought I to seek for Thee, and there observe "wherein evil itself was;" that is, whence corruption comes, by which Thy substance can by no means be impaired. For corruption does no ways impair our God; by no will, by no necessity, by no unlooked-for chance: because He is

God, and what He wills is good, and Himself is that good; but to be corrupted is not good. Nor art Thou against Thy will constrained to any thing, since Thy will is not greater than Thy power. But greater should it be, were Thyself greater than Thyself. For the will and power of God, is God Himself. And what can be unlooked-for by Thee, who knowest all things? Nor is there any nature in things, but Thou knowest it. And what should we more say, "why that substance which God is, should not be corruptible," seeing if it were so, it should not be God?

[V] 7 And I sought, "whence is evil," and sought in an evil way; and saw not the evil in my very search. I set now before the sight of my spirit, the whole creation, whatsoever we can see therein, (as sea, earth, air, stars, trees, mortal creatures;) yea, and whatever in it we do not see, as the firmament of heaven, all angels moreover, and all the spiritual inhabitants thereof. But these very beings, as though they were bodies, did my fancy dispose in place, and I made one great mass of Thy creation, distinguished as to the kinds of bodies; some, real bodies, some, what myself had feigned for spirits. And this mass I made huge, not as it was, (which I could not know,) but as I thought convenient, yet every way finite. But Thee, O Lord, I imagined on every part environing and penetrating it, though every way infinite: as if there were a sea, every where, and on every side, through unmeasured space, one only boundless sea, and it contained within it some sponge, huge, but bounded; that sponge must needs, in all its parts, be filled from that unmeasurable sea: so conceived I Thy creation, itself finite, full of Thee, the

Infinite; and I said, Behold God, and behold what God hath created; and God is good, yea, most mightily and incomparably better than all these: but yet He, the Good, created them good; and see how He environeth and fulfils them. Where is evil then, and whence, and how crept it in hither? What is its root, and what its seed? Or hath it no being? Why then fear we and avoid what is not? Or if we fear it idly, then is that very fear evil, whereby the soul is thus idly goaded and racked. Yea, and so much a greater evil, as we have nothing to fear, and yet do fear. Therefore either is that evil which we fear, or else evil is, that we fear. Whence is it then? seeing God, the Good, hath created all these things good. He indeed, the greater and chiefest Good, hath created these lesser goods; still both Creator and created, all are good. Whence is evil? Or, was there some evil matter of which He made, and formed, and ordered it, yet left something in it, which He did not convert into good? Why so then? Had He no might to turn and change the whole, so that no evil should remain in it, seeing He is Allmighty? Lastly, why would. He make any thing at all of it, and not rather by the same Allmightiness cause it not to be at all? Or, could it then be, against His will? Or if it were from eternity, why suffered He it so to be for infinite spaces of times past, and was pleased so long after to make something out of it? Or if He were suddenly pleased now to effect somewhat, this rather should the Allmighty have effected, that this evil matter should not be, and He alone be, the whole, true, sovereign, and infinite Good. Or if it was not good that He who was good, should not also frame and create something that were good, then, that evil matter being taken away and brought to nothing, He might form good matter, whereof to create all things. For He should not be Allmighty, if He might not create something good without the aid of that matter which Himself had not created. These thoughts I revolved in my miserable heart, overcharged with most gnawing cares, lest I should die ere I had found the truth; yet was the faith of Thy Christ our Lord and Saviour, professed in the Church Catholic, firmly fixed in my heart, in many points, indeed, as yet unformed, and fluctuating from the rule of doctrine; yet did not my mind utterly leave it, but rather daily took in more and more of it.

8 By this time also had I rejected the lying divinations and impious dotages of the astrologers. Let Thine own mercies, out of my very inmost soul, confess unto Thee for this also, O my God. For Thou, Thou altogether, (for who else calls us back from the death of all errors, save the Life which cannot die, and the Wisdom which needing no light enlightens the minds that need it, whereby the universe is directed, down to the whirling leaves of trees?) Thou madest provision for my obstinacy wherewith I struggled against Vindicianus,[4] an acute old man, and Nebridius, a young man of admirable talents; the first vehemently affirming, and the latter often (though with some doubtfulness) saying, "That there was no such art whereby to foresee things to come, but that men's conjectures were a sort of lottery, and that out of many things, which they said should come to pass, some actually did, unawares to them who spake it, who stumbled upon it, through their oft speaking." Thou

providedst then a friend for me, no negligent consulter of the astrologers; nor yet well skilled in those arts, but (as I said) a curious consulter with them, and yet knowing something, which he said he had heard of his father, which how far it went to overthrow the estimation of that art, he knew not. This man then, Firminus by name, having had a liberal education, and well taught in Rhetoric, consulted me, as one very dear to him, what, according to his so-called constellations, I thought on certain affairs of his, wherein his worldly hopes had risen, and I, who had herein now begun to incline towards Nebridius' opinion, did not altogether refuse to conjecture, and tell him what came into my unresolved mind; but added, that I was now almost persuaded, that these were but empty and ridiculous follies. Thereupon he told me, that his father had been very curious in such books, and had a friend as earnest in them as himself, who with joint study and conference fanned the flame of their affections to these toys, so that they would observe the moments, whereat the very dumb animals, which bred about their houses, gave birth, and then observed the relative position of the heavens, thereby to make fresh experiments in this so-called art. He said then that he had heard of his father, that what time his mother was about to give birth to him, Firminus, a woman-servant of that friend of his father's, was also with child, which could not escape her master, who took care with most exact diligence to know the births of his very puppies. And so it was, that (the one for his wife, and the other for his servant, with the most careful observation, reckoning days, hours, nay, the lesser divisions of the hours,) both were delivered at the same instant; so that both were constrained to allow the same constellations, even to the minutest points, the one for his son, the other for his newborn slave. For so soon as the women began to be in labour, they each gave notice to the other what was fallen out in their houses, and had messengers ready to send to one another, so soon as they had notice of the actual birth, of which they had easily provided, each in his own province, to give instant intelligence. Thus then the messengers of the respective parties met, he averred, at such an equal distance from either house, that neither of them could make out any difference in the position of the stars, or any other minutest points; and yet Firminus, born in a high estate in his parents' house, ran his course through the gilded paths of life, was increased in riches, raised to honours; whereas that slave continued to serve his masters, without any relaxation of his yoke, as Firminus, who knew him, told me.

9 Upon hearing and believing these things, told by one of such credibility, all that my resistance gave way; and first I endeavoured to reclaim Firminus himself from that curiosity, by telling him, that upon inspecting his constellations, I ought, if I were to predict truly, to have seen in them, parents eminent among their neighbours, a noble family in its own city, high birth, good education, liberal learning. But if that servant had consulted me upon the same constellations, since they were his also, I ought again (to tell him too truly) to see in them a lineage the most abject, a slavish condition, and every thing else, utterly at variance with the former. Whence then if I spake the

truth, I should, from the same constellations, speak diversely, or if I spake the same, speak falsely: thence it followed most certainly, that whatever, upon consideration of the constellations, was spoken truly, was spoken not out of art, but chance; and whatever spoken falsely, was not out of ignorance in the art, but the failure of the chance.

10 An opening thus made, ruminating with myself on the like things, that no one of those dotards (who lived by such a trade, and whom I longed to attack, and with derision to confute) might urge against me, that Firminus had informed me falsely, or his father him; I bent my thoughts on those that are born twins, who for the most part come out of the womb so near one to other, that the small interval (how much force soever in the nature of things folk may pretend it to have) cannot be noted by human observation, or be at all expressed in those figures which the Astrologer is to inspect, that he may pronounce truly. Yet they cannot be true: for looking into the same figures, he must have predicted the same of Esau and Jacob, whereas the same happened not to them. Therefore he must speak falsely; or if truly, then, looking into the same figures, he must not give the same answer. Not by art, then, but by chance, would he speak truly. For Thou, O Lord, most righteous Ruler of the Universe, while consulters and consulted know it not, dost by Thy hidden inspiration effect that the consulter should hear what according to the hidden deservings of souls, he ought to hear, out of the unsearchable depth of Thy just judgment, to Whom let no man say, What is this? Why that? Let him not so say, for he is man.

[VII] 11 Now then, O my Helper, hadst Thou loosed me from those fetters: and I sought "whence is evil," and found no way. But Thou sufferedst me not by any fluctuations of thought to be carried away from the Faith whereby I believed Thee both to be, and Thy substance to be unchangeable, and that Thou hast a care of, and wouldest judge men, and that in Christ, Thy Son, our Lord, and the holy Scriptures, which the authority of Thy Catholic Church pressed upon me, Thou hadst set the way of man's salvation, to that life which is to be after this death. These things being safe and immoveably settled in my mind, I sought anxiously "whence was evil?" What were the pangs of my teeming heart, what groans, O my God! yet even there were Thine ears open, and I knew it not: and when in silence I vehemently sought, those silent contritions of my soul were strong cries unto Thy mercy. Thou knewest what I suffered, and no man. For, what was that which was thence through my tongue distilled into the ears of my most familiar friends? Did the whole tumult of my soul, for which neither time nor utterance sufficed, reach them? Yet went up the whole to Thy hearing, all which I roared out from the groanings of my heart; and my desire was before Thee, and the light of mine eyes was not with me: for that was within, I without: nor was that confined to place, but I was intent on things contained in place, but there found I no resting-place, nor did they so receive me, that I could say, "It is enough," "it is well:" nor did they yet suffer me to turn back, where it might be well enough with me. For to these things was I superior, but inferior to Thee; and Thou art my true joy when subjected to Thee, and Thou hadst subjected to me, what

Thou createdst below me. And this was the true temperament,[5] and middle region of my safety, to remain in Thy Image, and by serving Thee, rule the body. But when I rose proudly against Thee, and *ran against the Lord with my neck, with the thick bosses of my buckler,* even these inferior things were set above me, and pressed me down, and no where was there respite or space of breathing. They met my sight on all sides by heaps and troops, and in thought the images thereof presented themselves unsought, as I would return to Thee, as if they would say unto me, "Whither goest thou, unworthy and defiled?" And these things had grown out of my wound; for Thou "humbledst the proud like one that is wounded," and through my own swelling was I separated[6] from Thee; yea, my pride-swollen face closed up mine eyes.

[VIII] 12 But Thou, Lord, *abidest for ever,* yet not for ever art Thou angry with us; because Thou pitiest our dust and ashes, and it was pleasing in Thy sight to reform my deformities; and by inward goads didst Thou rouse me, that I should be ill at ease, until Thou wert manifested to my inward sight. Thus, by the secret hand of Thy medicining, was my swelling abated, and the troubled and bedimmed eyesight of my mind, by the smarting anointings of healthful sorrows, was from day to day healed.

[IX] 13 And Thou, willing first to shew me, how Thou *resistest the proud, but givest grace unto the humble,* and by how great an act of Thy mercy Thou hadst traced out to men the way of humility, in that Thy WORD was made flesh, and dwelt among men:—Thou procuredst for me, by means of one puffed up with most unnatural pride, certain books of the Platonists,[7] translated from Greek into Latin. And therein[8] I read, not indeed in the very words, but to the very same purpose, enforced by many and divers reasons, that *In the beginning was the Word, and the Word was with God, and the Word was God: the Same was in the beginning with God: all things were made by Him, and without Him was nothing made: that which was made by Him is life, and the life was the light of men, and the light shineth in the darkness, and the darkness comprehended it not.* And that the soul of man,[9] though it *bears witness to the light,* yet itself *is not that light;* but the Word of God, being God, *is that true light that lighteth every man that cometh into the world. And that He was in the world, and the world was made by Him, and the world knew Him not.* But, that *He came unto His own, and His own received Him not; but as many as received Him, to them gave He power to become the sons of God, as many as believed in His name;* this I read not there.

14 Again I read there, that *God the Word was born not of flesh nor of blood, nor of the will of man, nor of the will of the flesh, but of God.*[10] But that *the Word was made flesh, and dwelt among us,* I read not there. For I traced in those books, that it was many and divers ways said, that *the Son was in the form of the Father, and thought it not robbery to be equal with God,* for that naturally He was the Same Substance. But that *He emptied himself, taking the form of a servant, being made in the likeness of men, and found in fashion as a man, humbled Himself, and became obedient unto death, and that the death of the cross: wherefore God*

exalted Him from the dead, *and gave Him a name above every name, that at the name of Jesus every knee should bow, of things in heaven, and things in earth, and things under the earth; and that every tongue should confess that the Lord Jesus Christ is in the glory of God the Father;* those books have not. For that before all times and above all times Thy Only-Begotten Son remaineth unchangeably, co-eternal with Thee, and that *of his fulness souls receive,* that they may be blessed; and that by participation of wisdom abiding in them, they are renewed, so as to be wise, is there. But that *in due time He died for the ungodly;* and that *Thou sparedst not Thine Only Son, but deliveredst Him for us all,* is not there. *For Thou hiddest these things from the wise, and revealedst them to babes;* that they *that labour and are heavy laden, might come unto Him, and He refresh them, because He is meek and lowly in heart; and the meek He directeth in judgment, and the gentle He teacheth His ways, beholding our lowliness and trouble, and forgiving all our sins.* But such as are lifted up in the lofty walk of some would-be sublimer learning, hear not Him, saying, *Learn of Me, for I am meek and lowly in heart, and ye shall find rest to your souls. Although they knew God, yet they glorify Him not as God, nor are thankful, but wax vain in their thoughts; and their foolish heart is darkened; professing that they were wise, they became fools.*

15 And therefore did I read there also, that they had *changed the glory of Thy incorruptible nature* into idols and divers shapes, *into the likeness of the image of corruptible man, and birds, and beasts, and creeping things;* namely into that Egyptian food,[11] for which Esau lost his birth-

right, for that Thy first-born people worshipped the head of a four-footed beast instead of Thee; turning in heart back towards Egypt; and bowing Thy image, their own soul, before the image of *a calf that eateth hay.* These things found I here, but I fed not on them. For it pleased Thee, O Lord, to take away the reproach of diminution from Jacob, *that the elder should serve the younger:* and Thou calledst the Gentiles into Thine inheritance. And I had come to Thee from among the Gentiles; and I set my mind upon the gold which Thou willedst Thy people to take from Egypt, seeing Thine it was, wheresoever it were. And to the Athenians Thou saidst by Thy Apostle, *that in Thee we live, move, and have our being, as one of their own poets had said.* And verily these books came from thence. But I set not my mind on the idols of Egypt, *whom they served with Thy gold, who changed the truth of God into a lie, and worshipped and served the creature more than the Creator.*[12]

[X] 16 And being thence admonished to return to myself, I entered even into my inward self, Thou being my Guide: and able I was, for Thou wert become my Helper. And I entered and beheld with the eye of my soul, (such as it was,) above the same eye of my soul, above my mind, the Light Unchangeable. Not this ordinary light, which all flesh may look upon,[13] nor as it were a greater of the same kind, as though the brightness of this should be manifold brighter, and with its greatness take up all space. Not such was this light, but other, yea, far other from all these. Nor was it above my soul, as oil is above water, nor yet as heaven above earth: but above to my soul, because

It made me; and I below It, because I was made by It. He that knows the Truth, knows what that Light is; and he that knows It, knows eternity. Love knoweth it. O Truth Who art Eternity! and Love Who art Truth! and Eternity Who art Love![14] Thou art my God, to Thee do I sigh night and day. Thee when I first knew, Thou liftedst me up, that I might see there was what I might see, and that I was not yet such as to see. And Thou didst beat back the weakness of my sight, streaming forth Thy beams of light upon me most strongly, and I trembled with love and awe: and I perceived myself to be far off from Thee, in the region of unlikeness,[15] as if I heard this Thy voice from on high: "I am the food of grown men; grow, and thou shalt feed upon Me; nor shalt thou convert Me, like the food of thy flesh, into thee, but thou shalt be converted into Me." And I learned, that *Thou for iniquity chastenest man, and Thou madest my soul to consume away like a spider.* And I said, "Is Truth therefore nothing because it is not diffused through space finite or infinite?" And Thou criedst to me from afar; "Yea verily, *I AM that I AM.*" And I heard, as the heart heareth, nor had I room to doubt, and I should sooner doubt that I live, than that Truth is not, *which is clearly seen being understood by those things which are made.*

[XI] 17 And I beheld the other things below Thee, and I perceived, that they neither altogether are, nor altogether are not, for they are, since they are from Thee, but are not, because they are not, what Thou art. For that truly is, which remains unchangeably.[16] *It is good then for me to hold fast unto God;* for if I remain not in Him, I cannot in myself; but *He remaining in himself, reneweth all things. And Thou art the Lord* my God, since Thou *standest not in need of my goodness.*

[XII] 18 And it was manifested unto me, that those things be good, which yet are corrupted; which neither were they sovereignly good, nor unless they were good, could be corrupted: for if sovereignly good, they were incorruptible, if not good at all, there were nothing in them to be corrupted. For corruption injures, but unless it diminished goodness, it could not injure. Either then corruption injures not, which cannot be; or which is most certain, all which is corrupted is deprived of good. But if they be deprived of all good, they shall cease to be. For if they shall be, and can now no longer be corrupted, they shall be better than before, because they shall abide incorruptibly. And what more monstrous, than to affirm things to become better by losing all their good? Therefore, if they shall be deprived of all good, they shall no longer be. So long therefore as they are, they are good: therefore whatsoever is, is good. That evil then which I sought, whence it is, is not any substance: for were it a substance, it should be good. For either it should be an incorruptible substance, and so a chief good: or a corruptible substance; which unless it were good, could not be corrupted. I perceived therefore, and it was manifested to me, that Thou madest all things good, nor is there any substance at all, which Thou madest not; and for that Thou madest not all things equal, therefore are all[17] things; because each is good, and altogether very good, because our God *made all things very good.*

[XIII] 19 And to Thee is nothing whatsoever evil: yea, not only to Thee, but also to Thy creation as a whole, because there is nothing without, which may break in, and corrupt that order which Thou hast appointed it. But in the parts thereof some things, because unharmonizing with other some, are accounted evil: whereas those very things harmonize[18] with others, and are good; and in themselves are good. And all these things which harmonize not together, do yet with the inferior part, which we call Earth, having its own cloudy and windy sky harmonizing with it. Far be it then that I should say, "These things should not be:" for should I see nought but these, I should indeed long for the better; but still must even for these alone praise Thee; for that Thou art to be *praised, do shew from the earth, dragons, and all deeps, fire, hail, snow, ice, and stormy wind, which fulfil Thy word; mountains, and all hills, fruitful trees, and all cedars; beasts, and all cattle, creeping things, and flying fowls; kings of the earth, and all people, princes, and all judges of the earth; young men and maidens, old men and young, praise Thy Name.* But when, from heaven, these *praise Thee, praise Thee, our God, in the heights, all Thy angels, all Thy hosts, sun and moon, all the stars and light, the Heaven of heavens, and the waters that be above the heavens, praise Thy Name;* I did not now long for things better, because I conceived of all: and with a sounder judgment I apprehended that the things above were better than these below, but all together better than those above by themselves.

[XIV] 20 There is no soundness in them, whom aught of Thy creation displeaseth: as neither in me, when much which Thou hast made, displeased me. And because my soul durst not be displeased at my God, it would fain not account that Thine, which displeased it. Hence it had gone into the opinion of two substances, and had no rest, but talked idly. And returning thence, it had made to itself a God, through infinite measures of all space; and thought it to be Thee, and placed it in its heart; and had again become the temple of its own idol, to Thee abominable. But after Thou hadst soothed my head, unknown to me, and closed *mine eyes that they should not behold vanity*, I ceased somewhat of my former self, and my phrenzy was lulled to sleep; and I awoke in Thee, and saw Thee infinite, but in another way, and this sight was not derived from the flesh.

[XV] 21 And I looked back on other things; and I saw that they owed their being to Thee; and were all bounded in Thee: but in a different way; not as being in space; but because Thou containest all things in Thine hand in Thy Truth; and all things are true so far as they be; nor is there any falsehood, unless when that is thought to be, which is not. And I saw that all things did harmonize, not with their places only, but with their seasons. And that Thou, who only art Eternal, didst not begin to work after innumerable spaces of times spent; for that all spaces of times, both which have passed, and which shall pass, neither go nor come, but through Thee, working, and abiding.[19]

[XVI] 22 And I perceived and found it nothing strange, that bread which is pleasant to a healthy palate, is loathsome to one distempered: and to sore eyes light is offensive, which to the sound is delightful. And Thy righteousness displeaseth the wicked; much more the viper and reptiles, which Thou hast created good, fitting in with the inferior portions of Thy Creation, with which the very wicked also fit in; and that the more, by how much they be unlike Thee; but with the superior creatures, by how much they become more like to Thee. And I enquired what iniquity was, and found it to be no substance, but the perversion of the will, turned aside from Thee, O God, the Supreme, towards these lower things, and *casting out its bowels*,[20] and puffed up outwardly.

[XVII] 23 And I wondered that I now loved Thee, and no phantasm for Thee. And yet did I not press on to enjoy my God; but was borne up to Thee by Thy beauty, and soon borne down from Thee by mine own weight, sinking with sorrow into these inferior things. This weight was carnal custom. Yet dwelt there with me a remembrance of Thee; nor did I any way doubt, that there was One to Whom I might cleave, but that I was not yet such as to cleave to Thee: for that *the body which is corrupted, presseth down the soul, and the earthly tabernacle weigheth down the mind that museth upon many things*. And most certain I was, *that Thy invisible works from the creation of the world are clearly seen, being understood by the things that are made, even Thy eternal power and Godhead*. For examining, whence it was that I admired the beauty of bodies celestial or terrestrial; and what aided me in judging soundly on things mutable, and pronouncing, "This ought to be thus, this not;" examining, I say, whence it was that I so judged, seeing I did so judge, I had found the unchangeable and true Eternity of Truth, above my changeable mind. And thus by degrees, I passed from bodies to the soul, which through the bodily senses perceives; and thence to its inward[21] faculty, to which the bodily senses represent things external, whitherto reaches the faculties of beasts; and thence again to the reasoning faculty, to which what is received from the senses of the body, is referred to be judged. Which finding itself also to be in me a thing variable, raised itself up to its own understanding, and drew away my thoughts from the power of habit, withdrawing itself from those troops of contradictory phantasms;[22] that so it might find what that light was, whereby it was bedewed,[23] when, without all doubting, it cried out, "That the unchangeable was to be preferred to the changeable;" whence also it knew That Unchangeable, which, unless it had in some way known, it had had no sure ground to prefer it to the changeable. And thus with the flash of one trembling glance it arrived at THAT WHICH IS. And then I saw Thy *invisible things understood by the things which are made.* But I could not fix my gaze thereon; and my infirmity being struck back, I was thrown again on my wonted habits, carrying along with me only a loving memory thereof, and a longing for what I had, as it were, perceived the odour of, but was not yet able to feed on.

[XVIII] 24 Then I sought a way of obtaining strength, sufficient to enjoy Thee; and found it not, until I embraced *that Mediator betwixt God and men, the Man Christ Jesus, who is over all, God blessed for evermore,* calling unto me, and saying, *I am the way, the truth, and the life*, and mingling that food which I was unable to receive, with our flesh. *For the Word was made flesh*, that Thy wisdom, whereby Thou createdst all things, might provide milk for our infant state. For I did not hold to my Lord Jesus Christ, I humbled to the humble; nor knew I yet whereto His infirmity would guide us. For Thy Word, the Eternal Truth, far above the higher parts of Thy Creation, raises up the subdued[24] unto Itself: but in this lower world built for Itself a lowly habitation of our clay, whereby to abase from themselves such as would be subdued, and bring them over to Himself; allaying their swelling, and fomenting their love; to the end they might go on no further in self-confidence, but rather consent to become weak, seeing before their feet the Divinity weak by taking our *coats of skin*;[25] and wearied, might cast themselves down upon It, and It rising, might lift them up.

[XIX] 25 But I thought otherwise; conceiving only of my Lord Christ, as of a man of excellent wisdom, whom no one could be equalled unto; especially, for that being wonderfully born of a Virgin, He seemed, in conformity therewith, through the Divine care for us, to have attained that great eminence of authority, for an ensample of despising things temporal for the obtaining of immortality. But what mystery there lay in, *"The Word was made flesh,*" I could not even imagine. Only I had learnt out of what is delivered to us in writing of Him, that He did eat, and drink, sleep, walk, rejoiced in spirit, was sorrowful, discoursed; that, flesh did not cleave by itself unto Thy Word, but with the human soul and mind. All know this, who know the unchangeableness of Thy Word, which I now knew, as far as I could, nor did I at all doubt thereof. For, now to move the limbs of the body by will, now not, now to be moved by some affection, now not, now to deliver wise sayings through human signs, now to keep silence, belong to soul and mind subject to variation. And should these things be falsely written of Him, all the rest also would risk the charge, nor would there remain in those books any saving faith for mankind. Since then they were written truly, I acknowledged a perfect man[26] to be in Christ; not the body of a man only, nor, with the body, a sensitive soul without a rational, but very man; whom, not only as being a form[27] of Truth, but for a certain great excellency of human nature and a more perfect participation of wisdom, I judged to be preferred before others. But Alypius imagined the Catholics to believe God to be so clothed with flesh, that besides God and flesh, there was no soul at all in Christ, and did not think that a human mind was ascribed to Him. And because he was well persuaded, that the actions recorded of Him, could only be performed by a vital and a rational creature, he moved the more slowly towards the Christian Faith. But understanding afterwards, that this was the error of the Apollinarian[28] heretics, he joyed in and was conformed to the Catholic Faith. But somewhat later, I confess, did I learn, how in that saying, *The Word was made flesh*, the Catholic Truth is distinguished from the falsehood of Photinus.[29] For the rejection of heretics makes the tenets of Thy Church and sound doctrine to stand out more clearly. *For there must also be heresies, that the approved may be made manifest among the weak.*

[XX] 26 But having then read those books of the Platonists, and thence been taught to search for incorporeal truth, I saw Thy *invisible things, understood by those things which are made*; and though cast back, I perceived what that was, which through the darkness of my mind I was hindered from contemplating, being assured, "That Thou wert, and wert infinite, and yet not diffused in space, finite or infinite; and that Thou truly art who art the same ever,[30] in no part nor motion, varying; and that all other things are from Thee, on this most sure ground alone, that they are." Of these things I was assured, yet too unsure to enjoy Thee. I prated as one well skilled; but had I not sought Thy way in Christ our Saviour, I had proved to be, not skilled, but killed.[31] For now I had begun to wish to seem wise, being filled with mine own punishment, yet I did not mourn, but rather scorn,[32] puffed up with knowledge. For where was that charity building upon the *foundation* of humility, *which is Christ Jesus?* or when should these books teach me it? Upon these, I believe, Thou therefore willedst that I should fall, before I studied Thy Scriptures, that it might be imprinted on my memory, how I was affected by them; and that afterwards when my spirits were tamed through Thy books, and my wounds touched by Thy healing fingers, I might discern and distinguish between presumption and confession; between those who saw whither they were to go, yet saw not the way,[33] and the way that leadeth not to behold only but to dwell in the beatific country. For had I first been formed in Thy Holy Scriptures, and hadst Thou, in the familiar use of them, grown sweet unto me, and had I then fallen upon those other volumes, they might perhaps have withdrawn me from the solid ground of piety, or, had I continued in that healthful frame which I had thence imbibed, I might have thought, that it might have been obtained by the study of those books alone.

[XXI] 27 Most eagerly then did I seize that venerable writing of Thy Spirit; and chiefly the Apostle Paul. Whereupon those difficulties vanished away, wherein he once seemed to me to contradict himself, and the text of his discourse not to agree with the testimonies of the Law and the Prophets. And the face of that pure word appeared to me one and the same; and I learned to *rejoice with trembling*. So I began; and whatsoever truth I had read in those other books, I found here amid the praise of Thy Grace;[34] that whoso sees, may not *so glory as if he had not received*, not only what he sees, but also that he sees, (*for what hath he, which he hath not received?*) and that he may be not only admonished to behold Thee, *Who art* ever *the same*, but also healed, to hold Thee; and that *he who cannot see afar off*, may yet walk on the way, whereby he may arrive, and behold, and hold Thee. For, though a man *be delighted with the law of God after the inner man*, what shall he do with that *other law in his members which warreth against the law of his mind, and bringeth him into captivity to the law of sin which is in his members?* For, *Thou art righteous, O Lord, but we have sinned and committed iniquity, and have done wickedly,* and Thy hand is grown heavy upon us, and *we are justly delivered over* unto that antient sinner, the king of death; because he persuaded our will to be like his will, whereby *he abode not in Thy truth. What shall wretched man do? who shall deliver him from the body of this death, but only Thy Grace, through Jesus Christ our Lord,* whom Thou hast begotten coeternal, and *formedst*[35] *in the beginning of Thy ways, in whom the prince of this world found nothing worthy of death,* yet killed he Him;[36] and *the handwriting, which was contrary to us, was blotted out?* This those writings contain not. Those pages present not the image of this piety, the tears of confession, Thy *sacrifice, a troubled spirit, a broken and a contrite heart,* the salvation of the people, the *Bridal City,* the *earnest of the Holy Ghost, the Cup of our Redemption.* No man signs there, *Shall not my soul be submitted unto God? for of Him cometh my salvation. For he is my God and my salvation, my guardian, I shall no more be moved.* No one there hears Him call, *Come unto Me all ye that labour.* They scorn to *learn of Him, because He is meek and lowly in heart; for these things hast Thou hid from the wise and prudent, and hast revealed them unto babes.* For it is one thing, from the mountain's shaggy top to see the land of peace, and to find no way thither; and in vain to essay through ways unpassable, opposed and beset by fugitives and deserters, under their captain *the lion and the dragon:* and another to keep on the way that leads thither, guarded by the host of the heavenly General; where they spoil not who have deserted the heavenly army; for they avoid it, as very torment. These things did wonderfully sink into my bowels, when I read that *least of Thy Apostles*,[37] and had meditated upon Thy works, and trembled exceedingly.

BOOK VIII

Aug.'s thirty-second year. He consults Simplicianus, from him hears the history of the conversion of Victorinus, and longs to devote himself entirely to God, but is mastered by his old habits; is still further roused by the history of St. Antony, and the conversion of two courtiers; during a severe struggle, hears a voice from heaven, opens Scripture, and is converted, with his friend Alypius. His mother's vision fulfilled.

[I] 1 O my God, let me, with thanksgiving, remember, and confess unto Thee Thy mercies on me. *Let my bones be bedewed with Thy love, and let them say unto Thee, Who is like unto Thee, O Lord? Thou hast broken my bonds in sunder, I will offer unto Thee the sacrifice of thanksgiving*. And how Thou hast broken them, I will declare; and all who worship Thee, when they hear this, shall say, "Blessed be the Lord, in heaven and in earth, great and wonderful is His name." Thy words had stuck fast in my heart, and *I was hedged round about on all sides by Thee*. Of Thy eternal life I was now certain, though I saw it in a figure and as *through a glass*. Yet I had ceased to doubt that there was an incorruptible substance, whence was all other substance; nor did I now desire to be more certain of Thee, but more steadfast in Thee. But for my temporal life, all was wavering, and *my heart had to be purged from the old leaven. The Way*, the Saviour Himself, well pleased me, but as yet I shrunk from going through its straitness. And Thou didst put into my mind, and it seemed good in my eyes, to go to Simplicianus,[1] who seemed to me a good servant of Thine; and Thy grace shone in him. I had heard also, that from his very youth he had lived most devoted unto Thee. Now he was grown into years; and by reason of so great age spent in such zealous following of Thy ways he seemed to me likely to have learned much experience; and so he had. Out of which store, I wished that he would tell me (setting before him my anxieties) which were the fittest way for one in my case to walk in Thy paths.

2 For, I saw the church full; and one went this way, and another that way. But I was displeased, that I led a secular life; yea now that my desires no longer inflamed me, as of old, with hopes of honour and profit, a very grievous burden it was to undergo so heavy a bondage. For, in comparison of Thy sweetness, *and the beauty of Thy house which I loved*, those things delighted me no longer. But still I was enthralled with the love of woman; nor did the Apostle forbid me to marry, although he advised me to something better, chiefly wishing *that all men were as himself was*. But I being weak, chose the more indulgent place; and because of this alone, was tossed up and down in all beside, faint and wasted with withering cares, because in other matters, I was constrained against my will to conform myself to a married life, to which I was given up and inthralled. I had heard from the mouth of

the Truth, *that there were some eunuchs, which had made themselves eunuchs for the kingdom of heaven's sake: but,* saith He, *let him who can receive it receive it. Surely vain are all men who are ignorant of God, and could not out of the good things which are seen, find out Him who is good.* But I was no longer in that vanity; I had surmounted it; and by the common witness of all Thy creatures, had found Thee our Creator, and Thy Word, God with Thee, and together with Thee one God, by whom Thou createdst all things. There is yet another kind of ungodly, *who knowing God, glorified Him not as God, neither were thankful.* Into this also had I fallen, but *Thy right hand upheld me,* and took me thence, and Thou placedst me where I might recover. For Thou hadst said unto man, *Behold, the fear of the Lord is wisdom,* and, *Desire not to seem wise;* because they *who affirmed themselves to be wise, became fools.* But I had now *found the goodly pearl, which, selling all that I had,* I ought to have *bought,* and I hesitated.

[II] 3 To Simplicianus then I went, the father of Ambrose (a Bishop now) in receiving Thy grace,[2] and whom Ambrose truly loved as a father. To him I related the mazes of my wanderings. But when I mentioned that I had read certain books of the Platonists, which Victorinus, sometime Rhetoric Professor of Rome, (who had died a Christian, as I had heard,) had translated into Latin, he testified his joy that I had not fallen upon the writings of other philosophers, full of *fallacies and deceits, after the rudiments of this world,* whereas the Platonists[3] many ways led to the belief in God, and His Word. Then to exhort me to the humility of Christ, *hidden from the wise, and revealed to little ones*, he spoke of Victorinus[4] himself whom while at Rome he had most intimately known: and of him he related what I will not conceal. For it contains great *praise of Thy grace*, to be confessed unto Thee, how that aged man, most learned and skilled in the liberal sciences, and who had read, and weighed so many works of the philosophers; the instructor of so many noble Senators, who also, as a monument of his excellent discharge of his office, had (which men of this world esteem a high honour) both deserved and obtained a statue in the Roman Forum; he, to that age a worshipper of idols, and a partaker of the sacrilegious rites, to which almost all the nobility of Rome were given up, and had inspired the people with the love of

> Anubis, barking Deity, and all
> The monster Gods of every kind, who fought
> 'Gainst Neptune, Venus, and Minerva:[5]

whom Rome once conquered, now adored, all which the aged Victorinus had with thundering eloquence so many years defended;—he now blushed not to be the child of Thy Christ, and the new-born babe of Thy fountain; submitting his neck to the yoke of humility, and subduing his forehead to the reproach of the Cross.

4 O Lord, Lord, *Which hast bowed the heavens and come down, touched the mountains and they did smoke*, by what means didst Thou convey Thyself into that breast? He used to read (as Simplicianus said) the holy

Scripture, most studiously sought and searched into all the Christian writings, and said to Simplicianus, (not openly, but privately and as a friend,) "Understand that I am already a Christian." Whereto he answered, "I will not believe it, nor will I rank you among Christians, unless I see you in the Church of Christ." The other, in banter, replied, "Do walls then make Christians?" And this he often said, that he was already a Christian; and Simplicianus as often made the same answer, and the conceit of the "walls" was by the other as often renewed. For he feared to offend his friends, proud dæmon-worshippers, from the height of whose Babylonian dignity, as from *cedars of Libanus*, which *the Lord* had not yet *broken down*, he supposed the weight of enmity would fall upon him. But after that by reading and earnest thought he had gathered firmness, and feared to be *denied by Christ before the holy angels, should he now be afraid to confess him before men*, and appeared to himself guilty of a heavy offence, in being ashamed of the Sacraments of the humility of Thy Word, and not being ashamed of the sacrilegious rites of those proud dæmons, whose pride he had imitated and their rites adopted, he became bold-faced against vanity, and shame-faced towards the truth, and suddenly and unexpectedly said to Simplicianus, (as himself told me,) "Go we to the Church; I wish to be made a Christian." But he, not containing himself for joy, went with him. And having been admitted to the first Sacrament and become a Catechumen, not long after he further gave in his name, that he might be regenerated by baptism, Rome wondering, the Church rejoicing.

The proud *saw, and were wroth; they gnashed with their teeth, and melted away*. But the *Lord* God *was the hope* of Thy servant, and *he regarded not vanities and lying* madness.

5 To conclude, when the hour was come for making profession of his faith, (which at Rome they, who are about to approach to Thy grace, deliver, from an elevated place, in the sight of all the faithful, in a set form of words[6] committed to memory,) the presbyters, he said, offered Victorinus[7] (as was done to such, as seemed likely through bashfulness to be alarmed) to make his profession more privately: but he chose rather to profess his salvation in the presence of the holy multitude. "For it was not salvation that he taught in rhetoric, and yet that he had publicly professed. How much less then ought he, when pronouncing Thy word, to dread Thy meek flock, who, when delivering his own words, had not feared a mad multitude!" When, then, he went up to make his profession, all, as they knew him, whispered his name one to another with the voice of congratulation. And who there knew him not? and there ran a low murmur through all the mouths of the rejoicing multitude, Victorinus! Victorinus! Sudden was the burst of rapture, that they saw him; suddenly were they hushed that they might hear him. He pronounced the true faith with an excellent boldness, and all wished to draw him into their very heart: yea by their love and joy they drew him thither; such were the hands wherewith they drew him.

[III] 6 Good God! what takes place in man, that he should more rejoice at the salvation of a soul despaired of, and freed from greater peril, than if there had always been hope of him, or the danger had been less? For so Thou also, merciful Father, *dost more rejoice over one penitent, than over ninety-nine just persons, that need no repentance.* And with much joyfulness do we hear, so often as we hear with what joy *the sheep which had strayed, is brought back upon the shepherd's shoulder,* and *the groat is restored to Thy treasury, the neighbours rejoicing with the woman who found it;* and the joy of the solemn service of Thy house forceth to tears, when in Thy house it is read of Thy *younger son, that he was dead, and lived again; had been lost, and is found.* For Thou *rejoicest* in us, and in Thy holy angels, holy through holy charity. For Thou art ever the same; for all things which abide not the same nor for ever, Thou for ever knowest in the same way.

7 What then takes place in the soul, when it is more delighted at finding or recovering the things it loves, than if it had ever had them? yea, and other things witness hereunto; and all things are full of witnesses, crying out, "so is it." The conquering commander triumpheth; yet had he not conquered, unless he had fought; and the more peril there was in the battle, so much the more joy is there in the triumph. The storm tosses the sailors, threatens shipwreck; all wax pale at approaching death; sky and sea are calmed, and they are exceeding joyed, as having been exceeding afraid. A friend is sick, and his pulse threatens danger; all who long for his recovery, are sick in mind with him. He is restored, though as yet he walks not with his

CONFESSIONS OF ST. AUGUSTINE

former strength; yet there is such joy, as was not, when before he walked sound and strong. Yea, the very pleasures of human life men acquire by difficulties, not those only which fall upon us unlooked for, and against our wills, but even by self-chosen, and pleasure-seeking trouble. Eating and drinking have no pleasure, unless there precede the pinching of hunger and thirst. Men, given to drink, eat certain salt meats, to procure a troublesome heat, which the drink allaying, causes pleasure. It is also ordered, that the affianced bride should not at once be given, lest as a husband he should hold cheap whom, as betrothed, he sighed not after.

8 This law holds in foul and accursed joy; this in permitted and lawful joy; this in the very purest perfection of friendship; this, in him *who was dead, and lived again; had been lost, and was found.* Every where the greater joy is ushered in by the greater pain. What means this, O Lord my God, whereas Thou art everlastingly joy to Thyself, and some things around Thee evermore rejoice in Thee?[8] What means this, that this portion of things thus ebbs and flows alternately displeased and reconciled? Is this their allotted measure? Is this all Thou hast assigned to them, whereas from the highest heavens to the lowest earth, from the beginning of the world to the end of ages, from the angel to the worm, from the first motion to the last, Thou settest each in its place, and realizest each in their season, every thing good after its kind? Woe is me! how high art Thou in the highest, and how deep in the deepest! and Thou never departest, and we scarcely return to Thee.

[IV] 9 Up, Lord, and do; stir us up, and recall us; kindle and draw us; inflame, grow sweet unto us; let us now love, *let us run*. Do not many, out of a deeper hell of blindness than Victorinus, return to Thee, approach, and are enlightened, receiving that *Light*, which *they who receive, receive power from Thee to become Thy sons?* But if they be less known to the nations, even they that know them, joy less for them. For when many joy together, each also has more exuberant joy; for that they are kindled and inflamed one by the other. Again, because those known to many, influence the more towards salvation, and lead the way with many to follow. And therefore do they also who preceded them, much rejoice in them, because they rejoice not in them alone. For far be it, that in Thy tabernacle the persons of the rich should be accepted before the poor, or the noble before the ignoble; seeing rather *Thou hast chosen the weak things of the world, to confound the strong; and the base things of this world, and the things despised hast Thou chosen, and those things which are not, that Thou mightest bring to nought things that are*. And yet even that *least of* Thy *apostles*, by whose tongue Thou soundedst forth these words, when through his warfare, Paulus the Proconsul, his pride conquered, was made to pass under the *easy yoke* of Thy Christ, and became a provincial of the great King; he also for his former name Saul, was pleased to be called Paul,[9] in testimony of so great a victory. For the enemy is more overcome in one, of whom he hath more hold; by whom he hath hold of more. But the proud he hath more hold of, through their nobility; and by them, of more through their authority. By how much the more welcome then the heart of Victorinus was esteemed, which the devil had held as an impregnable possession, the tongue of Victorinus, with which mighty and keen weapon he had slain many; so much the more abundantly ought Thy sons to rejoice, for that our King *hath bound the strong man*, and they saw his *vessels taken from him and cleansed*, and *made meet for Thy honour*, and become *serviceable for the Lord, unto every good work*.

[V] 10 But when that man of Thine, Simplicianus, related to me this of Victorinus, I was on fire to imitate him; for for this very end had he related it. But when he had subjoined also, how in the days of the Emperor Julian, a law was made, whereby Christians were forbidden to teach the liberal sciences or oratory; and how he, obeying this law, chose rather to give over the wordy school, than Thy *Word*, by which Thou *makest eloquent the tongues of the dumb*; he seemed to me not more resolute than blessed, in having thus found opportunity to wait on Thee only. Which thing I was sighing for, bound as I was, not with another's irons, but by my own iron will. My will the enemy held, and thence had made a chain for me, and bound me. For of a froward will, was a lust made; and a lust served, became custom; and custom not resisted, became necessity. By which links, as it were, joined together (whence I called it a chain) a hard bondage held me enthralled. But that new will which had begun to be in me, freely to serve Thee, and to wish to enjoy Thee, O God, the only assured pleasantness, was not yet able to overcome my former wilfulness, strengthened by age.

Thus did my two wills, one new, and the other old, one carnal, the other spiritual, struggle within me; and by their discord, undid my soul.

11 Thus I understood, by my own experience, what I had read, how *the flesh lusteth against the spirit and the spirit against the flesh*. Myself verily either way;[10] yet more myself, in that which I approved in myself, than in that which in myself I disapproved. For in this last, it was now for the more part not myself, because in much I rather endured against my will, than acted willingly. And yet it was through me, that custom had obtained this power of warring against me, because I had come willingly, whither I willed not. And who has any right to speak against it, if just punishment follow the sinner? Nor had I now any longer my former plea, that I therefore as yet hesitated to be above the world and serve Thee, for that the truth was not altogether ascertained to me; for now it too was. But I, still under service to the earth, refused to fight under Thy banner, and feared as much to be freed of all incumbrances, as we should fear to be encumbered with it.

12 Thus with the baggage of this present world was I held down pleasantly, as in sleep: and the thoughts wherein I meditated on Thee, were like the efforts of such as would awake, who yet overcome with a heavy drowsiness, are again drenched therein. And as no one would sleep for ever, and in all men's sober judgment, waking is better, yet a man for the most part, feeling a heavy lethargy in all his limbs, defers to shake off sleep, and, though half displeased, yet, even after it is time to

rise, with pleasure yields to it, so was I assured, that much better were it for me to give myself up to thy charity, than to give myself over to mine own cupidity; but though the former course satisfied me and gained the mastery, the latter pleased me and held me mastered,[11] Nor had I any thing to answer Thee calling to me, *Awake, thou that sleepest, and arise from the dead, and Christ shall give thee light.* And when Thou didst on all sides shew me, that what Thou saidst was true, I, convicted by the truth, had nothing at all to answer, but only those dull and drowsy words, "Anon, anon," "presently;" "leave me but a little." But "presently, presently," had no present, and my "little while" went on for a long while; in vain I *delighted in Thy law according to the inner man,* when *another law in my members, rebelled against the law of my mind, and led me captive under the law of sin which was in my members.* For the law of sin is the violence of custom, whereby the mind is drawn and holden, even against its will; but deservedly, for that it willingly fell into it. *Who then should deliver me thus wretched from the body of this death, but Thy grace only, through Jesus Christ our Lord?*

[VI] 13 And how Thou didst deliver me out of the bonds of desire, wherewith I was bound most straitly to carnal concupiscence, and out of the drudgery of worldly things, I will now declare, and confess unto Thy name, *O Lord, my helper and my redeemer.* Amid increasing anxiety, I was doing my wonted business, and daily sighing unto Thee. I attended Thy Church, whenever free from the business under the burden of which I groaned. Alypius was with me, now after the third sitting released from his law business, and awaiting to whom to sell his counsel, as I sold the skill of speaking, if indeed teaching can impart it. Nebridius had now, in consideration of our friendship, consented to teach under Verecundus, a citizen and a grammarian of Milan, and a very intimate friend of us all; who urgently desired, and by the right of friendship challenged from our company, such faithful aid as he greatly needed. Nebridius then was not drawn to this by any desire of advantage, (for he might have made much more of his learning had he so willed,) but as a most kind and gentle friend, he would not be wanting to a good office, and slight our request. But he acted herein very discreetly, shunning to become known to personages great according to this world, avoiding the distraction of mind thence ensuing, and desiring to have it free and at leisure, as many hours as might be, to seek, or read, or hear something concerning wisdom.

14 Upon a day then, Nebridius being absent, (I recollect not why,) lo, there came to see me and Alypius, one Pontitianus, our countryman so far as being an African, in high office in the Emperor's court. What he would with us, I know not, but we sat down to converse, and it happened that upon a table for some game, before us, he observed a book, took, opened it, and contrary to his expectation, found it the Apostle Paul; for he had thought it some of those books, which I was wearing myself in teaching. Whereat smiling, and looking at me, he expressed his joy and wonder, that he had on a sudden found this book, and this only before my eyes. For he was a Christian, and baptized, and often bowed himself before

Thee our God in the Church, in frequent and continued prayers. When then I had told him, that I bestowed very great pains upon those Scriptures, a conversation arose (suggested by his account) on Antony[12] the Egyptian Monk: whose name was in high reputation among Thy servants, though to that hour unknown to us. Which when he discovered, he dwelt the more upon that subject, informing and wondering at our ignorance of one so eminent. But we stood amazed, hearing Thy wonderful works[13] most fully attested, in times so recent, and almost in our own, wrought in the true Faith and Church Catholic. We all wondered; we, that they were so great, and he, that they had not reached us.

15 Thence his discourse turned to the flocks in the Monasteries, and their holy ways, a sweet smelling savour unto Thee, and the fruitful deserts[14] of the wilderness, whereof we knew nothing. And there was a Monastery at Milan,[15] full of good brethren, without the city walls, under the fostering care of Ambrose, and we knew it not. He went on with his discourse, and we listened in intent silence. He told us then how one afternoon at Triers, when the Emperor was taken up with the Circensian games, he and three others, his companions, went out to walk in gardens near the city walls, and there as they happened to walk in pairs, one went apart with him, and the other two wandered by themselves; and these, in their wanderings, lighted upon a certain cottage, inhabited by certain of thy servants, *poor in spirit, of whom is the kingdom of heaven*, and there they found a little book, containing the life of Antony. This one of them began to

read, admire, and kindle at it; and as he read, to meditate on taking up such a life, and giving over his secular service to serve Thee. And these two were of those whom they style[16] agents for the public affairs. Then suddenly, filled with an holy love, and a sober shame, in anger with himself he cast his eyes upon his friend, saying, "Tell me, I pray thee, what would we attain by all these labours of ours? what aim we at? what serve we for? Can our hopes in court rise higher than to be the Emperor's favourites? and in this, what is there not brittle, and full of perils? and by how many perils arrive we at a greater peril? And when arrive we thither? But a friend of God, if I wish it, I become now at once." So spake he. And in pain with the travail of a new life, he turned his eyes again upon the book, and read on, and was changed inwardly, where Thou sawest, and his mind was stripped of the world, as soon appeared. For as he read, and rolled up and down the waves of his heart, he stormed at himself a while, then discerned, and determined on a better course; and now being Thine, said to his friend, "Now have I broken loose from those our hopes, and am resolved to serve God; and this, from this hour, in this place, I begin upon. If thou likest not to imitate me, oppose not." The other answered, he would cleave to him, to partake so glorious a reward, so glorious a service. Thus both being now Thine, were *building* the *tower* at the necessary *cost, the forsaking all that they had, and following Thee.* Then Pontitianus and the other with him, that had walked in other parts of the garden, came in search of them to the same place; and finding them, reminded them to return, for the day was now far spent. But they relating their resolution and purpose, and how that will was begun, and settled in them, begged them, if they would not join, not to molest them. But the others, though nothing altered from their former selves, did yet bewail themselves, (as he affirmed,) and piously congratulated them, recommending themselves to their prayers; and so, with hearts lingering on the earth, went away to the palace. But the other two, fixing their heart on heaven, remained in the cottage. And both had affianced brides, who when they heard hereof, also dedicated their virginity unto God.

[VII] 16 Such was the story of Pontitianus; but Thou, O Lord, while he was speaking, didst turn me round towards myself, taking me from behind my back, where I had placed me, unwilling to observe myself; and setting me before my face, that I might see how foul I was, how crooked and defiled, bespotted and ulcerous. And I beheld and stood aghast; and whither to flee from myself I found not. And if I sought to turn mine eye from off myself, he went on with his relation, and Thou again didst set me over against myself, and thrustedst me before my eyes, that *I might find out mine iniquity, and hate it*. I had known it, but made as though I saw it not, winked at it, and forgot it.

17 But now, the more ardently I loved those, whose healthful affections I heard of, that they had resigned themselves wholly to Thee to be cured, the more did I abhor myself,[17] when compared with them. For many of my years (some twelve) had now run out with me since my nineteenth, when, upon the reading of Cicero's Hortensius,[18] I was stirred to an earnest love of wisdom; and still I was deferring to reject mere earthly felicity,

and give myself to search out that, whereof not the finding only, but the very search, was to be preferred to the treasures and kingdoms of the world, though already found, and to the pleasures of the body, though spread around me at my will. But I wretched, most wretched, in the very commencement of my early youth, had begged chastity of Thee, and said, "Give me chastity and continency, only not yet." For I feared lest Thou shouldest hear me soon, and soon cure me of the disease of concupiscence, which I wished to have satisfied, rather than extinguished. And I had wandered through crooked ways in a sacrilegious superstition,[19] not indeed assured thereof, but as preferring it to the others which I did not seek religiously, but opposed maliciously.

18 And I had thought, that I therefore deferred from day to day to reject the hopes of this world, and follow Thee only, because there did not appear aught certain, whither to direct my course. And now was the day come wherein I was to be laid bare to myself, and my conscience was to upbraid me. "Where art thou now, my tongue? Thou saidst, that for an uncertain truth thou likedst not to cast off the baggage of vanity; now, it is certain, and yet that burthen still oppresseth thee, while they who neither have so worn themselves out with seeking it, nor for ten years and more have been thinking thereon, have had their shoulders lightened, and received wings to fly away." Thus was I gnawed within, and exceedingly confounded with an horrible shame, while Pontitianus was so speaking. And he having brought to a close his tale and the business he came for, went his way; and I into

myself. What said I not against myself? With what scourges of condemnation lashed I not my soul, that it might follow me, striving to go after Thee! Yet it drew back; refused, but excused not itself. All arguments were spent and confuted; there remained a mute shrinking; and she feared, as she would death, to be restrained from the flux of that custom, whereby she was wasting to death.

[VIII] 19 Then in this great contention of my inward dwelling, which I had strongly raised against my soul, in *the chamber* of my heart, troubled in mind and countenance, I turned upon Alypius. "What ails us?" I exclaim: "what is it? what heardest thou? The unlearned start up and *take heaven by force*, and we with our learning, and without heart, lo, where we wallow in flesh and blood! Are we ashamed to follow, because others are gone before, and not ashamed not even to follow?" Some such words I uttered, and my fever of mind tore me away from him, while he, gazing on me in astonishment, kept silence. For it was not my wonted tone; and my forehead, cheeks, eyes, colour, tone of voice, spake my mind more than the words I uttered. A little garden there was to our lodging, which we had the use of, as of the whole house; for the master of the house, our host, was not living there. Thither had the tumult of my breast hurried me, where no man might hinder the hot contention wherein I had engaged with myself, until it should end as Thou knewest, I knew not. Only I was healthfully distracted and dying, to live; knowing what evil thing I was, and not knowing what good thing I was shortly to become. I retired then into the garden, and Alypius, on my steps. For his presence did not lessen my privacy; or how could he forsake me so disturbed? We sate down as far removed as might be from the house. I was troubled in spirit, most vehemently indignant that I entered not into Thy will and covenant, O my God, which *all my bones cried out* unto me to enter, and praised it to the skies. And therein we enter not by ships, or chariots, or feet, no, move not so far as I had come from the house to that place where we were sitting. For, not to go only, but to go in thither was nothing else but to will to go, but to will resolutely and thoroughly; not to turn and toss, this way and that, a maimed and half-divided will, struggling, with one part sinking as another rose.

20 Lastly, in the very fever of my irresoluteness, I made with my body many such motions as men sometimes would, but cannot, if either they have not the limbs, or these be bound with bands, weakened with infirmity, or any other way hindered. Thus, if I tore my hair, beat my forehead, if locking my fingers I clasped my knee; I willed, I did it. But I might have willed, and not done it, if the power of motion in my limbs had not obeyed. So many things then I did, when "to will" was not in itself "to be able;" and I did not what both I longed incomparably more to do, and which soon after, when I should will, I should be able to do; because soon after, when I should will, I should will thoroughly. For in these things the ability was one with the will, and to will was to do; and yet was it not done: and more easily did my body obey the weakest willing of my soul, in moving its limbs at its nod, than the soul obeyed itself to accomplish in the will alone this its momentous will.

[IX] 21 Whence is this monstrousness? and to what end? Let Thy mercy gleam that I may ask, if so be the secret penalties of men, and those darkest pangs of the sons of Adam, may perhaps answer me. Whence is this monstrousness? and to what end? The mind commands the body, and it obeys instantly; the mind commands itself, and is resisted.[20] The mind commands the hand to be moved; and such readiness is there, that command is scarce distinct from obedience. Yet the mind is mind, the hand is body. The mind commands the mind, its own self, to will, and yet it doth not. Whence this monstrousness? and to what end? It commands itself, I say, to will, and would not command, unless it willed, and what it commands is not done. But it willeth not entirely: therefore doth it not command entirely. For so far forth it commandeth, as it willeth: and, so far forth is the thing commanded, not done, as it willeth not. For the will commandeth that there be a will; not another, but itself. But it doth not command entirely, therefore what it commandeth, is not. For were the will entire, it would not even command it to be, because it would already be. It is therefore no monstrousness partly to will, partly to nill, but a disease of the mind, that it doth not wholly rise, by truth up-borne, borne down by custom. And therefore are there two wills, for that one of them is not entire: and what the one lacketh, the other hath.

[X] 22 *Let them perish from Thy presence*, O God, as perish *vain talkers, and seducers* of the soul: who[21] observing that in deliberating there were two wills, affirm, that there are two minds in us of two kinds, one good, the other evil.

Themselves are truly evil, when they hold these evil things; and themselves shall become good, when they hold the truth, and assent unto the truth, that Thy Apostle may say to them, *Ye were sometimes darkness, but now light in the Lord.* But they, wishing to be light, not *in the Lord*, but in themselves, imagining the nature of the soul to be that which God is,[22] are made more gross darkness through a dreadful arrogancy; for that they *went back farther from Thee, the true Light that enlighteneth every man that cometh into the world.* Take heed what you say, and blush for shame: *draw near unto Him and be enlightened, and your faces shall not be ashamed.* Myself when I was deliberating upon serving the Lord my God now, as I had long purposed, it was I who willed, I who nilled, I, I myself. I neither willed entirely, nor nilled entirely. Therefore was I at strife with myself, and rent asunder by myself. And this rent befel me against my will, and yet indicated, not the presence of another mind, but the punishment of my own.[23] *Therefore it was no more I that wrought it, but sin that dwelt in me;* the punishment of a sin more freely committed, in that I was a son of Adam.

23 For if there be so many contrary natures, as there be conflicting wills; there shall now be not two only, but many. If a man deliberate, whether he should go to their conventicle, or to the theatre; these Manichees cry out, Behold, here are two natures: one good, draws this way; another bad, draws back that way. For whence else is this hesitation between conflicting wills? But I say, that both be bad: that which draws to them, as that which draws back to the theatre. But they believe not that will to be

other than good, which draws to them. What then if one of us should deliberate, and amid the strife of his two wills be in a strait, whether he should go to the theatre, or to our church? would not these Manichees also be in a strait what to answer? For either they must confess, (which they fain would not,) that the will which leads to our church is good, as well as theirs, who have received and are held by the mysteries of theirs: or they must suppose two evil natures, and two evil souls conflicting in one man, and it will not be true, which they say, that there is one good and another bad; or they must be converted to the truth, and no more deny, that where one deliberates, one soul fluctuates between contrary wills.

24 Let them no more say then, when they perceive two conflicting wills in one man, that the conflict is between two contrary souls, of two contrary substances, from two contrary principles, one good, and the other bad. For Thou, O true God, dost disprove, check, and convict them; as when, both wills being bad, one deliberates, whether he should kill a man by poison, or by the sword; whether he should seize this or that estate of another's, when he cannot both; whether he should purchase pleasure by luxury, or keep his money by covetousness; whether he go to the circus, or the theatre, if both be open on one day; or, thirdly, to rob another's house, if he have the opportunity; or, fourthly, to commit adultery, if at the same time he have the means thereof also; all these meeting together in the same juncture of time, and all being equally desired, which cannot at one time be acted: for they rend the mind amid four, or even (amid the vast variety of things desired)

more, conflicting wills, nor do they yet allege that there
are so many divers substances. So also in wills which are
good. For I ask them, is it good to take pleasure in reading
the Apostle?[24] or good to take pleasure in a sober Psalm?
or good to discourse on the Gospel? They will answer to
each, "It is good." What then if all give equal pleasure, and
all at once? Do not divers wills distract the mind, while
he deliberates, which he should rather choose? yet are
they all good, and are at variance till one be chosen,
whither the one entire will may be borne, which before
was divided into many. Thus also, when, above, eternity
delights us, and the pleasure of temporal good holds us
down below, it is the same soul which willeth not this or
that with an entire will; and therefore is rent asunder with
grievous perplexities, while out of truth it sets this first,
but out of habit sets not that aside.

[XI] 25 Thus soul-sick was I, and tormented, accusing
myself much more severely than my wont, rolling and
turning me in my chain, till that were wholly broken,
whereby I now was but just, but still was, held. And
Thou, O Lord, pressedst upon me in my inward parts by
a severe mercy, redoubling the lashes of fear and shame,
lest I should again give way, and not bursting that same
slight remaining tie, it should recover strength, and bind
me the faster. For I said within myself, "Be it done now,
be it done now." And as I spake, I all but enacted it. I all
but did it, and did it not: yet sunk not back to my former
state, but kept my stand hard by, and took breath. And
I essayed again, and wanted somewhat less of it, and
somewhat less, and all but touched and laid hold of it; and

yet came not at it, nor touched, nor laid hold of it:
hesitating to die to death and to live to life: and the worse
whereto I was inured,[25] prevailed more with me than the
better, whereto I was unused: and the very moment
wherein I was to become other than I was, the nearer it
approached me, the greater horror did it strike into me;
yet did it not strike me back, nor turned me away, but
held me in suspense.

26 The very toys of toys, and vanities of vanities, my
ancient mistresses, still held me; they plucked my fleshly
garment, and whispered softly, "Dost thou cast us off?
and from that moment shall we no more be with thee for
ever? and from that moment shall not this or that be
lawful for thee for ever?" And what was it which they
suggested in that I said, "this or that," what did they
suggest, O my God? Let Thy mercy turn it away from the
soul of Thy servant. What defilements did they suggest!
what shame! And now I much less than half heard them,
and not openly shewing themselves and contradicting
me, but muttering as it were behind my back, and privily
plucking me, as I was departing, but to look back on
them. Yet they did retard me, so that I hesitated to burst
and shake myself free from them, and to spring over
whither I was called; a violent habit saying to me,
"Thinkest thou, thou canst live without them?"

27 But now it spake very faintly. For on that side whither
I had set my face, and whither I trembled to go, there
appeared unto me the chaste dignity of Continency,
serene, yet not relaxedly gay, honestly alluring me to

come, and doubt not; and stretching forth to receive and embrace me, her holy hands full of multitudes of good examples. There were so many young men and maidens here, a multitude of youth and every age, grave widows and aged virgins; and Continence herself in all, not barren, but a *fruitful mother of children* of joys, by Thee her Husband, O Lord. And she smiled on me with a persuasive mockery, as would she say, "Canst not thou what these youths, what these maidens can? or can they either in themselves, and not rather in the Lord their God? The Lord their God gave me unto them. Why standest thou in thyself, and so standest not? Cast thyself upon Him, fear not He will not withdraw Himself that thou shouldest fall; cast thyself fearlessly upon Him, He will receive, and will heal thee." And I blushed exceedingly, for that I yet heard the muttering of those toys, and hung in suspense. And she again seemed to say, "Stop thine ears against *those* thy unclean *members on the earth, that they may be mortified. They tell thee of delights, but not as doth the law of the Lord thy God.*" This controversy in my heart was self against self only. But Alypius sitting close by my side, in silence waited the issue of my unwonted emotion.

[XII] 28 But when a deep consideration had from the secret bottom of my soul drawn together and heaped up all my misery in the sight of my heart; there arose a mighty storm, bringing a mighty shower of tears. Which that I might pour forth wholly, in its natural expressions, I rose from Alypius: solitude was suggested to me as fitter for the business of weeping; so I retired so far that even his presence could not be a burthen to me. Thus was it then with me, and he perceived something of it; for something I suppose I had spoken, wherein the tones of my voice appeared choked with weeping, and so had risen up. He then remained where we were sitting, most extremely astonished. I cast myself down I know not how, under a certain fig-tree, giving full vent to my tears; and the floods of mine eyes gushed out, an *acceptable sacrifice to Thee*. And, not indeed in these words, yet to this purpose, spake I much unto Thee: *And Thou, O Lord, how long? how long, Lord, wilt Thou be angry, for ever? Remember not our former iniquities*, for I felt that I was held by them. I sent up these sorrowful words; How long? how long, "to-morrow, and to-morrow?" Why not now? why not is there this hour an end to my uncleanness?

29 So was I speaking, and weeping in the most bitter contrition of my heart, when, lo! I heard from a neighbouring house a voice, as of boy or girl, I know not, chanting, and oft repeating, "Take up and read; Take up and read." Instantly, my countenance altered, I began to think most intently, whether children were wont in any kind of play to sing such words: nor could I remember ever to have heard the like. So checking the torrent of my tears, I arose; interpreting it to be no other than a command from God, to open the book, and read the first chapter I should find. For I had heard of Antony,[26] that coming in during the reading of the Gospel, he received the admonition, as if what was being read, was spoken to him; *Go, sell all that thou hast, and give to the poor, and thou shall have treasure in heaven, and come and follow me*. And by such oracle he was forthwith converted unto

Thee. Eagerly then I returned to the place where Alypius was sitting; for there had I laid the volume of the Apostle, when I arose thence. I seized, opened, and in silence read that section, on which my eyes first fell: *Not in rioting and drunkenness, not in chambering and wantonness, not in strife and envying: but put ye on the Lord Jesus Christ, and make not provision for the flesh,* in concupiscence. No further would I read; nor needed I: for instantly at the end of this sentence, by a light as it were of serenity infused into my heart, all the darkness of doubt vanished away.

30 Then putting my finger between, or some other mark, I shut the volume, and with a calmed countenance made it known to Alypius. And what was wrought in him, which I knew not, he thus shewed me. He asked to see what I had read: I shewed him; and he looked even further than I had read, and I knew not what followed. This followed, *him that is weak in the faith, receive;* which he applied to himself, and disclosed to me. And by this admonition was he strengthened; and by a good resolution and purpose, and most corresponding to his character, wherein he did always very far differ from me, for the better, without any turbulent delay he joined me. Thence we go into my mother; we tell her; she rejoiceth: we relate in order how it took place; she leaps for joy, and triumpheth, and blesseth Thee, *Who art able to do above that which we ask or think;* for she perceived that Thou hadst given her more for me, than she was wont to beg by her pitiful and most sorrowful groanings. For Thou convertedst me unto Thyself, so that I sought neither wife, nor any hope of this world, standing in that rule of

faith, where Thou hadst shewed me unto her in a vision, so many years before. And Thou didst *convert her mourning into joy*, much more plentiful than she had desired, and in a much more precious and purer way than she erst required by having grandchildren of my body.

BOOK IX

Aug. determines to devote his life to God, and to abandon his profession of Rhetoric, quietly however; retires to the country to prepare himself to receive the grace of Baptism, and is baptized with Alypius, and his son Adeodatus. At Ostia, in his way to Africa, his mother Monnica dies, in her fifty-sixth year, the thirty-third of Augustine. Her life and character.

[I] 1 *O Lord, I am Thy servant; I am Thy servant, and the son of Thy handmaid: Thou hast broken my bonds in sunder. I will offer to Thee the sacrifice of praise.* Let my heart and my tongue praise Thee; yea let *all my bones say, O Lord, who is like unto Thee?* Let them say, and answer Thou me, and *say unto my soul, I am thy salvation.* Who am I, and what am I? What evil have not been either my deeds, or if not my deeds, my words, or if not my words, my will? But Thou, O Lord, art good and merciful, and Thy right hand had respect unto the depth of my death, and from the bottom of my heart emptied that abyss of corruption. And this Thy whole gift was, to nill what I willed, and to will what Thou willedst. But where through all those years, and out of what low and deep recess was my free-will called forth in a moment, whereby to submit my neck to Thy *easy yoke,* and my shoulders unto Thy *light burthen,* O Christ Jesus, *my Helper and my Redeemer?* How

sweet did it at once become to me, to want the sweet-
nesses of those toys! and what I feared to be parted from,
was now a joy to part with. For Thou didst cast them
forth from me, Thou true and highest sweetness.¹ Thou
castest them forth, and for them enteredst in Thyself,
sweeter than all pleasure, though not to flesh and blood;
brighter than all light, but more hidden than all depths,
higher than all honour, but not to the high in their own
conceits. Now was my soul free from the biting cares of
canvassing and getting, and weltering in filth, and
scratching off the itch of lust. And my infant tongue
spake freely to Thee, my brightness, and my riches, and
my health, the Lord my God.

[II] 2 And I resolved in Thy sight, not tumultuously to
tear, but gently to withdraw, the service of my tongue
from the marts of lip-labour: that the young, no students
in Thy law, nor in Thy peace, but in lying dotages and
law-skirmishes, should no longer buy at my mouth arms
for their madness. And very seasonably, it now wanted
but very few days unto the² Vacation of the Vintage, and
I resolved to endure them, then in a regular way to take
my leave, and having been purchased by Thee, no more
to return for sale. Our purpose then was known to Thee;
but to men, other than our own friends, was it not known.
For we had agreed among ourselves not to let it out abroad
to any: although to us, now ascending from the *valley of
tears*, and singing that *song of degrees*, Thou hadst given
sharp arrows, and *destroying coals* against the *subtile
tongue*,³ which as though advising for us, would thwart,
and would out of love devour us, as it doth its meat.

3 Thou hadst pierced our hearts with Thy charity, and we carried Thy words as it were fixed in our entrails: and the examples of Thy servants, whom for black Thou hadst made bright, and for dead, alive, being piled together in the receptacle of our thoughts, kindled and burned up that our heavy torpor, that we should not sink down to the abyss; and they fired us so vehemently, that all the blasts of *subtle tongues* from gainsayers might only inflame us the more fiercely, not extinguish us. Nevertheless, because for *Thy Name's* sake which Thou hast *hallowed* throughout the earth, this our vow and purpose might also find some to commend it, it seemed like ostentation not to wait for the vacation now so near, but to quit beforehand a public profession, which was before the eyes of all; so that all looking on this act of mine, and observing how near was the time of vintage which I wished to anticipate, would talk much of me, as if I had desired to appear some great one. And what end had it served me, that people should repute and dispute upon my purpose, and that *our good should be evil spoken of?*

4 Moreover, it had at first troubled me, that in this very summer my lungs[4] began to give way, amid too great literary labour, and to breathe deeply with difficulty, and by the pain in my chest to shew that they were injured, and to refuse any full or lengthened speaking; this had troubled me, for it almost constrained me of necessity, to lay down that burthen of teaching, or, if I could be cured and recover, at least to intermit it. But when the full wish for leisure, that I might see *how that Thou art the Lord,* arose, and was fixed, in me; my God, Thou knowest, I

began even to rejoice that I had this secondary, and that no feigned, excuse, which might something moderate the offence taken by those, who for their sons' sake, wished me never to have the freedom of Thy sons. Full then of such joy, I endured till that interval of time were run; it may have been some twenty days, yet they were endured manfully; endured, for the covetousness which aforetime bore a part of this heavy business, had left me, and I remained alone, and had been overwhelmed, had not patience taken its place. Perchance, some of Thy servants, my brethren, may say, that I sinned in this, that with a heart fully set on Thy service, I suffered myself to sit even one hour in the chair of lies. Nor would I be contentious. But hast not Thou, O most merciful Lord, pardoned and remitted this sin also, with my other most horrible and deadly sins, in the holy water?

[III] 5 Verecundus was worn down with care about this our blessedness, for that being held back by bonds, whereby he was most straitly bound, he saw that he should be severed from us. For himself was not yet a Christian, his wife one of the faithful; and yet hereby, more rigidly than by any other chain, was he let and hindered from the journey which we had now essayed. For he would not, he said, be a Christian on any other terms than on those he could not. However, he offered us courteously to remain at his country-house, so long as we should stay there. Thou, O Lord, shalt reward him *in the resurrection of the just*, seeing thou hast already given him *the lot* of the righteous. For although, in our absence, being now at Rome, he was seized with bodily sickness, and therein being made a Christian, and one of the faithful, he departed this life; yet *hadst Thou mercy not on him only, but on us also:* lest remembering the exceeding kindness of our friend towards us, yet unable to number him among Thy flock, we should be agonized with intolerable sorrow. Thanks unto Thee, our God, we are Thine: Thy suggestions and consolations tell us, Faithful in promises, Thou now requitest Verecundus for his country-house of Cassiacum, where from the fever of the world we reposed in Thee, with the eternal freshness of Thy Paradise: for that Thou hast forgiven him his sins upon earth, in that rich mountain,[5] that mountain which yieldeth milk, Thine own mountain.

6 He then had at that time sorrow, but Nebridius joy. For although he also, not being yet a Christian, had fallen into the pit of that most pernicious error, believing the flesh of Thy Son to be a phantom: yet emerging thence, he believed as we did; not as yet indued with any Sacraments of Thy Church, but a most ardent searcher out[6] of truth. Whom, not long after our conversion and regeneration by Thy Baptism, being also a faithful member of the Church Catholic, and serving Thee in perfect chastity and continence amongst his people in Africa, his whole house having through him first been made Christian, didst Thou release from the flesh; and now he lives in Abraham's bosom.[7] Whatever that be, which is signified by that bosom, there lives my Nebridius, my sweet friend, and Thy child, O Lord, adopted of a freed man; there he liveth. For what other place is there for such a soul? There he liveth, whereof he asked much of me, a poor

inexperienced man. Now lays he not his ear to my mouth, but his spiritual mouth unto Thy fountain, and drinketh as much as he can receive, wisdom in proportion to his thirst, endlessly happy. Nor do I think that he is so inebriated therewith, as to forget me; seeing Thou, Lord, Whom he drinketh, art mindful of us. So were we then, comforting Verecundus, who sorrowed, as far as friendship permitted, that our conversion was of such sort; and exhorting him to become faithful, according to his measure, namely, of a married estate; and awaiting Nebridius to follow us, which, being so near, he was all but doing: and so, lo! those days rolled by at length; for long and many they seemed, for the love I bare to the easeful liberty, that I might sing to Thee from my inmost marrow, *My heart hath said unto Thee, I have sought Thy face: Thy face, Lord, will I seek.*

[IV] 7 Now was the day come, wherein I was in deed to be freed of my Rhetoric Professorship, whereof in thought I was already freed. And it was done. Thou didst rescue my tongue, whence Thou hadst before rescued my heart. And I blessed Thee, rejoicing; retiring with all mine to the villa.[8] What I there did in writing, which was now enlisted in Thy service, though still, in this breathing-time as it were, panting from the school of pride, my books may witness,[9] as well what I debated with others, as what with myself alone,[10] before Thee: what with Nebridius, who was absent, my Epistles[11] bear witness. And when shall I have time to rehearse all Thy great benefits towards us at that time, especially when hasting on to yet greater mercies? For my remembrance recalls me, and pleasant is it to me, O Lord, to confess to Thee, by what inward goads Thou tamedst me; and how Thou hast evened me, *lowering the mountains and hills of my high imaginations, straightening my crookedness, and smoothing my rough ways;* and how Thou also subduedst the brother of my heart, Alypius, unto the Name of Thy Only Begotten, our Lord and Saviour Jesus Christ, which he would not at first vouchsafe to have inserted in our writings. For rather would he have them savour of the lofty *cedars* of the Schools, which *the Lord* hath now *broken down,* than of the wholesome herbs of the Church, the antidote against serpents.

8 Oh in what accents spake I unto Thee, my God, when I read the Psalms of David, those faithful songs, and sounds of devotion, which allow of no swelling spirit, as yet a Catechumen, and a novice in Thy real love, resting in that villa, with Alypius, a Catechumen, my mother cleaving to us, in female garb with masculine faith, with the tranquillity of age, motherly love, Christian piety. Oh, what accents did I utter unto Thee in those Psalms, and how was I by them kindled towards Thee, and on fire to rehearse them, if possible, through the whole world, against the pride of mankind. And yet they are sung through the whole world, nor can *any hide himself from Thy heat.* With what vehement and bitter sorrow was I angered at the Manichees! and again I pitied them, for that they knew not those Sacraments, those medicines, and were mad against the antidote, which might have recovered them of their madness. How I would they had then been somewhere near me, and without my knowing that they were there, could have beheld my countenance,

and heard my words, when I read the fourth Psalm in that time of my rest, and how that Psalm wrought upon me, *When I called, the God of my righteousness heard me; in tribulation Thou enlargedst me. Have mercy upon me, O Lord, and hear my prayer.* Would that what I uttered on these words, they could hear, without my knowing whether they heard, lest they should think I spake it for their sakes! Because in truth neither should I speak the same things, nor in the same way, if I perceived that they heard and saw me; nor if I spake them would they so receive them, as when I spake by and for myself before Thee, out of the natural feelings of my soul.

9 I trembled for fear, and again kindled with hope, and with rejoicing in Thy mercy, O Father; and all issued forth both by mine eyes and voice, when Thy good Spirit turning unto us, said, *O ye sons of men, how long slow of heart? why do ye love vanity, and seek after leasing?* For I had *loved vanity, and sought after leasing. And Thou, O Lord,* hadst already *magnified Thy Holy One, raising Him from the dead, and setting Him at Thy right hand,* whence *from on high* He should *send His promise,* the *Comforter, the Spirit of truth.* And He had already sent Him, but I knew it not; He had sent Him, because He was now magnified, rising again from the dead, and ascending into heaven. For till then, *the Spirit was not yet given, because Jesus was not yet glorified.* And the prophet cries out, *How long, slow of heart? why do ye love vanity, and seek after leasing? Know this, that the Lord hath magnified his Holy One.* He cries out, *How long?* He cries out, *Know this:*

and I so long, not knowing, *loved vanity, and sought after leasing:* and therefore I heard and trembled, because it was spoken unto such as I remembered myself to have been. For in those phantoms which I had held for truths, was there *vanity and leasing;* and I spake aloud many things earnestly and forcibly, in the bitterness of my remembrance. Which would they had heard, who yet *love vanity and seek after leasing!* They would perchance have been troubled, and have vomited it up; and *Thou wouldest hear them when they cried unto Thee;* for by a true death in the flesh did He die for us, who now *intercedeth unto Thee for us.*

10 I further read, *Be angry, and sin not.* And how was I moved, O my God, who had now learned to be angry at myself for things past, that I might not sin in time to come! Yea, to be justly angry; for that it was not another nature of a people of darkness which sinned for me, as they say who are not angry at themselves, and *treasure up* wrath *against the day of* wrath, *and of the revelation of Thy just judgment.* Nor were my *good things*[12] now without, nor sought with the eyes of flesh in that earthly sun;[13] for they that would have joy from without soon become vain, and waste themselves on the things seen, and temporal,[14] and in their famished[15] thoughts do lick their very shadows. Oh that they were wearied out with their famine,[16] and said, *Who will shew us good things?* And we would say, and they hear, *The light of Thy countenance is sealed upon us.* For we are not *that light which enlighteneth every man,* but we are enlightened by Thee; that *having been sometimes darkness, we may be light in Thee.* Oh that

they could see the eternal Internal, which having tasted, I was grieved that I could not shew It them, so long as they brought me their heart in their eyes, roving abroad from Thee, while they said, *Who will shew us good things?* For there, where I was *angry* within myself *in my chamber*, where I was inwardly pricked, where I had sacrificed, slaying my old man and commencing the purpose of a new life, *putting my trust in Thee,*—there hadst Thou begun to grow sweet unto me, and *hadst put gladness in my heart*. And I cried out, as I read this outwardly, finding it inwardly. Nor would I be multiplied[17] with worldly goods; wasting away time, and wasted by time; whereas I had in thy eternal Simple Essence other *corn, and wine, and oil*.

11   And with a loud cry of my heart I cried out in the next verse, O *in peace*, O for *The Self-Same!* O what said he, *I will lay me down and sleep,*[18] for who shall hinder us, when *cometh to pass that saying which is written, Death is swallowed up in victory?* And Thou surpassingly art the Self-same, Who *art not changed;* and in Thee is rest which forgetteth all toil, for there is none other with Thee, nor are we to seek those many other things, which are not what Thou art: but Thou, Lord, *alone* hast *made me dwell in hope*. I read, and kindled; nor found I what to do to those deaf and dead, of whom myself had been, a pestilent person, a bitter and a blind bawler against those writings, which are honied with the honey of heaven, and lightsome with Thine own light: and I was consumed with zeal at the enemies of this Scripture.

12 When shall I recall all which passed in those holy-days? Yet neither have I forgotten, nor will I pass over the severity of Thy scourge, and the wonderful swiftness of Thy mercy. Thou didst then torment me with pain in my teeth; which when it had come to such height, that I could not speak,[19] it came into my heart to desire all my friends present to pray for me to Thee, the God of all manner of health. And this I wrote on wax, and gave it them to read. Presently so soon as with humble devotion we had bowed our knees, that pain went away. But what pain? or how went it away? I was affrighted, O my Lord, my God; for from infancy I had never experienced the like. And the power of Thy Nod was deeply conveyed to me, and rejoicing in faith, I praised Thy Name. And that faith suffered me not to be at ease about my past sins, which were not yet forgiven me by Thy baptism.

[V] 13 The vintage-vacation ended, I gave notice to the Milanese to provide their scholars with another master to sell words to them; for that I had both made choice to serve Thee, and through my difficulty of breathing and pain in my chest, was not equal to the Professorship. And by letters I signified to Thy Prelate, the holy man Ambrose, my former errors and present desires, begging his advice what of Thy Scriptures I had best read, to become readier and fitter for receiving so great grace. He recommended Isaiah[20] the Prophet: I believe, because he above the rest is a more clear foreshewer of the Gospel and of the calling of the Gentiles. But I, not understanding the first lesson in him, and imagining the whole to be like it, laid it by, to be resumed when better practised in our Lord's own words.

[VI] 14 Thence, when the time was come, wherein I was to give in my name,[21] we left the country and returned to Milan. It pleased Alypius also to be with me born again in Thee, being already clothed with the humility befitting Thy Sacraments; and a most valiant tamer of the body, so as, with unwonted venture, to wear the frozen ground of Italy with his bare feet. We joined with us the boy Adeodatus, born after the flesh, of my sin. Excellently hadst Thou made him. He was not quite fifteen,[22] and in wit surpassed many grave and learned men. I confess unto Thee Thy gifts, O Lord my God, Creator of all, and abundantly able to reform our deformities: for I had no part in that boy, but the sin. For that we brought him up in Thy discipline, it was Thou, none else, had inspired us with it. I confess unto Thee Thy gifts. There is a book of ours entitled The Master;[23] it is a dialogue between him and me. Thou knowest, that all there ascribed to the person conversing with me, were his ideas, in his sixteenth year. Much besides, and yet more admirable, I found in him. That talent struck awe into me. And who but Thou could be the workmaster of such wonders? Soon didst Thou take his life from the earth: and I now remember him without anxiety, fearing nothing for his childhood or youth, or his whole self. Him we joined with us, our contemporary in grace, to be brought up in Thy discipline; and we were baptized,[24] and anxiety for our past life vanished from us. Nor was I sated in those days with the wondrous sweetness of considering the depth of Thy counsels concerning the salvation of mankind. How did I weep, in Thy Hymns and Canticles, touched to the quick by the voices of Thy sweet-attuned Church! The voices flowed into mine ears, and the Truth distilled into my heart, whence the affections of my devotion overflowed, and tears ran down, and happy was I therein.

[VII] 15 Not long had the Church of Milan begun to use this kind of consolation and exhortation, the brethren zealously joining with harmony of voice and hearts. For it was a year, or not much more, that Justina, mother to the Emperor Valentinian, a child, persecuted[25] Thy servant Ambrose, in favour of her heresy, to which she was seduced by the Arians. The devout people kept watch in the Church, ready to die with their Bishop Thy servant. There my mother Thy handmaid, bearing a chief part of those anxieties and watchings, lived for prayer. We, yet unwarmed by the heat of Thy Spirit, still were stirred up by the sight of the amazed and disquieted city. Then it was first instituted that after the manner of the Eastern Churches,[26] Hymns and Psalms should be sung, lest the people should wax faint through the tediousness of sorrow: and from that day to this the custom is retained, divers, yea, almost all Thy congregations, throughout other parts of the world, following herein.

16 Then didst Thou by a vision discover to Thy forenamed Bishop, where the bodies of Gervasius and Protasius[27] the martyrs lay hid, (whom Thou hadst in Thy secret treasury stored uncorrupted so many years,)

whence Thou mightest seasonably produce them to repress the fury of a woman, but an Empress. For when they were discovered and dug up, and with due honour translated to the Ambrosian Basilica, not only they who were vexed with unclean spirits[28] (the devils confessing themselves) were cured, but a certain man, who had for many years been blind,[29] a citizen, and well known to the city, asking and hearing the reason of the people's confused joy, sprang forth, desiring his guide to lead him thither. Led thither, he begged to be allowed to touch with his handkerchief the bier of Thy *saints, whose death is precious in Thy sight*. Which when he had done, and put to his eyes, they were forthwith opened. Thence did the fame spread, thence Thy praises glowed, shone; thence the mind of that enemy, though not turned to the soundness of believing, was yet turned back from her fury of persecuting. Thanks to Thee, O my God. Whence and whither hast Thou thus led my remembrance, that I should confess these things also unto Thee? Which great though they be, I had passed by in forgetfulness. And yet then, when *the odour of Thy ointments was so fragrant*, did we not *run after Thee*. Therefore did I more weep among the singing of Thy Hymns, formerly sighing after Thee, and at length breathing in Thee, as far as the breath may enter into this our house of grass.

[VIII] 17 Thou *that makest men to dwell of one mind in one house*, didst join with us Euodius also, a young man of our own city. Who being an officer of Court,[30] was before us converted to Thee and baptized: and quitting his secular warfare, girded himself to Thine. We were together,[31] about to dwell together in our devout purpose. We sought where we might serve Thee most usefully, and were together returning to Africa: whitherward being as far as Ostia, my mother departed this life. Much I omit, as hastening much. Receive my confessions and thanksgivings, O my God, for innumerable things whereof I am silent. But I will not omit whatsoever my soul would bring forth concerning that Thy handmaid, who brought me forth, both in the flesh, that I might be born to this temporal light, and in heart, that I might be born to Light eternal.[32] Not her gifts, but Thine in her, would I speak of; for neither did she make nor educate herself. Thou createdst her; nor did her father and mother know what a one should come from them. And the sceptre of Thy Christ, the discipline of Thine only Son, in a Christian house, a good member of Thy Church, educated her in Thy fear. Yet for her good discipline, was she wont to commend not so much her mother's diligence, as that of a certain decrepit maid-servant, who had carried her father when a child, as little ones used to be carried at the backs of elder girls. For which reason, and for her great age, and excellent conversation, was she, in that Christian family, well respected by its heads. Whence also the charge of her master's daughters was entrusted to her, to which she gave diligent heed, restraining them earnestly, when necessary, with a holy severity, and teaching them with a grave discretion. For, except at those hours wherein they were most temperately fed at their parents' table, she would not suffer them, though parched with thirst, to drink even water; preventing an evil custom, and adding this wholesome advice; "Ye drink water now, because you have not wine in your power; but when you come to be married, and be made mistresses of cellars and cupboards, you will scorn water, but the custom of drinking will abide." By this method of instruction, and the authority she had, she refrained the greediness of childhood, and moulded their very thirst to such an excellent moderation, that what they should not, that they would not.[33]

18 And yet (as Thy handmaid told me her son) there had crept upon her a love of wine. For when (as the manner was) she, as though a sober maiden, was bidden by her parents to draw wine out of the hogshead, holding the vessel under the opening, before she poured the wine into the flagon, she sipped a little with the tip of her lips; for more her instinctive feelings refused. For this she did, not out of any desire of drink, but out of the exuberance of youth, whereby it boils over in mirthful freaks, which in youthful spirits are wont to be kept under by the gravity of their elders. And thus by adding to that little, daily littles, (*for whoso despiseth little things, shall fall by little and little,*) she had fallen into such a habit, as greedily to drink off her little cup brimfull almost of wine. Where was then that discreet old woman, and that her earnest countermanding? Would aught avail against a secret disease, if Thy healing hand, O Lord, watched not over us? Father, mother, and governors absent, Thou present, who createdst, who callest, who also by those set over us, workest something towards the salvation of our souls, what didst Thou then, O my God? how didst Thou cure her? how heal her? didst Thou not out of another

soul bring forth a hard and a sharp taunt, like a lancet out of Thy secret store, and with one touch remove all that foul stuff? For a maid-servant with whom she used to go to the cellar, falling to words (as it happens) with her little mistress, when alone with her, taunted her with this fault, with most bitter insult, calling her wine-bibber. With which taunt she, stung to the quick, saw the foulness of her fault, and instantly condemned and forsook it. As flattering friends pervert, so reproachful enemies mostly correct. Yet not what by them Thou doest, but what themselves purposed, dost Thou repay them. For she in her anger sought to vex her young mistress, not to amend her; and did it in private, either for that the time and place of the quarrel so found them; or lest herself also should have anger, for discovering it thus late. But Thou, Lord, Governor of all in heaven and earth, who turnest to Thy purposes the deepest currents, and the ruled turbulence of the tide of times,[34] didst by the very unhealthiness of one soul, heal another; lest any, when he observes this, should ascribe it to his own power, even when another, whom he wished to be reformed, is reformed through words of his.

[IX] 19 Brought up thus modestly and soberly, and made subject rather by Thee to her parents, than by her parents to Thee, so soon as she was of marriageable age, being bestowed upon a husband, she served him as her lord; and did her diligence to win him unto Thee, preaching Thee unto him by her conversation; by which Thou ornamentedst her, making her reverently amiable, and admirable unto her husband. And she so endured the wronging of her bed, as never to have any quarrel with her husband thereon. For she looked for Thy mercy upon him, that believing in Thee, he might be made chaste. But besides this, he was fervid, as in his affections, so in anger: but she had learnt, not to resist an angry husband, not in deed only, but not even in word. Only when he was smoothed and tranquil, and in a temper to receive it, she would give an account of her actions, if haply he had overhastily taken offence. In a word, while many matrons, who had milder husbands, yet bore even in their faces marks of shame, would in familiar talk blame their husbands' lives, she would blame their tongues, giving them, as in jest, earnest advice; "That from the time they heard the marriage writings read to them, they should account them as indentures, whereby they were made servants; and so, remembering their condition, ought not to set themselves up against their lords." And when they, knowing what a choleric husband she endured, marvelled, that it had never been heard, nor by any token perceived, that Patricius had beaten his wife, or that there had been any domestic difference between them, even for one day, and confidentially asking the reason, she taught them her practice above mentioned. Those wives who observed it found the good, and returned thanks; those who observed it not, found no relief, and suffered.

20 Her mother-in-law also, at first by whisperings of evil servants incensed against her, she so overcame by observance and persevering endurance and meekness, that she of her own accord discovered to her son the meddling tongues, whereby the domestic peace betwixt

her and her daughter-in-law had been disturbed, asking him to correct them. Then, when in compliance with his mother, and for the well-ordering of the family, and the harmony of its members, he had with stripes corrected those discovered, at her will who had discovered them, she promised the like reward to any who, to please her, should speak ill of her daughter-in-law to her: and, none now venturing, they lived together with a remarkable sweetness of mutual kindness.

21 This great gift also Thou bestowedst, O my God, my mercy, upon that good handmaid of Thine, in whose womb Thou createdst me, that between any disagreeing and discordant parties where she was able, she shewed herself such a peacemaker, that hearing on both sides most bitter things, such as swelling and indigested choler uses to break out into, when the crudities of enmities are breathed out in sour discourses to a present friend against an absent enemy, she never would disclose aught of the one unto the other, but what might tend to their reconcilement. A small good this might appear to me, did I not to my grief know numberless persons, who through some horrible and wide-spreading contagion of sin, not only disclose to persons mutually angered things said in anger, but add withal things never spoken, whereas to humane humanity, it ought to seem a light thing, not to foment or increase ill will by ill words, unless one study withal by good words to quench it. Such was she, Thyself, her most inward Instructor, teaching her in the school of the heart.

22 Finally, her own husband, towards the very end of his earthly life, did she gain unto Thee; nor had she to complain of that in him as a believer, which before he was a believer she had borne from him. She was also the servant of thy servants; whosoever of them knew her, did in her much praise and honour and love Thee; for that through the witness of the fruits of a holy conversation[35] they perceived Thy presence in her heart. For she had been *the wife of one man*, had *requited her parents, had governed her house* piously, *was well reported of for good works, had brought up children*, so often *travailing in birth of them*, as she saw them swerving from Thee. Lastly, of all of us Thy servants, O Lord, (whom on occasion of Thy own gift Thou sufferest to speak,) us, who before her sleeping in Thee lived united together, having received the grace of Thy baptism, did she so take care of, as though she had been mother of us all; so served us, as though she had been child to us all.

[X] 23 The day now approaching whereon she was to depart this life, (which day Thou well knewest, we knew not,) it came to pass, Thyself, as I believe, by Thy secret ways so ordering it, that she and I stood alone, leaning in a certain window, which looked into the garden of the house where we now lay, at Ostia; where removed from the din of men, we were recruiting from the fatigues of a long journey, for the voyage. We were discoursing then together, alone, very sweetly; and *forgetting those things which are behind, and reaching forth unto those things which are before*, we were enquiring between ourselves in the presence of the Truth, which Thou art, of what sort the eternal life of the saints was to be, *which eye hath not seen, nor ear heard, nor hath it entered into the heart of man*. But yet we gasped with the mouth of our heart, after those heavenly streams of Thy fountain, *the fountain of life*, which is *with Thee;* that being bedewed thence according to our capacity, we might in some sort meditate upon so high a mystery.

24 And when our discourse was brought to that point, that the very highest delight of the earthly senses, in the very purest material light, was, in respect of the sweetness of that life, not only not worthy of comparison, but not even of mention; we raising up ourselves with a more glowing affection towards the "Self-same,"[36] did by degrees pass through all things bodily, even the very heaven, whence sun and moon, and stars shine upon the earth; yea, we were soaring higher yet, by inward musing, and discourse, and admiring of Thy works; and we came to our own minds, and went beyond them,[37] that we might arrive at that region of never-failing plenty, where *Thou feedest Israel* for ever with the food of truth, and where life is the *Wisdom by whom all* these *things are made*, and what have been, and what shall be, and she is not made, but is, as she hath been, and so shall she be ever; yea rather, to "have been," and "hereafter to be," are not in her, but only "to be," seeing she is eternal. For to "have been," and to "be hereafter," are not eternal. And while we were discoursing and panting after her, we slightly touched on her with the whole effort of our heart; and we sighed, and there we leave bound *the first fruits of the Spirit;* and returned to vocal expressions of our mouth,

where the word spoken has beginning and end. And what is like unto Thy Word, our Lord, who *endureth in Himself* without becoming old, and *maketh all things new?*

25 We were saying then: If to any the tumult of the flesh were hushed, hushed the images of earth, and waters, and air, hushed also the poles of heaven, yea the very soul be hushed to herself, and by not thinking on self surmount self, hushed all dreams and imaginary revelations, every tongue and every sign, and whatsoever exists only in transition, since if any could hear, all these say, *We made not ourselves, but He made us that abideth for ever*—If then having uttered this, they too should be hushed, having roused only our ears to Him who made them, and He alone speak, not by them, but by Himself, that we may hear His Word, not through any tongue of flesh, nor Angel's voice, nor sound of thunder, nor in the dark riddle of a similitude, but, might hear Whom in these things we love, might hear His Very Self without these, (as we two now strained ourselves, and in swift thought touched on that Eternal Wisdom, which abideth over all;)—could this be continued on, and other visions of kind far unlike be withdrawn, and this one ravish, and absorb, and wrap up its beholder amid these inward joys, so that life might be for ever like that one moment of understanding which now we sighed after; were not this, *Enter into thy Master's joy?* And when shall that be? When *we shall all rise again*, though we *shall not all be changed?*

26 Such things was I speaking, and even if not in this very manner, and these same words, yet, Lord, Thou knowest, that in that day when we were speaking of these things, and this world with all its delights became, as we spake, contemptible to us, my mother said, "Son, for mine own part I have no further delight in any thing in this life. What I do here any longer, and to what end I am here, I know not, now that my hopes in this world are accomplished. One thing there was, for which I desired to linger for a while in this life, that I might see thee a Catholic Christian before I died. My God hath done this for me more abundantly, that I should now see thee withal, despising earthly happiness, become His servant: what do I here?"

[XI] 27 What answer I made her unto these things, I remember not. For scarce five days after, or not much more, she fell sick of a fever; and in that sickness one day she fell into a swoon, and was for a while withdrawn from these visible things. We hastened round her; but she was soon brought back to her senses; and looking on me and my brother[38] standing by her, said to us enquiringly, "Where was I?" And then looking fixedly on us, with grief amazed; "Here," saith she, "shall you bury your mother." I held my peace and refrained weeping; but my brother spake something, wishing for her, as the happier lot, that she might die, not in a strange place, but in her own land. Whereat, she with anxious look, checking him with her eyes, for that he still *savoured such things*, and then looking upon me; "Behold," saith she, "what he saith:" and soon after to us both, "Lay," she saith, "this body any where; let not the care for that any way disquiet you: this only I request, that you would remember me at the Lord's altar, wherever you be." And having delivered this sentiment in what words she could, she held her peace, being exercised by her growing sickness.

28 But I, considering Thy gifts, Thou unseen God, which Thou instillest into the hearts of Thy faithful ones, whence wondrous fruits do spring, did rejoice and give thanks to Thee, recalling what I before knew, how careful and anxious she had ever been, as to her place of burial, which she had provided and prepared for herself by the body of her husband. For because they had lived in great harmony together, she also wished (so little can the human mind embrace things divine) to have this addition to that happiness, and to have it remembered among men, that after her pilgrimage beyond the seas, what was earthly of this united pair had been permitted to be united beneath the same earth. But when this emptiness had through the fulness of Thy goodness begun to cease in her heart, I knew not, and rejoiced admiring what she had so disclosed to me; though indeed in that our discourse also in the window, when she said, "What do I here any longer?" there appeared no desire of dying in her own country. I heard afterwards also, that when we were now at Ostia, she with a mother's confidence, when I was absent, one day discoursed with certain of my friends about the contempt of this life, and the blessing of death: and when they were amazed at such courage which Thou hadst given to a woman, and asked, "Whether she were not afraid to leave her body so far

from her own city?" she replied, "Nothing is far to God; nor was it to be feared lest at the end of the world, He should not recognize whence He were to raise me up." On the ninth day then of her sickness, and the fifty-sixth year of her age, and the three and thirtieth of mine, was that religious and holy soul freed from the body.

[XII] 29 I closed her eyes; and there flowed withal a mighty sorrow into my heart, which was overflowing into tears; mine eyes at the same time, by the violent command of my mind, drank up their fountain wholly dry; and woe was me in such a strife! But when she breathed her last, the boy Adeodatus burst out into a loud lament; then, checked by us all, held his peace. In like manner also a childish feeling in me, which was, through my heart's youthful voice, finding its vent in weeping, was checked and silenced. For we thought it not fitting to solemnize that funeral with tearful lament, and groanings: for thereby do they for the most part express grief for the departed, as though unhappy, or altogether dead; whereas she was neither unhappy in her death, nor altogether dead. Of this, we were assured on good grounds, the testimony of her good conversation and her *faith unfeigned*.

30 What then was it which did grievously pain me within, but a fresh wound wrought through the sudden wrench of that most sweet and dear custom of living together? I joyed indeed in her testimony, when, in that her last sickness, mingling her endearments with my acts of duty, she called me "dutiful," and mentioned, with great affection of love, that she never had heard any harsh

or reproachful sound uttered by my mouth against her. But yet, O my God, Who madest us, what comparison is there betwixt that honour that I paid to her, and her slavery for me? Being then forsaken of so great comfort in her, my soul was wounded, and that life rent asunder as it were, which, of hers and mine together, had been made but one.

31 The boy then being stilled from weeping, Euodius took up the Psalter, and began to sing, our whole house answering him, the Psalm, *I will sing of mercy and judgment to Thee, O Lord*.[39] But hearing what we were doing, many brethren and religious women came together; and whilst they (whose office it was) made ready for the burial, as the manner is, I (in a part of the house, where I might properly), together with those who thought not fit to leave me, discoursed upon something fitting the time; and by this balm of truth, assuaged that torment, known to Thee, they unknowing and listening intently, and conceiving me to be without all sense of sorrow. But in Thy ears, where none of them heard, I blamed the weakness of my feelings, and refrained my flood of grief, which gave way a little unto me; but again came, as with a tide, yet not so as to burst out into tears, nor to a change of countenance; still I knew what I was keeping down in my heart. And being very much displeased, that these human things had such power over me, which in the due order and appointment of our natural condition, must needs come to pass, with a new grief I grieved for my grief, and was thus worn by a double sorrow.

32 And behold, the corpse was carried to the burial; we went and returned without tears. For neither in those prayers which we poured forth unto Thee, when the sacrifice of our ransom⁴⁰ was offered for her, when now the corpse was by the grave's side, as the manner there is, previous to its being laid therein, did I weep even during those prayers; yet was I the whole day in secret heavily sad, and with troubled mind prayed Thee, as I could, to heal my sorrow, yet Thou didst not; impressing, I believe, upon my memory by this one instance, how strong is the bond of all habit, even upon a soul, which now feeds upon no deceiving Word. It seemed also good to me to go and bathe, having heard that the bath had its name (balneum) from the Greek βαλανετον, for that it drives sadness from the mind. And this also I confess unto Thy mercy, *Father of the fatherless*, that I bathed, and was the same as before I bathed. For the bitterness of sorrow could not exsude out of my heart. Then I slept, and woke up again, and found my grief not a little softened; and as I was alone in my bed, I remembered those true verses of Thy Ambrose. For Thou art the

> Maker of all, the Lord,
>> And Ruler of the height,
> Who, robing day in light, hast poured
>> Soft slumbers o'er the night,
> That to our limbs the power
>> Of toil may be renew'd,
> And hearts be rais'd that sink and cower,
>> And sorrows be subdu'd;

33 And then by little and little I recovered my former thoughts of Thy handmaid, her holy conversation towards Thee, her holy tenderness and observance towards us, whereof I was suddenly deprived: and I was minded to weep in Thy sight, for her and for myself, in her behalf and in my own. And I gave way to the tears which I before restrained, to overflow as much as they desired; reposing my heart upon them; and it found rest in them, for it was in Thy ears, not in those of man, who would have scornfully interpreted my weeping. And now, Lord, in writing I confess it unto Thee. Read it, who will, and interpret it, how he will: and if he finds sin therein, that I wept my mother for a small portion of an hour, (the mother who for the time was dead to mine eyes, who had for many years wept for me, that I might live in Thine eyes,) let him not deride me; but rather, if he be one of large charity, let him weep himself for my sins unto Thee, the Father of all the brethren of Thy Christ.

[XIII] 34 But now, with a heart cured of that wound, wherein it might seem blameworthy for an earthly feeling, I pour out unto Thee, our God, in behalf of that Thy handmaid, a far different kind of tears, flowing from a spirit shaken by the thoughts of the dangers of every soul *that dieth in Adam*. And although she having been quickened in Christ, even before her release from the flesh, had lived to the praise of Thy name for her faith and conversation; yet dare I not say that from what time Thou regeneratedst her by baptism, no word issued from her mouth against Thy Commandment. Thy Son, the Truth, hath said, *Whosoever shall say unto his brother, Thou fool, shall be in danger of hell fire.* And woe be even unto the commendable life of men, if, laying aside mercy, Thou shouldest examine it. But because Thou art not extreme in inquiring after sins, we confidently hope to find some place with Thee. But whosoever reckons up his real merits to Thee, what reckons he up to Thee, but[41] Thine own gifts? O that men would know themselves to be men; *and that he that glorieth, would glory in the Lord.*

35 I therefore, O my Praise and my Life, God of my heart, laying aside for a while her good deeds, for which I give thanks to Thee with joy, do now beseech Thee for the sins of my mother. Hearken unto me, I entreat Thee, by the Medicine of our wounds, Who hung upon the tree, and now *sitting at Thy right hand maketh intercession to Thee for us.* I know that she dealt mercifully, and from her heart *forgave her debtors their debts; do Thou also forgive her debts,* whatever she may have contracted in so many years, since the water of salvation. Forgive her, Lord, forgive, I beseech Thee; *enter not into judgment with her. Let Thy mercy be exalted above Thy justice,* since Thy words are true, and *Thou hast promised mercy unto the merciful;* which Thou gavest them to be, *who wilt have mercy on whom Thou wilt have mercy;* and wilt *have compassion, on whom Thou hast had compassion.*

36 And, I believe, Thou hast already done what I ask; but *accept, O Lord, the free-will offerings of my mouth.* For she, the day of her dissolution now at hand, took no thought to have her body sumptuously wound up, or embalmed with spices; nor desired she a choice monument, or to be

buried in her own land. These things she enjoined us not; but desired only to have her name commemorated at Thy Altar, which she had served without intermission of one day: whence she knew that holy sacrifice to be dispensed, by which the *hand-writing that was against us, is blotted out*; through which the enemy was triumphed over, who summing up our offences, and seeking what to lay to our charge, *found nothing in Him*, in Whom we conquer. Who shall restore to Him the innocent blood? Who repay Him the price wherewith He bought us, and so take us from Him?[42] Unto the Sacrament of which our ransom, Thy handmaid bound her soul by the bond of faith. Let none sever her from Thy protection: let neither *the lion nor the dragon* interpose himself by force or fraud. For she will not answer that she owes nothing, lest she be convicted and seized by the crafty accuser: but she will answer, that *her sins are forgiven* her by Him, to Whom none can repay that price, which He, Who owed nothing, paid for us.

37 May she rest then in peace with the husband, before and after whom she had never any; whom she obeyed, *with patience bringing forth fruit* unto Thee, that she might win him also unto Thee. And inspire, O Lord my God, inspire Thy servants my brethren, Thy sons my masters, whom with voice, and heart, and pen I serve, that so many as shall read these Confessions, may at Thy Altar remember Monnica Thy handmaid, with Patricius, her sometimes husband, by whose bodies Thou broughtest me into this life, how, I know not. May they with devout affection remember my parents in this transitory light, my brethren under Thee our Father in our Catholic Mother,

and my fellow citizens in that eternal Jerusalem, which Thy pilgrim people sigheth after from their Exodus, even unto their return thither. That so, my mother's last request of me, may through my confessions, more than through my prayers, be, through the prayers of many, more abundantly fulfilled to her.

BOOK X

Having in the former books spoken of himself before his receiving the grace of Baptism, in this Aug. confesses what he then was. But first, he enquires by what faculty we can know God at all, whence he enlarges on the mysterious character of the memory, wherein God, being made known, dwells, but which could not discover Him. Then he examines his own trials under the triple division of temptation, "lust of the flesh, lust of the eyes, and pride;" what Christian continency prescribes as to each. On Christ the Only Mediator, who heals and will heal all infirmities.

[I] 1 Let me know Thee, O Lord, who knowest me: *let me know Thee, as I am known*. Power of my soul, enter into it, and fit it for Thee, that Thou mayest have and hold it *without spot or wrinkle*. This is my hope, *therefore do I speak*; and in this hope do I rejoice, when I rejoice healthfully. Other things of this life are the less to be sorrowed for, the more they are sorrowed for; and the more to be sorrowed for, the less men sorrow for them. For behold, Thou *lovest the truth*, and *he that doth it, cometh to the light*. This would I do in my heart before Thee in confession: and in my writing, before many witnesses.

[II] 2 And from Thee, O Lord, *unto whose eyes* the abyss of man's conscience is naked, what could be hidden in me though I would not confess it? For I should hide Thee from me, not me from Thee. But now, for that my groaning is witness, that I am displeased with myself, Thou shinest out, and art pleasing, and beloved, and longed for; that I may be ashamed of myself, and renounce myself, and choose Thee, and neither please Thee, nor myself, but in Thee. To Thee therefore, O Lord, am I open, whatever I am; and with what fruit I confess unto Thee, I have said. Nor do I it with words and sounds of the flesh, but with the words of my soul, and the cry of the thought which Thy ear knoweth. For when I am evil, then to confess to Thee, is nothing else than to be displeased with myself: but when holy, nothing else than not to ascribe it to myself: because Thou, O Lord, *blessest the godly*, but first Thou *justifieth him when ungodly*. My confession then, O my God, in Thy sight, is made silently, and not silently. For in sound, it is silent; in affection, it cries aloud. For neither do I utter any thing right unto men, which Thou hast not before heard from me; nor dost Thou hear any such thing from me, which Thou hast not first said unto me.

[III] 3 What then have I to do with men, that they should hear my confessions; as if they could *heal all my infirmities*? A race, curious to know the lives of others, slothful to amend their own. Why seek they to hear from me what I am; who will not hear from Thee what themselves are? And how know they, when from myself they hear of myself, whether I say true; seeing *no man knows what is in man, but the spirit of man which is in him*? But if they hear from Thee of themselves, they cannot say, "The Lord lieth," For what is it to hear from Thee of themselves, but to know themselves? and who knoweth and saith, "It is false," unless himself lieth? But because *charity believeth all things*; (that is, among those whom knitting unto itself it maketh one,) I also, O Lord, will in such wise confess unto Thee, that men may hear, to whom I cannot demonstrate whether I confess truly; yet they believe me, whose ears charity openeth unto me.

4 But do Thou, my inmost Physician, make plain unto me, what fruit I may reap by doing it. For the confessions of my past sins, which Thou hast *forgiven and covered*, that Thou mightest bless me in Thee, changing my soul by Faith and Thy Sacrament, when read and heard, stir up the heart, that it sleep not in despair and say, "I cannot," but awake in the love of Thy mercy and the sweetness of Thy grace, whereby, whoso *is weak, is strong*, when by it he became conscious of his own weakness. And the good delight to hear of the past evils of such as are now freed from them, not because they are evils, but because they have been and are not. With what fruit then, O Lord my God, to Whom my conscience daily confesseth, trusting more in the hope of Thy mercy than in their own innocency, with what fruit, I pray, do I by this book, confess to men also in Thy presence, what I now am, not what I have been? For that other fruit I have seen and spoken of. But what I now am, at the very time of making these confessions, divers desire to know, who have or have not known me, who have heard from me or of me; but their ear is not at my heart, where I am, whatever I am. They wish then to hear me confess

what I am within; whither neither their eye, nor ear, nor understanding, can reach; they wish it, as ready to believe—but will they know? For charity, whereby they are good, telleth them, that in my confessions I lie not; and she in them, believeth me.

[IV] 5 But for what fruit would they hear this? do they desire to joy with me, when they hear how near, by Thy gift, I approach unto Thee? and to pray for me, when they shall hear how much I am held back by my own weight? To such will I discover myself. For it is no mean fruit, O Lord my God, *that by many thanks should be given* to Thee *on our behalf*, and Thou be by many intreated for us. Let the brotherly mind love in me, what Thou teachest is to be loved, and lament in me, what Thou teachest is to be lamented. Let a brotherly, not a stranger, mind, not that of the *strange children, whose mouth talketh of vanity, and their right hand is a right hand of iniquity*, but that brotherly mind which when it approveth, rejoiceth for me, and when it disapproveth me, is sorry for me; because whether it approveth or disapproveth, it loveth me. To such will I discover myself: they will breathe freely[1] at my good deeds, sigh for my ill. My good deeds are Thine appointments, and Thy gifts; my evil ones, are my offences, and Thy judgments.[2] Let them breathe freely at the one, sigh at the other; and let hymns and weeping go up into Thy sight, out of the hearts of my brethren, Thy *censers*. And do Thou, O Lord, be pleased with the incense of Thy holy temple, *have mercy upon me according to Thy great mercy for Thine own name's sake*; and no ways forsaking what Thou hast begun, perfect my imperfections.

6 This is the fruit of my confessions of what I am, not of what I have been, to confess this, not before Thee only, in a secret *exultation with trembling*, and a secret sorrow with hope; but in the ears also of the believing sons of men, sharers of my joy, and partners in my mortality, my fellow citizens, and fellow pilgrims, who are gone before, or are to follow on, companions of my way. These are Thy servants, my brethren, whom Thou willest to be Thy sons; my masters whom Thou commandest me to serve, if I would live with Thee, of Thee. But this Thy Word, were little did it only command by speaking, and not go before in performing. This then I do in deed and word, this I do *under Thy wings*; in over great peril, were not my soul subdued unto Thee under Thy wings, and my infirmity known unto Thee. I am a little one, but my Father ever liveth, and my Guardian is *sufficient for me*. For He is the same who begat me, and defends me: and Thou Thyself art all my good; Thou, Almighty, Who art with me, yea, before I am with Thee. To such then whom Thou commandest me to serve will I discover, not what I have been, but what I now am, and what I yet am. *But neither do I judge myself.* Thus therefore I would be heard.

[V] 7 For *Thou, Lord, dost judge me*: because, although *no man knoweth the things of a man, but the spirit of a man which is in him*, yet is there something of man, which neither *the spirit of man that is in him*, itself *knoweth*. But Thou, Lord, knowest all of him, Who hast made him. Yet I, though in Thy sight I despise myself, and account myself *dust and ashes*; yet know I something of Thee, which I know not of myself. And truly, *now we see through a glass darkly*, not *face to face* as yet. So long therefore as *I be absent from Thee*, I am more present with myself than with Thee; and yet know I Thee that Thou art in no ways passible;[3] but I, what temptations I can resist, what I cannot, I know not. And there is hope, because *Thou art faithful, Who will not suffer us to be tempted above that we are able; but wilt with the temptation also make a way to escape, that we may be able to bear it.* I will confess then what I know of myself, I will confess also what I know not of myself. And that because what I do know of myself, I know by Thy shining upon me; and what I know not of myself, so long know I not it, until *my darkness be made as the noon-day* in Thy countenance.

[VI] 8 Not with doubting, but with assured consciousness, do I love Thee, Lord. Thou hast stricken my heart with Thy word, and I loved Thee. Yea also *heaven, and earth, and all that therein is*, behold, on every side they bid me love Thee; nor cease to say so unto all, *that they may be without excuse.* But more deeply *wilt Thou have mercy on whom Thou wilt have mercy, and wilt have compassion on whom Thou hast had compassion:* else in deaf ears do the heaven and the earth speak Thy praises. But what do I love, when I love Thee? not beauty of bodies, nor the fair harmony of time, nor the brightness of the light, so gladsome to our eyes, nor sweet melodies of varied songs, nor the fragrant smell of flowers, and ointments, and spices, not manna and honey, not limbs acceptable to embracements of flesh. None of these I love, when I love my God; and yet I love a kind of light, and melody, and fragrance, and meat, and embracement, when

I love my God, the light, melody, fragrance, meat, embracement of my inner man: where there shineth unto my soul, what space cannot contain, and there soundeth, what time beareth not away, and there smelleth, what breathing disperseth not, and there tasteth, what eating diminisheth not, and there clingeth, what satiety divorceth not. This is it which I love, when I love my God.

9 And what is this? I asked[4] the earth, and it answered me, "I am not He;" and whatsoever are in it, confessed the same. I asked the sea and the deeps, and the living creeping things, and they answered, "We are not thy God, seek above us." I asked the moving air; and the whole air with his inhabitants answered, "Anaximenes was deceived, I am not God." I asked the heavens, sun, moon, stars, "Nor (say they) are we the God whom thou seekest." And I replied unto all the things which encompass the door of my flesh; "Ye have told me of my God, that ye are not He; tell me something of Him." And they cried out with a loud voice, "He made us." My questioning them, was my thoughts on them: and their form of beauty gave the answer.[5] And I turned myself unto myself, and said to myself, "Who art thou?" And I answered, "A man." And behold, in me there present themselves to me soul, and body, one without, the other within. By which of these ought I to seek my God? I had sought Him in the body from earth to heaven, so far as I could send messengers, the beams of mine eyes. But the better is the inner, for to it as presiding and judging, all the bodily messengers reported the answers of heaven and earth, and all things therein, who said, "We are not God, but He made us." These things did my inner man know by

the ministry of the outer: I the inner, knew them; I, the mind, through the senses of my body. I asked the whole frame of the world about my God; and it answered me, "I am not He, but He made me."

10 Is not this corporeal figure apparent to all whose senses are perfect? why then speaks it not the same to all? Animals small and great see it, but they cannot ask it: because no reason is set over their senses to judge on what they report. But men can ask, so that *the invisible things of God are clearly seen, being understood by the things that are made;* but by love of them, they are made subject unto them: and subjects cannot judge. Nor yet do the creatures answer such as ask, unless they can judge: nor yet do they change their voice, (i.e. their appearance,) if one man only sees, another seeing asks, so as to appear one way to this man, another way to that; but appearing the same way to both, it is dumb to this, speaks to that; yea rather it speaks to all; but they only understand, who compare its voice received from without, with the truth within. For truth saith unto me, "Neither heaven, nor earth, nor any other body is thy God." This, their very nature saith to him that seeth them; "They are a mass; a mass is less in a part thereof, than in the whole." Now to thee I speak, O my soul, thou art my better part: for thou quickenest the mass of my body, giving it life, which no body can give to a body: but thy God is even unto thee the Life of thy life.

[VII] 11 What then do I love, when I love my God? who is He above the head of my soul? By my very soul will I ascend to Him. I will pass beyond that power whereby I am united to my body, and fill its whole frame with life. Nor can I by that power find my God; for so *horse and mule that have no understanding*, might find Him; seeing it is the same power, whereby even their bodies live. But another power there is, not that only whereby I animate, but that too whereby I imbue with sense my flesh, which the Lord hath framed for me: commanding the eye not to hear, and the ear not to see; but the eye, that through it I should see, and the ear, that through it I should hear; and to the other senses severally, what is to each their own peculiar seats and offices; which, being divers, I the one mind, do through them enact. I will pass beyond this power of mine also; for this also have the horse and mule, for they also perceive through the body.

[VIII] 12 I will pass then beyond this power of my nature also, rising by degrees unto Him, who made me. And I come to the fields and spacious palaces of my memory, where are the treasures of innumerable images, brought into it from things of all sorts perceived by the senses. There is stored up, whatsoever besides we think, either by enlarging or diminishing, or any other way varying those things which the sense hath come to; and whatever else hath been committed and laid up, which forgetfulness hath not yet swallowed up and buried. When I enter there, I require what I will, to be brought forth, and something instantly comes; others must be longer sought after, which are fetched, as it were, out of some inner receptacle; others rush out in troops, and while one thing is desired and required, they start forth, as who should say, "Is it perchance I?" These I drive away with the hand of my heart, from the face of my remembrance; until what I wished for be unveiled, and appear in sight, out of its secret place. Other things come up readily, in unbroken order, as they are called for; those in front making way for the following; and as they make way, they are hidden from sight, ready to come when I will. All which takes place, when I repeat a thing by heart.

13 There are all things preserved distinctly and under general heads, each having entered by its own avenue: as light, and all colours and forms of bodies, by the eyes; by the ears all sorts of sounds; all smells by the avenue of the nostrils; all tastes by the mouth; and by the sensation of the whole body, what is hard or soft; hot or cold; smooth or rugged; heavy or light; either outwardly or inwardly to the body. All these doth that great harbour of the memory receive in her numberless secret and inexpressible windings, to be forthcoming, and brought out at need; each entering in by his own gate, and there laid up. Nor yet do the things themselves enter in; only the images of the things perceived, are there in readiness, for thought to recall. Which images, how they are formed, who can tell, though it doth plainly appear by which sense each hath been brought in and stored up? For even while I dwell in darkness and silence, in my memory I can produce colours, if I will, and discern betwixt black and white, and what others I will: nor yet do sounds break in, and disturb the image drawn in by my eyes, which I am reviewing, though they also are there, lying dormant, and laid up, as it were, apart. For these too I call for, and forthwith they appear. And

though my tongue be still, and my throat mute, so can I sing as much as I will; nor do those images of colours, which notwithstanding be there, intrude themselves and interrupt, when another store is called for, which flowed in by the ears. So the other things, piled in and up by the other senses, I recall at my pleasure. Yea, I discern the breath of lilies from violets, though smelling nothing; and I prefer honey to sweet wine, smooth before rugged, at the time neither tasting, nor handling, but remembering only.

14 These things do I within, in that vast court of my memory. For there are present with me, heaven, earth, sea, and whatever I could think on therein, besides what I have forgotten. There also meet I with myself, and recall myself, and when, where, and what I have done, and under what feelings. There be all which I remember, either on my own experience, or others' credit. Out of the same store do I myself with the past continually combine fresh and fresh likenesses of things, which I have experienced, or, from what I have experienced, have believed: and thence again infer future actions, events and hopes, and all these again I reflect on, as present. "I will do this or that," say I to myself, in that great receptacle of my mind, stored with the images of things so many and so great, "and this or that will follow." "O that this or that might be!" "God avert this or that!" So speak I to myself: and when I speak, the images of all I speak of are present, out of the same treasury of memory; nor would I speak of any thereof, were the images wanting.

15 Great is this force of memory, excessive great, O my God; a large and boundless chamber! who ever sounded the bottom thereof? yet is this a power of mine, and belongs unto my nature; nor do I myself comprehend all that I am. Therefore is the mind too strait to contain itself. And where should that be, which it containeth not of itself? Is it without it, and not within? how then doth it not comprehend itself? A wonderful admiration surprises me, amazement seizes me upon this. And men go abroad to admire the heights of mountains, the mighty billows of the sea, the broad tides of rivers, the compass of the ocean, and the circuits of the stars, and pass themselves by; nor wonder, that when I spake of all these things, I did not see them with mine eyes, yet could not have spoken of them, unless I then actually saw the mountains, billows, rivers, stars, which I had seen, and that ocean which I believe to be, inwardly in my memory, and that, with the same vast spaces between, as if I saw them abroad. Yet did not I by seeing draw them into myself, when with mine eyes I beheld them; nor are they themselves with me, but their images only. And I know by what sense of the body, each was impressed upon me.

[IX] 16 Yet not these alone does the unmeasurable capacity of my memory retain. Here also is all, learnt of the liberal sciences and as yet unforgotten; removed as it were to some inner place, which is yet no place: nor are they the images thereof, but the things themselves. For, what is literature, what the art of disputing, how many kinds of questions there be, whatsoever of these I know, in such manner exists in my memory, as that I have not taken in the image, and left out the thing, or that it should have sounded and passed away like a voice fixed on the ear by that impress, whereby it might be recalled, as if it sounded, when it no longer sounded; or as a smell while it passes, and evaporates into air affects the sense of smell, whence it conveys into the memory an image of itself, which remembering, we renew, or as meat, which verily in the belly hath now no taste, and yet in the memory still in a manner tasteth; or as any thing which the body by touch perceiveth, and which when removed from us, the memory still conceives. For those things are not transmitted into the memory, but their images only are with an admirable swiftness caught up, and stored as it were in wondrous cabinets, and thence wonderfully by the act of remembering, brought forth.

[X] 17 But now when I hear that there be three kinds of questions, "Whether the thing be? what it is? of what kind it is?" I do indeed hold the images of the sounds, of which those words be composed, and that those sounds, with a noise passed through the air, and now are not. But the things themselves which are signified by those sounds, I never reached with any sense of my body, nor ever discerned them otherwise than in my mind; yet in my memory have I laid up not their images, but themselves. Which how they entered into me, let them say if they can; for I have gone over all the avenues of my flesh, but cannot find by which they entered. For the eyes say, "if those images were coloured, we reported of them." The ears say, "if they sound, we gave knowledge of them." The nostrils say, "if they smell, they passed by us." The taste says, "unless they have a savour, ask me not." The touch says, "if it have not size, I handled it not; if I handled it not, I gave no notice of it." Whence and how entered these things into my memory? I know not how. For when I learned them, I gave not credit to another man's mind, but recognized them in mine; and approving them for true, I commended them to it, laying them up as it were, whence I might bring them forth when I willed. In my heart then they were, even before I learned them, but in my memory they were not. Where then? or wherefore, when they were spoken, did I acknowledge them, and said, "So is it, it is true," unless that they were already in the memory, but so thrown back and buried as it were in deeper recesses, that had not the suggestion of another drawn them forth, I had perchance been unable to conceive of them?

[XI] 18 Wherefore we find, that to learn these things whereof we imbibe not the images by our senses, but perceive within by themselves, without images, as they are, is nothing else, but by conception to receive, and by marking to take heed that those things which the memory did before contain at random and unarranged, be laid up at hand as it were in that same memory, where before they lay unknown, scattered and neglected, and so readily occur to the mind familiarized to them. And how many things of this kind does my memory bear which have been already found out, and as I said, placed as it were at hand, which we are said to have learned and come to know; which were I for some short space of time to cease to call to mind, they are again so buried, and glide back, as it were, into the deeper recesses, that they must again, as if new, be thought out thence, for other abode they have none: but they must be drawn together again, that they may be known; that is to say, they must as it were be collected together from their dispersion: whence the word "cogitation" is derived. For *cogo* (collect) and *cogito* (re-collect) have the same relation to each other as *ago* and *agito*, *facio* and *factito*. But the mind hath appropriated to itself this word (cogitation), so that, not what is "collected" any how, but what is "recollected," i.e. brought together, in the mind, is properly said to be cogitated, or thought upon.

[XII] 19 The memory containeth also reasons and laws innumerable of numbers and dimensions, none of which hath any bodily sense impressed; seeing they have neither colour, nor sound, nor taste, nor smell, nor touch. I have heard the sound of the words whereby when discussed they are denoted: but the sounds are other than the things. For the sounds are other in Greek than in Latin: but the things are neither Greek, nor Latin, nor any other language. I have seen the lines of architects, the very finest, like a spider's thread; but those are still different, they are not the images of those lines, which the eye of flesh shewed me: he knoweth them, whosoever without any conception whatsoever of a body, recognizes them within himself. I have perceived also the numbers of the things with which we number all the senses of my body; but those numbers wherewith we number, are different, nor are they the images of these, and therefore they indeed are. Let him who seeth them not, deride me for saying these things, and I will pity him, while he derides me.

[XIII] 20 All these things I remember, and how I learnt them I remember. Many things also most falsely objected against them have I heard, and remember; which though they be false, yet is it not false that I remember them; and I remember also that I have discerned betwixt those truths and these falsehoods objected to them. And I perceive, that the present discerning of these things is different from remembering that I oftentimes discerned them, when I often thought upon them. I both remember then to have often understood these things; and what I now discern and understand, I lay up in my memory, that hereafter I may remember that I understood it now. So then I remember also to have remembered; as, if hereafter I shall call to remembrance, that I have now been able to remember these things, by the force of memory shall I call it to remembrance.

[XIV] 21 The same memory contains also the affections of my mind, not in the same manner that my mind itself contains them, when it feels them; but far otherwise, according to a power of its own. For without rejoicing I remember myself to have joyed; and without sorrow do I recollect my past sorrow. And that I once feared, I review without fear; and without desire call to mind a past desire. Sometimes, on the contrary, with joy do I remember my fore-past sorrow, and with sorrow, joy. Which is not wonderful, as to the body; for mind is one thing, body another. If I therefore with joy remember some past pain of body, it is not so wonderful. But now seeing this very memory itself is mind, (for when we give a thing in charge, to be kept in memory, we say, "See that you keep it in mind;"[6] and when we forget, we say, "It did not come to my mind," and, "It slipped out of my mind," calling the memory itself the mind;) this being so, how is it, that when with joy I remember my past sorrow, the mind hath joy, the memory hath sorrow; the mind upon the joyfulness which is in it, is joyful, yet the memory upon the sadness which is in it, is not sad? Does the memory perchance not belong to the mind? Who will say so? The memory then is, as it were, the belly of the mind, and joy and sadness, like sweet and bitter food; which, when committed to the memory, are, as it were, passed into the belly, where they may be stowed, but cannot taste. Ridiculous it is to imagine these to be alike; and yet are they not utterly unlike.

22 But, behold, out of my memory I bring it, when I say there be four perturbations of the mind, desire, joy, fear, sorrow; and whatsoever I can dispute thereon, by dividing each into its subordinate species, and by defining it, in my memory find I what to say, and thence do I bring it: yet am I not disturbed by any of these perturbations, when by calling them to mind, I remember them; yea, and before I recalled and brought them back, they were there; and therefore could they, by recollection, thence be brought. Perchance, then, as meat is by chewing the cud brought up out of the belly, so by recollection these out of the memory. Why then does not the disputer, thus recollecting, taste in the mouth of his musing the sweetness of joy, or the bitterness of sorrow? Is the comparison unlike in this, because not in all respects like? For who would willingly speak thereof, if

so oft as we name grief or fear, we should be compelled to be sad or fearful? And yet could we not speak of them, did we not find in our memory, not only the sounds of the names according to the images impressed by the senses of the body, but notions of the very things themselves which we never received by any avenue of the body, but which the mind itself perceiving by the experience of its own passions, committed to the memory, or the memory of itself retained, without being committed unto it.

[XV] 23 But whether by images or no, who can readily say? Thus, I name a stone, I name the sun, the things themselves not being present to my senses, but their images to my memory. I name a bodily pain, yet it is not present with me, when nothing aches: yet unless its image were present to my memory, I should not know what to say thereof, nor in discoursing discern pain from pleasure. I name bodily health; being sound in body, the thing itself is present with me; yet, unless its image also were present in my memory, I could by no means recal what the sound of this name should signify. Nor would the sick, when health were named, recognize what were spoken, unless the same image were by the force of memory retained, although the thing itself were absent from the body. I name numbers whereby we number; and not their images, but themselves are present in my memory. I name the image of the sun, and that image is present in my memory. For I recal not the image of its image, but the image itself is present to me, calling it to mind. I name memory, and I recognize what I name. And where do I recognize it, but in the memory itself? Is it also present to itself by its image, and not by itself?

[XVI] 24 What, when I name forgetfulness, and withal recognize what I name? Whence should I recognize it, did I not remember it? I speak not of the sound of the name, but of the thing which it signifies: which if I had forgotten, I could not recognize what that sound signifies. When then I remember memory, memory itself is, through itself, present with itself: but when I remember forgetfulness, there are present both memory and forgetfulness; memory whereby I remember, forgetfulness which I remember. But what is forgetfulness, but the privation of memory? How then is it present that I remember it, since when present I cannot remember? But if what we remember we hold it in memory, yet, unless we did remember forgetfulness, we could never at the hearing of the name, recognize the thing thereby signified, then forgetfulness is retained by memory. Present then it is, that we forget not, and being so, we forget. It is to be understood from this, that forgetfulness, when we remember it, is not present to the memory by itself, but by its image: because if it were present by itself, it would not cause us to remember, but to forget. Who now shall search out this? who shall comprehend how it is?

25 Lord, I truly, toil therein, yea and toil in myself; I am become a heavy soil requiring over-much *sweat of the brow*. For we are not now searching out the regions of heaven, or measuring the distances of the stars, or

enquiring the balancings of the earth. It is I myself who remember, I the mind. It is not so wonderful, if what I myself am not, be far from me. But what is nearer to me than myself? And lo, the force of mine own memory is not understood by me; though I cannot so much as name myself without it. For what shall I say, when it is clear to me that I remember forgetfulness? Shall I say that that is not in my memory, which I remember? or shall I say that forgetfulness is for this purpose in my memory, that I might not forget? Both were most absurd. What third way is there? How can I say that the image of forgetfulness is retained by my memory, not forgetfulness itself, when I remember it? How could I say this either, seeing that when the image of any thing is impressed on the memory, the thing itself must needs be first present, whence that image may be impressed? For thus do I remember Carthage, thus all places where I have been, thus men's faces whom I have seen, and things reported by the other senses; thus the health or sickness of the body. For when these things were present, my memory received from them images, which, being present with me, I might look on and bring back in my mind, when I remembered them in their absence. If then this forgetfulness is retained in the memory through its image, not through itself, then plainly, itself was once present, that its image might be taken. But when it was present, how did it write its image in the memory, seeing that forgetfulness by its presence, effaces even what it finds already noted? And yet, in whatever way, although that way be past conceiving and explaining, yet certain am I that I remember forgetfulness itself also, whereby what we remember is effaced.

[XVII] 26 Great is the power of memory, a fearful thing, O my God, a deep and boundless manifoldness; and this thing is the mind, and this am I myself. What am I then, O my God? What nature am I? A life various and manifold, and exceeding immense. Behold in the plains, and caves, and caverns of my memory, innumerable and innumerably full of innumerable kinds of things, either through images, as all bodies; or by actual presence, as the arts; or by certain notions or impressions, as the affections of the mind, which, even when the mind doth not feel, the memory retaineth, while yet whatsoever is in the memory, is also in the mind—over all these do I run, I fly; I dive on this side and on that, as far as I can, and there is no end. So great is the force of memory, so great the force of life, even in the mortal life of man. What shall I do then, O Thou my true life, my God? I will pass even beyond this power of mine which is called memory: yea, I will pass beyond it, that I may approach unto Thee, O sweet Light. What sayest Thou to me? See, I am mounting up through my mind towards Thee who abidest above me. Yea I now will pass beyond this power of mine which is called memory, desirous to arrive at Thee, whence Thou mayest be arrived at; and to cleave unto Thee, whence one may cleave unto Thee. For even beasts and birds have memory; else could they not return to their dens and nests, nor many other things they are used unto: nor indeed could they be used to any thing, but by memory. I will pass then beyond memory also, that I may arrive at Him who hath separated me from the four-footed beasts and made me wiser than the fowls of the air, I will pass beyond memory also, and where shall I find Thee, Thou truly good and certain sweetness? And where shall I find Thee? If I find Thee without my memory, then do I not retain Thee in my memory. And how shall I find Thee, if I remember Thee not?

[XVIII] 27 For the woman that had lost her groat, and sought it with a light; unless she had remembered it, she had never found it. For when it was found, whence should she know whether it were the same, unless she remembered it? I remember to have sought and found many a thing; and this I thereby know, that when I was seeking any of them, and was asked, "Is this it?" "Is that it?" so long said I "No," until that were offered me which I sought. Which had I not remembered (what ever it were) though it were offered me, yet should I not find it, because I could not recognize it. And so it ever is, when we seek and find any lost thing. Notwithstanding, when any thing is by chance lost from the sight, not from the memory, (as any visible body,) yet its image is still retained within, and it is sought until it be restored to sight; and when it is found, it is recognized by the image which is within: nor do we say that we have found what was lost, unless we recognize it; nor can we recognize it, unless we remember it. But this was lost to the eyes, but retained in the memory.

[XIX] 28 But what when the memory itself loses any thing, as falls out when we forget and seek that we may recollect? Where in the end do we search, but in the memory itself? and there, if one thing be perchance offered instead of another, we reject it, until what we seek meets us; and when it doth, we say, "This is it;" which we should not unless we recognized it, nor recognize it unless we remembered it. Certainly then we had forgotten it. Or, had not the whole escaped us, but by the part whereof we had hold, was the lost part sought for; in that the memory felt that it did not carry on together all which it was wont, and maimed, as it were, by the curtailment of its ancient habit, demanded the restoration of what it missed? For instance, if we see or think of some one known to us, and having forgotten his name, try to recover it; whatever else occurs, connects itself not therewith; because it was not wont to be thought upon together with him, and therefore is rejected, until that present itself, whereon the knowledge reposes equably as its wonted object. And whence does that present itself, but out of the memory itself? for even when we recognize it, on being reminded by another, it is thence it comes. For we do not believe it as something new, but, upon recollection, allow what was named to be right. But were it utterly blotted out of the mind, we should not remember it, even when reminded. For we have not as yet utterly forgotten that, which we remember ourselves to have forgotten. What then we have utterly forgotten, though lost, we cannot even seek after.

[XX] 29 How then do I seek Thee, O Lord? For when I seek Thee, my God, I seek a happy life. *I will seek Thee, that my soul may live*. For my body liveth by my soul; and my soul by Thee. How then do I seek a happy life, seeing I have it not, until I can say, where I ought to say it, "It

is enough?" How seek I it? By remembrance, as though I
had forgotten it, remembering that I had forgotten it? Or,
desiring to learn it as a thing unknown, either never
having known, or so forgotten it, as not even to remember
that I had forgotten it? Is not a happy life what all will,
and no one altogether wills it not?[7] Where have they
known it, that they so will it? where seen it, that they so
love it? Truly we have it, how, I know not. Yea, there is
another way, wherein when one hath it, then is he happy;
and there are, who are blessed, in hope. These have it in
a lower kind, than they who have it in very deed; yet are
they better off than such as are happy neither in deed,
nor in hope. Yet even these, had they it not in some sort,
would not so will to be happy, which that they do will,
is most certain. They have known it then, I know not
how, and so have it by some sort of knowledge, what, I
know not, and am perplexed whether it be in the memory,
which if it be, then we have been happy once; whether
all severally, or in that man who first sinned, *in whom* also
we all died, and from whom we are all born with misery,
I now enquire not; but only, whether the happy life be in
the memory? For neither should we love it, did we not
know it. We hear the name, and we all confess that we
desire the thing; for we are not delighted with the mere
sound. For when a Greek hears it in Latin, he is not
delighted, not knowing what is spoken; but we Latins
are delighted, as would he too, if he heard it in Greek;
because the thing itself is neither Greek nor Latin, which
Greeks and Latins, and men of all other tongues, long for
so earnestly. Known therefore it is to all, for could they
with one voice be asked, "would they be happy?" they

would answer without doubt, "they would." And this could not be, unless the thing itself whereof it is the name, were retained in their memory.

[XXI] 30 But is it so, as one remembers Carthage who hath seen it? No. For a happy life is not seen with the eye, because it is not a body. As we remember numbers then? No. For these, he that hath in his knowledge, seeks not further to attain unto; but a happy life, we have in our knowledge, and therefore love it, and yet still desire to attain it, that we may be happy. As we remember eloquence then? No. For although upon hearing this name also, some call to mind the thing, who still are not yet eloquent, and many who desire to be so, whence it appears that it is in their knowledge; yet these have by their bodily senses observed others to be eloquent, and been delighted, and desire to be the like; (though indeed they would not be delighted but for some inward knowledge thereof, nor wish to be the like, unless they were thus delighted;) whereas a happy life, we do by no bodily sense experience in others. As then we remember joy? Perchance; for my joy I remember, even when sad, as a happy life, when unhappy; nor did I ever with bodily sense see, hear, smell, taste, or touch my joy; but I experienced it in my mind, when I rejoiced; and the knowledge of it clave to my memory, so that I can recall it with disgust sometimes, at others with longing, according to the nature of the things, wherein I remember myself to have joyed. For even from foul things have I been immersed in a sort of joy; which now recalling, I detest and execrate; otherwhiles in good and honest things, which I recall with longing, although perchance no longer present; and therefore with sadness I recall former joy.

31 Where then and when did I experience my happy life, that I should remember, and love, and long for it? Nor is it I alone, or some few besides, but we all would fain be happy; which, unless by some certain knowledge we knew, we should not with so certain a will desire. But how is this, that if two men be asked whether they would go to the wars, one, perchance, would answer that he would, the other, that he would not; but if they were asked, whether they would be happy, both would instantly without any doubting say they would; and for no other reason would the one go to the wars, and the other not, but to be happy. Is it perchance, that as one looks for his joy in this thing, another in that, all agree in their desire of being happy, as they would, (if they were asked,) that they wished to have joy, and this joy they call a happy life? Although then one obtains this joy by one means, another by another, all have one end, which they strive to attain, namely, joy. Which being a thing, which all must say they have experienced, it is therefore found in the memory, and recognized whenever the name of a happy life is mentioned.

[XXII] 32 Far be it, Lord, far be it from the heart of Thy servant who here confesseth unto Thee, far be it, that, be the joy what it may, I should therefore think myself happy. For there is a *joy* which is *not* given *to the ungodly,* but to those who love Thee for Thine own sake, whose joy

Thou Thyself art. And this is the happy life, to rejoice to Thee, of Thee, for Thee; this is it, and there is no other.[8] For they who think there is another, pursue some other and not the true joy. Yet is not their will turned away from some semblance of joy.

[XXIII] 33 It is not certain then that all wish to be happy, inasmuch as they who wish not to joy in Thee, which is the only happy life, do not truly desire the happy life. Or do all men desire this, but *because the flesh lusteth against the Spirit, and the Spirit against the flesh, that they cannot do what they would,* they fall upon that which they can, and are content therewith; because, what they are not able to do, they do not will so strongly, as would suffice to make them able?[9] For I ask any one, had he rather joy in truth, or in falsehood? They will as little hesitate to say, "in the truth," as to say, "that they desire to be happy;" for a happy life is joy in the truth: for this is a joying in Thee, Who art *the Truth,* O God *my light, health of my countenance, my God.* This is the happy life which all desire; this life which alone is happy, all desire; to joy in the truth all desire.[10] I have met with many that would deceive; who would be deceived, no one. Where then did they know this happy life, save where they knew the truth also? For they love it also, since they would not be deceived. And when they love a happy life, which is no other than joying in the truth, then also do they love the truth; which yet they would not love, were there not some notice of it in their memory. Why then joy they not in it? why are they not happy? because they are more strongly taken up with other things which have more power to make them miserable, than that which they so faintly remember to make them happy.[11] For there is yet a little light in men; let them walk, let them *walk, that the darkness overtake them not.*

34 But why doth "truth generate hatred,"[12] and the *man of thine*, preaching the truth, become an enemy to them? whereas a happy life is loved, which is nothing else but joying in the truth; unless that truth is in that kind loved, that they who love any thing else, would gladly have that which they love to be the truth; and because they would not be deceived, would not be convinced that they are so? Therefore do they hate the truth, for that thing's sake, which they love instead of the truth. They love truth when she enlightens, they hate her when she reproves. For since they would not be deceived, and would deceive, they love her, when she discovers herself unto them, and hate her, when she discovers them. Whence she shall so repay them, that they who would not be made manifest by her, she both against their will makes manifest, and herself becometh not manifest unto them. Thus, thus, yea thus doth the mind of man, thus blind and sick, foul and ill-favoured, wish to be hidden, but that aught should be hidden from it, it wills not. But the contrary is requited it, that itself should not be hidden from the Truth; but the Truth is hid from it. Yet even thus miserable, it had rather joy in truths than in falsehoods. Happy then will it be, when, no distraction interposing, it shall joy in that only Truth, by Whom all things are true.

[XXIV] 35 See what a space I have gone over in my memory seeking Thee, O Lord; and I have not found Thee, without it. Nor have I found any thing concerning Thee, but what I have kept in memory, ever since I learnt Thee. For since I learnt Thee, I have not forgotten Thee. For where I found Truth, there found I my God, the Truth Itself;[13] which since I learnt, I have not forgotten. Since then I learned Thee, Thou residest in my memory; and there do I find Thee, when I call Thee to remembrance, and delight in Thee. These be my holy delights, which Thou hast given me in Thy mercy, having regard to my poverty.

[XXV] 36 But where in my memory residest Thou, O Lord, where residest Thou there? what manner of lodging hast Thou framed for Thee? what manner of sanctuary hast Thou builded for Thee? Thou hast given this honour to my memory, to reside in it; but in what quarter of it Thou residest, that am I considering. For in thinking on Thee, I passed[14] beyond such parts of it, as the beasts also have, for I found Thee not there among the images of corporeal things: and I came to those parts to which I committed the affections of my mind, nor found Thee there. And I entered into the very seat of my mind, (which it hath in my memory, inasmuch as the mind remembers itself also,) neither wert Thou there: for as Thou art not a corporeal image, nor the affection of a living being; (as when we rejoice, condole, desire, fear, remember, forget, or the like;) so neither art Thou the mind itself; because Thou art the Lord God of the mind; and all these are changed, but Thou remainest unchangeable over all, and yet hast vouchsafed to dwell in my memory, since I learnt Thee. And why seek I now, in what place thereof Thou dwellest, as if there were places therein? Sure I am, that in it Thou dwellest, since I have remembered Thee, ever since I learnt Thee, and there I find Thee, when I call Thee to remembrance.

[XXVI] 37 Where then did I find Thee, that I might learn Thee? For in my memory Thou wert not, before I learned Thee. Where then did I find Thee, that I might learn Thee, but in Thee above me? Place there is none; *we go backward and forward*, and there is no place. Every where, O Truth, dost Thou give audience to all who ask counsel of Thee, and at once answerest all, though on manifold matters they ask Thy counsel. Clearly dost Thou answer, though all do not clearly hear. All consult Thee on what they will, though they hear not always what they will. He is thy best servant, who looks not so much to hear that from Thee, which himself willeth; as rather to will that, which from Thee he heareth.

[XXVII] 38 Too late loved I Thee, O Thou Beauty of ancient days, yet ever new! too late I loved Thee! And behold, Thou wert within, and I abroad, and there I searched for Thee; deformed I, plunging amid those fair forms, which Thou hadst made.[15] Thou wert with me, but I was not with Thee. Things held me far from Thee, which, unless they were in Thee, were not at all.[16] Thou calledst, and shoutedst, and burstest, my deafness. Thou flashedst, shonest, and scatteredst my blindness. Thou breathedst odours, and *I drew in breath* and *pant for Thee.* I tasted, and *hunger and thirst.* Thou touchedst me, and I burned for Thy peace.

[XXVIII] 39. When I shall with my whole self cleave to Thee, I shall no where have sorrow, or labour; and my life shall wholly live, as wholly full of Thee. But now since whom Thou fillest, Thou liftest up, because I am not full of Thee I am a burthen to myself. Lamentable joys strive with joyous sorrows: and on which side is the victory, I know not. Woe is me! Lord, have pity on me. My evil sorrows strive with my good joys; and on which side is the victory, I know not. Woe is me! Lord, have pity on me. Woe is me! lo! I hide not my wounds; Thou art the Physician, I the sick; Thou merciful, I miserable. *Is not the life of man upon earth all trial?* Who wishes for troubles and difficulties? Thou commandest them to be endured, not to be loved. No man loves what he endures, though he love to endure. For though he rejoices that he endures, he had rather there were nothing for him to endure. In adversity, I long for prosperity, in prosperity I fear adversity. What middle place is there betwixt these two, where *the life of man is* not *all trial?* Woe to the prosperities of the world, once and again, through fear of adversity, and corruption of joy! Woe to the adversities of the world, once and again, and the third time, from the longing for prosperity, and because adversity itself is a hard thing, and lest it shatter endurance. Is not the *life of man upon earth all trial,* without any interval?

[XXIX] 40 And all my hope is no where but in Thy exceeding great mercy. Give what Thou enjoinest, and enjoin what Thou wilt.[17] Thou enjoinest us continency;[18] and *when I knew*, saith one, *that no man can be continent, unless God give it, this also was a part of wisdom to know whose gift she is.* By continency verily, are we bound up and brought back into One, whence we were dissipated into many. For too little doth he love Thee, who loves any thing with Thee, which he loveth not for Thee.[19] O love, who ever burnest and never consumest! O charity, my God! kindle me. Thou enjoinest continency: give me what Thou enjoinest, and enjoin what Thou wilt.

[XXX] 41 Verily Thou enjoinest me continency from the *lust of the flesh, the lust of the eyes, and the ambition of the world.*[20] Thou enjoinest continency from concubinage; and, for wedlock itself, Thou has counselled something better than what Thou hast permitted. And since Thou gavest it, it was done, even before I became a dispenser of Thy Sacrament. But there yet live in my memory (whereof I have much spoken) the images of such things, as my ill custom there fixed; which haunt me, strengthless when I am awake: but in sleep, not only so as to give pleasure, but even to obtain assent, and what is very like reality. Yea, so far prevails the illusion of the image, in my soul and in my flesh, that, when asleep, false visions persuade to that which when waking, the true cannot. Am I not then myself, O Lord my God? And yet there is so much difference betwixt myself and myself, within that moment wherein I pass from waking to sleeping, or return from sleeping to waking! Where is reason then, which, awake, resisteth such suggestions? And should the things themselves be urged on it, it remaineth unshaken. Is it clasped up with the eyes? is it lulled asleep with the senses of the body? And whence is it that often even in sleep we resist, and mindful of our purpose, and abiding most chastely in it, yield no assent to such enticements? And yet so much difference there is, that when it happeneth otherwise, upon waking we return to peace of conscience: and by this very difference discover that we did not, what yet we be sorry that in some way it was done in us.

42 Art Thou not mighty, God Almighty, so as to *heal all the diseases of my soul*, and by Thy more abundant grace to quench even the impure motions of my sleep? Thou wilt increase, Lord, Thy gifts more and more in me, that my soul may follow me to Thee, disentangled from the bird-lime of concupiscence; that it rebel not against itself, and even in dreams not only not, through images of sense, commit those debasing corruptions, even to pollution of the flesh, but not even to consent unto them. For that nothing of this sort should have, over the pure affections even of a sleeper, the very least influence, not even such as a thought would restrain,—to work this, not only during life, but even at my present age, is not hard for the Almighty, Who art *able to do above all that we ask or think*. But what I yet am in this kind of my evil, have I confessed unto my good Lord; *rejoicing with trembling*, in that which Thou hast given me, and bemoaning that wherein I am still imperfect; hoping, that Thou wilt perfect Thy mercies in me, even to perfect peace, which my outward and inward man shall have with Thee, when *death shall be swallowed up in victory.*

[XXXI] 43 There is another *evil of the day*, which I would were *sufficient for it*. For by eating and drinking we repair the daily decays of our body, until Thou *destroy both belly and meat*, when Thou shalt slay my emptiness with a wonderful fulness, and *clothe this incorruptible with* an eternal *incorruption*. But now the necessity is sweet unto me, against which sweetness I fight, that I be not taken captive; and carry on a daily war by fastings; often *bringing my body into subjection*, and my pains are removed by pleasure. For hunger and thirst are in a manner pains; they burn and kill like a fever, unless the medicine of nourishments come to our aid. Which since it is at hand through the consolations of Thy gifts, with which land, and water, and air serve our weakness, our calamity is termed gratification.

44 This hast Thou taught me, that I should set myself to take food as physic. But while I am passing from the discomfort of emptiness to the content of replenishing, in the very passage the snare of concupiscence besets me. For that passing, is pleasure, nor is there any other way to pass thither, whither we needs must pass. And health being the cause of eating and drinking, there joineth itself as an attendant a dangerous pleasure, which mostly endeavours to go before it, so that I may for her sake do what I say I do, or wish to do, for health's sake. Nor have each the same measure; for what is enough for health, is too little for pleasure. And oft it is uncertain, whether it be the necessary care of the body which is yet asking for sustenance, or whether a voluptuous deceivableness of greediness is proffering its services. In this uncertainty

the unhappy soul rejoiceth, and therein prepares an excuse to shield itself, glad that it appeareth not what sufficeth for the moderation of health, that under the cloak of health, it may disguise the matter of gratification. These temptations I daily endeavour to resist, and I call on Thy right hand, and to Thee do I refer my perplexities; because I have as yet no settled counsel herein.

45 I hear the voice of my God commanding, *Let not your hearts be overcharged with surfeiting and drunkenness*. Drunkenness is far from me; Thou wilt have mercy that it come not near me. But full-feeding sometimes creepeth upon Thy servant; Thou wilt have mercy, that it may be far from me. For *no one can be continent unless Thou give it*. Many things Thou givest us, praying for them; and what good soever we have received before we prayed, from Thee we received it; yea to the end we might afterwards know this, did we before receive it. Drunkard was I never, but drunkards have I known made sober by Thee. From Thee then it was, that they who never were such, should not so be, as from Thee it was, that they who have been, should not ever so be; and from Thee it was, that both might know from Whom it was. I heard another voice of Thine, *Go not after thy lusts, and from thy pleasure turn away*. Yea by Thy favour have I heard that which I have much loved; *neither if we eat, shall we abound; neither if we eat not, shall we lack;* which is to say, neither shall the one make me plenteous, nor the other miserable. I heard also another, *for I have learned in whatsoever state I am, therewith to be content; I know how to abound, and how to suffer need. I can do all things through Christ that*

strengtheneth me. Behold a soldier of the heavenly camp, not the dust which we are. But *remember*, Lord, *that we are dust, and that of dust thou hast made man; and he was lost and is found*. Nor could he of himself do this, because he whom I so loved, saying this through the in-breathing of Thy inspiration, was of the same dust. *I can do all things* (saith he) *through Him that strengtheneth me*. Strengthen me, that *I can*. Give what Thou enjoinest, and enjoin what Thou wilt.[21] He confesses to have received, and when *he glorieth, in the Lord he glorieth*. Another have I heard begging that he might receive, *Take from me* (saith he) *the desires of the belly*; whence it appeareth, O my holy God, that Thou givest, when that is done which Thou commandest to be done.

46 Thou hast taught me, good Father, that *to the pure, all things are pure*; but that *it is evil unto the man that eateth with offence*; and, that *every creature of Thine is good, and nothing to be refused, which is received with thanksgiving*; and that *meat commendeth us not to God*; and, that *no man should judge us in meat or drink*; and, that *he which eateth, let him not despise him that eateth not; and let not him that eateth not, judge him that eateth*. These things have I learned, thanks be to Thee, praise to Thee, my God, my Master, knocking at my ears, enlightening my heart; deliver me out of all temptation. I fear not uncleanness of meat, but the uncleanness of lusting. I know, that Noah was permitted to eat all kind of flesh[22] that was good for food; that Elijah was fed with flesh; that John, endued with an admirable abstinence, was not polluted by feeding on living creatures, locusts.[23] I know also that

Esau was deceived by lusting for lentiles; and that David blamed himself for desiring a draught of water; and that our King was tempted, not concerning flesh, but bread. And therefore the people in the wilderness also deserved to be reproved, not for desiring flesh, but because, in the desire of food, they murmured against the Lord.

47 Placed then amid these temptations, I strive daily against concupiscence in eating and drinking. For it is not of such nature, that I can settle on cutting it off once for all, and never touching it afterward, as I could of concubinage. The bridle of the throat then is to be held attempered between slackness and stiffness. And who is he, O Lord, who is not somewhit transported beyond the limits of necessity? whoever he is, he is a great one; let him make Thy Name great. But I am not such, for *I am a sinful man*. Yet do I too magnify Thy name; and *He maketh intercession to Thee* for my sins, who *hath overcome the world;* numbering me among the *weak members* of His *body;* because *thine eyes have seen* that of Him which is *imperfect, and in Thy book shall all be written.*[24]

[XXXII] 48 With the allurements of smells, I am not much concerned. When absent, I do not miss them; when present, I do not refuse them; yet ever ready to be without them. So I seem to myself; perchance I am deceived. For that also is a mournful darkness, whereby my abilities within me, are hidden from me; so that my mind making enquiry into herself of her own powers, ventures not readily to believe herself; because even what is in it, is mostly hidden, unless experience reveal it.[25] And no one ought to be secure in that life, the whole whereof is called *a trial*, that he who hath been capable, of worse to be made better, may not likewise of better be made worse. Our only hope, only confidence, only assured promise, is Thy mercy.

[XXXIII] 49 The delights of the ear, had more firmly entangled and subdued me; but Thou didst loosen, and free me. Now, in those melodies which Thy words breathe soul into, when sung with a sweet and attuned voice, I do a little repose; yet not so as to be held thereby, but that I can disengage myself when I will. But with the words which are their life and whereby they find admission into me, themselves seek in my affections a place of some estimation, and I can scarcely assign them one suitable. For at one time I seem to myself to give them more honour than is seemly, feeling our minds to be more holily and fervently raised unto a flame of devotion, by the holy words themselves when thus sung, than when not; and that the several affections of our spirit, by a sweet variety, have their own proper measures in the voice and singing, by some hidden correspondence wherewith they are stirred up. But this contentment of the flesh, to which the soul must not be given over to be enervated, doth oft beguile me, the sense not so waiting upon reason, as patiently to follow her; but having been admitted merely for her sake, it strives even to run before her, and lead her. Thus in these things I unawares sin, but afterwards am aware of it.

50 At other times, shunning over-anxiously this very deception, I err in too great strictness; and sometimes to that degree, as to wish the whole melody of sweet music which is used to David's Psalter, banished from my ears, and the Church's too; and that mode seems to me safer, which I remember to have been often told me of Athanasius Bishop of Alexandria, who made the reader of the psalm utter it with so slight inflection of voice that it was nearer speaking than singing. Yet again, when I remember the tears I shed at the Psalmody of Thy Church, in the beginning of my recovered faith; and how at this time, I am moved, not with the singing, but with the things sung, when they are sung with a clear voice and modulation most suitable, I acknowledge the great use of this institution. Thus I fluctuate between peril of pleasure, and approved wholesomeness; inclined the rather (though not as pronouncing an irrevocable opinion) to approve of the usage of singing in the church; that so by the delight of the ears, the weaker minds may rise to the feeling of devotion. Yet when it befalls me to be more moved with the voice than the words sung, I confess to have sinned penally, and then had rather not hear music. See now my state; weep with me, and weep for me, ye, who so regulate your feelings within, as that good action ensues. For you who do not act, these things touch not you. But Thou, O Lord my God, hearken; behold, and see, and *have mercy, and heal me*, Thou, in whose presence I have become a problem to myself; and *that is my infirmity*.

[XXXIV] 51 There remains the pleasure of these eyes of my flesh, on which to make my confessions in the hearing of the ears of Thy temple, those brotherly and devout ears; and so to conclude the temptations of the *lust of the flesh*, which yet assail me, *groaning earnestly, and desiring to be clothed upon with my house from heaven*. The eyes love fair and varied forms, and bright and soft colours. Let not these occupy my soul; let God rather occupy it, *who made these* things, *very good* indeed, yet is He my good, not they. And these affect me, waking, the whole day, nor is any rest given me from them, as there is from musical, sometimes, in silence, from all voices. For this queen of colours, the light, bathing all which we behold, wherever I am through the day, gliding by me in varied forms, sooths me when engaged on other things, and not observing it. And so strongly doth it entwine itself, that if it be suddenly withdrawn, it is with longing sought for, and if absent long, saddeneth the mind.

52 O Thou Light, which Tobias saw, when, these eyes closed, he taught his son the way of life; and himself went before with the feet of charity, never swerving. Or which Isaac saw, when his fleshly *eyes being heavy* and closed by old age, it was vouchsafed him, not, knowingly to bless his sons, but by blessing to know them. Or which Jacob saw, when he also, blind through great age, with illumined heart, in the persons of his sons shed light on the different races of the future people, in them foresignified; and laid his hands, mystically crossed, upon his grandchildren by Joseph, not as their father by his outward eye corrected them, but as himself

inwardly discerned. This is the light, it is one, and all are one, who see and love it. But that corporeal light whereof I spake, it seasoneth the life of this world for her blind lovers, with an enticing and dangerous sweetness. But they who know how to praise Thee for it, "O All-creating Lord,"[26] take it up[27] in Thy hymns, and are not taken up with it in their sleep. Such would I be. These seductions of the eyes I resist, lest my feet wherewith I walk upon Thy way be ensnared; and I lift up mine invisible eyes to Thee, that Thou wouldest *pluck my feet out of the snare.* Thou dost ever and anon pluck them out, for they are ensnared. Thou ceasest not to pluck them out, while I often entangle myself in the snares on all sides laid; because *Thou that keepest Israel shalt neither slumber nor sleep.*

53 What innumerable toys, made by divers arts and manufactures, in our apparel, shoes, utensils and all sort of works, in pictures also and divers images, and these far exceeding all necessary and moderate use and all pious meaning, have men added to tempt their own eyes withal; outwardly following what themselves make, inwardly forsaking Him by whom themselves were made, and destroying that which themselves have been made! But I, my God and my Glory, do hence also sing a hymn to Thee, and do consecrate praise to Him who consecrateth me,[28] because those beautiful patterns which through men's souls are conveyed into their cunning hands,[29] come from that Beauty, Which is above our souls, Which my soul day and night sigheth after. But the framers and followers of the outward beauties, derive thence the rule of judging

of them, but not of using[30] them. And He is there, though they perceive Him not,[31] that so they might not wander, but *keep their strength for Thee*, and not scatter it abroad upon pleasureable wearinesses. And I, though I speak and see this, entangle my steps with these outward beauties; but Thou pluckest me out, O Lord, Thou pluckest me out; *because Thy loving-kindness is before my eyes.* For I am taken miserably, and Thou pluckest me out mercifully; sometimes not perceiving it, when I had but lightly lighted upon them; otherwhiles with pain, because I had stuck fast in them.

[XXXV] 54 To this is added, another form of temptation more manifoldly dangerous. For besides that concupiscence of the flesh which consisteth in the delight of all senses and pleasures, wherein its slaves, who *go far from Thee*, waste and *perish*, the soul hath, through the same senses of the body, a certain vain and curious desire, veiled under the title of knowledge and learning, not of delighting in the flesh, but of *making experiments through the flesh*. The seat whereof being in the appetite of knowledge, and sight being the sense chiefly used for attaining knowledge, it is in Divine language called, *The lust of the eyes.* For, to see, belongeth properly to the eyes; yet we use this word of the other senses also, when we employ them in seeking knowledge. For we do not say, hark how it flashes, or smell how it glows, or taste how it shines, or feel how it gleams; for all these are said to be seen. And yet we say not only, see how it shineth, which the eyes alone can perceive; but also, see how it soundeth, see how it smelleth, see how it tasteth, see how hard it is.

And so the general experience of the senses, as was said, is called *The lust of the eyes*, because the office of seeing, wherein the eyes hold the prerogative, the other senses by way of similitude take to themselves, when they make search after any knowledge.

55 But by this may more evidently be discerned, wherein pleasure and wherein curiosity is the object of the senses; for pleasure seeketh objects beautiful, melodious, fragrant, savoury, soft; but curiosity, for trial's sake, the contrary as well, not for the sake of suffering annoyance, but out of the lust of making trial and knowing them. For what pleasure hath it, to see in a mangled carcase what will make you shudder? and yet if it be lying near, they flock thither, to be made sad, and to turn pale. Even in sleep they are afraid to see it. As if when awake, any one forced them to see it, or any report of its beauty drew them thither! Thus also in the other senses, which it were long to go through. From this disease of curiosity, are all those strange sights exhibited in the theatre. Hence men go on to search out the hidden powers of nature, (which is besides our end,) which to know profits not, and wherein men desire nothing but to know.[32] Hence also, if with that same end of perverted knowledge magical arts be enquired by. Hence also in religion itself, is God tempted, when signs and wonders are demanded of Him, not desired for any good end, but merely to make trial of.

56 In this so vast wilderness, full of snares and dangers, behold many of them I have cut off, and thrust out of my heart, as Thou hast given me, O God of my salvation. And

yet when dare I say, since so many things of this kind buzz on all sides about our daily life—when dare I say, that nothing of this sort engages my attention, or causes in me an idle interest? True, the theatres do not now carry me away, nor care I to know the courses of the stars, nor did my soul ever consult ghosts departed; all sacrilegious mysteries I detest. From Thee, O Lord my God, to whom I owe humble[33] and single-hearted service, by what artifices and suggestions doth the enemy deal with me to desire some sign! But I beseech thee by our King, and by our pure and holy country, Jerusalem, that as any consenting thereto is far from me, so may it ever be further and further. But when I pray Thee for the salvation of any, my end and intention is far different. Thou givest and wilt give me to *follow Thee* willingly, doing what Thou *wilt*.

57 Notwithstanding, in how many most petty and contemptible things is our curiosity daily tempted, and how often we give way, who can recount? How often do we begin, as if we were tolerating people telling vain stories, lest we offend the weak; then by degrees we take interest therein! I go not now to the circus to see a dog coursing a hare; but in the field, if passing, that coursing peradventure will distract me even from some weighty thought, and draw me after it: not that I turn aside the body of my beast, yet still incline my mind thither. And unless Thou, having made me see my infirmity, didst speedily admonish me either through the sight itself, by some contemplation to rise towards Thee, or altogether to despise and pass it by, I dully stand fixed therein. What, when

sitting at home, a lizard catching flies, or a spider entangling them rushing into her nets, oft-times takes my attention? Is the thing different, because they are but small creatures? I go on from them to praise Thee the wonderful Creator and Orderer of all, but this does not first draw my attention. It is one thing to rise quickly, another not to fall. And of such things is my life full; and my one hope is Thy wonderful great mercy. For when our heart becomes the receptacle of such things, and is over-charged with throngs of this abundant vanity, then are our prayers also thereby often interrupted and distracted, and whilst in Thy presence we direct the voice of our heart to Thine ears, this so great concern is broken off, by the rushing in of I know not what idle thoughts. Shall we then account this also among things of slight concernment, or shall ought bring us back to hope, save Thy complete mercy, since Thou hast begun to change us?

[XXXVI] 58 And Thou knowest how far Thou hast already changed me, who first healedst me of the lust of vindicating myself, that so Thou mightest *forgive all* the rest of my *iniquities, and heal all my infirmities, and redeem my life from corruption, and crown me with mercy and pity, and satisfy my desire with good things:* who didst curb my pride with Thy fear, and tame my neck to Thy *yoke.* And now I bear it and it is *light* unto me, because so hast Thou promised, and hast made it; and verily so it was, and I knew it not, when I feared to take it.

59 But, O Lord, Thou alone Lord without pride, because Thou art the only true Lord, who hast no lord; hath this third kind of temptation also ceased from me, or can it cease through this whole life? To wish, namely, to be feared and loved of men, for no other end, but that we may have a joy therein which is no joy? A miserable life this, and a foul boastfulness! Hence especially it comes, that men do neither purely love, nor fear Thee. And therefore *dost Thou resist the proud, and givest grace to the humble:* yea, Thou thunderest down upon the ambitions of the world, and *the foundations of the mountains tremble.* Because now certain offices of human society make it necessary to be loved and feared of men, the adversary of our true blessedness layeth hard at us, every where spreading his snares of "well-done, well-done;" that greedily catching at them, we may be taken unawares, and sever our joy from Thy truth, and set it in the deceivingness of men; and be pleased at being loved and feared, not for Thy sake, but in Thy stead: and thus having been made like him, he may have them for his own, not in the bands of charity, but in the bonds of punishment: who purposed to *set his throne in the north,* that dark and chilled they might serve him, pervertedly and crookedly imitating Thee. But we, O Lord, behold we are Thy *little flock;* possess us as Thine, stretch Thy wings over us, and let us fly under them. Be Thou our glory; let us be loved for Thee, and Thy word feared in us. Who would be praised of men, when Thou blamest, will not be defended of men, when Thou judgest; nor delivered, when Thou condemnest. But when—not *the sinner is praised in the desires of his soul,* nor he *blessed who doth ungodlily,* but—

a man is praised for some gift which Thou hast given him, and he rejoices more at the praise for himself than that he hath the gift for which he is praised, he also is praised, while Thou dispraisest; and better is he who praised than he who is praised. For the one took pleasure in the gift of God in man; the other was better pleased with the gift of man, than of God.

[XXXVII] 60 By these temptations we are assailed daily, O Lord; without ceasing are we assailed. Our daily *furnace* is the tongue of men. And in this way also Thou commandest us continence. Give what Thou enjoinest, and enjoin what Thou wilt. Thou knowest on this matter the groans of my heart, and the floods of mine eyes. For I cannot learn how far I am more cleansed from this plague, and I much fear my *secret sins*, which Thine eyes know, mine do not. For in other kinds of temptations I have some sort of means of examining myself; in this, scarce any. For, in refraining my mind from the pleasures of the flesh, and idle curiosity, I see how much I have attained to, when I do without them; foregoing, or not having them.[34] For then I ask myself how much more or less trouble-some it is to me, not to have them? Then, riches, which are desired, that they may serve to some one or two or all of the three concupiscences,[35] if the soul cannot discern, whether, when it hath them, it despiseth them, they may be cast aside, that so it may prove itself. But to be without praise, and therein essay our powers, must we live ill, yea so abandonedly and atrociously, that no one should know without detesting us? What greater madness can be said, or thought of? But if praise useth and ought to accompany a good life and good works, we ought as little to forego its company, as good life itself. Yet I know not, whether I can well or ill be without any thing, unless it be absent.

61 What then do I confess unto Thee in this kind of temptation, O Lord? What, but that I am delighted with praise, but with truth itself, more than with praise? For were it proposed to me, whether I would, being phrenzied in error on all things, be praised by all men, or being consistent and most settled in the truth be blamed by all, I see which I should choose. Yet fain would I, that the approbation of another should not even increase my joy for any good in me. Yet I own, it doth increase it, and not so only, but dispraise doth diminish it. And when I am troubled at this my misery, an excuse occurs to me, which of what value it is, Thou God knowest, for it leaves me uncertain. For since Thou hast commanded us not continency alone, that is, from what things to refrain our love, but righteousness also, that is, whereon to bestow it, and hast willed us to love not Thee only, but our neighbour also; often, when pleased with intelligent praise, I seem to myself to be pleased with the proficiency or towardliness of my neighbour, or to be grieved for evil in him, when I hear him dispraise either what he understands not, or is good. For sometimes I am grieved at my own praise, either when those things be praised in me, in which I mislike myself, or even lesser and slight goods are more esteemed, than they ought. But again how know I whether I am therefore thus affected, because I would not have him who praiseth me, differ from me

about myself; not as being influenced by concern for him, but because those same good things which please me in myself, please me more when they please another also? For some how I am not praised when my judgment of myself is not praised; forasmuch as either those things are praised, which displease me; or those more, which please me less. Am I then doubtful of myself in this matter?

62 Behold, in Thee, O Truth, I see, that I ought not to be moved at my own praises, for my own sake, but for the good of my neighbour.[36] And whether it be so with me, I know not. For herein I know less of myself, than of Thee.[37] I beseech now, O my God, discover to me myself also, that I may confess unto my brethren, who are to pray for me, wherein I find myself maimed. Let me examine myself again more diligently. If in my praise I am moved with the good of my neighbour, why am I less moved if another be unjustly dispraised than if it be myself? Why am I more stung by reproach cast upon myself, than at that cast upon another, with the same injustice, before me? Know I not this also? or is it at last that I *deceive myself*, and do not the truth before Thee in my heart and tongue? This madness put far from me, O Lord, lest mine own mouth be to me the *sinner's oil to make fat my head. I am poor and needy;* yet best, while in hidden groanings I displease myself, and seek Thy mercy, until what is lacking in my defective state be renewed and perfected, on to that peace which the eye of the proud knoweth not.

[XXXVIII] 63 Yet the word, which cometh out of the mouth, and deeds known to men, bring with them a most dangerous temptation through the love of praise: which, to establish a certain excellency of our own, solicits and collects men's suffrages. It tempts, even when it is reproved by myself in myself, on the very ground that it is reproved; and often glories more vainly of the very contempt of vain-glory; and so it is no longer contempt of vain-glory, whereof it glories; for it doth not contemn when it glorieth.

[XXXIX] 64 Within also, within is another evil, arising out of a like temptation; whereby men become vain, pleasing themselves in themselves, though they please not, or displease, or care not to please others. But pleasing themselves, they much displease Thee, not only taking pleasure in things not good, as if good, but in Thy good things, as though their own;[38] or even if as thine, yet as though for their own merits; or even if as though from Thy grace, yet not with brotherly rejoicing, but envying that grace to others. In all these and the like perils and travails, Thou seest the trembling of my heart; and I rather feel my wounds to be cured by Thee, than not inflicted by me.

[XL] 65 Where hast Thou not walked with me, O Truth, teaching me what to beware, and what to desire; when I referred to Thee what I could discover here below, and consulted Thee? With my outward senses, as I might, I surveyed the world, and observed the life, which my body hath from me, and these my senses. Thence entered

I the recesses of my memory, those manifold and spacious chambers, wonderfully furnished with innumerable stores; and I considered, and stood aghast; being able to discern nothing of these things without Thee, and finding none of them to be Thee. Nor was I myself, who found out these things, who went over them all, and laboured to distinguish and to value every thing according to its dignity, taking some things upon the report of my senses, questioning about others which I felt to be mingled with myself, numbering and distinguishing the reporters themselves, and in the large treasure-house of my memory, revolving some things, storing up others, drawing out others. Nor yet was I myself when I did this, i.e. that my power whereby I did it, neither was it Thou, for Thou art the abiding light, which I consulted concerning all these, whether they were, what they were, and how to be valued; and I heard Thee directing and commanding me; and this I often do, this delights me, and as far as I may be freed from necessary duties, unto this pleasure have I recourse. Nor in all these which I run over consulting Thee, can I find any safe place for my soul, but in Thee; whither my scattered[39] members may be gathered, and nothing of me depart from Thee. And sometimes Thou admittest me to an affection, very unusual, in my inmost soul; rising to a strange sweetness, which if it were perfected in me, I know not what in it would not belong to the life to come. But through my miserable encumbrances I sink down again into these lower things, and am swept back by former custom, and am held, and greatly weep, but am greatly held. So much doth the burthen of a bad custom weigh us down. Here I can stay, but would not; there I would, but cannot; both ways, miserable.

[XLI] 66 Thus then have I considered the sicknesses of my sins in that threefold concupiscence,[40] and have called Thy right hand to my help. For with a wounded heart have I beheld Thy brightness, and stricken back I said, "who can attain thither? *I am cast away from the sight of Thine eyes.*" Thou art the Truth who presidest over all, but I through my covetousness,[41] would not indeed forego Thee, but would with Thee possess a lie; as no man would in such wise speak falsely, as himself to be ignorant of the truth. So then I lost Thee, because Thou vouchsafest not to be possessed with a lie.

[XLII] 67 Whom could I find to reconcile me to Thee? was I to have recourse to Angels? by what prayers? by what sacraments? Many endeavouring to return unto Thee, and of themselves unable, have, as I hear, tried this, and fallen into the desire of curious visions, and been accounted worthy to be deluded. For they, being high minded, sought Thee by the pride of learning, swelling out rather, than smiting upon, their breasts, and so by the agreement of their heart, drew unto themselves the *princes of the air*, the fellow-conspirators of their pride, by whom, through magical influences, they were deceived, seeking a mediator, by whom they might be purged, and there was none. For the devil it was, *transforming himself into an Angel of light*. And it much enticed proud flesh, that he had no body of flesh. For they were mortal, and sinners; but Thou, Lord, to whom they proudly sought to be reconciled, art immortal, and without sin. But a mediator between God and man, must have something like to God, something like to men; lest being in both like to man, he should be far from God: or if in both like God, too unlike man: and so not be a mediator. That deceitful mediator then, by whom in Thy secret judgments pride deserved to be deluded, hath one thing in common with man, that is sin; another, he would seem to have in common with God; and not being clothed with the mortality of flesh,[42] would vaunt himself to be immortal. But since *the wages of sin is death*, this hath he in common with men, that with them he should be condemned to death.

[XLIII] 68 But the true Mediator, Whom in Thy secret mercy Thou hast shewed to the humble, and sentest, that by His example also they might learn that same humility, that *Mediator between God and man, the Man Christ Jesus*, appeared betwixt mortal sinners and the immortal Just One; mortal with men, just with God: that because the wages of righteousness is life and peace, He might by a righteousness conjoined with God, make void that death of sinners, now made righteous, which He willed to have in common with them. Hence He was shewed forth to holy men of old; that so they, through faith in His Passion to come, as we through faith of it passed, might be saved. For as Man, He was a Mediator; but as the Word, not in the middle between God and man, because equal to God, and God with God, and together one God.

69 How hast Thou loved us,[43] good Father, who *sparedst not Thine only Son, but deliveredst Him up for us ungodly!* How hast Thou loved us, for whom, *He that thought it no robbery to be equal with Thee, was made subject even to the death of the cross,* He alone *free among the dead,*[44] having power to lay down His life, and power to take it again: for us to Thee both Victor and Victim, and therefore Victor, because the Victim; for us to Thee Priest and Sacrifice, and therefore Priest because the Sacrifice; making us to Thee, of servants, sons, by being born of Thee, and serving us. Well then is my hope strong in Him, that Thou *wilt heal all my infirmities,* by Him Who *sitteth at Thy right hand and maketh intercession for us;* else should I despair. For many and great are my infirmities, many they are, and great; but Thy medicine is mightier. We might imagine that Thy Word was far from any union with man, and despair of ourselves, unless He had been *made flesh and dwelt among us.*

70 Affrighted with my sins and the burthen of my misery, I had cast in my heart, and had purposed to *flee to the wilderness:* but Thou forbaddest me, and strengthenedst me, saying, *Therefore Christ died for all, that they which live may now no longer live unto themselves, but unto Him that died for them.* See, Lord, I *cast my care upon Thee,* that I may live, and *consider wondrous things out of Thy law.* Thou knowest my unskilfulness, and my infirmities; teach me, and heal me. He Thine only Son, *in Whom are hid all the treasures of wisdom and knowledge,* hath redeemed me with His blood. *Let not the proud speak evil of me;* because I meditate on my ransom, and eat and

drink, and communicate it; and *poor*, desired to be *satisfied* from Him, amongst those that *eat and are satisfied, and they shall praise the Lord who seek Him.*

––––––––––

Here, where Aug. breaks off the account of his life, it may be well to subjoin his own view of that wretched portion of it, which preceded his conversion and baptism. This he gives incidentally in answer to the Donatists, who, affecting great purity of discipline, would fain have undervalued his defences of the Faith on account of his sins, when he as yet belonged not to the Faith, being a heretic and unbaptized. (Serm. 3. in Ps. 36. sec. 19.) "Let them speak then against us what they will; we will love them, though against their will. For we know, brethren, we know their speeches; for which let us not be angry with them; bear it patiently with us. For they see that they have nothing to allege in the matter itself; so they turn their speeches against us, and begin to speak evil of us, many things which they know, many which they know not. For we were once, as the Apostle saith, 'foolish and unbelieving, and to every good work reprobate.' We were foolish and phrensied in a perverse error, we deny it not; and in proportion as we deny not what has past in us, do we the more praise God, Who hath forgiven us. Why then dost thou, after the manner of heretics, leave the matter, and betake thyself to the person? For what am I? What am I? Am I the Catholic Church? Am I the heritage of Christ diffused throughout all nations? Enough for me, that I am in it. Thou revilest my past ills; what great thing dost thou herein? I am severer against my ills, than thou; what thou revilest, I have condemned. Would thou wouldest imitate me, and thy error also might become past! Those are past ills, which they know of especially in this city. [Carthage. See b. iii.] For here we lived ill, which I confess; and in proportion as I rejoice in the

grace of God, so do I for my past sins—what shall I say?—
grieve? I should grieve, were it still I. But what shall I say?
joy? Neither can I say this; for would I had never been! Yet
whatsoever I have been, in the Name of Christ, it is past. But
what they now censure, they know not. For there are things
for which they may yet blame me, but it is too much for them
to know these. For I do toil much in my thoughts, struggling
against my evil suggestions, and having lasting and almost
continual conflict with the temptations of the enemy, who
would subvert me. I groan to God in my infirmity; and He
knoweth what my heart laboureth with, Who knoweth what
it bringeth forth. 'But to me it is a very small thing that I be
judged by you, or of man's judgment,' saith the Apostle, 'yea,
I judge not my own self.' For I know myself better than they,
and God better than myself. Let them not then reproach you
on our account, let them not, Christ forbid! For they say, 'And
who are they? and whence are they? we knew them evil here;
where were they baptized?' If they knew us well, they know
that once we sailed hence; they know that we tarried in a
foreign land; they know that we went and returned, different
men. We were not baptized here; but the Church, where we
were baptized, is known to the whole world. And there are
many of our brethren, who both know that we were baptized,
and were baptized with us. It is easy then to know this, if any
of the brethren are concerned on this account."

BOOK XI

A ug. breaks off the history of the mode whereby God led him to holy Orders, in order to "confess" God's mercies in opening to him the Scripture. Moses is not to be understood, but in Christ, not even the first words *In the beginning God created the heaven and the earth.* Answer to cavillers who asked, what did God before He created the heaven and the earth, and whence willed He at length to make them, whereas He did not make them before. Inquiry into the nature of Time.

[I] 1 Lord, since eternity is Thine, art Thou ignorant of what I say to Thee? or dost Thou see in time, what passeth in time? Why then do I lay in order before Thee so many relations? Not, of a truth, that Thou mightest learn them through me, but to stir up mine own and my readers' devotions towards Thee, that we may all say, *Great is the Lord, and greatly to be praised.* I have said already, and again will say, for love of Thy love do I this. For we pray also, and yet Truth hath said, *Your Father knoweth what you have need of, before you ask.* It is then our affections which we lay open unto Thee, confessing our own miseries, and Thy mercies upon us, that Thou mayest free us wholly, since Thou hast begun, that we may cease to be wretched in ourselves, and be blessed in Thee; seeing Thou hast called us, to become *poor in spirit, and meek, and mourners, and hungering and athirst after righteousness, and merciful, and pure in heart, and peace-makers*. See, I have told Thee many things, as I could and as I would, because Thou first wouldest that I should confess unto Thee, my Lord God. *For Thou art good, for Thy mercy endureth for ever*.

[II] 2 But how shall I suffice with the tongue of my pen to utter all Thy exhortations, and all Thy terrors, and comforts, and guidances, whereby Thou broughtest me to preach Thy Word, and dispense Thy Sacrament¹ to Thy people? And if I suffice to utter them in order, the drops² of time are precious with me; and long have I burned to *meditate in Thy law*, and therein to confess to Thee my skill and unskilfulness, the day-break of Thy enlightening, and the remnants of my darkness, until infirmity be swallowed up by strength. And I would not have aught besides steal away those hours which I find free from the necessities of refreshing my body and the powers of my mind, and of the service which we owe to men,³ or which though we owe not, we yet pay.

3 O Lord my God, give ear unto my prayer, and let Thy mercy hearken unto my desire: because it is anxious not for myself alone, but would serve brotherly charity; and Thou seest my heart, that so it is. I would sacrifice to Thee the service of my thought and tongue; do Thou give me, what I may offer Thee. For *I am poor and needy, Thou rich to all that call upon Thee*; Who, inaccessible to care,

carest for us. *Circumcise* from all rashness and all lying both *my* inward and outward *lips:* let Thy Scriptures be my pure delights: let me not be deceived in them, nor deceive out of them. Lord, hearken and pity, O Lord my God, Light of the blind, and Strength of the weak; yea also Light of those that see, and Strength of the strong; hearken unto my soul, and hear it *crying out of the depths.* For if thine ears be not with us in the depths also, whither shall we go? whither cry? *The day is Thine, and the night is Thine;* at Thy beck the moments flee by. Grant thereof a space for our meditations in the *hidden things of Thy law,* and close it not against us who *knock.* For not in vain wouldest Thou have the darksome secrets[4] of so many pages written; nor are those forests without their harts[5] which retire therein and range and walk; feed, lie down, and ruminate.[6] *Perfect* me, O Lord, and *reveal* them *unto me.* Behold, Thy voice is my joy; Thy voice exceedeth the abundance of pleasures. Give what I love: for I do love; and this hast Thou given: forsake not Thy own gifts, nor despise Thy green herb that thirsteth. Let me confess unto Thee whatsoever I shall find in Thy books, and *hear the voice of praise,* and drink-in Thee, and meditate on the *wonderful things out of Thy law;* even from the *beginning,* wherein *Thou madest the heaven and the earth,* unto the everlasting reigning of Thy holy city with Thee.

4 *Lord, have mercy on me, and hear my desire.* For it is not, I deem, of the earth, not of gold and silver, and precious stones, or gorgeous apparel, or honours and offices, or the pleasures of the flesh, or necessaries for the body and for this life of our pilgrimage: *all which shall be added*

unto those that seek Thy kingdom and Thy righteousness. Behold, O Lord my God, wherein is my desire. *The wicked have told me of delights, but not such as Thy law, O Lord.* Behold, wherein is my desire. Behold, Father, behold, and see and approve; and be it pleasing in the sight of Thy mercy, that I may find grace before Thee, that the inward parts of Thy words be *opened* to me *knocking.* I beseech by our Lord Jesus Christ Thy Son, *the Man of Thy right hand, the Son of man, whom Thou hast established for Thyself,* as Thy Mediator and ours, through Whom Thou soughtest us, not seeking Thee, but soughtest us, that we might seek Thee,—Thy *Word, through Whom Thou madest all things,* and among them, me also;—Thy Only-Begotten, through Whom Thou calledst to adoption the believing people, and therein me also;—I beseech Thee by Him, who *sitteth at Thy right hand, and intercedeth with Thee for us, in Whom are hidden all the treasures of wisdom and knowledge.* These do I seek in Thy books. *Of Him did Moses write;* this saith Himself; this saith the Truth.

[III] 5 I would hear and understand, how "In the Beginning Thou madest the heaven and earth." Moses wrote this, wrote and departed, passed hence from Thee to Thee; nor is he now before me. For if he were, I would hold him and ask him, and beseech him by Thee to open these things unto me, and would lay the ears of my body to the sounds bursting out of his mouth. And should he speak Hebrew, in vain will it strike on my senses, nor would aught of it touch my mind; but if Latin, I should know what he said. But whence should I know, whether he spake truth? Yea, and if I knew this also, should I know it from him? Truly within me, within, in the chamber of my thoughts, Truth, neither Hebrew, nor Greek, nor Latin, nor barbarian, without organs of voice or tongue, or sound of syllables, would say, "It is truth," and I forthwith should say confidently to that man of Thine, "thou sayest truly." Whereas then I cannot enquire of him, Thee, Thee I beseech, O Truth, full of Whom he spake truth, Thee, my God, I beseech, forgive my sins; and Thou, who gavest him Thy servant to speak these things, give to me also to understand them.

[IV] 6 Behold, the heavens and the earth are; they proclaim that they were created; for they change and vary.[7] Whereas whatsoever hath not been made, and yet is, hath nothing in it, which before it had not; and this it is, to change and vary. They proclaim also, that they made not themselves; "therefore we are, because we have been made; we were not therefore, before we were, so as to make ourselves." Now the evidence of the thing, is the voice of the speakers. Thou therefore, Lord, madest them; who art beautiful, for they are beautiful; who art good, for they are good; who Art, for they are; yet are they not beautiful nor good, nor are they, as Thou their Creator art; compared with Whom, they are neither beautiful, nor good, nor are. This we know, thanks be to Thee. And our knowledge, compared with Thy knowledge, is ignorance.

[V] 7 But how didst Thou *make the heaven and the earth?* and what the engine of Thy so mighty fabric? For it was not as a human artificer, forming one body from another, according to the discretion of his mind, which can in some way invest with such a form, as it seeth in itself by its inward eye.[8] And whence should he be able to do this, unless Thou hadst made that mind? and he invests with a form what already existeth, and hath a being, as clay, or stone, or wood, or gold, or the like. And whence should they be, hadst not Thou appointed them? Thou madest the artificer his body, Thou the mind commanding the limbs, Thou the matter whereof he makes any thing; Thou the apprehension whereby to take in his art, and see within what he doth without; Thou the sense of his body, whereby, as by an interpreter, he may from mind to matter, convey that which he doth, and report to his mind what is done; that it within may consult the truth, which presideth over itself, whether it be well done or no. All these praise Thee, the Creator of all. But how dost Thou make them? how, O God, didst Thou *make heaven and earth?* Verily, neither in the heaven, nor in the earth, didst Thou *make heaven and earth;* nor in the air, or waters, seeing these also belong to *the heaven and the earth;* nor in the whole world didst Thou make the whole world; because there was no place where to make it, before it was made, that it might be. Nor didst Thou hold any thing in Thy hand, whereof to make heaven and earth. For whence shouldest Thou have this, which Thou hadst not made, thereof to make any thing? For what is, but because Thou art? Therefore *Thou spakest, and they were made,* and *in Thy Word Thou madest them.*

[VI] 8 But how didst Thou speak? In the way that the *voice* came *out of the cloud, saying, This is my beloved Son?* For that voice passed by and passed away, began and ended; the syllables sounded and passed away, the second after the first, the third after the second, and so forth in order, until the last after the rest, and silence after the last. Whence it is abundantly clear and plain that the motion of a creature expressed it, itself temporal, serving Thy eternal will. And these Thy words, created for a time, the outward ear reported to the intelligent soul, whose inward ear lay listening to Thy Eternal Word. But she compared these words sounding in time, with that Thy Eternal Word in silence, and said "It is different, far different. These words are far beneath me, nor are they, because they flee and pass away; but the *Word of* my *Lord abideth* above me *for ever.*" If then in sounding and passing words Thou saidst that *heaven and earth should be made,* and so *madest heaven and earth,* there was a corporeal creature before heaven and earth, by whose motions in time that voice might take his course in time. But there was nought corporeal before *heaven and earth;* or if there were, surely thou hadst, without such a passing voice, created that, whereof to make this passing voice, by which to say, *Let the heaven and the earth be made.* For whatsoever that were, whereof such a voice were made, unless by Thee it were made, it could not be at all. By what Word then didst Thou speak, that a body might be made, whereby these words again might be made?

[VII] 9 Thou callest us then to understand the *Word, God, with* Thee *God,* Which is spoken eternally, and by It are all things spoken eternally. For what was spoken was not spoken successively, one thing concluded that the next might be spoken, but all things together and eternally.[9] Else have we time and change; and not a true eternity nor true immortality. This I know, O my God, and give thanks. I know, I confess to Thee, O Lord, and with me there knows and blesses Thee, whoso is not unthankful to assured Truth. We know, Lord, we know; since inasmuch as any thing is not which was, and is, which was not, so far forth it dieth and ariseth. Nothing then of Thy Word doth give place or replace, because It is truly immortal and eternal. And therefore unto the Word coeternal with Thee Thou dost at once and eternally say all that Thou dost say; and whatever Thou sayest shall be made is made; nor dost Thou make, otherwise than by saying; and yet are not all things made together, or everlasting, which Thou makest by saying.

[VIII] 10 Why, I beseech Thee, O Lord my God? I see it in a way; but how to express it, I know not, unless it be, that whatsoever begins to be, and leaves off to be, begins then, and leaves off then, when in Thy eternal Reason it is known, that it ought to begin or leave off; in which Reason nothing beginneth or leaveth off. This is Thy Word, which is also "the Beginning,[10] because also It speaketh unto us." Thus in the Gospel He speaketh through the flesh; and this sounded outwardly in the ears of men; that it might be believed and sought inwardly, and found in the eternal Verity; where the *good* and only

Master teacheth all His disciples. There, Lord, hear I Thy voice speaking unto me; because He speaketh unto us, who teacheth us; but He that teacheth us not, though He speaketh, to us He speaketh not. Who now teacheth us, but the unchangeable Truth? for even when we are admonished through a changeable creature; we are but led to the unchangeable Truth; where we learn truly, *while we stand and hear Him,* and *rejoice greatly because of the Bridegroom's voice,* restoring us to Him, from Whom we are. And therefore the Beginning, because unless It abided, there should not, when we went astray, be whither to return.[11] But when we return from error, it is through knowing that we return; and that we may know, He teacheth us, *because* He is *the Beginning, and speaking unto us.*

[IX] 11 In this *Beginning,* O God, *hast Thou made heaven and earth,* in Thy Word, in Thy Son, in Thy Power, in Thy Wisdom, in Thy Truth; wondrously speaking, and wondrously making. Who shall comprehend? Who declare it? What is that which gleams through me, and strikes my heart without hurting it; and I shudder and kindle? I shudder, inasmuch as I am unlike it; I kindle, inasmuch as I am like it. It is Wisdom, Wisdom's self which gleameth through me; severing my cloudiness which yet again mantles over me, fainting from it, through the darkness which for my punishment gathers upon me. For *my strength is brought down in need,* so that I cannot support my blessings, till Thou, Lord, Who hast been *gracious to all mine iniquities,* shalt *heal all my infirmities.* For *Thou shalt also redeem my life from corruption,*

and crown me with loving kindness and tender mercies, and
shalt satisfy my desire with good things, because my youth
shall be renewed like an eagle's. For *in hope we are saved,*
wherefore *we through patience wait for* Thy promises. Let
him that is able, Hear Thee inwardly discoursing out of
Thy oracle: I will boldly cry out, *How wonderful are Thy*
works, O Lord, in Wisdom hast Thou made them all; and
this *Wisdom* is the *Beginning,* and in that *Beginning* didst
Thou *make heaven and earth.*

[X] 12 Lo are they not full of their old leaven, who say
to us, "What was God doing before *He made heaven and*
earth?" "For if (say they) He were unemployed and
wrought not, why does He not also henceforth, and for
ever, as He did heretofore? For did any new motion arise
in God, and a new will to make a creature, which He had
never before made, how then would that be a true
eternity, where there ariseth a will, which was not? For
the will of God is not a creature, but before the creature;
seeing nothing could be created, unless the will of the
Creator had preceded. The will of God then belongeth to
His very Substance. And if aught have arisen in God's
Substance, which before was not, that Substance cannot
be truly called eternal. But if the will of God has been
from eternity that the creature should be, why was not
the creature also from eternity?"

[XI] 13 Who speak thus, do not yet understand Thee, O
Wisdom of God, Light of souls, understand not yet how
the things be made, which by Thee, and in Thee are made:
yet they strive to comprehend things eternal, whilst their

heart fluttereth between the motions of things past and to come, and is still unstable. Who shall hold it, and fix it, that it be settled awhile, and awhile catch the glory of that ever-fixed Eternity, and compare it with the times which are never fixed, and see that it cannot be compared; and that a long time cannot become long, but out of many motions passing by, which cannot be prolonged altogether; but that in the Eternal nothing passeth, but the whole is present; whereas no time is all at once present: and that all time past, is driven on by time to come, and all to come followeth upon the past; and all past and to come, is created, and flows out of that which is ever present? Who shall hold the heart of man, that it may stand still, and see how eternity ever still-standing, neither past nor to come, uttereth the times past and to come? Can my hand do this, or the hand of my mouth by speech bring about a thing so great?

[XII] 14 See, I answer him that asketh, "What did God before He *made heaven and earth?*" I answer not as one is said to have done merrily, (eluding the pressure of the question,) "He was preparing hell (saith he) for pryers into mysteries." It is one thing to answer enquiries, another to make sport of enquirers. So I answer not; for rather had I answer, "I know not," what I know not, than so as to raise a laugh at him who asketh deep things and gain praise for one who answereth false things. But I say that Thou, our God, art the Creator of every creature: and if by the name "heaven and earth," every creature be understood; I boldly say, "that before God made heaven and earth, He did not make any thing." For if He made, what did He make but a creature? And would I knew whatsoever I desire to know to my profit, as I know, that no creature was made, before there was made any creature.

[XIII] 15 But if any excursive brain rove over the images of forepassed times, and wonder that Thou the God Almighty and All-creating and All-supporting, Maker of heaven and earth, didst for innumerable ages forbear from so great a work, before Thou wouldest make it; let him awake and consider, that he wonders at false conceits. For whence could innumerable ages pass by, which Thou madest not, Thou the Author and Creator of all ages? or what times should there be, which were not made by Thee?[12] or how should they pass by, if they never were? Seeing then Thou are the Creator of all times, if any time was before Thou *madest heaven and earth*, why say they that Thou didst forego working? For that very time didst Thou make, nor could times pass by, before Thou madest those times. But if before *heaven and earth* there was no time, why is it demanded, what Thou then didst? For there was no "then," when there was no time.

16 Nor dost Thou by time, precede time: else shouldest Thou not precede all times. But Thou precedest all things past, by the sublimity of an ever-present eternity; and surpassest all future because they are future, and when they come, they shall be past; *but Thou art the Same, and Thy years fail not*. Thy years neither come nor go; whereas ours both come and go, that they all may come. Thy years stand together, because they do stand; nor are departing

thrust out by coming years, for they pass not away; but ours shall all be, when they shall no more be. Thy years are one day; and Thy day is not daily, but To-day, seeing Thy To-day gives not place unto to-morrow, for neither doth it replace yesterday. Thy To-day, is Eternity;[13] therefore didst Thou beget The Coeternal, to whom Thou saidst, *This day have I begotten Thee.* Thou hast made all things; and before all times Thou art: neither in any time was time not.

[XIV] 17 At no time then hadst Thou not made any thing, because time itself Thou madest. And no times are coeternal with Thee, because Thou abidest; but if they abode, they should not be times. For what is time? Who can readily and briefly explain this? Who can even in thought comprehend it, so as to utter a word about it? But what in discourse do we mention more familiarly and knowingly, than time? And, we understand, when we speak of it; we understand also, when we hear it spoken of by another. What then is time? If no one asks me, I know: if I wish to explain it to one that asketh, I know not: yet I say boldly, that I know, that if nothing passed away, time past were not; and if nothing were coming, a time to come were not; and if nothing were, time present were not. Those two times then, past and to come, how are they, seeing the past now is not, and that to come is not yet? But the present, should it always be present, and never pass into time past, verily it should not be time, but eternity. If time present (if it is to be time) only cometh into existence, because it passeth into time past, how can we say that either this is, whose cause of being is, that it shall not be; so, namely, that we cannot truly say that time is, but because it is tending not to be?

[XV] 18 And yet we say, "a long time" and "a short time;" still, only of time past or to come. A long time past (for example) we call an hundred years since; and a long time to come, an hundred years hence. But a short time past, we call (suppose) ten days since; and a short time to come, ten days hence. But in what sense is that long or short, which is not? For the past, is not now; and the future, is not yet. Let us not then say, "it is long;" but of the past, "it hath been long;" and of the future, "it will be long." O my Lord, my Light, shall not here also Thy Truth mock at man? For that past time which was long, was it long when it was now past, or when it was yet present? For then might it be long, when there was, what could be long; but when past, it was no longer; wherefore neither could that be long, which was not at all. Let us not then say, "time past hath been long:" for we shall not find, what hath been long, seeing that since it was past, it is no more; but let us say, "that present time was long;" because, when it was present, it was long. For it had not yet passed away, so as not to be; and therefore there was, what could be long; but after it was past, that ceased also to be long, which ceased to be.

19 Let us see then, thou soul of man, whether present time can be long: for to thee it is given to feel and to measure length of time. What wilt thou answer me? Are an hundred years, when present, a long time? See first,

whether an hundred years can be present. For if the first of these years be now current, it is present, but the other ninety and nine are to come, and therefore are not yet, but if the second year be current, one is now past, another present, the rest to come. And so if we assume any middle year of this hundred to be present, all before it, are past; all after it, to come; wherefore an hundred years cannot be present. But see at least whether that one which is now current, itself is present; for if the current month be its first, the rest are to come; if the second, the first is already past, and the rest are not yet. Therefore, neither is the year now current present; and if not present as a whole, then is not the year present. For twelve months are a year; of which whatever be the current month is present; the rest past, or to come. Although neither is that current month present; but one day only; the rest being to come, if it be the first; past, if the last; if any of the middle, then amid past and to come.

20 See how the present time, which alone we found could be called long, is abridged to the length scarce of one day. But let us examine that also; because neither is one day present as a whole. For it is made up of four and twenty hours of night and day: of which, the first hath the rest to come; the last hath them past; and any of the middle hath those before it past, those behind it to come. Yea, that one hour passeth away in flying particles. Whatsoever of it hath flown away, is past; whatsoever remaineth, is to come. If an instant of time be conceived, which cannot be divided into the smallest particles of moments, that alone is it, which may be called present. Which yet flies with

such speed from future to past, as not to be lengthened
out with the least stay. For if it be, it is divided into past
and future. The present hath no space. Where then is the
time, which we may call long? Is it to come? Of it we do
not say, "it is long;" because it is not yet, so as to be long;
but we say, "it will be long." When therefore will it be?
For if even then, when it is yet to come, it shall not be
long, (because what can be long, as yet is not,) and so it
shall then be long, when from future which as yet is not,
it shall begin now to be, and have become present, that
so there should exist what may be long; then does time
present cry out in the words above, that it cannot be long.

[XVI] 21 And yet, Lord, we perceive intervals of times,
and compare them, and say, some are shorter, and others
longer. We measure also, how much longer or shorter this
time is than that; and we answer, "This is double, or
treble; and that, but once, or only just so much as that."
But we measure times as they are passing, by perceiving
them; but past, which now are not, or the future, which
are not yet, who can measure? unless a man shall presume
to say, that can be measured, which is not. When then
time is passing, it may be perceived and measured; but
when it is past, it cannot, because it is not.

[XVII] 22 I ask, Father, I affirm not: O my God, rule and
guide me. "Who will tell me that there are not three times,
(as we learned when boys, and taught boys,) past, present,
and future; but present only, because those two are not? Or
are they also; and when from future it becometh present,
doth it come out of some secret place; and so, when retiring,

from present it becometh past? For where did they, who foretold things to come, see them, if as yet they be not? For that which is not, cannot be seen. And they who relate things past, could not relate them, if in mind they did not discern them, and if they were not, they could no way be discerned. Things then past and to come are."

[XVIII] 23 Permit me, Lord, to seek further. O my hope, let not my purpose be confounded. For if times past and to come be, I would know where they be. Which yet if I cannot, yet I know, wherever they be, they are not there as future, or past, but present. For if there also they be future, they are not yet there; if there also they be past, they are no longer there. Wheresoever then is whatsoever is, it is only as present. Although when past facts are related, there are drawn out of the memory, not the things themselves which are past, but words which, conceived by the images of the things, they, in passing, have through the senses left as traces in the mind. Thus my childhood, which now is not, is in time past, which now is not: but now when I recall its image, and tell of it, I behold it in the present, because it is still in my memory. Whether there be a like cause of foretelling things to come also; that of things which as yet are not, the images may be perceived before, already existing, I confess, O my God, I know not. This indeed I know, that we generally think before on our future actions, and that that forethinking is present, but the action whereof we forethink is not yet, because it is to come. Which, when we have set upon, and have begun to do what we were forethinking, then shall that action be; because then it is no longer future, but present.

24 Which way soever then this secret fore-perceiving of things to come be; that only can be seen, which is. But what now is, is not future, but present. When then things to come are said to be seen, it is not themselves which as yet are not, (that is, which are to be,) but their causes perchance or signs are seen, which already are. Therefore they are not future but present to those who now see that, from which the future, being fore-conceived in the mind, is foretold. Which fore-conceptions again now are; and those who foretel those things, do behold the conceptions present before them. Let now the numerous variety of things furnish me some example. I behold the day-break, I foreshew, that the sun is about to rise. What I behold, is present; what I foresignify, to come; not the sun, which already is; but the sun-rising, which is not yet. And yet did I not in my mind imagine the sun-rising itself, (as now while I speak of it,) I could not foretel it. But neither is that day-break which I discern in the sky, the sun-rising, although it goes before it; nor that imagination of my mind; which two are seen now present, that the other which is to be may be foretold. Future things then are not yet: and if they be not yet, they are not: and if they are not, they cannot be seen; yet foretold they may be from things present, which are already, and are seen.

[XIX] 25 Thou then, Ruler of Thy creation, by what way dost Thou teach souls things to come? For Thou didst teach Thy Prophets. By what way dost Thou, to whom nothing is to come, teach things to come; or rather of the future, dost teach things present? For, what is not, neither can it be taught. Too far is this way out of my ken:

it is too mighty for me, I cannot attain unto it; but from Thee I can, when Thou shalt vouchsafe it, O sweet light of my hidden eyes.

[XX] 26 What now is clear and plain is, that neither things to come nor past are. Nor is it properly said, "there be three times, past, present, and to come:" yet perchance it might be properly said, "there be three times; a present of things past, a present of things present, and a present of things future." For these three do exist in some sort, in the soul, but otherwhere do I not see them; present of things past, memory; present of things present, sight; present of things future, expectation. If thus we be permitted to speak, I see three times, and I confess there are three. Let it be said too, "there be three times, past, present, and to come:" in our incorrect way. See, I object not, nor gainsay, nor find fault, if what is so said be but understood, that neither what is to be, now is, nor what is past. For but few things are there, which we speak properly, most things improperly; still the things intended are understood.

[XXI] 27 I said then even now, we measure times as they pass, in order to be able to say, this time is twice so much as that one; or, this is just so much as that; and so of any other parts of time, which be measurable. Wherefore, as I said, we measure times as they pass. And if any should ask me, "How knowest thou?" I might answer, "I know, that we do measure, nor can we measure things that are not; and things past and to come, are not." But time present how do we measure, seeing it hath no space? It is measured while passing, but when it shall have passed, it is not measured; for there will be nothing to be measured. But whence, by what way, and whither passes it while it is a measuring? whence, but from the future? Which way, but through the present? whither, but into the past? From that therefore, which is not yet, through that, which hath no space, into that, which now is not. Yet what do we measure, if not time in some space? For we do not say, single, and double, and triple, and equal, or any other like way that we speak of time, except of spaces of times. In what space then do we measure time passing? In the future, whence it passeth through? But what is not yet, we measure not. Or in the present, by which it passes? but no space, we do not measure: or in the past, to which it passes? But neither do we measure that, which now is not.

[XXII] 28 My soul is on fire to know this most intricate enigma. Shut it not up, O Lord my God, good Father; through Christ I beseech Thee, do not shut up these usual, yet hidden things, from my desire, that it be hindered from piercing into them; but let them dawn through Thy enlightening mercy, O Lord. Whom shall I enquire of concerning these things? and to whom shall I more fruitfully confess my ignorance, than to Thee, to Whom these my studies, so vehemently kindled toward Thy Scriptures, are not troublesome? Give what I love; for I do love, and this hast Thou given me. Give, Father, Who *truly knowest to give good gifts unto Thy children.* Give, because I have taken upon me to know, and trouble is before me until Thou openest it. By Christ I beseech Thee, in His Name, Holy of holies, let no man disturb me. For *I believed, and therefore do I speak*. This is my hope, for this do I live, that *I may contemplate the delights of the Lord*. Behold, *Thou hast made my days* old, and they pass away, and how, I know not. And we talk of time, and time, and times, and times, "How long time is it since he said this;" "how long time since he did this;" and "how long time since I saw that;" and "this syllable hath double time to that single short syllable." These words we speak, and these we hear, and are understood, and understand. Most manifest and ordinary they are, and the self-same things again are but too deeply hidden, and the discovery of them were new.

[XXIII] 29 I heard once from a learned man, that the motions of the sun, moon, and stars, constituted time, and I assented not. For why should not the motions of all bodies rather be times? Or, if the lights of heaven should cease, and a potter's wheel run round, should there be no time by which we might measure those whirlings, and say, that either it moved with equal pauses, or if it turned sometimes slower, otherwhiles quicker, that some rounds were longer, other shorter? Or, while we were saying this, should we not also be speaking in time? Or, should there in our words be some syllables short, others long, but because those sounded in a shorter time, these in a longer? God, grant to men to see in a small thing notices common to things great and small. The stars and lights of heaven, are also *for signs, and for seasons, and for years, and for days;* they are; yet neither should I say, that the going round of that wooden wheel was a day, nor yet he, that it was therefore no time.

30 I desire to know the force and nature of time, by which we measure the motions of bodies, and say (for example) this motion is twice as long as that. For I ask, Seeing "day" denotes not the stay only of the sun upon the earth, (according to which day is one thing, night another;) but also its whole circuit from east to east again; according to which we say, "there passed so many days," the night being included when we say, "so many days," and the nights not reckoned apart;—seeing then a day is completed by the motion of the sun and by his circuit from east to east again, I ask, does the motion alone make the day, or the stay in which that motion is completed, or both? For if the first be the day; then should we have a day, although the sun should finish that course in so small a space of time, as one hour comes to. If the second, then should not that make a day, if between one sun-rise and another there were but so short a stay, as one hour comes to; but the sun must go four and twenty times about, to complete one day. If both, then neither could that be called a day, if the sun should run his whole round in the space of one hour; nor that, if, while the sun stood still, so much time should overpass, as the sun usually makes his whole course in, from morning to morning. I will not therefore now ask, what that is which is called day; but, what time is, whereby we, measuring the circuit of the sun, should say that it was finished in half the time it was wont, if so be it was finished in so small a space as twelve hours; and comparing both times, should call this a single time, that a double time; even supposing the sun to run his round from east to east, sometimes in that single, sometimes in that double time. Let no man then tell me, that the motions

of the heavenly bodies constitute times, because, when at the prayer of one, the sun had stood still, till he could achieve his victorious battle, the sun stood still, but time went on. For in its own allotted space of time was that battle waged and ended. I perceive time then to be a certain extension. But do I perceive it, or seem to perceive it? Thou, Light and Truth, wilt shew me.

[XXIV] 31 Dost Thou bid me assent, if any define time to be "motion of a body?" Thou dost not bid me. For that no body is moved, but in time, I hear; this Thou sayest; but that the motion of a body is time, I hear not; thou sayest it not. For when a body is moved, I by time measure, how long it moveth, from the time it began to move, until it left off? And if I did not see whence it began; and it continue to move so that I see not when it ends, I cannot measure, save perchance from the time I began, until I cease to see. And if I look long, I can only pronounce it to be a long time, but not how long; because when we say "how long," we do it by comparison; as, "this is as long as that," or "twice so long as that," or the like. But when we can mark the distances of the places, whence and whither goeth the body moved, or his parts, if it moved as in a lathe, then can we say precisely, in how much time the motion of that body or his part, from this place unto that, was finished. Seeing therefore the motion of a body is one thing, that by which we measure how long it is, another; who sees not, which of the two is rather to be called time? For and if a body be sometimes moved, sometimes stands still, then we measure, not his motion only, but his standing still too by time; and we say, "it stood still, as much as it moved;" or "it stood still twice or thrice so long as it moved;" or any other space which our measuring hath either ascertained, or guessed; more or less, as we use to say. Time then is not the motion of a body.

[XXV] 32 And I confess to Thee, O Lord, that I yet know not what time is, and again I confess unto Thee, O Lord, that I know that I speak this in time, and that having long spoken of time, that very "long" is not long, but by the pause of time. How then know I this, seeing I know not what time is? or is it perchance that I know not how to express what I know? Woe is me, that do not even know, what I know not. Behold, O my God, before Thee I lie not; but as I speak, so is my heart. *Thou shalt light my candle; Thou, O Lord my God, wilt enlighten my darkness.*

[XXVI] 33 Does not my soul most truly confess unto Thee, that I do measure times? Do I then measure, O my God, and know not what I measure? I measure the motion of a body in time; and the time itself do I not measure? Or could I indeed measure the motion of a body how long it were, and in how long space it could come from this place to that, without measuring the time in which it is moved? This same time then, how do I measure? do we by a shorter time measure a longer, as by the space of a cubit, the space of a rood? for so indeed we seem by the space of a short syllable, to measure the space of a long syllable, and to say that this is double the other. Thus measure we the spaces of stanzas, by the spaces of the verses, and the spaces of the verses, by the spaces of the feet, and the spaces of the feet, by the spaces of the syllables, and the spaces of long, by the spaces of short syllables; not measuring by pages, (for then we measure spaces, not times;) but when we utter the words and they pass by, and we say "it is a long stanza, because composed of so many verses; long verses, because consisting of so many feet; long feet, because prolonged by so many syllables; a long syllable because double to a short one." But neither do we this way obtain any certain measure of time; because it may be, that a shorter verse, pronounced more fully, may take up more time than a longer, pronounced hurriedly. And so for a verse, a foot, a syllable. Whence it seemed to me, that time is nothing else than protraction; but of what, I know not; and I marvel, if it be not of the mind itself? For what I beseech Thee, O my God, do I measure, when I say, either indefinitely "this is a longer time than that," or definitely "this is double that?" That I measure time, I know; and yet I measure not time to come, for it is not yet; nor present, because it is not protracted by any space; nor past, because it now is not. What then do I measure? Times passing, not past? for so I said.

[XXVII] 34 Courage, my mind, and press on mightily. God is our helper, He *made us, and not we ourselves*. Press on where truth begins to dawn. Suppose, now, the voice of a body begins to sound, and does sound, and sounds on, and list, it ceases; it is silence now, and that voice is past, and is no more a voice. Before it sounded, it was to come, and could not be measured, because as yet it was not, and now it cannot, because it is no longer. Then therefore while it sounded, it might; because there then was what might be measured. But yet even then it was not at a stay; for it was passing on, and passing away. Could it be measured the rather, for that? For while passing, it was being extended into some space of time, so that it might be measured, since the present hath no space. If therefore then it might, then, lo, suppose another voice hath begun to sound, and still soundeth in one continued tenor without any interruption; let us measure it while it sounds; seeing when it hath left sounding, it will then be past, and nothing left to be measured; let us measure it verily, and tell how much it is. But it sounds still, nor can it be measured but from the instant it began in, unto the end it left in. For the very space between is the thing we measure, namely, from some beginning unto some end. Wherefore, a voice that is not yet ended, cannot be measured, so that it may be said how long, or short it is; nor can it be called equal to another, or double to a single, or the like. But when ended, it no longer is. How may it then be measured? And yet we measure times; but yet neither those which are not yet, nor those which no longer are, nor those which are not lengthened out by some pause, nor those which have no bounds. We measure neither times to come, nor past, nor present, nor passing; and yet we do measure times.

35 "Deus Creator omnium," this verse of eight syllables alternates between short and long syllables. The four short then, the first, third, fifth, and seventh, are but single, in respect of the four long, the second, fourth, sixth, and eighth. Every one of these, to every one of

those, hath a double time: I pronounce them, report on them, and find it so, as one's plain sense perceives. By plain sense then, I measure a long syllable by a short, and I sensibly find it to have twice so much; but when one sounds after the other, if the former be short, the latter long, how shall I detain the short one, and how, measuring, shall I apply it to the long, that I may find this to have twice so much; seeing the long does not begin to sound, unless the short leaves sounding? And that very long one do I measure as present, seeing I measure it not till it be ended? Now his ending is his passing away. What then is it I measure? where is the short syllable by which I measure? where the long which I measure? Both have sounded, have flown, passed away, are no more; and yet I measure, and confidently answer (so far as is presumed on a practised sense) that as to space of time this syllable is but single, that double. And yet I could not do this, unless they were already past and ended. It is not then themselves, which now are not, that I measure, but something in my memory, which there remains fixed.

36 It is in thee, my mind, that I measure times. Interrupt me not, that is, interrupt not thyself with the tumults of thy impressions. In thee I measure times; the impression, which things as they pass by cause in thee, remains even when they are gone; this it is which still present, I measure, not the things which pass by to make this impression. This I measure, when I measure times. Either then this is time, or I do not measure times. What when we measure silence, and say that this silence hath held as long time as did that voice? do we not stretch out our thought to the measure

of a voice, as if it sounded that so we may be able to report of the intervals of silence in a given space of time? For though both voice and tongue be still, yet in thought we go over poems, and verses, and any other discourse, or dimensions of motions, and report as to the spaces of times, how much this is in respect of that, no otherwise than if vocally we did pronounce them. If a man would utter a lengthened sound, and had settled in thought how long it should be, he hath in silence already gone through a space of time, and committing it to memory, begins to utter that speech, which sounds on, until it be brought unto the end proposed. Yea it hath sounded, and will sound; for so much of it as is finished, hath sounded already, and the rest will sound. And thus passeth it on, until the present intent conveys over the future into the past; the past increasing by the diminution of the future, until by the consumption of the future, all is past.

[XXVIII] 37 But how is that future diminished or consumed, which as yet is not? or how that past increased, which is now no longer, save that in the mind which enacteth this, there be three things done? For it expects, it considers, it remembers; that so that which it expecteth, through that which it considereth, passeth into that which it remembereth. Who therefore denieth, that things to come are not as yet? and yet, there is in the mind an expectation of things to come. And who denies past things to be now no longer? and yet is there still in the mind a memory of things past. And who denieth that the present time hath no space, because it passeth away in a moment? and yet our consideration continueth, through which that which shall be present proceedeth to become absent. It is not then future time, that is long, for as yet it is not: but a "long future," is "a long expectation of the future," nor is it time past, which now is not, that is long; but a long past, is "a long memory of the past."

38 I am about to repeat a Psalm that I know. Before I begin, my expectation is extended over the whole; but when I have begun, how much soever of it I shall separate off into the past, is extended along my memory; thus the life of this action of mine is divided between my memory as to what I have repeated, and expectation as to what I am about to repeat; but "consideration" is present with me, that through it what was future, may be conveyed over, so as to become past. Which the more it is done again and again, so much the more the expectation being shortened, is the memory enlarged; till the whole expectation be at length exhausted, when that whole action being ended, shall have passed into memory. And this which takes place in the whole Psalm, the same takes place in each several portion of it, and each several syllable; the same holds in that longer action, whereof this Psalm may be a part; the same holds in the whole life of man, whereof all the actions of man are parts; the same holds through the whole age of the sons of men, whereof all the lives of men are parts.

[XXIX] 39 But because *Thy loving kindness is better than all lives*, behold, my life is but a distraction, and *Thy right hand upheld me*, in my Lord the *Son of man*, the *Mediator betwixt Thee*, The One, and us many, many[14] also through our manifold distractions amid many things, that by Him *I may apprehend in Whom I have been appre- hended*, and may be re-collected from my old conversation, to follow The One, *forgetting what is behind, and* not distended but *extended*, not to things which shall be and shall pass away, but *to those things which are before*, not distractedly but intently, *I follow on for the prize of my heavenly calling*, where I may *hear the voice of* Thy *praise*, and *contemplate* Thy *delights*, neither to come, nor to pass away. But now *are my years spent in mourning*. And Thou, O Lord, art my comfort, my Father everlasting, but I have been severed amid times, whose order I know not; and my thoughts, even the inmost bowels of my soul, are rent and mangled with tumultuous varieties, until I flow together into Thee, purified and molten by the fire of Thy love.

[XXX] 40 And now will I stand, and become firm in Thee, in my mould, Thy truth; nor will I endure the questions of men, who by a penal disease thirst for more than they can contain, and say, "what did God before He *made heaven and earth?*" "Or, how came it into His mind to make any thing, having never before made any thing?" Give them, O Lord, well to bethink themselves what they say, and to find, that "never" cannot be predicated, when "time" is not. This then that He is said "never to have made;" what else is it to say, than "in 'no time' to have made?" Let them see therefore, that time cannot be without created being,[15] and cease to *speak* that *vanity*. May they also be *extended towards those things which are before;* and understand Thee before all times, the eternal

Creator of all times, and that no times be coeternal with Thee, nor any creature, even if there be any creature before all times.

[XXXI] 41 O Lord my God, what a depth is that recess of Thy mysteries, and how far from it have the consequences of my transgressions cast me! Heal mine eyes, that I may share the joy of Thy light. Certainly, if there be a mind gifted with such vast knowledge and fore-knowledge, as to know all things past and to come, as I know one well-known Psalm, truly that mind is passing wonderful, and fearfully amazing; in that nothing past, nothing to come in after-ages, is any more hidden from him, than when I sung that Psalm, was hidden from me what, and how much of it had passed away from the beginning, what, and how much there remained unto the end. But far be it that Thou the Creator of the Universe, the Creator of souls and bodies, far be it, that Thou shouldest in such wise know all things past and to come. Far, far more wonderfully, and far more mysteriously, dost thou know them. For not, as the feelings of one who singeth what he knoweth, or heareth some well-known song, are through expectation of the words to come, and the remembering of those that are past, varied, and his senses divided,—not so doth any thing happen unto Thee, unchangeably eternal, that is, the eternal[16] Creator of minds. Like then as Thou *in the Beginning* knewest *the heaven and the earth*, without any variety of Thy knowledge, so *madest* Thou *in the Beginning heaven and earth*, without any distraction of Thy action. Whoso understandeth, let him confess unto Thee; and whoso understandeth not, let him confess unto Thee. Oh how high art Thou, and yet the humble in heart are Thy dwelling-place; for Thou *raisest up those that are bowed down*, and they fall not, whose elevation Thou art.

BOOK XII

Aug. proceeds to comment on Gen. l. 1, and explains the "heaven" to mean that spiritual and incorporeal creation, which cleaves to God unintermittingly, always beholding His countenance; "earth," the formless matter whereof the corporeal creation was afterwards formed. He does not reject, however, other interpretations, which he adduces, but rather confesses that such is the depth of Holy Scripture, that manifold senses may and ought to be extracted from it, and that whatever truth can be obtained from its words, does, in fact, lie concealed in them.

[I] 1 My heart, O Lord, touched with the words of Thy holy Scripture, is much busied, amid this poverty of my life. And therefore mosttimes, is the poverty of human understanding copious in words, because enquiring hath more to say than discovering, and demanding is longer than obtaining, and our hand that knocks, hath more work to do, than our hand that receives. We hold the promise, who shall make it null? *If God be for us, who can be against us? Ask, and ye shall have; seek, and ye shall find; knock, and it shall be opened unto you. For every one that asketh, receiveth; and he that seeketh, findeth; and to him that knocketh, shall it be opened.* These be Thine own promises: and who need fear to be deceived, when the Truth promiseth?

[II] 2 The lowliness of my tongue confesseth unto Thy Highness, that Thou *madest heaven and earth;* this heaven which I see, and this earth that I tread upon, whence is this earth that I bear about me; Thou madest it. But where is that *heaven of heavens,* O Lord, which we hear of in the words of the Psalm, *The heaven of heavens*[1] *are the Lord's; but the earth hath he given to the children of men?* Where is that heaven which we see not, to which all this which we see is earth? For this corporeal whole, not being wholly every where, hath in such wise received its portion of beauty in these lower parts, whereof the lowest is this our earth; but to that *heaven of heavens,* even the heaven of our earth, is but earth: yea both these great bodies, may not absurdly be called *earth,* to that unknown *heaven, which is the Lord's, not the sons' of men.*

[III] 3 And now this *earth* was *invisible* and *without form,* and there was I know not what depth of abyss, upon which there was no light, because it had no shape. Therefore didst Thou command it to be written, that *darkness was upon the face of the deep;* what else than the absence of light?[2] For had there been light, where should it have been but by being over all, aloft, and enlightening? Where then light was not, what was the presence of darkness, but the absence of light? *Darkness* therefore *was upon* it, because light was not upon it; as where sound is not, there is silence. And what is it to have silence there, but to have no sound there? Hast not Thou, O Lord, taught this soul, which confesseth unto Thee? Hast not Thou taught me, Lord, that before Thou formedst and diversifiedst this formless matter, there was nothing, neither colour, nor figure, nor body, nor spirit? and yet not altogether nothing; for there was a certain formlessness, without any beauty.

[IV] 4 How then should it be called, that it might be in some measure conveyed to those of duller mind, but by some ordinary word? And what, among all parts of the world can be found nearer to an absolute formlessness, than *earth* and *deep*? For, occupying the lowest stage, they are less beautiful than the other higher parts are, transparent all and shining. Wherefore then may I not conceive the formlessness of matter (which Thou hadst created without beauty, whereof to make this beautiful world) to be suitably intimated unto men, by the name of *earth invisible and without form*.

[V] 5 So that when thought seeketh what the sense may conceive under this, and saith to itself, "It is no intellectual form, as life, or justice; because it is the matter of bodies; nor object of sense, because being *invisible*, and without form, there was in it no object of sight or sense;"—while man's thought thus saith to itself, it may endeavour either to know it, by being ignorant of it; or to be ignorant, by knowing it.

[VI] 6 But I, Lord, if I would, by my tongue and my pen, confess unto Thee the whole, whatever Thyself hath taught me of that matter,—the name whereof hearing before, and not understanding, when they who understood it not, told me of it, so I conceived³ of it as having innumerable forms and diverse, and therefore did not conceive it at all, my mind tossed up and down foul and horrible "forms" out of all order, but yet "forms;" and I called it *without form* not that it wanted all form, but because it had such as my mind would, if presented to it, turn from, as unwonted and jarring, and human frailness would be troubled at. And still that which I conceived, was *without form,* not as being deprived of all form, but in comparison of more beautiful forms; and true reason did persuade me, that I must utterly uncase it of all remnants of form whatsoever, if I would conceive matter absolutely *without form*; and I could not; for sooner could I imagine that not to be at all, which should be deprived of all form, than conceive a thing betwixt form and nothing, neither formed, nor nothing, a formless almost nothing. So my mind gave over to question thereupon with my spirit, it being filled with the images of formed bodies, and changing and varying them, as it willed; and I bent myself to the bodies themselves, and looked more deeply into their changeableness, by which they cease to be what they have been, and begin to be what they were not; and this same shifting from form to form, I suspected to be through a certain formless state,⁴ not through a mere nothing; yet this I longed to know, not to suspect only. —If then my voice and pen would confess unto Thee the whole, whatsoever knots Thou

CONFESSIONS OF ST. AUGUSTINE

didst open for me in this question, what reader would hold out to take in the whole? Nor shall my heart for all this cease to give Thee honour, and a song of praise, for those things which it is not able to express. For the changeableness of changeable things, is itself capable of all those forms, into which these changeable things are changed. And this changeableness, what is it? Is it soul? Is it body? Is it that which constituteth soul or body? Might one say, "a nothing something," an "is, is not,"[5] I would say, this were it: and yet in some way was it even then, as being capable of receiving these visible and compound figures.

[VII] 7 But whence had it this degree of being, but from Thee, from Whom are all things, so far forth as they are? But so much the further from Thee, as the unliker Thee; for it is not farness of place. Thou therefore, Lord, Who art not one in one place, and otherwise in another, but the Self-same,[6] and the Self-same, and the Self-same, *Holy, Holy, Holy, Lord God Almighty,* didst *in the Beginning,* which is of Thee, in Thy Wisdom, which was born of Thine own Substance, create something, and that out of nothing. For Thou *createdst heaven and earth*; not out of Thyself;[7] for so should they have been equal to Thine Only Begotten Son, and thereby to Thee also; whereas no way were it right that aught should be equal to Thee, which was not of Thee. And aught else besides Thee was there not, whereof Thou mightest create them, O God, One Trinity, and Trine Unity; and therefore out of nothing didst Thou *create heaven and earth*; a great thing, and a small thing; for Thou art Almighty and Good, to make all things good, even the great heaven, and the petty earth. Thou wert, and nothing was there besides, out of which Thou *createdst heaven and earth*; things of two sorts; one near Thee, the other near to nothing;[8] one, to which Thou alone shouldest be superior; the other, to which nothing should be inferior.

[VIII] 8 But that *heaven of heavens was for Thyself, O Lord*; but the *earth* which *Thou gavest to the sons of men*, to be seen and felt, was not such as we now see and feel. For it was *invisible, without form*, and there was a *deep*, upon which there was no light; or, *darkness was* above *the deep*, that is, more than in the deep. Because this *deep* of waters, visible now, hath even in his depths, a light proper for its nature; perceivable in whatever degree unto the fishes, and creeping things in the bottom of it. But that whole deep was almost nothing, because hitherto it was altogether *without form*; yet there was already that which could be formed. For Thou, Lord, madest the world of a matter *without form*, which out of nothing, Thou madest next to nothing, thereof to make those great things, which we sons of men wonder at. For very wonderful is this corporeal heaven; of which *firmament between water and water*, the second day, after the creation of light, Thou saidst, *Let it be made, and it was made.* Which *firmament* Thou *calledst heaven*; the heaven, that is, to this earth and sea, which Thou madest the third day, by giving a visible figure to the formless matter, which Thou madest before all days. For already hadst Thou made both an heaven, before all days; but that was the heaven of this heaven; because *In the beginning Thou* hadst *made heaven and earth*. But this same earth which Thou madest, was formless matter, because *it was invisible and without form, and darkness was upon the deep*, of which *invisible earth* and *without form*, of which formlessness, of which almost nothing, Thou mightest make all these things of which this changeable world consists, but subsists not;⁹ whose very changeableness appears therein, that times can be observed and numbered in it. For times are made by the alterations of things, while the figures, the matter whereof is the invisible earth aforesaid, are varied and turned.

[IX] 9 And therefore the Spirit, the Teacher of Thy servant,¹⁰ when It recounts Thee to have *In the Beginning created heaven and earth*, speaks nothing of times, nothing of days. For verily that *heaven of heavens* which Thou *createdst in the Beginning*, is some intellectual creature, which, although no ways coeternal unto Thee, the Trinity, yet partaketh of Thy eternity, and doth through the sweetness of that most happy contemplation of Thyself, strongly restrain its own changeableness; and without any fall since its first creation, cleaving close unto Thee, is placed beyond all the rolling vicissitude of times. Yea, neither is this very formlessness of the *earth invisible, and without form*, numbered among the days. For where no figure nor order is, there does nothing come, or go; and where this is not, there plainly are no days, nor any vicissitude of spaces of times.

[X] 10 O let the Light, the Truth, the Light of my heart, not mine own darkness, speak unto me. I fell off into that, and became darkened; but even thence, even thence I loved Thee. I went astray, and remembered Thee. *I heard Thy voice behind me*, calling to me to return, and scarcely heard it, through the tumultuousness of the enemies of peace.[11] And now, behold, I return in distress and panting after Thy fountain. Let no man forbid me! of this will I drink, and so live. Let me not be mine own life; from myself I lived ill, death was I to myself; and I revive in Thee. Do Thou speak unto me, do Thou discourse unto me. I have believed Thy Books, and their words be most full of mystery.

[XI] 11 Already Thou hast told me with a strong voice, O Lord, in my inner ear, that Thou art eternal, *Who only hast immortality*:[12] since Thou canst not be changed as to figure or motion, nor is Thy will altered by times: seeing no will which varies is immortal. This is in Thy sight clear to me, and let it be more and more cleared to me, I beseech Thee; and in the manifestation thereof, let me with sobriety abide under Thy wings. Thou hast told me also with a strong voice, O Lord, in my inner ear, that Thou hast made all natures and substances, which are not what Thyself is, and yet are; and that only is not from Thee, which is not, and the motion of the will from Thee who Art, unto that which in a less degree is, because such motion is transgression and sin;[13] and that no man's sin doth either hurt 'Thee, or disturb the order of Thy government, first or last.[14] This is in Thy sight clear unto me, and let it be more and more cleared to me, I beseech Thee: and in the manifestation thereof, let me with sobriety abide under Thy wings.

12 Thou hast told me also with a strong voice, in my inner ear, that neither is that creature coeternal unto Thyself, whose happiness Thou only art, and which with a most persevering purity, drawing its nourishment from Thee, doth in no place and at no time put forth its natural mutability; and, Thyself being ever present with it, unto Whom with its whole affection it keeps itself, having neither future to expect, nor conveying[15] into the past what it remembereth, is neither altered by any change, nor distracted into any times. O blessed creature, if such there be, for cleaving unto Thy Blessedness; blest in Thee, its eternal Inhabitant and its Enlightener! Nor do I find by what name I may the rather call *the heaven of heavens* which *is the Lord's,* than Thine house, which contemplateth Thy delights without any defection of going forth to another; one pure mind, most harmoniously one, by that settled estate of peace of holy spirits,[16] the citizens of Thy city in *heavenly places;* far above those heavenly places that we see.

13 By this may the soul, whose pilgrimage is made long and far away, by this may she understand, if she now *thirsts for Thee,* if *her tears be* now *become her bread, while they daily say unto her, Where is thy God?* if she now *seeks of Thee one thing,* and *desireth it, that she may dwell in Thy house all the days of her life;* (and what is her life, but Thou? and what Thy days, but Thy eternity, as *Thy years* which *fail not, because Thou art ever the same?*) by this then may the soul that is able, understand how far Thou art, above all times, eternal; seeing Thy house which at no time went into a far country, although it be not

coeternal with Thee, yet by continually and unfailingly cleaving unto Thee, suffers no changeableness of times. This is in Thy sight clear unto me, and let it be more and more cleared unto me, I beseech Thee, and in the manifestation thereof, let me with sobriety abide under Thy wings.

14 There is, behold, I know not what formlessness in those changes of these last and lowest creatures: and who shall tell me, (unless such a one as through the emptiness of his own heart, wanders and tosses himself up and down amid his own fancies?) who but such a one would tell me, that if all figure be so wasted and consumed away, that there should only remain that formlessness, through which the thing was changed and turned from one figure to another, that that could exhibit the vicissitudes of times? For plainly it could not, because, without the variety of motions, there are no times: and no variety, where there is no figure.

[XII] 15 These things considered, as much as Thou givest, O my God, as much as Thou stirrest me up to *knock*, and as much as Thou *openest* to me *knocking*, two things I find that Thou hast made, not within the compass of time, neither of which is coeternal with Thee. One, which is so formed, that without any ceasing of contemplation, without any interval of change, though changeable, yet not changed, it may thoroughly enjoy Thy eternity and unchangeableness; the other which was so formless, that it had not that, which could be changed from one form into another, whether of motion, or of repose, so as to become subject unto time. But this Thou didst not leave thus formless, because before all days, Thou *in the Beginning didst create Heaven and Earth*; the two things that I spake of. *But the Earth was invisible and without form, and darkness was upon the deep*. In which words, is the formlessness conveyed unto us, (that such capacities may hereby be drawn on by degrees, as are not able to conceive an utter privation of all form, without yet coming to nothing,) out of which another Heaven might be created, together with a visible and well-formed earth: and the waters diversly? ordered, and whatsoever further is in the formation of the world, recorded to have been, not without days, created; and that, as being of such nature, that the successive changes of times may take place in them, as being subject to appointed alterations of motions and of forms.

[XIII] 16 This then is what I conceive, O my God, when I hear Thy Scripture saying, *In the beginning God made Heaven and Earth: and the Earth was invisible and without form, and darkness was upon the deep*, and not mentioning what day Thou createdst them; this is what I conceive, that because of the *Heaven of heavens*,—that intellectual Heaven, whose Intelligences know all at once, not *in part*, not *darkly*, not *through a glass*, but as a whole, *in manifestation, face to face*; not, this thing now, and that thing anon; but (as I said) know all at once, without any succession of times;—and because of the *earth invisible and without form*,[17] without any succession of times, which succession presents "this thing now, that thing anon;" because where is no form, there is no distinction of things:—it is, then, on account of these two, a primitive formed, and a primitive formless; the one, *heaven* but *the Heaven of heaven*, the other *earth* but the earth *invisible and without form*; because of these two do I conceive, did Thy Scripture say without mention of days, *In the Beginning God created Heaven and Earth*. For forthwith it subjoined what earth it spake of; and also, in that the *Firmament* is recorded to be created the second day, and *called Heaven*, it conveys to us of which Heaven He before spake, without mention of days.

[XIV] 17 Wondrous depth of Thy words! whose surface, behold! is before us, inviting to little ones; yet are they a wondrous depth, O my God, a wondrous depth! It is awful to look therein; an awfulness of honour, and a trembling of love. *The enemies*[18] *thereof I hate* vehemently; oh that Thou wouldest *slay* them with Thy *two-edged sword*, that they might no longer be enemies unto it: for so do I love to have them slain unto themselves, that they may live unto Thee. But behold others not fault-finders, but extollers of the book of Genesis; "The Spirit of God," say they, "Who by His servant Moses wrote these things, would not have those words thus understood; He would not have it understood, as thou sayest, but otherwise, as we say." Unto Whom Thyself, O Thou God of us all, being Judge, do I thus answer.

[XV] 18 "Will you affirm that to be false, which with a strong voice Truth tells me in my inner ear, concerning the Eternity of the Creator, that His substance is no ways changed by time, nor His will separate from His substance? Wherefore He willeth not one thing now, another anon, but once, and at once, and always, He willeth all things that He willeth; not again and again, nor now this, now that; nor willeth afterwards, what before He willed not, nor willeth not, what before He willed; because such a will is mutable; and no mutable thing is eternal: but our God is eternal. Again, what He tells me in my inner ear, the expectation of things to come becomes sight, when they are come, and this same sight becomes memory, when they be past. Now all thought which thus varies is mutable; and no mutable is eternal: but our God is eternal." These things I infer, and put together, and find that my God, the eternal God, hath not upon any new will made any creature, nor doth His knowledge admit of any thing transitory.

19 "What will ye say then, O ye gainsayers? Are these things false?" "No," they say; "What then? Is it false, that every nature already formed, or matter capable of form, is not but from Him Who is supremely good, because He is supremely?" "Neither do we deny this," say they. "What then? do you deny this, that there is a certain sublime creature, with so chaste a love cleaving unto the true and truly eternal God, that although not coeternal with Him, yet is it not detached from Him, nor dissolved into the variety and vicissitude of times, but reposeth in the most true contemplation of Him only?" Because Thou, O God, unto him that loveth Thee so much as Thou commandest, dost shew Thyself, and sufficest him; and therefore doth he not decline from Thee, nor toward himself.[19] This is the house of God,[20] not of earthly mould, nor of any celestial bulk corporeal, but spiritual,

and partaker of Thy eternity, because without defection for ever. *For Thou hast made it fast for ever and ever, Thou hast given it a law which it shall not pass.* Nor yet is it coeternal with Thee, O God, because not without beginning; for it was made.

20 For although we find no time before it, for *wisdom was created before all things;* not that Wisdom which is altogether equal and coeternal unto Thee, our God, His Father, and by Whom all things were created, and *in* Whom, as *the Beginning, Thou createdst heaven and earth;* but that wisdom which is created, that is, the[21] intellectual nature, which by contemplating the light, is light. For this, though created, is also called wisdom. But what difference there is betwixt the Light which enlighteneth, and which is enlightened,[22] so much is there betwixt the Wisdom that createth, and that created; as betwixt the Righteousness which justifieth, and the righteousness which is made by justification. For we also are called Thy *righteousness:* for so saith a certain servant of Thine, *That we might be made the righteousness of God in Him.* Therefore since a certain created wisdom was created before all things, the rational and intellectual mind of that chaste city of Thine, *our mother which is above, and is free and eternal in the heavens;* (in what heavens, if not in those that *praise Thee, the Heaven of heavens?* Because this is also the *Heaven of heavens for the Lord;*)—though we find no time before it, (because that which hath been created before all things, precedeth also the creature of time,) yet is the Eternity of the Creator Himself before it, from Whom, being created, it took the beginning, not indeed of time, (for time itself was not yet,) but of its creation.

21 Hence it is so of Thee, our God, as to be altogether other than Thou, and not the Self-same: because though we find time neither before it, nor even in it, (it being meet ever to behold Thy face, nor is ever drawn away from it, wherefore it is not varied by any change,) yet is there in it a liability to change, whence it would wax dark, and chill, but that by a strong affection cleaving unto Thee, like perpetual noon, it shineth and gloweth from Thee. O *house* most lightsome and delightsome! *I have loved thy beauty, and the place of the habitation of the glory of my Lord*, thy builder and possessor. Let my wayfaring sigh after thee; and I say to Him that made thee, let Him take possession of me also in thee, seeing He hath made me likewise. *I have gone astray like a lost sheep: yet upon the shoulders of my Shepherd*, thy builder, hope I to be brought back to thee.

22 "What say ye to me, O ye gainsayers that I was speaking unto, who yet believe Moses to have been the holy servant of God, and his books the oracles of the Holy Ghost? Is not this *house* of God, not coeternal indeed with God, yet after its measure, *eternal in the heavens*, when you seek for changes of times in vain, because you will not find them? For that, to which it is ever *good to cleave fast to God*, surpasses all extension, and all revolving periods of time." "It is," say they. "What then of all that which my heart loudly uttered unto my God, when inwardly it *heard the voice of* His *praise*, what part thereof do you affirm to be false? Is it that the matter was *without form*, in which because there was no *form*, there was no order. But where no order was, there could be no vicissi-

tude of times: and yet this 'almost nothing', inasmuch as it was not altogether nothing, was from Him certainly, from Whom is whatsoever is, in what degree soever it is." "This also," say they, "do we not deny."

[XVI] 23 With these would I now parley a little in Thy presence, O my God, who grant all these things to be true, which Thy Truth whispers unto my soul. For those who deny these things, let them bark and deafen themselves as much as they please; I will essay to persuade them to quiet, and to open in them a way for Thy word. But if they refuse, and repel me; I beseech, O my God, *be not Thou silent to me*. Speak Thou truly in my heart; for only Thou so speakest: and I will let them alone blowing upon the dust without, and raising it up into their own eyes: and myself will *enter my chamber*, and sing there a song of loves unto Thee; groaning *with groanings unutterable*, in my wayfaring, and remembering Jerusalem, with heart lifted up towards it, Jerusalem my country, Jerusalem my mother, and Thyself that rulest over it, the Enlightener, Father, Guardian, Husband, the pure and strong delight, and solid joy, and all good things unspeakable, yea all at once, because the One Sovereign and true Good. Nor will I be turned away, until Thou gather all that I am, from this dispersed[23] and disordered estate, into the peace of that our most dear mother, where the *first-fruits of my spirit*[24] be already, (whence I am ascertained of these things,) and Thou conform and confirm it for ever, O my God, my Mercy. But those who do not affirm all these truths to be false, who honour Thy holy Scripture, set forth by holy Moses, placing it, as we, on the summit of authority to be followed, and do yet contradict me in some thing, I answer thus; Be Thyself Judge, O our God, between my Confessions and these men's contradictions.

[XVII] 24 For they say, "Though these things be true, yet did not Moses intend those two, when, by revelation of the Spirit, he said, *In the beginning God created heaven and earth*. He did not under the name of *heaven*, signify that spiritual or intellectual creature which always beholds the face of God; nor under the name of *earth*, that formless matter. "What then?" "That man of God," say they, "meant as we say, this declared he by those words." "What?" "By the name of *heaven* and *earth* would he first signify," say they, "universally and compendiously, all this visible world; so as afterwards by the enumeration of the several days, to arrange in detail, and, as it were, piece by piece, all those things, which it pleased the Holy Ghost thus to enounce. For such were that rude and carnal people to which he spake, that he thought them fit to be entrusted with the knowledge of such works of God only as were visible." They agree, however, that under the words *earth invisible and without form*, and that darksome *deep* (out of which it is subsequently shewn, that all these visible things which we all know, were made and arranged during those "days") may, not incongruously, be understood of this formless (first) matter.

25 What now if another should say, "That this same formlessness and confusedness of matter, was for this reason first conveyed under the name of *heaven and earth*, because out of it was this visible world with all

those natures which most manifestly appear in it, which is ofttimes called by the name of *heaven and earth*, created and perfected?" What again if another say, "that invisible and visible nature is not indeed inappropriately called *heaven and earth*; and so, that the universal creation, which God *made* in His Wisdom, that is, *in the Beginning*, was comprehended under those two words? Notwithstanding, since all things be made not of the substance of God, but out of nothing, (because they are not the same that God is, and there is a mutable nature in them all, whether they abide, as doth the eternal house of God, or be changed, as the soul and body of man are:) therefore the common matter of all things visible and invisible, (as yet unformed though capable of form,) out of which was to be created both *heaven and earth*, (i.e. the invisible and visible creature when formed,) was entitled by the same names given to the *earth invisible and without form* and the *darkness upon the deep*, but with this distinction, that by the *earth invisible and without form* is understood corporeal matter, antecedent to its being qualified by any form; and by the *darkness upon the deep*, spiritual matter, before it underwent any restraint of its unlimited fluidness, or received any light from Wisdom?"

26 It yet remains for a man to say, if he will, "that the already perfected and formed natures, visible and invisible, are not signified under the name of *heaven and earth*, when we read, *In the beginning God made heaven and earth*, but that the yet unformed commencement of things, the stuff apt to receive form and making, was called by these names, because therein were confusedly

contained, not as yet distinguished by their qualities and forms, all those things which being now digested into order, are called *Heaven* and *Earth*, the one being the spiritual, the other the corporeal, creation."

[XVIII] 27 All which things being heard and well considered, I will not *strive about words:* for that is *profitable to nothing, but the subversion of the hearers. But the law is good to edify, if a man use it lawfully: for that the end of it is charity, out of a pure heart and good conscience, and faith unfeigned.* And well did our Master know, upon which *two commandments* He *hung all the Law and the Prophets.* And what doth it prejudice me, O my God, Thou light of my eyes in secret, zealously confessing these things, since divers things may be understood under these words which yet are all true,— what, I say, doth it prejudice me, if I think otherwise than another thinketh the writer thought? All we readers verily strive to trace out and to understand his meaning whom we read; and seeing we believe him to speak truly, we dare not imagine him to have said any thing, which ourselves either know or think to be false. While every man endeavours then to understand in the holy Scriptures, the same as the writer understood, what hurt is it, if a man understand what Thou, the light of all true-speaking minds, dost shew him to be true, although he whom he reads, understood not this, seeing he also understood a Truth, though not this truth?

[XIX] 28 For true it is, O Lord, that Thou *madest heaven and earth*; and it is true too, that *the Beginning* is Thy *Wisdom*, in Which *Thou createdst all:* and true again, that this visible world hath for its greater parts the *heaven and the earth*, which briefly comprise all made and created natures. And true too, that whatsoever is mutable, gives us to understand a certain want of form, whereby it receiveth a form, or is changed, or turned. It is true, that that is subject to no times, which so cleaveth to the unchangeable Form, as, though subject to change, never to be changed. It is true, that that formlessness which is almost nothing, cannot be subject to the alteration of times. It is true, that that whereof a thing is made, may by a certain mode of speech, be called by the name of the thing made of it; whence that formlessness, whereof heaven and earth were made, might be called *heaven and earth*. It is true, that of things having form, there is not any nearer to having no form, than the *earth* and the *deep*. It is true, that not only every created and formed thing, but whatsoever is capable of being created and formed, Thou madest, *of whom are all things*. It is true, that whatsoever is formed out of that which had no form, was unformed before it was formed.

[XX] 29 Out of these truths, of which they doubt not whose inward eye Thou hast enabled to see such things, and who unshakenly believe Thy servant Moses to have spoken in the Spirit of truth;—of all these then, he taketh one, who saith, *In the Beginning God made the heaven and the earth*, that is, "in His word coeternal with Himself, God made the intelligible and the sensible, or the spiritual and the corporeal creature." He another, that saith, *In the Beginning God made heaven and earth;* that is, "in His Word coeternal with Himself, did God make the universal bulk of this corporeal world, together with all those apparent and known creatures, which it containeth." He another, that saith, *In the Beginning God made heaven and earth:* that is, "in His Word coeternal with Himself, did God make the formless matter[25] of creatures spiritual and corporeal." He another, that saith, *In the Beginning God created heaven and earth;* that is, "in His Word coeternal with Himself, did *God create* the formless matter of the creature corporeal, wherein *heaven and earth* lay as yet confused, which, being now distinguished and formed, we at this day see in the bulk of this world." He another, who saith, *In the Beginning God made heaven and earth,* that is, "in the very beginning of creating and working, did God *make* that formless matter, confusedly containing in itself both *heaven and earth;* out of which, being formed, do they now stand out, and are apparent, with all that is in them."

[XXI] 30 And with regard to the understanding of the words following, out of all those truths, he chooses one to himself, who saith, *But the earth was invisible, and without form, and darkness was upon the deep;* that is, "that corporeal thing that God made, was as yet a formless matter of corporeal things, without order, without light." Another he who says, *The earth was invisible and without form, and darkness was upon the deep;* that is, "this all, which is called *heaven and earth,* was still a formless and darksome matter, of which the corporeal heaven and the corporeal earth were to be made, with all things in them, which are known to our corporeal senses." Another he who says, *The earth was invisible and without form, and darkness was upon the deep;* that is, "this all, which is called *heaven and earth,* was still a formless and a darksome matter; out of which was to be made, both that intelligible *heaven,* otherwise called the *Heaven of heavens,* and the *earth,* that is, the whole corporeal nature, under which name is comprised this corporeal heaven also; in a word, out of which every visible and invisible creature was to be created." Another he who says, *The earth was invisible and without form, and darkness was upon the deep,* "the Scripture did not call that formlessness by the name of *heaven and earth;* but that formlessness, saith he, already was, which he called *the earth invisible without form, and darkness upon the deep;* of which he had before said, that *God* had *made heaven and earth,* namely, the spiritual and corporeal creature." Another he who says, *The earth was invisible and without form, and darkness was upon the deep;* that is, "there already was a certain formless matter, of which the Scripture said before, that *God made heaven and earth;* namely, the whole corporeal bulk of the world, divided into two great parts, upper and lower, with all the common and known creatures in them."

[XXII] 31 For should any attempt to dispute against these two last opinions, thus, "If you will not allow, that this formlessness of matter seems to be called by the name of *heaven and earth;* Ergo, there was something which God had not made, out of which to *make heaven and earth;* for neither hath Scripture told us, that God made this matter, unless we understand it to be signified by the name of *heaven and earth*, or of *earth* alone, when it is said, *In the Beginning God made the heaven and earth*; that so in what follows, *and the earth was invisible and without form*, (although it pleased Him so to call the formless matter,) we are to understand no other matter, but that which God made, whereof is written above, *God made heaven and earth*." The maintainers of either of those two latter opinions will, upon hearing this, return for answer, "we do not deny this formless matter to be indeed created by God, that God of Whom are all things, very good; for as we affirm that to be a greater good, which is created and formed, so we confess that to be a lesser good which is made capable of creation and form, yet still good. We say however that Scripture hath not set down, that God made this formlessness, as also it hath not many others; as the *Cherubim*, and *Seraphim*, and those which the Apostle distinctly speaks of, *Thrones, Dominions, Principalities, Powers*. All which that God made, is most apparent. Or if in that which is said, *He made heaven and earth*, all things be comprehended, what shall we say of the *waters, upon* which *the Spirit of God moved*? For if they be comprised in this word *earth*; how then can formless matter be meant in that name of *earth*, when we see the *waters* so beautiful? Or if it be so taken; why then is it written, that out of the same formlessness, the *firmament* was made, and *called heaven*; and *that the waters were made*, is not written? For the waters remain not formless and invisible, seeing we behold them flowing in so comely a manner. But if they then received that beauty, when God said, *Let the water which is under the firmament be gathered together*, that so the gathering together, be itself the forming of them; what will be answered as to those *waters which be above the firmament?* Seeing neither if formless would they have been worthy of so honourable a seat, nor is it written, by what word they were formed. If then Genesis is silent as to God's making of any thing, which yet that God did make neither sound faith nor well-grounded understanding doubteth, nor again will any sober teaching dare to affirm these *waters* to be coeternal with God, on the ground that we find them to be mentioned in the book of Genesis, but when they were created, we do not find; why (seeing truth teaches us) should we not understand that formless matter (which this Scripture calls the *earth invisible and without form, and darksome deep*) to have been created of God out of nothing, and therefore not to be coeternal to Him; notwithstanding this history hath omitted to shew when it was created?"

[XXIII] 32 These things then being heard and perceived, according to the weakness of my capacity, (which I confess unto Thee, O Lord, that knowest it,) two sorts of disagreements I see may arise, when a thing is in words related by true reporters; one, concerning the truth of the things, the other, concerning the meaning of the relater. For we enquire one way about the making of the creature, what is true; another way, what Moses, that excellent minister of Thy Faith, would have his reader and hearer understand by those words. For the first sort, away with all those who imagine themselves to know as a truth, what is false; and for this other, away with all them too, which imagine Moses to have written things that be false. But let me be united in Thee, O Lord, with those, and delight myself in Thee, with them that feed on Thy truth, in the largeness of charity, and let us approach together unto the words of Thy book, and seek in them for Thy meaning, through the meaning of Thy servant, by whose pen Thou hast dispensed them.

[XXIV] 33 But which of us shall, among those so many truths, which occur to enquirers in those words, as they are differently understood, so discover that one meaning, as to affirm, "this Moses thought," and "this would he have understood in that history;" with the same confidence as he would, "this is true," whether Moses thought this or that? For behold, O my God, I Thy servant, who have in this book vowed a sacrifice of confession unto Thee, and pray, that by Thy mercy I may *pay my vows unto Thee*, can I, with the same confidence wherewith I affirm, that in Thy incommutable world Thou createdst all things visible and invisible, affirm also, that Moses meant no other than this, when he wrote, *In the Beginning God made heaven and earth*? No. Because I see not in his mind, that he thought of this when he wrote these things, as I do see it in Thy truth to be certain. For he might have his thoughts upon God's commencement of creating, when he said *In the beginning;* and by *heaven and earth*, in this place he might intend no formed and perfected nature whether spiritual or corporeal, but both of them inchoate and as yet formless. For I perceive, that whichsoever of the two had been said, it might have been truly said; but which of the two he thought of in these words, I do not so perceive. Although, whether it were either of these, or any sense beside, (that I have not here mentioned,) which this so great man saw in his mind, when he uttered these words, I doubt not but that he saw it truly, and expressed it aptly.

[XXV] 34 Let no man harass me then, by saying, Moses thought not as you say, but as I say: for if he should ask me, "How know you that Moses thought that which you infer out of his words?" I ought to take it in good part,[26] and would answer perchance as I have above, or something more at large, if he were unyielding. But when he saith, "Moses meant not what you say, but what I say," yet denieth not that what each of us say, may both be true, O my God, life of the poor, in Whose bosom is no contradiction, pour down a softening dew into my heart, that I may patiently bear with such as say this to me, not because they have a divine Spirit, and have seen in the heart of Thy servant what they speak, but because they be proud; not knowing Moses' opinion, but loving their own, not because it is truth, but because it is theirs. Otherwise they would equally love another true opinion, as I love what they say, when they say true: not because it is theirs, but because it is true; and on that very ground not theirs because it is true. But if they therefore love it, because it is true, then is it both theirs, and mine; as being in common to all lovers of truth. But whereas they contend that Moses did not mean what I say, but what they say, this I like not, love not: for though it were so, yet that their rashness belongs not to knowledge, but to overboldness, and not insight but vanity was its parent. And therefore, O Lord, are Thy judgments terrible; seeing Thy truth is neither mine, nor his, nor another's; but belonging to us all, whom Thou callest publicly to partake of it, warning us terribly, not to account it private to ourselves, lest we be deprived of it. For whosoever challenges that as proper to himself, which Thou propoundest to all to enjoy, and would have that his own which belongs to all, is driven from what is in common to his own; that is, from truth, to a lie. For he *that speaketh a lie, speaketh it of his own.*

35 Hearken, O God, Thou best Judge; Truth Itself, hearken to what I shall say to this gainsayer, hearken, for before Thee do I speak, and before my brethren, who employ Thy *law lawfully, to the end of charity:* hearken and behold, if it please Thee, what I shall say to him. For this brotherly and peaceful word do I return unto Him: "If we both see that to be true that Thou sayest, and both see that to be true that I say, where, I pray Thee, do we see it? Neither I in thee, nor thou in me; but both in the unchangeable Truth itself, which is above our souls." Seeing then we strive not about the very light of the Lord our God, why strive we about the thoughts of our neighbour which we cannot so see, as the unchangeable Truth is seen: for that, if Moses himself had appeared to us and said, "This I meant;" neither so should we see it, but should believe it. Let us *not* then *be puffed up for one against another, above that which is written: let us love the Lord our God with all our heart, with all our soul, and with all our mind: and our neighbour as ourself.* With a

view to which two precepts of charity, unless we believe that Moses meant, whatsoever in those books he did mean, we shall *make God a liar*, imagining otherwise of our fellow servant's mind, than He hath taught us. Behold now, how foolish it is, in such abundance of most true meanings, as may be extracted out of those words, rashly to affirm, which of them Moses principally meant; and with pernicious contentions to offend charity itself, for whose sake he spake every thing, whose words we go about to expound.

[XXVI] 36. And yet I, O my God, Thou lifter up of my humility, and rest of my labour, Who hearest my confessions, and *forgivest my sins:* seeing Thou commandest me *to love my neighbour as myself,* I cannot believe that Thou gavest a less gift unto Moses Thy faithful servant, than I would wish or desire Thee to have given me, had I been born in the time he was, and hadst Thou set me in that office, that by the service of my heart and tongue those books might be dispensed, which for so long after were to profit all nations, and through the whole world from such an eminence of authority, were to surmount all sayings of false and proud teachings. I should have desired verily, had I then been Moses, (for we all come from the same lump, and *what is man, saving that Thou art mindful of him?*) I would then, had I been then what he was, and been enjoined by Thee to write the book of Genesis, have desired such a power of expression and such a style to be given me, that neither they who cannot yet understand how God created, might reject the sayings, as beyond their capacity; and they who had attained thereto, might find what true opinion soever they had by thought arrived at, not passed over in those few words of that Thy servant: and should another man by the light of truth have discovered another, neither should that fail of being discoverable in those same words.

[XXVII] 37 For as a fountain within a narrow compass, is more plentiful, and supplies a tide for more streams over larger spaces, than any one of those streams, which, after a wide interval, is derived from the same fountain; so the relation of that dispenser of Thine, which was to benefit many who were to discourse thereon, does out of a narrow scantling of language, overflow into streams of clearest truth, whence every man may draw out for himself such truth as he can upon these subjects, one, one truth, another, another, by larger circumlocutions of discourse. For some, when they read, or hear these words, conceive that God like a man or some mass endued with unbounded power, by some new and sudden resolution, did, exterior to itself, as it were at a certain distance, *create heaven and earth*, two great bodies above and below, wherein all things were to be contained. And when they hear, *God said, Let it be made, and it was made;* they conceive of words begun and ended, sounding in time, and passing away; after whose departure, that came into being, which was commanded so to do; and whatever of the like sort, men's acquaintance with the material world would suggest. In whom, being yet little ones and carnal, while their weakness is by this humble kind of speech, carried on, as in a mother's bosom, their faith is wholesomely built up, whereby they hold assured, that God made all natures, which in admirable variety their eye beholdeth around. Which words, if any despising, as too simple, with a proud weakness, shall stretch himself beyond the guardian nest; he will, alas, fall miserably. Have pity, O Lord God, lest they who go by the way trample on the unfledged bird, and send Thine angel to replace it into the nest, that it may live, till it can fly.

[XXVIII] 38 But others, unto whom these words are no longer a nest, but deep shady fruit-bowers, see the fruits concealed therein, fly joyously around, and with cheerful notes seek out, and pluck them. For reading or hearing these words, they see that all times past and to come, are surpassed by Thy eternal and stable abiding; and yet that there is no creature formed in time, not of Thy making. Whose will, because it is the same that Thou art, Thou madest all things, not by any change of will, nor by a will, which before was not, and that these things were not out of Thyself, in Thine own likeness, which is the form of all things, but out of nothing, a formless unlikeness, which should be formed by Thy likeness, (recurring to Thy Unity, according to their appointed capacity, so far as is given to each thing in his kind,) and might all be made very good; whether they abide around Thee, or being in gradation removed in time and place, make or undergo the beautiful variations of the Universe. These things they see, and rejoice, in the little degree they here may, in the light of Thy truth.

39 Another bends his mind on that which is said, *In the Beginning God made heaven and earth;* and beholdeth therein Wisdom, *the Beginning because*[27] *It also speaketh unto us.* Another likewise bends his mind on the same words, and by *Beginning* understands the commencement of things created; *In the beginning He made*, as if it were said, *He at first made.* And among them that understand *In the Beginning* to mean, "In Thy Wisdom *Thou createdst heaven and earth*," one believes the matter out of which the heaven and earth were to be created, to be there called *heaven and earth* another, natures already formed and distinguished; another, one formed nature, and that a spiritual, under the name *Heaven*, the other formless, of corporeal matter, under the name *Earth.* They again who by the names *heaven and earth*, understand matter as yet formless, out of which *heaven and earth* were to be formed, neither do they understand it in one way; but the one, that matter out of which both the intelligible and the sensible creature were to be perfected; another, that only, out of which this sensible corporeal mass was to be made, containing in its vast bosom these visible and ordinary natures. Neither do they, who believe the creatures already ordered and arranged, to be in this place called *heaven and earth*, understand the same; but the one, both the *invisible* and *visible*, the other, the *visible* only, in which we behold this lightsome heaven, and darksome earth, with the things in them contained.

[XXIX] 40 But he that no otherwise understands *In the Beginning He made*, than if it were said, *At first He made*, can only truly understand *heaven and earth* of the matter of *heaven and earth*, that is, of the universal intelligible and corporeal creation. For if he would understand thereby the universe, as already formed, it may be rightly demanded of him, "If God made this first, what made He afterwards?" and after the universe, he will find nothing; whereupon must he against his will hear another question; "How [did God make] this first, if nothing after?" But when he says, God made matter first formless, then formed, there is no absurdity, if he be but qualified to discern, what precedes by eternity, what by time, what by choice, and what in original. By eternity, as God is before all things; by time, as the flower before the fruit; by choice, as the fruit before the flower; by original, as the sound before the tune. Of these four, the first and last mentioned, are with extreme difficulty understood, the two middle, easily. For a rare and too lofty a vision is it, to behold Thy Eternity, O Lord, unchangeably making things changeable; and thereby before them. And who, again, is of so sharpsighted understanding, as to be able without great pains to discern, how the sound is therefore before the tune; because a tune is a formed sound; and a thing not formed, may exist; whereas that which existeth not, cannot be formed. Thus is the matter before the thing made;[28] not because it maketh it, seeing itself is rather made; nor is it before by interval of time; for we do not first in time utter formless sounds without singing, and subsequently adapt or fashion them into the form of a chant, as wood or silver, whereof a chest or vessel is fashioned. For such materials do by time also precede the forms of the things made of them, but in singing it is not so; for when it is sung, its sound is heard; for there is not first a formless sound, which is afterwards formed into a chant. For each sound, so soon as made, passeth away, nor canst thou find ought to recall and by art to compose. So then the chant is concentrated in its sound, which sound of his is his matter. And this indeed is formed, that it may be a tune; and therefore (as I said) the matter of the sound is before the form of the tune; not before, through any power it hath to make it a tune; for a sound is no way the workmaster of the tune; but is something corporeal, subjected to the soul which singeth, whereof to make a tune. Nor is it first in time; for it is given forth together with the tune; nor first in choice, for a sound is not better than a tune, a tune being not only a sound, but a beautiful sound. But it is first in original, because a tune receives not form to become a sound, but a sound receives a form to become a tune. By this example, let him that is able, understand how the matter of things was first made, and called *heaven and earth*, because *heaven and earth* were made out of it. Yet was it not made first in time; because the forms of things give rise to time;[29] but that was *without form;* but now is, in time, an object of sense together with its form. And yet nothing can be related of that matter, but as though prior in time, whereas in value it is last (because things formed are superior to things without form) and is preceded by the Eternity of the Creator: that so there might be out of nothing, whereof somewhat might be created.

[XXX] 41 In this diversity of the true opinions, let Truth herself produce concord. And our God have mercy upon us, that we may *use the law lawfully, the end of the commandment, pure charity.* By this if a man demands of me, "which of these was the meaning of Thy servant Moses;" this were not the language of my Confessions, should I not confess unto Thee, "I know not;" and yet I know that those senses are true, those carnal ones excepted, of which I have spoken what seemed necessary. And even those hopeful little ones who so think, [have this benefit that] the words of Thy Book affright them not, delivering high things lowlily, and with few words a copious meaning. And all we who, I confess, see and express the truth delivered in those words, let us love one another, and jointly love Thee our God, the fountain of truth, if we are athirst for it, and not for vanities; yea, let us so honour this Thy servant, the dispenser of this Scripture, full of Thy Spirit, as to believe that, when by Thy revelation he wrote these things, he intended that, which among them chiefly excels both for light of truth, and fruitfulness of profit.

[XXXI] 42 So when one says, "Moses meant as I do;" and another, "Nay, but as I do," I suppose that I speak more reverently, "Why not rather as both, if both be true?" And if there be a third, or a fourth, yea if any other seeth any other truth in those words, why may not he be believed to have seen all these, through whom the One God hath tempered the holy Scriptures to the senses of many, who should see therein things true but divers? For I certainly, (and fearlessly I speak it from my heart,) that were I to indite any thing to have supreme authority, I should prefer so to write, that whatever truth any could apprehend on those matters, might be conveyed

CONFESSIONS OF ST. AUGUSTINE

in my words, rather than set down my own meaning so clearly as to exclude the rest, which not being false, could not offend me. I will not therefore, O my God, be so rash, as not to believe, that Thou vouchsafedst as much to that great man. He without doubt, when he wrote those words, perceived and thought on what truth soever we have been able to find, yea and whatsoever we have not been able, nor yet are, but which may be found in them.

[XXXII] 43 Lastly, O Lord, who art God and not flesh and blood, if man did see less, could any thing be concealed from *Thy good Spirit*, (who shall *lead me into the land of uprightness*,) which Thou Thyself by those words wert about to reveal to readers in times to come, though he through whom they were spoken, perhaps among many true meanings, thought on some one? which if so it be, let that which he thought on be of all the highest. But to us, O Lord, do Thou, either reveal that same, or any other true one which Thou pleasest; that so, whether Thou discoverest the same to us, as to that Thy servant, or some other by occasion of those words, yet Thou mayest feed us, not error deceive us.[30] Behold, O Lord my God, how much we have written upon a few words, how much I beseech Thee! What strength of ours, yea what ages would suffice for all Thy books in this manner? Permit me then in these more briefly to confess unto Thee, and to choose some one true, certain, and good sense that Thou shalt inspire me, although many should occur, where many may occur; this being the law of my confession, that if I should say that which Thy minister intended, that is right and best; for this should I endeavour, which if I should not attain, yet I should say that, which Thy Truth willed by his words to tell me, which revealed also unto him, what It willed.

BOOK XIII

Continuation of the exposition of Gen. I; It contains the mystery of the Trinity, and a type of the formation, extension, and support of the Church.

[I] 1 I call upon Thee, O my God, my mercy, Who createdst me, and forgattest not me, forgetting Thee. I call Thee into[1] my soul, which, by the longing Thyself inspirest into her, Thou preparest for Thee. Forsake me not now calling upon Thee, whom Thou preventedst before I called, and urgedst me with much variety of repeated calls, that I would hear Thee from afar, and be converted, and call upon Thee, that calledst after me; for Thou, Lord, blottedst out all my evil deservings, so as not to repay into my hands, wherewith I fell from Thee; and Thou hast prevented all my well deservings, so as to repay the work of Thy hands wherewith Thou madest me; because before I was, Thou wert; nor was I any thing, to which Thou mightest grant to be; and yet behold, I am, out of Thy goodness, preventing all this which Thou hast made me, and whereof Thou hast made me. For neither hadst Thou need of me,[2] nor am I any such good, as to be helpful unto Thee, my Lord and God; not in serving Thee,[3] as though Thou wouldest tire in working; or lest Thy power might be less, if lacking my service: nor cultivating Thy service, as a land, that must remain

[348]

uncultivated, unless I cultivated[4] Thee: but serving and worshipping Thee, that I might receive a well-being from Thee, from whom it comes, that I have a being capable of well-being.

[II] 2 For of the fulness of Thy goodness, doth Thy creature subsist, that so a good, which could no ways profit Thee, nor was of Thee, (lest so it should be equal to Thee,) might yet be since it could be made of Thee. For what did *heaven and earth, which Thou madest in the Beginning*, deserve of Thee? Let those spiritual and corporeal natures which Thou madest in Thy Wisdom, say wherein they deserved of Thee, to depend thereon, (even in that their several inchoate and formless state, whether spiritual or corporeal, ready to fall away into an immoderate liberty and far-distant unlikeliness unto Thee;—the spiritual, though *without form*, superior to the corporeal though formed, and the corporeal though without form, better than were it altogether nothing,) and so to depend upon Thy Word, as formless, unless by the same Word they were brought back to Thy Unity, indued with form, and from Thee the One Sovereign Good were made all very good. How did they deserve of Thee, to be even *without form*, since they had not been even this, but from Thee?

3 How did corporeal matter deserve of Thee, to be even *invisible and without form*? seeing it were not even this, but that Thou madest it, and therefore because it was not, could not deserve of Thee to be made. Or how could the inchoate spiritual creature deserve of Thee, even to ebb

and flow darksomely like the deep,[5]—unlike Thee, unless it had been by the same Word turned to that, by Whom it was created, and by Him so enlightened, become light; though not equally, yet conformably to that Form which is equal unto Thee? For as in a body, to be, is not one with being beautiful, else could it not be deformed; so likewise to a created spirit to live, is not one with living wisely; else should it be wise unchangeably. But *good it is* for it always to *hold fast to Thee*;[6] lest what light it hath obtained by turning to Thee, it lose by turning from Thee, and relapse into life resembling the darksome deep. For we ourselves also, who as to the soul are a spiritual creature, turned away from Thee our light, *were* in that life *sometimes darkness;* and still labour amidst the relics of our darkness, until in Thy Only One we become *Thy righteousness, like the mountains of God.* For we have been *Thy judgments, which are like the great deep.*[7]

[III] 4 That which Thou saidst in the beginning of the creation, *Let there be light, and there was light;* I do, not unsuitably, understand of the spiritual creature: because there was already a sort of life, which Thou mightest illuminate. But as it had no claim on Thee for a life, which could be enlightened, so neither now that it was, had it any, to be enlightened. For neither could its formless estate be pleasing unto Thee, unless it became light, and that not by existing simply, but by beholding the illuminating light, and cleaving to it; so that, that it lived, and lived happily,[8] it owes to nothing but Thy grace, being turned by a better change unto That, which cannot be changed into worse or better; which Thou alone art, because Thou alone simply art; unto Thee it being not one thing to live, another to live blessedly, seeing Thyself art Thine own Blessedness.[9]

[IV] 5 What then could be wanting unto Thy good, which Thou Thyself art, although these things had either never been, or remained *without form;* which thou madest, not out of any want, but out of the fulness of Thy goodness, restraining them and converting them to form, not as though Thy joy were fulfilled by them? For to Thee being perfect, is their imperfection displeasing, and hence were they perfected by Thee, and please Thee; not as wert Thou imperfect, and by their perfecting wert also to be perfected. For Thy good Spirit indeed *was borne over the waters*, not borne up by them, as if He rested upon them. For those, *on* whom *Thy* good *Spirit* is said to *rest*, He causes to rest in Himself. But Thy incorruptible and unchangeable will, in itself all-sufficient for itself, *was borne upon* that life which Thou hadst created; to which, living is not one with happy living, seeing it liveth also, ebbing and flowing in its own darkness: for which it remaineth to be converted unto Him, by Whom it was made, and to live more and more by *the fountain of life, and in His light to see light*, and to be perfected, and enlightened, and beautified.

[V] 6 Lo, now the Trinity appears unto me in *a glass darkly*, which is Thou my God, because Thou, O Father, in Him Who is *the Beginning* of our wisdom, Which is Thy Wisdom, born of Thyself, equal unto Thee and coeternal, that is, in Thy Son, *createdst heaven and earth*.

Much now have we said of the *Heaven of heavens,* and of the earth *invisible and without form,* and of the darksome *deep,* in reference to the wandering instability of its spiritual deformity, unless it had been converted unto Him, from Whom it had its then degree of life, and by His enlightening became a beauteous life, and *the heaven of* that *heaven,* which was afterwards *set between water and water.* And under the name of God, I now held the Father, who made these things, and under the name of Beginning,[10] the Son, in whom He made these things; and believing, as I did, my God as the Trinity, I searched further in His holy words, and lo, Thy *Spirit moved upon the waters.* Behold the Trinity, my God, Father, and Son, and Holy Ghost, Creator of all creation.

[VI] 7 But what was the cause, O true-speaking Light?— unto Thee lift I up my heart, let it not teach me vanities, dispel its darkness; and tell me, I beseech Thee, by our mother charity, tell me the reason, I beseech Thee, why after the mention of heaven, and of the *earth invisible and without form, and darkness upon the deep,* Thy Scripture should then at length mention Thy Spirit?[11] Was it because it was meet that the knowledge of Him should be conveyed, as being "borne above;" and this could not be said, unless that were first mentioned, *over* which Thy Spirit may be understood to have been *borne.* For neither was He *borne above* the Father, nor the Son, nor could He rightly be said to be *borne above,* if He were *borne over* nothing. First then was that to be spoken of, *over* which He might be *borne;* and then He, whom it was meet not otherwise to be spoken of than as being *borne.* But wherefore was it not meet that the knowledge of Him should be conveyed otherwise, than as being *borne above?*

[VII] 8 Hence let him that is able, follow with his understanding Thy Apostle, where he thus speaks, *Because* Thy *love is shed abroad in our hearts by the Holy Ghost which is given unto us:* and where *concerning spiritual gifts,* he teacheth and *sheweth unto us a more excellent way* of charity; and where *he bows his knee, unto Thee for us,* that we may *know the supereminent knowledge of the love of Christ.* And therefore from the beginning, was He *borne* supereminent *above the waters.* To whom shall I speak this? how speak of the weight of evil desires, downwards to the steep abyss; and how charity raises up again by Thy Spirit which was *borne above the waters?* to whom shall I speak it? how speak it? For it is not in space that we are merged and emerge. What can be more, and yet what less like? They be affections, they be loves; the uncleanness of our spirit flowing away downwards with the love of cares, and the holiness of Thine raising us upward by love of unanxious repose;[12] that we may lift our hearts[13] unto Thee, where Thy Spirit is *borne above the waters;* and come to that supereminent repose, when our soul shall have passed through the *waters which yield no support.*[14]

[VIII] 9. Angels fell away, man's soul fell away, and thereby pointed out the abyss in that dark depth, ready for the whole spiritual creation, hadst not Thou said from the beginning, *Let there be light, and* there had been *light,* and every obedient intelligence of Thy heavenly City had cleaved to Thee, and rested in Thy Spirit, Which is *borne* unchangeably *over* every thing changeable. Otherwise, had even the *heaven of heavens* been in itself a darksome deep; but *now it is light in the Lord*. For even in that miserable restlessness of the spirits, who fell away and discovered their own darkness, when bared of the clothing of Thy light, dost Thou sufficiently reveal how noble Thou madest the reasonable creature; to which nothing will suffice to yield a happy rest, less than Thee;[15] and so not even herself. For Thou, *O our God, shalt lighten our darkness:* from Thee riseth our *garment* of *light;* and then *shall our darkness be as the noon day*. Give Thyself unto me, O my God, restore Thyself unto me: behold I love, and if it be too little, I would love more strongly. I cannot measure so as to know, how much love there yet lacketh to me, ere my life may run into Thy embracements, nor turn away, until it be *hidden in the hidden place*[16] *of Thy Presence*. This only I know, that woe is me except in Thee: not only without but within myself also; and all abundance, which is not my God, is emptiness to me.

[IX] 10 But was not either the Father, or the Son, *borne above the waters?* if this means, in space, like a body, then neither was the Holy Spirit; but if the unchangeable supereminence of Divinity above all things changeable, then were both Father, and Son, and Holy Ghost borne *upon the waters*. Why then is this said of Thy Spirit only, why is it said only of Him? As if He had been in place, Who is not in place, of Whom only it is written, that He is Thy gift?[17] In Thy Gift we rest; there we enjoy Thee. Our rest is our place. Love lifts us up thither, and Thy good

Spirit *lifts up* our lowliness *from the gates of death*. In Thy *good pleasure* is our *peace*. The body by its own weight strives towards its own place. Weight makes not downward only, but to his own place. Fire tends upward, a stone downward. They are urged by their own weight, they seek their own places. Oil poured below water, is raised above the water; water poured upon oil, sinks below the oil. They are urged by their own weights to seek their own places. When out of their order, they are restless; restored to order, they are at rest. My weight, is my love; thereby am I borne, whithersoever I am borne.[18] We are inflamed, by Thy Gift we are kindled; and are carried upwards; we glow inwardly, and go forwards. We *ascend Thy ways that be in our heart*, and sing *a song of degrees*; we glow inwardly with Thy fire, with Thy good fire, and we go; because we go upwards to *the peace of Jerusalem*: for *gladdened was I in those who said unto me, We will go up to the house of the Lord*. There hath Thy good pleasure placed us, that we may desire nothing else, but to abide there for ever.

[X] 11 Blessed creature, which being itself other than Thou, has known no other condition, than that, so soon as it was made, it was, without any interval, by Thy Gift, Which is *borne above* every thing changeable, borne aloft by that calling whereby Thou saidst, *Let there be light, and there was light*. Whereas in us this took place at different times, in that *we were darkness, and are made light:* but of that is only said, what it would have been, had it not been enlightened. And, this is so spoken, as if it had been unsettled and darksome before; that so the cause whereby it was made otherwise, might appear, namely, that being turned to the Light unfailing it became light. Whoso can, let him understand this; let him ask of Thee. Why should he trouble me, as if I could *enlighten* any man *that cometh into this world?*

[XI] 12 Which of us comprehendeth the Almighty Trinity? and yet which speaks not of It, if indeed it be It? Rare is the soul, which while it speaks of It, knows what it speaks of. And they contend and strive, yet, without peace, no man sees that vision. I would that men would consider these three, that are in themselves.[19] These three be indeed far other than the Trinity: I do but tell, where they may practise themselves, and there prove and feel how far they be. Now the three I spake of are, To Be, to Know, and to Will. For I Am, and Know, and Will: I Am Knowing and Willing: and I Know myself to Be, and to Will: and I Will to Be, and to Know. In these three then, let him discern that can, how inseparable a life there is, yea one life, one mind, and one essence, yea lastly how inseparable a distinction there is, and yet a distinction. Surely a man hath it before him; let him look into himself, and see, and tell me. But when he discovers and can say any thing of these, let him not therefore think that he has found that which is above these Unchangeable, which Is unchangeably, and Knows unchangeably, and Wills unchangeably; and whether because of these three, there is in God also a Trinity, or whether all three be in Each, so that the three belong to Each; or whether both ways at once, wondrously, simply and yet manifoldly, Itself a bound unto Itself within Itself, yet unbounded;[20] whereby It is, and is Known unto

Itself, and sufficeth to Itself, unchangeably the Self-same, by the abundant greatness of its Unity,—who can readily conceive this? who could any ways express it? who would, any way, pronounce thereon rashly?

[XII] 13 Proceed in thy confession, say to the Lord thy God, O my faith, *Holy, Holy, Holy, O Lord my God, in* Thy *Name have we been baptized, Father, Son, and Holy Ghost; in* Thy *Name do we baptize, Father, Son, and Holy Ghost,* because among us also, in His Christ did God *make heaven and earth,* namely, the spiritual and carnal people²¹ of His Church. Yea and our *earth,* before it received the *form of doctrine,* was *invisible and without form;* and we were covered with the darkness of ignorance. For Thou *chastenedst man for iniquity, and* Thy *judgments were like the great deep unto him.* But because Thy *Spirit was borne above the waters,* Thy mercy forsook not our misery, and Thou saidst, *Let there be light, Repent ye, for the kingdom of heaven is at hand. Repent ye, let there be*²² *light.* And because our *soul was troubled within* us, *we remembered Thee, O Lord, from the land of Jordan, and that mountain*²³ equal unto Thyself, but *little for our sakes:* and our darkness displeased us, we turned unto Thee *and there was light.* And, behold, *we were sometimes darkness, but now light in the Lord.*

[XIII] 14 But as yet *by faith and not by sight, for by hope we are saved; but hope that is seen, is not hope.* As yet doth *deep call unto deep,*²⁴ but now *in the voice of Thy waterspouts.* As yet doth he that saith, *I could not speak unto you as unto spiritual, but as unto carnal,* even he as yet, doth *not think himself to have apprehended*, and *forgetteth those things which are behind, and reacheth forth to those which are before*, and *groaneth being burthened*, and *his soul thirsteth after the Living God, as the hart after the water-brooks*, and saith, *When shall I come? desiring to be clothed upon with his house which is from heaven*, and calleth upon this *lower deep*, saying, *Be not conformed to this world, but be ye transformed by the renewing of your mind*. And, *be not children in understanding, but in malice, be ye children, that in understanding ye may be perfect;* and *O foolish Galatians, who hath bewitched you?* But now no longer in his own voice; but in Thine who sentest Thy *Spirit from above;* through Him *who ascended up on high*, and *set open the flood-gates* of His gifts, that *the force of His streams might make glad the city of God*. Him doth this *friend of the bridegroom* sigh after, having now the *first-fruits of the Spirit laid up with Him, yet still groaning within himself, waiting for the adoption, to wit, the redemption of his body;* to Him he sighs, a member of *the Bride;* for Him he is jealous, as being *a friend of the Bridegroom;* for Him he is jealous, not for himself; because *in the voice of Thy waterspouts*, not in his own voice, doth he call to that other depth, over whom being *jealous* he *feareth, lest as the serpent beguiled Eve through his subtilty*, so their minds should be corrupted from the purity that is in our Bridegroom Thy only Son. O what a light of beauty will that be, when we shall *see Him as He is*, and those tears be *passed away*, which have *been my meat day and night*, whilst they daily say unto me, *Where is now Thy God?*

[XIV] 15. Behold, I too say, O my God, Where art Thou?
see, where Thou art! in Thee I breathe a little, when *I pour
out my soul by myself in the voice of joy and praise*, the
sound of *him that keeps holy-day*. And yet again *it is sad*,
because it relapseth, and becomes *a deep*, or rather
perceives itself still to be *a deep*. Unto it speaks my faith
which Thou hast kindled to enlighten my feet in the night,
*Why art thou sad, O my soul, and why dost thou trouble me?
Hope in the Lord; His word is a lanthorn unto thy feet: hope*
and endure, until the night, the mother of the wicked,
until the *wrath* of the Lord, be overpast, whereof we also
were once *children*, who *were sometimes darkness*, relics
whereof we bearabout us in our *body, dead because of sin;
until the day break and the shadows fly away. Hope thou in
the Lord; in the morning*[25] I shall *stand in Thy presence, and
contemplate Thee: I shall for ever confess unto Thee. In the
morning I shall stand in Thy presence, and shall see the
health of my countenance, my God, Who also shall quicken
our mortal bodies, by the Spirit that dwelleth in us*, because
He hath in mercy been *borne over* our inner *darksome* and
floating deep: from Whom we have in this pilgrimage
received *an earnest*, that we should *now* be *light*: whilst we
are *saved by hope*, and *are* the *children of light, and the
children of the day, not the children of the night, nor of the
darkness*, which yet *sometimes* we *were. Betwixt* whom
and us, in this uncertainty of human knowledge, Thou
only *dividest*; Thou, who *provest* our *hearts*, and *callest the
light, day, and the darkness, night*. For who discerneth us,
but Thou? *And what have we, that we have not received of
Thee? out of the same lump vessels unto honour*, whereof
others also are made *unto dishonour*.

[XV] 16 Or who, except Thou, our God, made for us
that firmament of authority over us in Thy divine
Scripture? as it is said, For *heaven shall be folded up
like a scroll*; and now is it stretched over us like a skin.
For Thy Divine Scripture is of more eminent authority,
since those mortals by whom Thou dispensest it unto
us, underwent mortality. And Thou knowest, Lord,
Thou knowest, how Thou *with skins*[26] didst *clothe*
men, when they by sin became mortal. Whence Thou
hast *like a skin stretched out the firmament* of Thy
book, that is, Thy harmonizing words, which by the
ministry of mortal men Thou spreadest over us. For by
their very death was that solid *firmament*[27] of authority,
in Thy discourses set forth by them, more eminently
extended over all that be under it; which whilst they
lived here, was not so eminently extended. Thou
hadst not as yet *spread abroad the heaven like a skin*;
Thou hadst not as yet enlarged in all directions the glory
of their deaths.[28]

17 Let us *look*, O Lord, *upon the heavens, the work of Thy
fingers*; clear from our eyes that cloud, which Thou hast
spread under them. There is *Thy testimony, which giveth
wisdom unto the little ones: perfect*, O my God, Thy *praise
out of the mouth of babes and sucklings*. For we know no
other books, which so destroy pride, which so *destroy the
enemy and the defender*,[29] who resisteth Thy reconciliation
by defending his own sins. I know not, Lord, I know not
any other such *pure* words, which so persuade me to
confess, and make my neck pliant to Thy yoke, and invite
me to serve Thee for nought. Let me understand them,

good Father: grant this to me, who am placed under them: because for those placed under them, hast Thou established them.

18 Other *waters* there be *above* this *firmament*, I believe immortal, and separated from earthly corruption. Let them praise Thy Name, let them praise Thee, the supercelestial people, Thine angels, who have no need to gaze up at this firmament, or by reading to know of Thy Word.[30] For they *always behold* Thy *face*, and there read without any syllables in time, what willeth Thy eternal will; they read, they choose, they love.[31] They are ever reading; and that never passes away which they read; for by choosing, and by loving, they read the very unchangeableness of Thy counsel. Their book is never closed, nor *their scroll folded up*; seeing Thou Thyself art this to them, and art eternally; because Thou hast ordained them above this *firmament*, which Thou hast firmly settled over the infirmity of the lower people, where they might gaze up and learn Thy mercy, announcing in time Thee Who madest times. For *Thy mercy, O Lord, is in the heavens, and Thy truth reacheth unto the clouds.* The clouds pass away, but the heaven abideth. The preachers of Thy word pass out of this life into another; but Thy Scripture is spread abroad over the people, even unto the end of the world. Yet *heaven and earth* also *shall pass away, but* Thy *words shall not pass away.* Because the *scroll* shall be *rolled together: and the grass* over which it was spread, *shall with the goodliness of it pass away;* but Thy *Word remaineth for ever,* which now appeareth unto us *under the dark image* of the clouds, and *through the glass* of the heavens, not *as*

it is: because we also, though the well-beloved of Thy Son, yet it *hath not yet appeared what we shall be. He looketh through the lattice* of our flesh, and He spake us tenderly, and kindled us, and we *ran after His odours. But when He shall appear, then shall we be like Him, for we shall see Him as He is. As He is,* Lord, will our sight be.

[XVI] 19 For altogether, *as Thou art,* Thou only knowest; Who art unchangeably, and knowest unchangeably, and willest unchangeably. And Thy Essence Knoweth, and Willeth unchangeably; and Thy Knowledge Is, and Willeth unchangeably; and Thy Will Is, and Knoweth unchangeably. Nor seemeth it right in Thine eyes, that as the Unchangeable Light knoweth Itself, so should it be known by the thing enlightened, and changeable. Therefore is *my soul like a land where no water is,* because as it cannot of itself enlighten itself, so can it not of itself satisfy itself. For so *is the fountain of life with Thee,* like as *in Thy light we shall see light.*

[XVII] 20 Who *gathered* the embittered *together into one* society? For they have all one end, a temporal and earthly felicity, for attaining whereof they do all things, though they waver up and down with an innumerable variety of cares. Who, Lord, but Thou, saidst, *Let the waters be gathered together into one place, and let the dry land appear, which thirsteth after Thee?* For *the sea also is Thine, and Thou hast made it, and Thy hands prepared the dry land.* Nor is the bitterness of men's wills, but *the gathering together of the waters, called sea;* for Thou restrainest the wicked desires of men's souls, and *settest them their bounds, how far* they may be allowed to *pass*, that their waves may break one against another: and thus makest Thou it a sea. *by the order of Thy dominion over all things.*[32]

21 But the souls that *thirst after Thee*, and that *appear before Thee*, (being by other bounds divided from the society of the sea,) Thou waterest by a sweet spring, that *the earth may bring forth her fruit*,[33] and Thou, Lord God, so commanding, our soul may bud forth works of mercy *according to their kind, loving our neighbour* in the relief of his bodily necessities, *having seed in itself according to its likeness*, when from feeling of our infirmity, we compassionate so as to relieve the needy; helping them, *as we would* be helped, if we were in like need; not only in things easy, as in herb *yielding seed*, but also in the protection of our assistance, with our best strength, like *the tree yielding fruit:* that is, well-doing in rescuing him that suffers wrong, from the hand of the powerful, and giving him the shelter of protection, by the mighty strength of just judgment.

[XVIII] 22 So, Lord, so, I beseech Thee, let there spring up, as Thou doest, as Thou givest cheerfulness and ability, *let truth spring out of the earth, and righteousness look down from heaven*, and *let there be lights in the firmament. Let us break our bread to the hungry*, and *bring the* houseless *poor to our house.* Let us *clothe the naked, and despise not those of our own flesh.* Which fruits having sprung out of the earth, see *it is good:* and let our temporary *light break forth;* and ourselves, from this lower fruitfulness of action, arriving at the delightfulness of contemplation, obtaining the Word of Life above, appear *like lights in the world*, cleaving to the *firmament* of Thy Scripture. For there Thou instructest us, to *divide* between the things intellectual, and things of sense, as *betwixt the day and the night;* or between souls, given either to things intellectual, or things of sense, so that now not Thou only in the secret of Thy judgment, as before the firmament was made, *dividest between the light and the darkness*, but Thy spiritual children also *set* and ranked *in the* same *firmament*, (now that Thy grace is laid open throughout the world,) may *give light upon the earth, and divide betwixt the day and the night, and be for signs of times*, that *old things are passed away, and, behold, all things are become new;* and that *our salvation is nearer than when we believed:* and that *the night is far spent, and the day is at hand:* and that *Thou wilt crown Thy year with blessing, sending* the *labourers* of Thy *goodness into* Thy *harvest*, in sowing whereof, *others have laboured, sending* also into another field, whose *harvest* shall be *in the end.* Thus grantest Thou the prayers of him that asketh, and *blessest* the years of *the just; but Thou art the same, and in Thy years* which *fail not*, Thou preparest a garner for our passing years. For Thou by an eternal counsel dost in their proper seasons bestow heavenly blessings upon the earth.

23 *For to one is given by the Spirit the word of wisdom*, as it were *the greater light*, for their sakes who are delighted with the light of perspicuous truth, as it were *for the rule of the day. To another the word of knowledge by the same Spirit*, as it were *the lesser light: to another faith; to another*

the gift of healing; to another the working of miracles; to another prophecy; to another discerning of spirits; to another divers kinds of tongues. And all these as it were stars. For all these worketh the one and self-same spirit, dividing to every man his own as He will; and causing stars to appear manifestly, to profit withal. But the word of knowledge, wherein are contained all Sacraments, which are varied in their seasons[34] as it were the moon, and those other notices of gifts, which are reckoned up in order, as it were stars, inasmuch as they come short of that brightness of wisdom, which gladdens the forementioned day, are only for the rule of the night.[35] For they are necessary to such, as that Thy most prudent servant could not speak unto as unto spiritual, but as unto carnal; even he, who speaketh wisdom among those that are perfect. But the natural man, as it were a babe in Christ and fed on milk, until he be strengthened for solid meat and his eye be enabled to behold the Sun, let him not dwell in a night forsaken of all light, but be content[36] with the light of the moon and the stars. So dost Thou speak to us, our All-wise God, in Thy Book, Thy firmament; that we may discern all things, in an admirable contemplation; though as yet in signs, and in times, and in days, and in years.

[XIX] 24 But first, wash you, be clean;[37] put away evil from your souls, and from before mine eyes, that the dry land may appear. Learn to do good, judge the fatherless, plead for the widow, that the earth may bring forth the green herb for meat, and the tree bearing fruit; and come, let us reason together, saith the Lord, that there may be

*lights in the firmament of the heaven, and they may shine
upon the earth.* That *rich man* asked of the *good Master,
what he should do to attain eternal life.* Let the *good
Master* tell him, (whom he thought no more than man;
but He is *good* because He is *God,*) let Him tell him, *if he
would enter into life,* he must *keep the commandments:* let
him put away from him the bitterness *of malice and
wickedness; not kill, not commit adultery, not steal, not
bear false witness;* that *the dry land may appear,* and *bring
forth the honouring of father and mother, and the love of
our neighbour. All these* (saith he) *have I kept.* Whence
then so many thorns, if the earth be fruitful? Go, root up
the spreading thickets of covetousness; *sell that thou hast,*
and be filled with fruit, by *giving to the poor, and thou
shall have treasure in heaven;* and *follow* the Lord *if thou
will be perfect,* associated with them, among whom *He
speaketh wisdom,* Who knoweth what to distribute *to the
day,* and *to the night,* that thou also mayest know it, and
for thee there may be *lights in the firmament of heaven;*
which will not be, unless *thy heart be* there: nor will that
either be, unless *there thy treasure* be; as thou hast heard
of the *good Master.* But that barren earth *was grieved;*[38]
and *the thorns choked the word.*

25 But you, *chosen generation,* you *weak things of the
world,* who have *forsaken all,* that ye may *follow* the Lord;
go after Him, and *confound the mighty;* go after Him, ye
beautiful feet, and *shine* ye *in the firmament,* that *the
heavens* may *declare His glory, dividing between the light*
of the perfect, though not as the angels, *and the darkness*
of the little ones, though not despised. Shine over the

earth; and let *the day*, lightened by the *sun, utter unto day, speech* of *wisdom; and night*, shining with the *moon, shew unto night, the word of knowledge*. The moon and stars shine for the night; yet doth not the night obscure them, seeing they give it light in its degree. For behold God saying, as it were, *Let there be lights in the firmament of heaven;* there *came suddenly a sound from heaven, as it had been the rushing of a mighty wind, and there appeared cloven tongues like as of fire, and it sat upon each of them.* And there were *made lights in the firmament of heaven,* having the *word of life*. Run ye to and fro every where, ye holy fires, ye beauteous fires; for ye are the *light of the world*, nor are ye *put under a bushel;* He whom you cleave unto, is exalted, and hath exalted you. Run ye to and fro, and be known unto all nations.

[XX] 26 Let the sea also conceive and *bring forth* your works; and *let the waters bring forth the moving creature that hath life.* For ye, *separating the precious from the vile,* are made the mouth of God, by whom. He saith, *Let the waters bring forth*, not the *living creature* which the *earth brings forth*, but the *moving creature having* life, *and the fowls that fly above the earth.* For Thy Sacraments, O God, by the ministry of Thy holy ones, have moved amid the waves of temptations of the world, to hallow the Gentiles in Thy Name, in Thy Baptism. And amid these things, many great wonders were wrought, as it were *great whales:* and the voices of Thy messengers *flying above the earth, in the open firmament* of Thy Book; that being set over them, as their authority under which they were to fly, whithersoever they went. For *there is no speech nor language, where their voice is not heard:* seeing *their sound is gone through all the earth*, and *their words to the end of the world*, because Thou, Lord, *multipliedst* them by *blessing*.

27 Speak I untruly, or do I mingle and confound, and not distinguish between the lucid knowledge of these things *in the firmament of heaven*, and the material works in the wavy sea, and *under the firmament of heaven*? For of those things whereof the knowledge is substantial and defined, without any increase by generation, as it were lights of *wisdom and knowledge*, yet even of them, the material operations are many and divers; and one thing growing out of another, they are multiplied by Thy blessing, O God, who hast refreshed the fastidiousness of mortal senses; that so one thing in the understanding of our mind, may, by the motions of the body, be many ways[39] set out, and expressed. These Sacraments have the waters brought forth; but in Thy word. The[40] necessities of the people estranged from the eternity of Thy truth, have brought them forth, but in Thy Gospel; because the waters themselves cast them forth, the diseased bitterness whereof was the cause, why they were sent forth in Thy Word.

28 Now are all things fair that Thou hast made; but behold, Thyself art unutterably fairer, that madest all; from whom had not Adam fallen, the brackishness of the sea had never flowed out of him, that is, the human race so profoundly curious, and tempestuously swelling, and restlessly tumbling up and down; and then had there been no need of Thy dispensers to work in *many waters*, after a corporeal and sensible manner, mysterious doings and

sayings. For such those *moving* and and *flying creatures* now seem to me to mean, whereby people being initiated and consecrated by corporeal Sacraments, should not further profit, unless their soul had a spiritual life, and unless after the word of admission, it looked forwards to perfection.[41]

[XXI] 29 And hereby, in Thy Word, not the deepness of the sea, but the earth separated from the bitterness of the waters, brings forth, not the *moving creature that hath life*, but *the living soul*. For now hath it no more need of baptism, as the heathen have, and as itself had, when it was covered with the waters; (for no other *entrance* is there *into the kingdom of heaven*, since Thou hast appointed that this should be the entrance:) nor does it seek after wonderfulness of miracles to work belief; for it is not such, that *unless it sees signs and wonders, it will not believe*, now that the faithful *earth* is separated from the waters that were bitter with infidelity; and *tongues are for a sign, not to them that believe, but to them that believe not*. Neither then does that earth which *Thou hast founded upon the waters*,[42] need that *flying kind*, which at Thy word *the waters brought forth*. Send Thou Thy word into it by Thy messengers: for we speak of their working, yet it is Thou that workest in them that they may work out a *living soul* in it. The earth brings it forth, because the earth is the cause that they work this in the soul; as the sea was the cause that they wrought upon the *moving creatures that have life*, and *the fowls that fly under the firmament of heaven*, of whom the earth hath no need; although it feeds upon that fish which was taken out of the deep, upon that *table* which *Thou hast prepared in the presence* of them that believe. For therefore was[43] He taken out of the deep, that He might feed the dry land; and the *fowl*, though bred in the sea, is yet *multiplied upon the earth*. For of the first preachings of the Evangelists, man's infidelity was the cause; yet are the faithful also exhorted and blessed by them manifoldly, from day to day. But *the living soul* takes his beginning from the *earth:* for it profits only those already among the Faithful, to contain themselves from the love of this world, that so their soul may live unto Thee, which was *dead while it lived in pleasures;* in death-bringing pleasures, Lord, for Thou, Lord, art the life-giving delight of the pure heart.

30 Now then let Thy ministers work upon *the earth,*—not as upon the waters of infidelity, by preaching and speaking by miracles, and Sacraments, and mystic words; wherein ignorance, the mother of admiration might be intent upon them, out of a reverence towards those secret signs. For such is the entrance unto the Faith for the sons of Adam forgetful of Thee, while *they hide themselves from Thy face,* and become a darksome deep. But—let Thy ministers work now as on the *dry land,* separated from the whirlpools of the great deep: and let them be a pattern unto the Faithful, by living before them, and stirring them up to imitation. For thus do men hear, so as not to hear only, but to do also. *Seek the Lord, and your soul shall live,* that the *earth* may *bring forth the living soul. Be not conformed to the world.* Contain yourselves from it: the soul lives by avoiding what it dies by affecting. Contain yourselves from the ungoverned wildness of pride, the

sluggish voluptuousness of luxury, and the *false name of knowledge:*[44] that so the wild beasts may be tamed, the cattle broken to the yoke, the serpents, harmless. For these be the motions of our mind under an allegory; that is to say, the haughtiness of pride, the delight of lust, and the poison of curiosity, are the motions of a dead soul; for the soul dies not so as to lose all motion; because it dies[45] by *forsaking the fountain of life*, and so is taken up by this transitory world, and is *conformed unto it.*

31 But Thy word, O God, is the *fountain of life* eternal; and passeth not away: wherefore this departure of the soul is restrained by Thy word, when it is said unto us, *Be not conformed unto this world*; that so *the earth* may in the *fountain of life bring forth a living soul;* that is, a soul made continent in Thy Word, by Thy Evangelists, by *following* the *followers* of Thy *Christ*. For this is *after his kind*; because a man is wont to imitate his friend. *Be ye* (saith he) *as I am, for I also am as you are*. Thus in this *living soul* shall there be *good beasts*, in meekness of action; (for Thou hast commanded, *Go on with thy business in meekness, so shalt thou be beloved by* all men;) and *good cattle*, which *neither if they eat, shall they over-abound, nor, it they eat not, have any lack;* and *good serpents*, not dangerous, to do hurt, but *wise* to take heed; and only making so much search into this temporal nature, as may suffice that *eternity be clearly seen, being understood by the things that are made*. For these creatures are obedient unto reason,[46] when being restrained from deadly prevailing upon us, they live, and are good.

32 For behold, O Lord, our God, our Creator, when our affections have been restrained from the *love of the world*, by which we died through evil-living; and begun to be a *living soul*, through good living; and Thy word which Thou spakest by Thy apostle, is made good in us, *Be not conformed to this world:* there follows that also, which Thou presently subjoinedst, saying, *But be ye transformed by the renewing of your mind;* not now *after your kind*, as though following your neighbour who went before you, nor as living after the example of some better man, (for Thou saidst not, "Let man be made after his kind," but, *Let us make man after our own image and similitude*,) *that* we *might prove what* Thy *will is.* For to this purpose said that dispenser of Thine, (who *begat* children *by the Gospel*,) that he might not for ever have them *babes*, whom he must be fain to *feed with milk*, and *cherish as a nurse; be ye transformed* (saith he) *by the renewing of your mind, that ye may prove what is that good and acceptable and perfect will of God.* Wherefore Thou sayest not, "Let man be made," but *Let us make man.* Nor saidst Thou, "according to his kind;" but, *after our image and likeness.* For man being *renewed in his mind*, and beholding and understanding Thy truth, needs not man as his director, so as to follow *after his kind;* but by Thy direction *proveth what is that good, that acceptable, and perfect will of Thine:* yea, Thou teachest him, now made capable, to discern the Trinity of the Unity, and the Unity of the Trinity.[47] Wherefore to that said in the plural, *Let us make man*, is yet subjoined in the singular, *And God made man:* and to that said in the plural, *After our likeness*, is subjoined in the singular, *After the image of God.* Thus is man *renewed in the knowledge of God,*

after the image of Him that created him: and being made *spiritual, he judgeth all things,* (all things which are to be judged,) yet *himself is judged of no man.*

[XXIII] 33 But that he *judgeth all things,* this answers to his having *dominion over the fish of the sea, and over the fowls of the air,* and *over all cattle* and wild *beasts, and over all the earth, and over every creeping thing that creepeth upon the earth.* For this he doth by the under-standing of his mind, whereby he *perceiveth the things of the Spirit of God;* whereas otherwise, *man being placed in honour, had no understanding, and is compared unto the brute beasts, and is become like unto them.* In Thy Church therefore, O our God, according to Thy grace which Thou hast bestowed upon it, (*for we are Thy workmanship created unto good works,*) not those only who are spiritu-ally set over, but they also who spiritually are subject to those that are set over them,—for in this way didst Thou *make man male and female,* in Thy grace spiritual, where, according to the sex of body, *there is neither male nor female,* because *neither Jew nor Grecian, neither bond nor free.*)—*Spiritual* persons, (whether such as are set over, or such as obey;) do *judge* spiritually; not of that spiritual knowledge *which shines in the firmament,* (for they ought not to judge as to so supreme authority,) nor may they judge of Thy Book itself, even though something there shineth not clearly; for we submit our understanding unto it, and hold for certain, that even what is closed to our sight, is yet rightly and truly spoken. For so man, though now *spiritual and renewed in the knowledge of God after His image that created him,* ought to be *a doer of the*

law, not *a judge*. Neither doth he judge of that distinction
of spiritual and carnal men, who are known unto Thine
eyes, O our God, and have not as yet discovered themselves
unto us by works, that by *their fruits we might know them:*
but Thou, Lord, dost even now know them, and hast
divided and *called* them in secret, or ever the *firmament*
was *made*. Nor doth he, though *spiritual, judge* the unquiet
people of this world; *for what hath he to do, to judge them
that are without*, knowing not which of them shall
hereafter come into the sweetness of Thy grace; and which
continue in the perpetual bitterness of ungodliness?

34 *Man* therefore, whom Thou hast *made after* Thine
own *image*, received not *dominion* over *the lights of
heaven*, nor over that hidden heaven itself, nor over *the
day and the night*, which Thou *calledst* before the
foundation of the heaven, nor over the *gathering together
of the waters*, which is the *sea;* but He received *dominion
over the fishes of the sea, and the fowls of the air, and over
all cattle, and over all the earth, and over all creeping things
which creep upon the earth*. For He judgeth and approveth
what He findeth right, and He disalloweth what He
findeth amiss, whether in the celebration of those
Sacraments by which such are initiated, as Thy mercy
searches out in *many waters:* or in that, in which that
Fish[48] is set forth, which, taken out of the deep, the
devout earth feedeth upon: or in the expressions and
signs of words, subject to the authority of Thy Book,—
such signs, as proceed out of the mouth, and sound forth,
flying as it were under the firmament, by interpreting,
expounding, discoursing, disputing, consecrating, or

praying unto Thee, so that the people may answer, *Amen.*
The vocal pronouncing of all which words, is occasioned
by the deep of this world, and the blindness of the flesh,
which cannot see thoughts; so that there is need to speak
aloud into the ears; so that, although *flying fowls* be
multiplied upon the earth, yet they derive their beginning
from the waters. *The spiritual man judgeth* also by allowing
of what is right, and disallowing what he finds amiss, in
the works and lives of the faithful; their alms, as it were
the earth bringing forth fruit, and of the *living soul, living*
by the taming of the affections, in chastity, in fasting, in
holy meditations; and of those things, which are perceived
by the senses of the body. Upon all these is he now said
to *judge,* wherein he hath also power of correction.

35 But what is this, and what kind of mystery? Behold,
Thou *blessest mankind,* O Lord, that they *may increase*
and *multiply,* and *replenish the earth;* dost Thou not
thereby give us a hint to understand something? why
didst Thou not as well bless *the light,* which Thou *calledst
day;* nor *the firmament of heaven,* nor *the lights,* nor *the
stars,* nor *the earth,* nor *the sea?* I might say that Thou, O
God, who *created us after Thine Image,* I might say, that
it had been Thy good pleasure to bestow this blessing
peculiarly upon man; hadst: Thou not in like manner
blessed the fishes and the whales, that they *should
increase and multiply, and replenish the waters of the sea,*
and that the *fowls should be multiplied upon the earth.* I
might say likewise, that this blessing pertained properly
unto such creatures, as are bred of their own kind, had I
found it given to the fruit-trees, and plants, and beasts of

the earth. But now neither unto the herbs, nor the trees, nor the beasts, nor serpents is it said, *Increase and multiply;* notwithstanding all these as well as the fishes, fowls, or men, do by generation increase and continue their kind.

36 What then shall I say, O Truth my Light? "that it was idly said, and without meaning?" Not so, O Father of piety, far be it from a minister of Thy word to say so. And if I understand not what Thou meanest by that phrase, let my betters, that is, those of more under-standing than myself, make better use of it, according as Thou, my God, hast given to each man to understand. But let my confession also be pleasing in Thine eyes, wherein I confess unto Thee, that I believe, O Lord, that Thou spakest not so in vain; nor will I suppress, what this lesson suggests to me. For it is true, nor do I see what should hinder me from thus understanding the figurative sayings of Thy Bible. For I know a thing to be manifoldly signified by corporeal expressions, which is understood one way by the mind; and that understood many ways in the mind, which is signified one way by corporeal expression. Behold, the single love of God and our neighbour, by what manifold sacraments, and innumerable languages, and in each several language, in how innumerable modes of speaking, it is corporeally expressed. Thus do the offspring of the *waters increase and multiply.* Observe again, whosoever readest this; behold, what Scripture delivers, and the voice pronounces one only way, *In the Beginning God created heaven and earth;* is it not

understood manifoldly, not through any deceit of error, but by various kinds of true senses? Thus do man's offspring *increase and multiply*.

37 If therefore we conceive of the natures of the things themselves, not allegorically, but properly, then does the phrase *increase and multiply*, agree unto all things, that come of seed. But if we treat of the words as figuratively spoken, (which I rather suppose to be the purpose of the Scripture, which doth not, surely, superfluously ascribe this benediction to the offspring of aquatic animals and man only;) then do we find "multitude" to belong to creatures spiritual as well as corporeal, as in *heaven* and *earth*, and to souls both righteous and unrighteous, as in *light* and *darkness;* and to holy authors who have been the ministers of the Law unto us, as in the *firmament* which is settled betwixt the *waters* and the *waters;* and to the society of people yet in the bitterness of infidelity, as in *the sea;* and to the zeal of holy souls, as in *the dry land;* and to works of mercy belonging to this present life, as in the *herbs bearing seed*, and in *trees bearing fruit;* and to *spiritual gifts set forth for edification*, as in *the lights of heaven;* and to affections formed unto temperance, as in the *living soul*. In all these instances we meet with multitudes, abundance, and increase; but what shall in such wise *increase and multiply* that one thing may be expressed many ways, and one expression understood many ways; we find not, except in signs corporeally expressed, and in things mentally conceived. By signs corporeally pronounced we understand the generations of the waters, necessarily occasioned by the depth of the

flesh; by things mentally conceived, human generations, on account of the fruitfulness of reason. And for this end do we believe Thee, Lord, to have said to these kinds, *Increase and multiply*. For in this blessing, I conceive Thee to have granted us a power and a faculty, both to express several ways what we understand but one; and to understand several ways, what we read to be obscurely delivered but in one. Thus are the *waters of the sea replenished*, which are not moved but by several significations: thus with human increase is the *earth* also *replenished*, whose *dryness* appeareth in its longing,[49] and reason ruleth over it.

[XXV] 38 I would also say, O Lord my God, what the following Scripture minds me of; yea, I will say, and not fear. For I will say the truth, Thyself inspiring me with what Thou willedst me to deliver out of those words. But by no other inspiration than Thine, do I believe myself to speak truth, seeing Thou art *the Truth, and every man a liar. He* therefore *that speaketh a lie, speaketh of his own;* that therefore I may speak truth, I will speak of Thine. Behold, Thou hast given unto us *for food every herb bearing seed which is upon all the earth; and every tree, in which is the fruit of a tree yielding seed*. And not to us alone, but also *to all the fowls of the air, and to the beasts of the earth, and to all creeping things;* but unto the *fishes* and to the *great whales*, hast Thou not given them. Now we said that by these *fruits of the earth were signified*, and figured in an allegory, the works of mercy which are provided for the necessities of this life out of the *fruitful earth*. Such an *earth* was the devout *Onesiphorus, unto whose house Thou gavest mercy*, because he *often refreshed* Thy Paul, *and was not ashamed of his chain*. Thus did also *the brethren*, and such fruit did they bear, who *out of Macedonia supplied what was lacking to* him. But how grieved he for some *trees*, which did not *afford* him the *fruit* due unto him, where he saith, *At my first answer no man stood by me, but all men forsook me. I pray God that it may not be laid to their charge.* For these fruits are due to such as minister the spiritual[50] doctrine unto us out of their understanding of the divine mysteries; and they are due to them, as *men*; yea and due to them also, as the *living soul*, which giveth itself as an example, in all continency; and due unto them also, as *flying creatures*, for their blessings which are *multiplied upon the earth*, because *their sound went out into all lands*.

[XXVI] 39 But they are fed by these fruits, that are delighted with them; nor are they delighted with them, *whose God is their belly*. For neither in them that yield them, are the things yielded the fruit, but with what mind they yield them. He therefore *that served God, and not his own belly*, I plainly see why he rejoiced; I see it, and I rejoice with him. For he had *received* from the *Philippians*, what they had sent *by Epaphroditus* unto him: and yet I perceive why he rejoiced. For whereat he rejoiced upon that he fed; for, speaking in truth, *I rejoiced* (saith he) *greatly in the Lord, that now at the last your care of me hath flourished again, wherein ye were also careful*, but it had become wearisome unto you. These *Philippians* then had now dried up, with a long weariness, and withered as it were as to bearing 'his *fruit* of a good work; and he rejoiceth for them, that *they flourished again*, not for himself, that they supplied his wants. Therefore subjoins he, not that *I speak in respect of want, for I have learned in whatsoever state I am, therewith to be content. I know both how to be abased, and I know how to abound; every where and in all things I am instructed both to be full, and to be hungry; both to abound, and to suffer need. I can do all things through Him which strengtheneth me.*

40 Whereat then rejoicest thou, O great Paul? whereat rejoicest thou? whereon feedest thou, O *man, renewed in the knowledge* of God, *after the image of Him that created thee*, thou *living soul*, of so much continency, thou tongue like *flying fowls*, speaking mysteries? (for to such creatures, is this food due;) what is it that feeds thee? Joy. Hear we what follows: *notwithstanding, ye have well done, that ye did communicate with my affliction*. Hereat he rejoiceth, hereon feedeth; because they had well done, not because his strait was eased, who saith unto Thee, *Thou hast enlarged me when I was in distress*; for that he *knew to abound, and to suffer want*,[51] in Thee *Who strengthenest him. For ye Philippians also know*, (saith he,) *that in the beginning of the Gospel, when I departed from Macedonia, no Church communicated with me as concerning giving and receiving, but ye only. For even in Thessalonica ye sent once and again unto my necessity*. Unto these good works, he now rejoiceth that they are returned; and is gladdened that they flourished again, as when a fruitful field resumes its green.

41 Was it for his own necessities, because he said, *Ye sent unto my necessity*? Rejoiceth he for that? Verily not for that. But how know we this? Because himself says immediately, *not because I desire a gift, but I desire fruit*. I have learned of Thee, my God, to distinguish betwixt a *gift*, and *fruit*. A *gift*, is the thing itself which he gives, that imparts these necessaries unto us; as money, meat, drink, clothing, shelter, help: but the *fruit*, is the good and right will of the giver. For the Good Master said not only, *He that receiveth a prophet*, but added, *in the name of a prophet*: nor did He only say, *He that receiveth a righteous man*, but added, *in the name of a righteous man*. So verily shall the one *receive the reward of a prophet*, the other, *the reward of a righteous man*: nor saith He only, *He that shall give to drink a cup of cold water to one of my little ones*; but added, *in the name of a disciple*: and so concludeth, *Verily I say unto you, he shall not lose his reward*. The *gift* is, to *receive a prophet*, to *receive a righteous man*, to *give a cup of cold water to a disciple*: but the *fruit*, to do this *in the name of a prophet*, *in the name of a righteous man*, *in the name of a disciple*. With *fruit* was Elijah fed by the widow that knew she fed a man of God, and therefore fed him: but by the raven was he fed with a *gift*. Nor was the inner man of Elijah so fed, but the outer only; which might also for want of that food have perished.

[XXVII] 42 I will then speak what is true in Thy sight, O Lord, that when carnal men and infidels (for the gaining and initiating whom, the initiatory Sacraments and the mighty workings of miracles are necessary, which we suppose to be signified by the name of *fishes* and *whales*) undertake the bodily refreshment, or otherwise succour Thy servant with something useful for this present life; whereas they be ignorant, why this is to be done, and to what end; neither do they feed these, nor are these fed by them; because neither do the one do it out of an holy and right intent; nor do the other rejoice at their *gifts*, whose *fruit* they as yet behold not. For upon that is the mind fed, of which it is glad. And therefore do not the *fishes* and *whales* feed upon such *meats*, as the *earth brings* not *forth* until after it was separated and *divided* from the bitterness of the waves of *the sea*.

[XXVIII] 43 And *Thou, O God, sawest every thing that Thou hadst made, and, behold, it was very good*. Yea we also see the same, and behold, all things are *very good*. Of the several kinds of Thy works, when Thou hadst said "let them be," and they were, Thou sawest each *that it was good*. Seven times have I counted it to be written, that Thou *sawest that that which Thou madest was good*: and this is the eighth, that Thou *sawest every thing that Thou hadst made*, and, behold, it was not only *good*, but also *very good*, as being now altogether. For severally, they were only *good*; but altogether, both *good*, and *very good*. All beautiful bodies express the same; by reason that a body consisting of members all beautiful, is far more beautiful than the same members by themselves are, by whose well-ordered blending the whole is perfected; notwithstanding that the members severally be also beautiful.[52]

[XXIX] 44 And I looked narrowly to find, whether seven, or eight times Thou sawest that Thy works were good, when they pleased Thee; but in Thy seeing I found no times, whereby I might understand that Thou sawest so often, what Thou madest. And I said, "Lord, is not this Thy Scripture true, since Thou art true, and being Truth, hast set it forth? why then dost Thou say unto me, 'that in Thy seeing there be no times;' whereas this Thy Scripture tells me, that what Thou madest each day, Thou *sawest that it was good:* and when I counted them, I found how often." Unto this Thou answerest me, for Thou art my God, and with a strong voice tellest Thy servant in his inner ear, breaking through my deafness and crying, "O man, that which My Scripture saith, I say: and yet doth that speak in time; but time has no relation to My Word; because My Word exists in equal eternity with Myself. So the things which ye see through My Spirit, I see; like as what ye speak by My Spirit, I speak. And so when ye see those things in time, I see them not in time; as when ye speak in time, I speak them not in time."

[XXX] 45 And I heard, O Lord my God, and drank up a drop of sweetness out of Thy truth, and understood, that certain men there be who mislike Thy works; and say, that many of them Thou madest, compelled by necessity; such as the fabric of the heavens, and harmony of the stars; and that Thou madest them not of what was Thine, but that they were otherwhere and from other sources created, for Thee to bring together and compact and combine, when out of Thy conquered enemies Thou raisedst up the walls of the universe; that they, bound down by the structure, might not again be able to rebel against Thee. For other things, they say Thou neither madest them, nor even compactedst them, such as all flesh and all very minute creatures, and whatsoever hath its root in the earth; but that a mind at enmity with Thee, and another nature not created by Thee, and contrary unto Thee, did, in these lower stages of the world, beget and frame these things. Phrenzied are they who say thus, because they see not Thy works by Thy Spirit, nor recognize Thee in them.

[XXXI] 46 But they who by Thy Spirit see these things, Thou seest in them. Therefore when they see that these *things are good*, Thou seest that they are good; and whatsoever things for Thy sake please, Thou pleasest in them, and what through Thy Spirit please us, they please Thee in us. *For what man knoweth the things of a man, save the spirit of a man, which is in him? even so the things of God knoweth no one, but the Spirit of God. Now we* (saith he) *have received, not the spirit of this world, but the Spirit which is of God, that we might know the things that are freely given to us of God.* And I am admonished, "Truly *the things of God knoweth no one, but the Spirit of God:* how then do we also know, *what things are given us of God?*" Answer is made me; "because the things which we know by His Spirit, even these *no one knoweth, but the Spirit of God.* For as it is rightly said unto those that were to speak by the Spirit of God, *it is not ye that speak:* so is it rightly said to them that know through the Spirit of God, 'It is not ye that know.' And no less then is it rightly said to those that see through the Spirit of God, 'It is not ye that see;' so whatsoever through the Spirit of God they *see* to be *good*, it is not they, but God that *sees that it is good*." It is one thing then for a man to think that to be ill which is good, as the fore-named do; another, that that which is good, a man should see that it is good, (as Thy creatures be pleasing unto many, because they be good, whom yet Thou pleasest not in them, when they prefer to enjoy them, to Thee;) and another, that when a man sees a thing that it is good, God should in him see that it is good, so, namely, that He should be loved in that which He made,[53] Who cannot be loved, but by the Holy Ghost which He hath given. *Because the love of God is shed abroad in our hearts by the Holy Ghost, Which is given unto us:* by Whom we see that whatsoever in any degree is, is good. For from Him it is, who Himself Is not in degree, but what He Is, Is.

[XXXII] 47 Thanks to Thee, O Lord. We behold *the heaven and earth*, whether the corporeal part, superior and inferior, or the spiritual and corporeal creature; and in the adorning of these parts, whereof the universal pile of the world, or rather the universal creation, doth consist, we see *light* made, and *divided from the darkness*. We see the *firmament of heaven*, whether that primary body of the world, *between the* spiritual upper *waters and the* inferior corporeal *waters*,[54] or (since this also is called heaven) this space of air through which wander the fowls of heaven, *betwixt those waters* which are in vapours borne above them, and in clear nights distil down in dew; *and* those heavier *waters* which flow along the earth. We behold a face of *waters gathered together* in the fields of *the sea*; and *the dry land* both void, and formed so as to be visible and harmonized, yea and the matter of herbs and trees. We behold *the lights* shining from above, *the sun* to suffice for *the day, the moon and the stars* to cheer *the night*; and that by all these, *times* should be marked and signified. We behold on all sides a moist element, replenished with fishes, beasts, and birds; because the grossness of the air, which bears up the flights of birds, thickeneth itself by the exhalation of the waters.[55] We behold the face of the earth decked out with earthly creatures, and *man, created after Thy image and likeness*, even through that Thy very *image and likeness*, (that is the power of reason and understanding,) set over all irrational creatures. And as in his soul there is one power which has dominion by directing, another made subject, that it might obey; so was there for the man, corporeally also, made a woman, who in the mind of her reasonable understanding should have a parity of nature, but in the sex of her body, should be in like manner subject to the sex of her husband, as the appetite of doing is fain to conceive[56] the skill of right-doing, from the reason of the mind. These things we behold, and they are severally *good*, and altogether *very good*.

[XXXIII] 48 Let Thy works praise Thee, that we may love Thee; and let us love Thee, that Thy works may praise Thee, which from time have beginning and ending, rising and setting, growth and decay, form and privation. They have then their succession of morning and evening, part secretly, part apparently; for they were made of nothing, by Thee, not of Thee; not of any matter not Thine, or that was before, but of matter concreated, (that is, at the same time created by Thee,) because to its state *without form*, Thou without any interval of time didst give form. For seeing the matter of *heaven and earth* is one thing, and the form another, Thou madest the matter of merely nothing, but the form of the world out of the matter *without form:* yet both together, so that the form should follow the matter, without any interval of delay.

[XXXIV] 49 We have also examined what Thou willedst to be shadowed forth, whether by the creation, or the relation of things in such an order. And we have seen, that things singly *are good*, and together *very good*, in Thy Word, in Thy Only-Begotten, both *heaven and earth*, the Head and the body of the Church, in Thy predestination before all times, without *morning and evening*. But when Thou begannest to execute in time the things predestinated, to the end Thou mightest reveal hidden things, and rectify our *disorders;* for our sins hung over us, and we had sunk into the *dark deep*, and Thy good *Spirit was borne* over us, to help us *in due season;* and Thou didst *justify the ungodly*, and *dividest* them from the wicked; and Thou *madest the firmament* of authority of Thy Book between those placed *above*, who were to be docile unto Thee, and those *under*, who were to be subject to them: and Thou *gatheredst together* the society of unbelievers *into one* conspiracy, that the zeal of the faithful might appear, and they might *bring forth* works of mercy, even distributing to the poor their earthly riches, to obtain heavenly. And after this didst Thou kindle certain *lights in the firmament*, Thy Holy ones, having *the word of life;* and shining with an eminent authority set on high through spiritual gifts; after that again, for the initiation of the unbelieving Gentiles, didst Thou out of corporeal matter produce the Sacraments, and visible miracles, and forms of words according to the firmament of Thy Book, by which the faithful should be *blessed* and *multiplied*. Next didst Thou form the *living soul* of the faithful, through affections well ordered by the vigour of continency: and after that, the mind subjected to Thee alone and needing to imitate no human authority, hast Thou renewed *after* Thy *image and likeness;* and didst subject its rational actions to the excellency of the under-standing, as *the* woman to the man; and to all Offices of Thy Ministry, necessary for the perfecting of the faithful in this life, Thou willedst, that for their temporal uses, good things, fruitful to themselves in time to come, be given by the same faithful.[57] *All* these we see, and they are *very good*, because Thou seest them in us, Who hast given unto us Thy Spirit, by which we might see them, and in them love Thee.

[XXXV] 50 O Lord God, *give peace unto us:* (for Thou hast given us all things;) the peace of rest, the peace of the Sabbath, which hath no evening. For all this most goodly array of things *very good*, having finished their courses, is to pass away, for in them there *was morning and evening*.

[XXXVI] 51 But the seventh day hath no evening, nor hath it setting; because Thou hast sanctified it to an ever-lasting continuance; that that which Thou didst *after Thy works* which were *very good, resting the seventh day*, although Thou madest them in unbroken rest, that may the voice of Thy Book announce beforehand unto us, that we also after our works, (therefore *very good*, because Thou hast given them us,) shall *rest* in Thee also in the Sabbath of eternal life.

[XXXVII] 52 For then shalt Thou so rest in us, as now Thou workest in us; and so shall that be Thy rest through us, as these are Thy works through us.[58] But Thou, Lord, ever workest, and art ever at rest. Nor dost Thou see in time, nor art moved in time, nor restest in a time; and yet Thou makest things seen in time, yea the times themselves, and the rest which results from time.

[XXXVIII] 53 We therefore see these things which Thou madest, because they are: but they are, because Thou seest them. And we see without, that they are, and within, that they are good, but Thou sawest them there, when made, where Thou sawest them, yet to be made. And we were at a later time moved to do well, after our hearts had conceived of Thy Spirit; but in the former time we were moved to do evil, forsaking Thee; but Thou, the One, the Good God, didst never cease doing good. And we also have some *good works*, of Thy gift, but not eternal; *after them* we trust to *rest* in Thy great *hallowing*. But Thou, being the Good which needeth no good, art ever at rest, because Thy rest is Thou Thyself. And what man can teach man to understand this? or what Angel, an Angel? or what Angel, a man? Let it be *asked* of Thee, *sought* in Thee, *knocked* for at Thee; so, so shall it be *received*, so shall it be *found*, so shall it be *opened*. Amen.

GRATIAS TIBI DOMINE

NOTES

BOOK I

1 St. Ambrose; from whom were the beginnings of his conversion and by whom he was baptised.

2 Against the Manichees.

3 i.e. Let me see the face of God, though I die, (Ex. 33, 20.) since if I see it not, but it be turned away, I must needs die, and that "the second death."

4 So the Greek Versions and Vulg. rendering צֻרִים as צָרִים, as it elsewhere signifies "the proud," not "proud presumptuous sins." They interpret it of sins forced on a person by the enemy. "There are two sources of sins; one from one's self, the other from the persuasion of others; to which the prophet refers, I suppose, when he says, 'Cleanse me from my secret faults,' and ab alienis 'spare Thy servant.'" St. Aug. de Lib. Arb. I. iii. c. 10.

5 "Many cry in trouble and are not heard; but to their salvation, not (to give them) to foolishness." St. Aug. ad loc.

6 A rite in the Western Churches, on admission as a Catechumen, previous to Baptism, denoting the purity and uncorruptedness and discretion required of Christians. See St. Aug. de Catechiz, rudib. c. 26. Concil. Carth. 3. can. 5; and Liturgies in Assem. Cod. Liturg. t. i.

7 His unregenerate nature, on which the image of God was not yet impressed, rather than the regenerate.

8 The "vail" was an emblem of honour, used in places of worship, and subsequently in courts of law, Emperors' palaces, and even private houses. See Du Fresne and Hoffmann sub. v. That between the vestibule, or proscholium,

and the school itself, besides being a mark of dignity, may, as St. Aug. perhaps implies, have been intended to denote the hidden mysteries taught therein, and that the mass of mankind were not fit hearers of truth.

9 Cic. Tuscul, l. i. c. 26.

10 Coleman's Terence, Eunuch. act iii. sc. 5.

11 Lit, is careful not to say "inter hominibus," but takes no care, lest—he destroy "hominem ex hominibus."

12 To be, is no other than to be one. In as far, therefore, as anything attains unity, in so far it "is." For unity worketh congruity and harmony, whereby things composite are, in so far as they are: for things uncompounded are in themselves, because they are one; but things compounded, imitate unity by the harmony of their parts, and, so far as they attain to unity, they are. Wherefore order and rule secure being, disorder tends to not-being. Aug. de morib. Manich. c. 6

BOOK II

1 Ps. 93, 20. Vulg. Lit. "formest trouble in or as a precept." Thou makest to us a precept out of trouble, so that trouble itself shall be a precept to us, i.e. hast willed so to discipline and instruct those Thy sons, that they should not be without fear, lest they should love something else, and forget Thee, their true good. St. Aug. ad loc.

2 Formerly an episcopal city; now a small village. At this time the inhabitants were heathen. St. Aug. calls them "his fathers," in a letter persuading them to embrace the Gospel. Ep. 232.

3 Sallust. de Bell. Catil, c. 9.

4 After this will come just judgment, of which he (the Psalmist) so speaks, that we may understand that each man's own sin is the instrument of his punishment, and his iniquity is turned into his torment; that we may not think, that that serenity and ineffable light of God need produce out of Itself that whereby sins were to be punished; for He so disposeth sins, that what were delights to man sinning, are the instruments of the Lord punishing. St. Aug. in Ps. 7, 15.

5 Souls in their very sins seek but a sort of likeness of God, in a proud and perverted, and, so to say, slavish freedom. Aug. de Trin. l. xi. c. 5.

6 See iii. 7. vii. 12. (old ed.)

BOOK III

1 He alludes to the sea of Sodom, which is said to bubble out a pitchy slime, into which other rivers running, are there lost in it. And like the lake itself, remain unmoveable: wherefore it is called the Dead Sea. (old ed.) See Tacit. Hist. l. v.

2 Eversores. This appears to have been a name which a pestilent and savage set of persons gave themselves, licentious alike in speech and action. Aug. names them again, de Vera Relig. c. 40. Ep. 185. ad Bonifac. c. 4; and this book, l. 3. c. 12, whence they seem to have consisted mainly of Carthaginian students, whose savage life is mentioned again, ib. c. 8.

3 In the Preface to the book "On the Benefit of Believing," St. Aug. speaks further on the errors which betrayed him to the Manichees. He is writing to Honoratus, who was still detained among them, on the benefits of believing before we can see.

"Thou knowest, Honoratus, that the circumstance which led me among those men, was their profession, that, setting aside the terrors of authority, they would lead such as would listen to them, to God by the plain and simple way of reason, and would rescue them from all errors. For what else led me, for nearly nine years, despising the religion which was in my boyhood ingrafted into me by my parents, to follow and be a diligent hearer of those men, but that they alleged that we were terrified by superstition, and that faith was enjoined to us before reason, while they urged no one to believe, until the truth had been sifted and cleared? Who would not be attracted by such promises, especially such as they then found me, an youthful mind, longing for truth, but puffed up and prating by aid of the disputes of some even learned men in the school, despising things as old wives' fables, and longing to drink in and retain the open and unmixed truth which they promised? But what again recalled me from being altogether fixed among them, and held me in the class of 'Hearers,' as they term it, so that I let not go the hopes and cares of this world, but that I observed that they were rather fluent and copious in refuting others, than solid and settled in establishing their own views?"

4 "I fell among men, who held that that light which we see with our eyes, is to be worshipped as a chief object of reverence. I assented not; yet thought that under this covering they veiled something of great account, which they would afterwards lay open." Aug. de vita Beata, Præf.

5 Of this passage St. Aug. is probably speaking, when he says, "Praises bestowed on bread in simplicity of heart, let him (Petilian) defame, if he will, by the ludicrous title of poisoning and corrupting phrensy. Aug. meant in mockery, that by verses he could get his bread; his calumniator seems to have twisted the word to signify a love-potion, c. lit. Petiliani, l. iii. c. 16.

6 Evod. Tell me whence we do evil? Aug. You start a question, which, when rather young, greatly harassed me, and drove and cast me headlong and worn among the heretics. Through which fall I was so broken and overwhelmed by such heaps of empty fables, that unless my love of finding the truth had obtained for me the Divine aid, I could never have come out thence, or have breathed even so freely, as to be able to enquire at all. Aug. de lib. Arb. 1. i. sec. 4.

7 "In this world of sense, we must very earnestly consider the force of time and place; so as to understand, that what as a part, whether of time or place, gives pleasure, is, as a whole, far better; and again, what, as a part, offends, does, in the judgment of one well-skilled, only offend, because the whole is not seen, wherewith that part admirably harmonizes." Aug. de Ordine, 1. ii. sec. 51.

8 As in typical actions of the Patriarchs. "On this [the calumnies against the Patriarchs] I would first say, that not their words only, but their life was prophetic; and that the whole kingdom of the Hebrew nation was one great prophet, because the prophet of one Great One. Wherefore in those among them, who *were taught within by the Wisdom of God*, (Ps. 89, 12. Vulg.) we must, not in what they said only, but also in what they did, search for prophecy of the Christ who was to come, and His Church; but in the rest of that nation; collectively in those things, which were done in them or to them by God. For all these things, as the Apostle says, were our ensamples." (I Cor. 10, 6.) Aug. c. Faust. 1. xxii. c. 24. "God so accounted of these men, and at that time made them such heralds of His Son, that not only in what they said, but in what they did, or what happened to them, Christ is sought, Christ is found. Whatever Scripture saith of Abraham, both happened and is a prophecy." Id. Serm. 2. de Tentat. Abr. sec. 7. "We know that prophecy was given as

in words, so in deeds. Both in deeds and words is the resurrection preached beforehand." Tertull. de Resurr. Carnis, c. 28.

9 Augustine (Quæst. in Exod. 1. ii. qu. 71.) mentions the two modes of dividing the Ten Commandments, into three and seven, or four and six, and gives what appear to have been his own private reasons for preferring the first. Both commonly existed in his day, but the Anglican mode appears to have been the most usual. It occurs in Origen, Greg. Naz., Jerome, Ambrose, Chrys. St. Aug. alludes to his division again, Serm. 8. 9. de x chordis, and S. 33 on this Psalm. "To the first Commandment there belong three strings, because God is Trine. To the other, i.e. the love of our neighbour, seven strings. These let us join to those three, which belong to the love of God, if we would *on the psaltery of ten strings sing a new song*. If ye do it out of love, ye sing a new song; if ye do it from fear, but still do it, ye bear indeed the psaltery, but do not yet sing; but if ye do not even this, ye cast away the psaltery itself. Better even to bear, than cast away; but again, better with joy to sing, than to bear as burthensome. But to 'sing a new song,' he must be a new man."

10 "Man's true honor is the image and likeness of God, which is only retained by reference to Him by whom it is impressed. Men cleave then the more to God, the less they love any thing of their own." Aug. de Trin. xii. 11.

11 "What then doth Faustus object to the spoiling of the Egyptians, not knowing what he saith? In doing which Moses so far from sinned, that he had sinned had he not done it. For God had commanded it, who knoweth not merely from men's actions, but from their thoughts, what each should suffer and by whom."—And after assigning a reason, "there may have been other most hidden reasons, why this people should have been enjoined this by God, but to Divine commands we must

yield by obeying, not resist by disputing.—This I stedfastly affirm, that Moses might no other than God had said, so that with the Lord should be the counsel to command, with the servant the obedience to perform." Aug. c. Faust. l. xxii. c. 71. "We may not believe of Samson but that he was commanded by God to destroy himself. But when God commands, and intimates clearly and explicitly that He does command, who shall criminate obedience? who accuse the service of piety?" De Civ. Dei, i. i. c. 26.

12 The Patriarchs, See note 8.

13 He alludes here to that devout manner of the Eastern ancients, who used to lie flat on their faces in prayer. Old Ed.

14 "Two things principally, which readily captivate that unguarded age, overcame me; one, intimacy, creeping round me with a sort of semblance of good, entwining itself, like a twisted chain, manifoldly round the neck. The other, that I had frequently gained a pernicious victory in disputing with unskilful Christians, who yet would strive eagerly to defend their faith as best they might. And this success being very frequent, the excitement of youth gained ground, and recklessly pressed on its energies towards the great evil of obstinacy. And having commenced this sort of disputing, after I had heard them, whatever ability I attained, either by my own powers, (whatever they were,) or by other reading, I readily ascribed to them alone. So from their discourses there was daily excited in me ardent love for contests, and from the result of the contests, a love for them. Thus it happened, that whatever they said, I strangely assented to as true, not because I knew it, but because I wished it to be true. And so, although step by step, and cautiously, yet long did I follow men, who preferred a shining straw to a living soul." Aug. de duab. Anim. c. Manich. c. 9.

BOOK IV

1 "To be happy, by his own power, without superintendence, belongs to God only." Aug. de Gen. c. Manich. ii. 5.

2 "He alone is truly pure, who waiteth on God, and keepeth himself to Him alone." Aug. de vita beata, sec. 18. "Whoso seeketh God, is pure, because the soul hath in God her legitimate Husband. Whosoever seeketh of God any thing besides God, doth not love God purely. If a wife loved her husband, because he is rich, she is not pure, for she loveth not her husband, but the gold of her husband." Aug. Serm. 137. "Whoso seeks from God any other reward but God, and for it would serve God, esteems what he wishes to receive, more than Him from whom he would receive it. What then? hath God no reward? None, save Himself. The reward of God is God Himself. This it loveth; if it love aught beside, it is no pure love. You depart from the immortal flame, you will be chilled, corrupted. Do not depart; it will be thy corruption, will be fornication in thee," Aug. in Ps. 72. sec. 32. "The pure fear of the Lord (Ps. 19, 9.) is that, wherewith the Church, the more ardently she loveth her Husband, the more diligently she avoids offending Him, and therefore love when perfected casteth not out this fear, but it remaineth for ever and ever." Aug. in loc. "Under the name of pure fear, is signified that will, whereby we must needs be averse from sin, and avoid sin, not through the constant anxiety of infirmity, but through the tranquillity of affection." De Civ. Dei, xiv. sec. 65.

3 "Who loves what he knows not? And what is to know God but to behold, and firmly to perceive Him? But we must beware, lest the mind believing that it does not see, feign to itself something which is not, and hope and love something unreal. And if this be, it will no longer be love out of a pure conscience and faith unfeigned." Aug. de Trin. viii. 66.

4 Vindicianus, see p. 54 (chap. 6). St. Aug. Ep. 138. sec. 3. calls him "the great physician of our times."

5 See note 4 above.

6 The Manichæans, which St. Aug. then was, could not but reject Baptism, or any rite employing a material substance. They purified matter, not matter them. St. Aug, speaks again of his "mocking" at Baptism in his own case. L. v. sec. 16. "They hold that Baptism in water contributes nothing to the salvation of any, nor do they think that any of those whom they deceive, should be baptized." (Aug. de Hæres.) "The Manichæans say that the washing of regeneration, i.e. the water itself, is superfluous, and with a profane mind contend that it profits nothing.—The Manichæans destroy the visible element; the Pelagians also the invisible mystery." (c. 2. Epp. Pelag, ii. 2.) "What avails it them (The Pelagians) to confess that baptism is necessary for all ages, which the Manichæans say is superfluous in all." (ib. iv. 4.) "He knows not, or feigns he knows not, that among them [the Manichæans] the name Catechumens does not imply that any Baptism is in store for them." c. litt. Petil. iii. 17. These statements are so distinct, that *inferences* from others can have no weight. Moreover, in the de Mor. Cath. c. 35. St. Aug. is plainly speaking of Christians; in the Acta c. Fel. i. 19, Felix the Manichæan is speaking communicative; "If there is no adversary against God, why are we baptized? Why is there an Eucharist, why Christianity, if there is nothing against God?" He is arguing from conceded facts, and speaks, generally, in the first person, in the name of the whole body of Christians, without thereby implying that the Manichæans used this mystery. What was needed for his argument was, that the Catholics used it. The same argument is used by Faustus. 1. xxiv. and Manes himself, Ep. ad Menoch ap. Aug. Op. Imp. iii. 107, although there more plainly as an argumentum ad hominem. It may be,

in part, on this account, as a mercy to St. Augustine, that God Almighty made His sacrament administered to his unconscious friend, the instrument of his miraculous conversion.

7 "Were any to say, I had rather die than be unhappy, I should answer, 'Thou speakest false.' For now thou art unhappy, and willest not to die, for no other cause than to be; so then, though you will not to be unhappy, you do will to be. Give thanks then for that thou art, which thou dost will, that so what thou art against thy will may be removed from thee. For willingly thou art, but unwillingly art unhappy." Aug. de Lib. Arb. iii. sec. 10.

8 Hor. Carm. L. i. od. 3.

9 Ovid. Trist. l. iv. Eleg. iv. 72.

10 In confessing the misery of my mind at the death of my friend, saying, that our soul was, as it were, made out of two, one, I said, "and therefore perchance I feared," &c. which seems to me rather an empty declamation than a grave confession, although this folly in it may be somewhat tempered by the addition of "perchance." Aug. Retract. l. ii. c. 6.

11 See b. i. 2 and 3.

12 See sec. 13.

13 In this life men, with much toil, seek rest and freedom from care, but through perverse longings they find it not. They wish to find rest in things which rest and abide not, and these, since they are withdrawn by time and pass away, harass them with fears and sorrows, and will not let them be at rest. Aug. de Catechiz. Rud. sec. 14.

14 For the beauty of the whole discourse is not from the single letters, or syllables, but from the whole. Aug. de Gen. c. Manich. i. 21.

15 Wherever you turn, He speaketh to thee by traces, which He has impressed upon His works, and by the very forms of outward things recalls thee, when sinking down to things outward.—Woe to them who leave Thee as their guide, and go astray in the traces of Thee, who, for Thee, love these intimations of Thee, and forget what Thou intimatest! O Wisdom, Thou most sweet light of the cleansed mind; for Thou ceasest not to intimate to us what and how great Thou art, and these intimations of Thee is the universal beauty of creation. Aug. de lib. arb. ii. 16.

16 This God is not placed far from every one of us; for in Him we live and move and are. But by love must we hold and cleave to Him, that we may enjoy Him present with us, from whom we are, who, were He absent, we could not even be. Aug. de Trin. viii. sec. 5, 6.

17 Because men seeking things without, become strange even to themselves, the written law also was given them; not because it was not already written in their hearts, but because thou wert strayed, as a vagabond, from thy own heart, so He, who is everywhere, laid hold on thee, and recalled thee to thine own inward self. What then does the written law cry aloud to such as have forsaken the law written in their hearts? "return to your hearts, ye transgressors."—What then thou wouldest not have done to thee, do not to another. Thou decidest it to be evil, in that thou wouldest not endure it, and the inward law, written in thy very heart, forces thee to know this. Thou didst it, and men groaned at thy hands; how art thou forced to "go back into thy own heart," when thou endurest it at the hands of others. Aug. in Ps. 57. sec. 1.

18 Shame we, since other things are only loved, as being good, by cleaving to them to cease to love Him, through whom they are good. c. 3. Aug. de Trin. viii. 3.

19 Men revolt not to evil things but in an evil way, i.e. not to

evil natures, but therefore in an evil way, because against the natural order, they go from Him, who is the Highest, to things which in a lesser degree are. Aug. de Civ. Dei, xii. 8.

20 What so unjust as that good should be with him who deserteth what is good? Nor can it be. But sometimes the evil of the loss of the higher good is not felt, through the possession of the lower good, which men love. But it is the law of Divine justice, that whoso hath with his good-will lost what he ought to love, shall with sorrow lose what he hath loved. Aug. de Gen. ad litt. viii. 14.

21 It is a perverted loftiness, when men deserting that whereto the mind should cleave as to its first principle, would become and be, as it were, a first principle to itself.—There is then, strange to say, something in humility, which raises the heart upwards, and something in elation, which sinks it downwards.—A reverent humility makes one subject to him who is higher; but nothing is higher than God; and so humility, which makes subject to God, exalts. But a faulty elation, in that it rejects this subjection, sinks down from Him, than whom nothing is higher, and thereby becomes lower. Aug. de Civ. Dei, xiv. 13.

22 By the lowliness of repentance the soul recovers her high estate. Aug. de lib. Arb. iii. 5. He made a way for us through humility; because through pride we had departed from God, we could not return but through humility, and one to take as a pattern we had not. For the whole mortal nature of man was swelled with pride.—Lest then men should disdain to follow a humble man, God humbled Himself; that even the pride of the human race might not disdain to follow the track of God. Aug. in Ps. 33. Enarr. I. sec. 4.

23 Or "an unintelligent soul;" very good MSS. reading "sensu," the majority, it appears, "sexu;" if we read "sexu," the absolute unity of the first principle, or Monad, may be

insisted upon, and in the inferior principle, divided into "violence" and "lust," "violence" as implying strength may be looked on as the male, "lust" was, in mythology, represented as female; if we take "sensu," it will express the living, but unintelligent, soul of the world, in the Manichæan, as a Pantheistic, system.

24 All the relations of things were comprised by Aristotle under nine heads; quantity, quality, relation, action, passion, where, when, situation, clothing; and these with that wherein they might be found, or "substance," make up the ten categories or predicaments.

BOOK V

1 "On whatever place a man have fallen, thereon he must lean, that he may rise. Therefore we must lean on those very sensible forms, whereby we are held back, that we may know those, which sense tells us not of. Sensible I call, what can be perceived through the senses, i.e. the eyes, ears, and other senses of the body. These sensible or corporeal forms children must of necessity cling to and love; the young almost of necessity; thenceforward as age goes on, it is no longer necessary." Aug. de vera Relig. c. 24.

2 "As a picture, wherein a black colouring occurs in its proper place, so is the universe beautiful, if any could survey it, notwithstanding the presence of sinners, although, taken by themselves, their proper deformity makes them hideous." Aug. de Civ. Dei., xi. 23.

3 "Persons are in Scripture called the enemies of God, who,

not by nature but by sins, oppose His government; able to injure, not Him, but, themselves. For they are enemies through the will to resist, not through the power to hurt." ib. xii. 3.

4 "Nor by their wickedness do they effect that under the rule, power, and wisdom of the All-ruling God, the beauty and order of the universe should in any way be deformed, since to their wills of whatever sort, though evil, certain fitting bounds are assigned to their power, and the due measure to their deservings, so that even with them, thus placed under the fitting and due order, the universe is fair," Aug. de Gen. ad Lit. l. xi. c. 21.

5 "Faustus, of African origin, born at Milevis, of a sweet discourse and clever wit." Aug. c. Faust. l. i. init. St. Aug. speaks again of his talent, (whence Aug. the more suspected that he saw through the fallacy of his own arguments,) ib. xvi. 26. and (whereas he claimed exclusively for the Manichees the Evangelical blessings on poverty and self-denial,) his luxury, as being notorious to all the "Hearers" of the Manichees, especially at Rome, (ib. v. 7.) while he despised the poverty of his parents. (ib. c. 5.) He was, as a Manichee, banished to an island by the proconsul, the Christians however interceding for him. (ib. c. 8.)

6 "The beasts of the field are most aptly understood of men rejoicing in carnal pleasures, who mount up to nothing arduous, nothing laborious. The birds of the air, the proud, of whom it is said, 'they have set their face in the heaven.' Behold again the fishes of the sea, i.e. the carnally curious, who walk through the paths of the seas, i.e. in the depths of this world search out the things of time; which, like paths in the sea, vanish and perish as soon as the water is mingled together again, after yielding a passage to what has passed

through. For these three sorts of sins, i.e. pleasure of the flesh and pride and curiosity, include all sins." Aug. ad loe. vid. sup. iii. 8. inf. x. 30 sqq.

7 "He is the home whither we go, He the way whereby we go; go we by Him to Him and we shall not go astray. Aug. Serm. 92. Christ, as God, is the home whither we go; Christ, as man, is the way whereby we go. Ib. 123. Christ carrieth us on, as a leader, carrieth us in Him, as the way, carrieth us up to Him, as our home." Aug. in Ps. 60. sec. 4.

8 "More praiseworthy is the mind, which knoweth its very weakness, than that which, regarding it not, searches out the paths of the stars, yea though it shall, or doth already, know them, not knowing by what path he may enter upon his own salvation and abiding strength." Aug. de Trin. iv. l. St. Aug. has the same train of thought, as in these sections, Serm. 68. sec. 1, 2, which he closes, "Be not much concerned though thou knowest not the circuits of the stars, or the numbers of bodies celestial or terrestrial. Behold the *beauty* of the world, and praise the counsels of the Creator. Behold what He made; praise Him who made; hold this chiefly; love Him who made; for thee also, who lovest Him, He made in His own image."

9 See above on 1. vii. sec. 15.

10 This was the old fashion of the East; where the scholars had liberty to ask questions of their masters, and to move doubts as the professors were reading, or so soon as the lecture was done. Thus did our Saviour with the Doctors. (Luke 2, 46.) So it is still in some European Universities. (Old Ed.) See e.g. Statuta Oxon. Tit. iv. Sect. ii. sec. 4.

11 Man must not blush to confess he knows not what he doth not know, lest while he feigns that he knoweth, he bring on himself never to know. Aug. Ep. 190, sec. 16.

12 See above, l. iii. sec. 6.

13 The waters of Baptism. (Old Ed.)

14 Such [churches] as were built over the grave of any Martyr, or called by his name to preserve the memory of him, had usually the distinguishing title of Martyrium, or Confessio, or Memoria given them. The Latins instead of Martyrium commonly use the name of Memoria Martyrum for such kind of churches. As in that noted passage of St. Austin, (de Civ. Dei, xxii. 10,) where he says, "We do not build temples to our Martyrs as Gods, but only memorials of them, as dead men, whose spirits still live with God, nor do we erect altars to them in those memorials, or offer sacrifice thereon to our Martyrs, but to the only God, both theirs and ours." Bingham, Antiq. b. viii. c. I. sec. 8.

15 St. Aug. substitutes "by His Cross" for "by His flesh;" (Eph. 2, 14,) since, as a Manichee, he had not the true faith in the Incarnation of Christ, neither did his belief in the Cross avail him. "Christ," he would say, "saved not by His Cross, him who believed not in His flesh."

16 See ibid.

17 See above, b. i, sec. 10.

18 See note on b. iv. c. 8.

19 See above, I. iii. c. II, 12.

20 L. iii. c. 12. beg.

21 From the LXX. St. Aug. applies the passage to the Manichees at length in his Comm.

22 The ordinary opinion as to the Academics, was that they were universal sceptics; St. Aug. states his conviction that they held, concealed, positive truth, but publicly contented themselves with refuting the opposed errors. The grounds of this he states in two places: "The various sects were then so rife, that what was most to be feared, was, lest men should

adopt error. And when any was driven by argument from what he had held as firm and unshaken, he sought the more carefully and steadily somewhat else, in proportion to the greater perseverance of their character, and their conviction that truth lay most deeply and rootedly involved in the nature of things and of the mind. But now there is such shrinking from toil, and carelessness of valuable studies, that as soon as it is noised abroad, that very acute philosophers thought that nothing could be grasped, men let their minds loose, and close up the truth for ever." (Ep. I.) In the other, he gives the historical account, though not confidently: the account is necessarily abridged. "Plato believed that there were two worlds; one spiritual, wherein truth itself dwelt, the other, this of ours, tangible to sense. The former then he held to be true, this latter like to truth, and formed after the image of the other. And thus, that the truth, as to that former world, was cleared and unclouded to a mind which knew itself; but that in the minds of the vulgar there could be produced not a certain but a conjectural knowledge of this latter. Whatever then was done in this world, through those which he called civil virtues, being resemblances of other true virtues, known only to the few wise, could only be called like to truth. These and the like appear to have been preserved and kept as mysteries by his successors as far as they could. For that they were not easily understood, except by those, who, cleansing themselves from all stains, have risen to a more than human conversation, and whoever should knowingly teach them to persons of all sorts, would be very blameable. So then when Zeno, chief of the Stoics, having heard and received some things, came to the school left by Plato, then under Polemo, I imagine he was looked on with suspicion, and not thought fit to have those reverenced Platonic principles entrusted and laid open to him, until he should have unlearned, what he had derived from others, and brought with him into this school. Polemo dies and Arcesilas succeeds him, a fellow-disciple of Zeno, but under Polemo. Zeno then being taken with notions of his own about the world, and specially the soul, (over which true philosophy jealously watches,) affirming the soul to be mortal, and that there was nothing but this world of sense, and in it all was corporeal, (for he thought God Himself a fire,) Arcesilas seems to me to have done very wisely and carefully, in that (the evil spreading widely) he hid altogether the doctrine of the Academy, and buried it as treasure to be found by posterity. So then the vulgar being apt to go headlong into error, and, from being conversant with bodies, naturally but mischie-vously to think every thing bodily, this most acute and right-minded man, settled rather to unteach those who were ill-taught, than to teach those whom he did not think teachable. Hence arose those habits attributed as a peculiarity to the new Academy, because the old had no occasion for them." Cont. Academ. I. iii. c. 17. With the scepticism imputed to them, and which was then suggested to him, he contrasts the Christian's faith even on things not known. "The city of God altogether rejects such doubting as madness, having, of those things which by the mind and reason she comprehends, though (by reason of the corruptible body, which passeth down the 'mind,' since, as the Apostle says, 'we know in part,') a slight, yet a most certain, knowledge." De Civ. Dei, xix. 18.

23 See above on b. iii. c. 12 p. 48 note 1.

24 An undefilable substance is not therefore undefiled, because it toucheth nothing, but because, whatever it toucheth, it remaineth in its purity. For in like way do we call a body invulnerable or impenetrable, which is not struck by steel, or rather that, which being struck is not penetrated? So then it is the more proved that the Son of God could not be

defiled by the Virgin's womb, in that He was born of a woman, than if He had not been born of a woman, and had avoided that contact; for He might seem to have known that He could be defiled thereby, and so be considered by us less undefilable. Euod. de fide c. 24 in App. ad Aug. Opp. t. viii.

25 See above, I. iii. sec. 14.

26 See above, b.v. c. 20.

27 See b. iii. c. 3. end.

28 This was the main weapon of the Manichees.

29 See above, b.v. sec. 19.

30 St. Aug. relates this part of his life summarily in his "Benefit of Believing," c. 28. for the sake of his friend Honoratus, who was still a Manichee.

BOOK VI

1 Go not abroad, return unto thyself, in the inner man dwelleth truth. Aug. de vera Relig. c. 39. See above b. vii. c. 7. and 10.

2 Fidelem Catholicum, one baptized into the Catholic Faith.

3 Baptism. [Old Ed.] The text is quoted in the prayers for the consecration of the water of Baptism in the old Roman and Gallican Liturgies. See Assem. Cod. Liturg. t. ii. p. 6, 7. 33. 35. 41.

4 St. Aug. goes over some of these subjects in the Civ. Dei, l. viii. c. 27. It is addressed to heathens. "Nor do we make temples, priestly offices, rites, sacrifices, to these same

martyrs, since not they, but their God, is our God. We honour the chapels indeed erected in memory of them, as those of holy men of God, who have contended to the death of their bodies for the truth, that the true faith might be spread, the false and feigned convicted.—But who ever heard any Christian priest, even when standing at the altar built over the holy body of a martyr to the honour and worship of God, say in the prayers, 'I offer to thee a sacrifice, Peter or Paul or Cyprian,' whereas in these their monuments offerings are made to God, who made them both men and martyrs, and joined them in heavenly glory with His holy angels: that by those Holy rites we may both thank the true God for their victories; and by the renewal of their memories, and imploring His aid, may exert ourselves to gain the like crown. Whatever services then religious persons may perform in these spots, are adornings of the martyrs' churches, not oblations or sacrifices to the deceased, as though gods. They too, who bring their meals thither, (which the better sort of Christians does not do, and in most countries is no such custom,) yet they who do it, (and having done it they pray, and then remove to eat or give of them to the poor,) seek to have them sanctified through the acceptableness of the martyrs, in the name of the Lord of the martyrs. But that these are not sacrifices to the martyrs, he knoweth, who knows the One Christian Sacrifice, which also is there offered."

5 St. Aug. on the same ground, persuaded the Church of Hippo, before he became its Bishop, to abandon this practice (Ep. 29.), and wrote to urge Aurelius, Bishop of Carthage, to abolish it in his see, anticipating that the rest of Africa would follow the example of the chief see.

6 The holy Eucharist was always celebrated by the whole Church on the birthday, i.e. day of martyrdom, of the Martyr. See Bingham 13, 9. 5. and 20, 7. 7, 8.

7 This animal (the swine) is in the law classed as unclean, as not ruminating, not as being its fault but its nature. But there are men signified by this animal, unclean by their fault not by nature, who hearing the words of wisdom gladly, afterwards reflect not thereon. For to bring back whatever useful thing you have heard as it were from the interior of the memory to the mouth of reflection, what else is it than after a sort spiritually to ruminate? Which whoso doth not, is figured by that sort of animals, whence the very abstaining from their flesh forewarned us to avoid the like fault. For wisdom herself being such a desirable treasure, it is of this cleanness of ruminating, and uncleanness of not ruminating, that it is written in another place, "The desirable treasure resteth in the mouth of the wise, but the fool swalloweth it down." Aug. c. Faust. vi. 7.

8 Perhaps Valentinian the younger, whose court, according to Possidius, was at Milan, when Aug. was Professor of Rhetoric there. Aug. also writes (c. litt. Petil. iii. 25.) that "he recited on the first of January a panegyric to Bauto the consul, as required by his then profession of Rhetoric." (Ed. Ben.)

9 Alypius became Bishop of Thagaste. (Aug. de gestis c. Emerit. sec. 1 and 5.) On the necessity which Bishops were under of hearing secular causes, and its use, see Bingham, l. ii. c. 7.

10 The Lord High Treasurer of the Western Empire was called *Comes Sacrarum largitionum*: he had six other treasurers in so many provinces under him, whereof he of Italy was one. Sir Henry Spelman's Glossary, "Comes," who quotes Cassiodor. Var. l. v. c. 40. [Old Ed.]

11 Discederet, sc. in alia omnia. The old Ed. renders "gone off the Bench."

12 "Pretiis Prætorianis, 'Pretium regium' is the privilege of a king or lord to purchase things at a certain fixed price." Du Cange.

13 "'Nebridius, my friend, who being a most diligent and acute enquirer in difficult subjects, especially such as related to doctrines of faith, hated exceedingly a brief answer on a great question." Aug. Ep. 98, sec. 8.

14 The Church herself addresses you in tones of motherly affection, "I whose growth and fruitfulness through the whole world so much amazes you, was not always what you now behold me. They who at that time were believers in Judæa, taught the miraculous birth of a virgin, the Passion, Resurrection, and Ascension of Christ, all His divine words and deeds, witnesses the things witnessed. These ye have not seen, and so refuse to believe. Look then at this, reflect on this which you see; which is neither related to you, being past, nor foretold, being future, but pointed out to you as present. Is it in your eyes a slight thing, or without meaning; think you it none or a slight Divine miracle, that the whole human race wear the name of One crucified?" Aug. de fide rer. quæ non videntur, sec. 5 and 7.

15 "I was entangled in the life of this world, clinging to dull hopes, of a beauteous wife, the pomp of riches, the emptiness of honours, and the other hurtful and destructive pleasures." Aug. de util, credendi, sec. 3. "After I had shaken off the Manichæans and escaped, especially when I had crossed the sea, the Academics long detained me tossing in the waves, winds from all quarters beating against my helm. And so I came to this shore, and there found a pole-star, to whom to entrust myself. For I often observed in the discourses of our Priest [Ambrose] and sometimes in yours [Theodorus], that you had no corporeal notions when you thought of God, or even of the soul, which of all things is next to God. But I was withheld, I own, from casting myself speedily into the bosom of true wisdom, by the alluring hopes of marriage and honours; meaning when I had

obtained these, to press (as few singularly happy had before me) with oar and sail into that haven, and there rest." Aug. de Vita Beata, sec. 4.

16 Paullinus says, that "though he lived among the people and set over them, ruling the sheep of the Lord's fold, as a watchful shepherd, with anxious sleeplessness, yet by renunciation of the world, and denial of flesh and blood, he had made himself a wilderness, severed from the many, called among the few." Ap. Aug. Ep. 24. sec. 2. St. Jerome calls him "his holy and venerable brother, Father (Papa) Alypius." (Ep. 39. ib.) Earlier, Aug. speaks of him, as "abiding in union with him, to be an example to the brethren who wished to avoid the cares of this world," (Ep. 22.) and to Paullinus, (Ep. 27.) [Romanianus] "is a relation of the venerable and truly blessed Bishop, Alypius, whom you embrace with your whole heart; deservedly: for whosoever thinks favourably of that man, thinks of the great mercy of God, and of the wonderful gifts of God.—Soon, by the help of God, I shall transfuse Alypius wholly into your soul; [Paullinus had asked Alypius to write him his life, and Aug. had at Alypius' request undertaken to relieve him, and to do it;] for I feared chiefly, lest he should shrink from laying open all, which the Lord has bestowed upon him, lest, if read by any ordinary person (for it would not be read by you only), he should seem not so much to set forth the gifts of God committed to men, as to exalt himself."

17 Romanianus was a relation of Alypius, (Aug. Ep. 27. ad Paulin.) of talent, which astonished Aug. himself, (c. Acad. i. 1. ii. 1.) "surrounded by affluence from early youth, and snatched by what are thought adverse circumstances from the absorbing whirlpools of life." (Ib.) Aug. frequently mentions his great wealth, as also this vexatious suit, whereby he was harassed, (c. Acad. i. 1. ii. 1, 2.) and which so clouded his mind, that his talents were almost unknown; (c. Acad. ii. 2.)

as also his very great kindness to himself, when "as a poor
lad, setting out to foreign study, he had received him in his
house, supported, and (yet more) encouraged him; when
deprived of his father, comforted, animated, aided him; when
returning to Carthage, in pursuit of a higher employment,
supplied him with all necessaries"—"lastly," says Aug.
"whatever ease I now enjoy, that I have escaped the bonds of
useless desires, that, laying aside the weight of dead cares, I
breathe, recover, return to myself, that with all earnestness I
am seeking the truth, [Aug. wrote this the year before his
baptism.] that I am attaining it, that I trust wholly to arrive at
it, you encouraged, impelled, effected." (c. Acad. ii. 2.) Aug.
had "cast him headlong with himself," (as so many other of
his friends) into the Manichæan heresy, (ib. i. sec. 3.) and it is
to be hoped that he extricated him with himself, but we only
learn positively that he continued to be fond of the works of
Aug. (Ep. 27.) whereas in that which he dedicated to him, (c.
Acad.) Aug. writes very doubtingly to him, and afterwards
recommends him to Paulinus "to be cured wholly or in part
by his conversation." (Ep. 27.)

18 Pain which some think a primary evil, whether of mind or
body, cannot even exist except in bodies retaining some
soundness. For that which offers resistance, so as to suffer,
after a manner refuses to cease to be what it was, having been
to a degree good; but when it is constrained to something
better, the pain is useful, when to the worse, useless.—But
evils without pain are worse; for it is worse to rejoice in
iniquity, than to feel pain for corruption.—So in the body a
wound with pain is better than putrefaction without pain,
which especially is entitled mortification [corruption.] Aug.
de natura boni Manich. c. 20.

19 How great a good God is, is chiefly set forth by this, that it
is well with no one who forsaketh Him. Aug. de Gen. ad Lit.
I. xv. c. 5.

BOOK VII

1 "By what understanding shall man comprehend God, when he comprehendeth not his very intellect, whereby he would fain comprehend Him?" Aug. de Trin. v. sec. 2.

2 St. Aug. frequently uses this argument against the Manichees, (e.g. de Morib. Manich. c. 12. c. Secundin. M. c. 20. de fide c. Man. c. 18 and 35.) and when in the conference with Fortunatus, the latter had nothing to answer to it, Aug. subjoins, "I knew that you had nothing to say, and when I was a 'hearer' among you, I could never discover what to say; and this was to me a warning from God to leave that error, and turn, or rather return, to the Catholic faith, through His mercy, who allowed me not to be held fast for ever in these deceits." Disp. 2. c. Fortun. Manich. v. fin.

3 "Evil is of two sorts, one which a man doth, the other which he suffers. What he doth, is sin; what he suffereth, punishment. The Providence of God governing and controlling all things, man doth ill which he wills, so as to suffer ill which he wills not." Aug. c. Adim. c. 26. We answer the Manichees, "Evil is not out of (ex) God, nor coæternal with God; but evil arose out of the free will of our rational nature, which was created good by Him who is good; but his goodness is not equal to the goodness of his Creator, since he is not of His nature [as the Manichees taught] but His workmanship; therefore he was under the possibility, not the necessity of sinning. But he had not even been under the possibility, had he had the nature of God, Who neither wills to be able, nor is able to will, to sin." But on this Manichæus proceeds, "If evil arose out of the free-will of the rational nature, whence that numerous tribe of evils, with which we see that they are born, who have not yet the free exercise of will?"—We answer, "These evils also are derived from the

will of human nature, which greatly sinning, was corrupted and condemned with its offspring. Wherefore those so varied natural goods of this nature, come from the workmanship of God, the evils from His judgments, which evils, they do not see, cannot be natures or substances, but are therefore called natural, because men are born with them, the original stock, as it were, being corrupted." Aug. Op. Imp. c. Julian. Pelag. vi. 5.

4 See b. iv. c. 3.

5 "Let the soul, then, reflecting upon herself, seek her own place in conformity to her nature, under Him to Whom she is to be subjected, above the things over which she is to be placed; under Him, by Whom she ought to be ruled, above the things which she ought to rule." Aug. de Trin. l. x. c. 5. "For so is she ordered, in the order not of place but of existences, that above her should be no one, but Him." Ib. l. xiv. c. 14. "It is expedient that the inferior should be subjected to the superior, that so he who wishes to have what is inferior to him subjected to him, should himself be subjected to what is superior to him." Aug. in Ps. 143.

6 "For pride renders averse to wisdom—but whence this averseness, but that he whose good is God, would be his own good to himself, as God is to Himself?" Aug. de lib. Arb. iii. 24.

7 This was likely to be the Book of Amelius the Platonist, who hath indeed this beginning of St. John's Gospel, calling the Apostle a Barbarian. Euseb. Præp. Evang. l. i. c. 10. [Old Ed.] "When I had read a very few books of Plato, whom I hear that you study eagerly, and had compared with them, as far as I could, their authoritative statement, who have delivered to us the Divine mysteries, I was so kindled, that I wished to break away from all those anchors which held me, but for the influence of certain persons." Aug. de Vita Beata, sec. 4.

8 All the following contrasts turn on this, that the Platonists had a notion of a Divine Eternal Word or Logos, (believing Him however to be in no sense distinct from God the Father,) but of His humiliation in becoming man, none.

9 "Plotinus explaining the meaning of Plato asserts, that not even that soul of the universe, whose existence they believe, derives its happiness from any other source than ours, i.e. that light which itself is not, but by which it was created, whereby, being intellectually illumined, it giveth out its intellectual (intelligibiliter) light.—This great Platonist then says, that the rational, or rather perhaps intellectual soul, (whereto, he conceives, that the souls of the immortals and the blessed belong, who he doubteth not dwell in the heavenly mansions,) hath no nature above it, save that of God, Who made the world, by Whom also itself was made; and that those superior beings derive their blessed life, and light of understanding the truth, from no other source than we; in harmony with the Gospel, where it is written, 'There was a man sent by God—he was not that light.' (John 1, 6 sqq.) By which contrast it sufficiently appears, that the rational or intellectual soul, such as it was in John, cannot be a light to itself, but shines by the participation of another true light. This John himself confesses, when 'bearing Him witness,' he saith, 'Of His fulness have we all received.'" Aug. de Civ. Dei, x. 2. comp. Tert. de Testim. animæ.

10 "Natus est" for "nati sunt." This reading occurs in Irenæus, l. lii. c. 18 and 21. (in a third place, he understands the passage of the Christian new birth, l. v. c. 2.) Tertull. de carne Christi, c. 19 and 24. Ambros. Præf. in Ps. 37: but the received reading occurs in other places both of St. Ambrose and St. Aug. as in the other fathers. See Sabatier ad loc.

11 We find the lentile to be an Egyptian food, for in Egypt it abounds; whence the Alexandrian lentile is highly prized,

(cp. Num. 11, 5.) and is brought even to our country, as if the lentile did not grow here. Esau, then, by desiring the Egyptian food, lost his birth-right. So also the people of the Jews, of whom it is said, "In their heart they turned back into Egypt," after a sort longed for the lentiles, and so lost their birth-right. Aug. in Ps. 46. sec. 6. [ed. Ben.]

12 "Let every good and true Christian understand that truth, wherever he finds it, belongs to *his* Lord." Aug. de Doctr. Christ. l. ii. c. 18. "By whomsoever truth is said, it is said through His teaching Who is The Truth." Aug. Ep. 166. sec. 9. "Whatever those called philosophers, and especially the Platonists, may have said true and conformable to our faith, is not only not to be dreaded, but is to be claimed from them, as unlawful possessors, to our use. For as the Egyptians not only had idols and heavy burthens, which the people of Israel were to abhor and avoid, but also vessels and ornaments of gold and silver, and apparel, which that people, at its departure from Egypt, privily assumed for a better use, not on its own authority, but at the command of God, the very Egyptians unwittingly furnishing the things, which themselves used not well; so all the teaching of the Gentiles not only hath feigned and superstitious devices, and heavy burdens of an useless toil, which we severally, as, under the leading of Christ, we go forth out of the fellowship of the Gentiles, ought to abhor and avoid, but it also containeth liberal arts, fitter for the service of truth, and some most useful moral precepts: as also there are found among them some truths concerning the worship of the One God Himself, as it were their gold and silver, which they did not themselves form, but drew from certain veins of Divine Providence running throughout, and which they perversely and wrongfully abuse to the service of dæmons. These the Christian, when he severs himself from their wretched fellowship, ought to take from them for the right use of preaching the Gospel.—For what else have many excellent

members of our faith done? See we not how richly laden with gold and silver and apparel, that most persuasive teacher and most blessed martyr Cyprian departed out of Egypt? or Lactantius? or Victorinus, Optatus, Hilary, not to speak of the living? and Greeks innumerable? And this, Moses himself, that most faithful servant of God, first did, of whom it is written, that 'he was learned in all the wisdom of the Egyptians.'" de Doctr. Christ. l. ii. c. 40.

13 As he had thought, as a Manichee. Vid. sup. l. iii. see. 10 and 12. and l. iv. sec. 3. and vii. sec. 2. "God is light, not such as these eyes see, but as the heart seeth, when thou hearest, 'He is Truth.'" Aug. de Trin. viii. 2.

14 "We were created in the image of our Creator, Whose is True Eternity, Eternal Truth, Eternal and True Love, and He is the Eternal and True and Loving Trinity, neither 'confounded' nor 'divided.'" Aug. de Civ. Dei, xi. 28. "For the Essence of God, whereby He Is, hath in it nothing mutable, whether in Eternity, or in Truth, or in Will; for there Truth is eternal, Love eternal; and there Love is true, Eternity true; and there Eternity is loving, Truth loving." Aug. de Trin. iv. procem.

15 "By becoming unlike, thou hast gone far away; by becoming like, thou drawest near." Aug. Præf. Serm. ad Ps. 99.

16 For that is chiefly to be said to Be, which always exists in one and the same way; which is every way like itself; which can in no way be injured or changed; which is not subject to time; which cannot at one time be other than at another. For this is what is most truly said to Be. Aug. de mor. Manich. c. 1. Magnificently then and divinely did our God say to His servant, I AM THAT I AM, and "thou shalt say to the children of Israel, I AM hath sent me unto you;" for He truly Is, because He is unchangeable; for all change causes that which was, not to Be. He then truly Is, who is unchangeable. Aug. de nat. boni, c. 19.

17 And not one only; goodness is the essence of things, diversity of goodness their difference. "Since no nature whatever is evil, and the name [evil] belongeth only to privation of good, but from things earthly to things heavenly, from things invisible to things visible, some things are better than other, being good; being unequal to this end, that they all might *be*." Aug. de Civ. Dei, ii. 22.

18 See above, l. v. c. 1. and note 1.

19 See above, l. xi. c. 13 and 20.

20 "'Why is earth and ashes proud?—while he liveth he casteth away his bowels.' Eccli. 10, 9. Since the soul in itself is nothing, but whatever is life in it, is from God, while it abides in its assigned place, it is sustained in mind and conscience by the presence of God Himself. This then is its innermost good. Wherefore to swell with pride, this is to pass off into outermost things, and, so to speak, to empty itself and so less and less to be. But to pass off into outermost things, what is this other than to *cast out its innermost parts*, i.e. to remove itself far from God, not by distance of space, but by the affections of the mind?" Aug. de Mus. l. vi. sec. 40.

21 Vid. sup. c. 10. init.

22 "'Phantasms' are nothing else than figments drawn by the bodily senses from bodily forms; which, to commit to memory, as they have been received, to divide, multiply, contract, enlarge, order, disarrange, or in any other way image in the mind by thinking, is very easy; but to avoid and escape, where truth is sought, difficult." Aug. de vera Relig. c. 10.

23 "Distinct from the soul is that Light Itself, whereby it is so enlightened, that it may behold all things, whether in itself or in Him, understanding them truly. For that Light is God Himself; but the soul, although rational and intellectual, is a

creature made after His image, which, when it endeavours to behold that Light, quivers through weakness, and is unable. Yet still thence is derived whatever it understands, as it is able. When then it is borne away thither, and withdrawn from the bodily senses, it is placed more expressly in the presence of That Vision, then, not in local space, but in a way of its own, it sees even above itself That, whereby being aided it sees also whatever, by understanding, it does see in itself" Aug. de Gen. ad Litt. xii. 31.

24 "He exalts those who follow humbly, who shrunk not from descending to them when lying prostrate." Aug. de Sancta Virginitate, c. 32.

25 "A 'skin' denotes mortality; wherefore our first parents, the authors of the sin of the human race,—having become mortal, were dismissed from paradise; but to denote their mortality, they were clothed with 'coats of skins;'—but skins are not taken but from dead animals; therefore by the name of skins, that mortality was figured." Aug. Enarr. in Ps. 103. s. 1. sec. 8. "Those, who ashamed of their nakedness, had made themselves aprons, He clothed with coats also, therefore of skin, that the death now attached to their corruptible bodies might be thereby figured." Op. Imp. c. Julian. iv. 37.

26 "The Word, the rational soul, and the flesh all together is Christ." Aug. Serm. 253. c. 4.

27 As the Manichees thought.

28 "——The faithful, I say, who believes and confesses in the Mediator, a real human, i.e. our, nature, although God the Word taking it in a singular manner, sublimated it into the Only Son of God, so that He who took it, and what He took, was One Person in the Trinity. For, after man was assumed, there became not a Quaternity, but remained the Trinity, that assumption making in an ineffable way, the truth of One Person in God and man. Since we do not say that Christ is

only God, as do the Manichæan heretics, nor only man, as the Photinian heretics, nor in such wise man as not to have any thing, which certainly belongs to human nature, whether the soul, or in the soul itself, the rational mind, or the flesh not taken of the woman, but made of the Word converted and changed into flesh, which three false and vain statements made three several divisions of the Apollinarian heretics; but we say that Christ is true God, born of God the Father, without any beginning of time, and also true man, born of a human mother in the fulness of time; and that His humanity, whereby He is inferior to the Father, does not derogate from His Divinity, whereby He is equal to the Father," Aug. de dono Persev. sec. ult. "There was formerly a heresy, its remnants perhaps still exist, of some called Apollinarians. Some of them said that that man, whom the Word took, when 'the Word was made flesh,' had not the human, (i.e. rational) mind, but was only a soul without human intelligence, but that the very Word of God was in that man instead of a mind. They were cast out; the Catholic Faith rejected them, and they made a heresy. It was established in the Catholic Faith, that that man, whom the Wisdom of God took, had nothing less than other men, with regard to the integrity of man's nature, but as to the excellency of His Person, had more than other men. For other men may be said to be partakers of the Word of God, having the Word of God, but none of them can be called the Word of God, which He was called when it is said, *The Word was made flesh*." (Aug. in Ps. 29. Enarr. 2. sec. 2.) "But when they reflected, that if their doctrine were true, they must confess, that the Only-Begotten Son of God, the Wisdom and Word of the Father, *by Whom all things were made*, is believed to have taken a sort of brute with the figure of a human body, they were dissatisfied with themselves, yet not so as to amend, and confess that the whole man was assumed by the Wisdom of God, without any diminution of nature; but still more boldly, denied to Him the soul itself, and every thing of any worth in man, and said that He took only human flesh." (De 83 Div. Quæst. qu. 80.) "These too the Catholic Church rejected, and expelled them from the sheep, and from the simple and true faith; and it was the more settled, that that Man, the Mediator, had every thing of men, save sin." (Aug. in Ps. 1. c.)

29 "The Photinians ascribe to the Son of God a beginning from the virgin's womb, and will not believe that He was before." Aug. Ep. 147. c. 7. See also b. vii. note 27 above.

30 "For to Be has chiefly reference to abiding; therefore that which is said in the highest and greatest sense to Be, is so called from its abiding in itself." Aug. de Mor. Manich, c. 6. See above c. xi.

31 Non peritus, sed periturus.

32 Non flebam sed inflabar.

33 "For thereby is He a Mediator, whereby He is man, thereby also He is the way. Since if between him, who goeth, and the place, whither he goes, there be the medium of a way, he has a hope of arriving; but if there be not, or he know not how he is to go, what avails it to know whither he is to go?" Aug. de Civ. Dei, l. xi. c. 2. "For what furthers it one, exalting himself, and so ashamed to embark on the wood [of the Cross], to see from afar his home beyond the sea? Or what hinders it the humble, that at so great a distance he sees it not, while he is drawing nigh it on that wood, whereon the other disdains to be carried?" Aug. de Trin. iv. 15. See also Tract. 2. in Joh. Evang.

34 "By a most deep and healthful mystery, the whole face, and (so to speak) countenance of Holy Scripture is found to admonish those who duly behold it, that *whose glorieth should glory in the Lord.*" Aug. Enchirid. c. 98.

35 Creasti, from the LXX, εκτισε. St. Aug. understands the passage (as is implied in this place,) of the human nature of our Lord, and "the beginning of His ways," of the beginning of coming to Him. "He who was pleased to give Himself not only as the possession of those who should come to the end, but also as the way to those who would come, was pleased to take upon Him flesh; whence also is that saying, 'The Lord created Me in the beginning of his ways,' that they should begin thence, who wished to come—from whom all must set off and begin their journey, who desire to come to the truth and abide in Eternal Life." Aug. de Doctr. Christ. i. sec. 38. "With reference to the 'form of God,' it is said, 'before the hills He begat Me,' i.e. before all the highest of creation, and, 'before the Morning star I begat Thee,' i.e. before all times and things of time; but with reference 'to the form of a servant,' it is said, 'The Lord formed Me in the beginning of His ways.' For as to the form of God He said, 'I am the Truth,' as to the form of a servant, 'I am the Way.' For because as the 'First-begotten from the dead,' He made a way for His Church to the kingdom of God to life eternal, being its Head for the immortality of the body also, therefore He was 'formed in the beginning of the ways of God towards His works.' For as to the form of God, He is 'the Beginning who also speaketh unto us,' (Joh. 8, 25.) in which 'Beginning God made heaven and earth.'—As to the form of God, 'He is the first-begotten of all creation.'" De Trin. i. sec. 24. "The same Wisdom which was begotten of God, deigned also to be created among men. Whereto belongeth, 'The Lord created Me,' &c. for 'the beginning of His ways' is the Head of the Church, which is Christ clothed with man, through whom an ensample of life might be given us, whereby to arrive at God." De fide et Symb. sec. 6. St. Athanas. in like way, Orat. ii. c. Ariann. sec. 47. "The Lord knowing His own Nature to be the Only-Begotten Wisdom, and Production of the Father, and other

than things of a produced and created nature, says in His love to man, 'The Lord, &c.' as if He had said, the Father 'prepared Me a body,' and created Me for man for the salvation of man. For as when we hear John say 'the Word became flesh,' we do not understand that the whole Word was flesh, but that it clothed itself with flesh and became man, or when we hear that 'Christ became a curse for us,' and that 'He made Him who knew no sin to be sin for us,' that He became wholly a curse and a sin, but that He took upon Him our curse and bore our sins, (Gal. 3, 13. Is. 53, 4. 1 Pet. 2, 24.) so when we hear in the Proverbs the word 'created,' we may not think that the Word is wholly a creature, but that God created Him 'having prepared for Him,' as is written, a created 'body,' that in Him we might be capable of being renewed and deified." (Comp. de Decret. Nic. Syn. sec. 14.) With regard to the difference of rendering ἐκτισε (ὁ Syr. Ch.) and ἐκτησατο (Aq. Theod. Symm. Jer.) it is in appearance more than in reality, for as St. Athanas. argues, (c. Arian. Orat. ii. sec. 48. comp. Dionysius ap. Athanas, de Decret. Nic. Syn. sec. 26. Hilar. de Synodis, sec. 17) "since 'creating,' in the sense of 'making,' is inconsistent with the fact of Sonship, therefore it must be taken in some other sense consistent with it, (as in Ps. 101, 19. ὁ 50, 12. Eph. 2, 15. Eph. 4, 24. Jer. 21, 22.) Wisdom is not here called a creature, though it is said God formed It," (ib.) that the question does not turn on words, "that the word is a thing indifferent, if the Nature be agreed upon, for words do not destroy the Nature, but rather the Nature draws over and changes the words into itself, for words were not before the natures but the reverse," (ib. sec. 3.) "that things created and made are external to the maker, but a son not so, but from the father who begat him; and a man forms (κτιζει) a house, but begets a son, and one could not convert these and say that the house or ship were begotten by the maker, but the son formed and made by him;" (de decr. Nic. Syn. sec. 13.) and "of human sons, if they be confessed to be sons, it matters not whether the word εγενοντο, (Job 1, 3.) or εκτησαμην, (Gen. 4, 1.) or εποιησα, (Is. 38, 19. 6.) be used for the nature of the case and the truth draw the meaning over to itself. Wherefore if any enquire, whether the Lord is a creature or made, you must first ask 'is He a Son and Word and Wisdom?' for if this be shewn, then all notion of a creature is cast out at once and at rest." Orat. ii. c. Arian. sec. 5. The passages then in which the Son is said to be "begotten," would be, in any case, a key to the meaning of εκτιοε in this. This argument will equally hold, if as Hilary (de Trin. xii. sec. 36.) seems to do, the passage be interpreted of the Coming forth προελευσιδ of the Son to create the worlds. And so one may admit without scruple that קבה has a sense which may be represented by κτιζει, "formed, produced" (not simply "possessed;") corresponding with חוללתי v. 24, 25. "brought forth" and in distinct contrast with "His works" (ספצליו). The modified meaning of κτιζει, (as of course all words used of Divine truths must be modified) in St. Athanas, corresponds best with that of קבה, which is not one of the words used of proper creation.

36 See above 1. ix. sec. 36. and note 42.

37 In giving an account of this period to his friend and patron Romanianus, St. Aug. seems to have blended together this and the history of his completed conversion, which was also wrought in connection with words in the same Apostle, but the account of which he uniformly suppresses, for fear probably of injuring the individual to whom he was writing. (See above on b. ix. sec. 4.) "Since that vehement flame, which was about to seize me, as yet was not, I thought that by which I was slowly kindled, was the very greatest. When lo! certain books—when they had distilled a very few drops of most precious unguent on that tiny flame, it is past belief,

Romanianus, past belief, and perhaps past what even you believe of me, (and what could I say more?) nay to myself also is it past belief; what a conflagration of myself they lighted. What ambition, what human show, what empty love of fame, or, lastly, what incitement or band of this mortal life could hold me then? I turned speedily and wholly back into myself. I cast but a glance, I confess, as one passing on, upon that religion which was implanted into us, as boys, and interwoven with our very inmost selves; but she drew me unknowing to herself. So then stumbling, hurrying, hesitating, I seized the Apostle Paul; 'for never,' said I, 'could they have wrought such things, or lived as it is plain they did live, if their writings and arguments were opposed to this so high good.' I read the whole most intently and carefully. But then, never so little light having now been shed thereon, such a countenance of wisdom gleamed upon me, that if I could exhibit it,—I say not to you, who ever hungeredst after her though unknown—but to your very adversary, (see on b. vi. sec. 24. note 17) casting aside and abandoning whatever now stimulates him so keenly to whatsoever pleasures, he would, amazed, panting, enkindled, fly to her Beauty." (c. Acad. ii. sec. 5.)

BOOK VIII

1 Simplicianus "became a successor of the most blessed Ambrose, Bishop of the Church of Milan." (Aug. Retract. ii. 1.) To him St. Aug. wrote two books "de diversis quæstionibus," (Opp. t. vi. p. 82 sqq.) and calls him "father," (ib.) speaks of his "fatherly affection from his most benevolent

heart not recent or sudden, but tried and known," (Ep. 37.) requests his "remarks and corrections of any books of his, which might chance to fall into his holy hands." (ib.) St. Ambrose mentions his "having traversed the whole world, for the sake of the Faith and of acquiring Divine knowledge, and having given the whole period of this life to daily reading, night and day; that he had an acute mind, whereby he took in intellectual studies, and was in the habit of proving how far the books of philosophy were gone astray from the truth." Ep. 65. see. 5. p. 1052. ed. Ben. See also Tillemont H. E. t. 10. Art. St. Simplicien.

2 St. Ambrose so ends a letter to him, "Farewell, and cherish us with a parent's affection, as you do." (Ambr. Ep. 65. and Simplic.) "I recognise therein the feelings of ancient friendship, and which is more, the affection of fatherly goodness." (Id. Ep. 35.) Some conjecture that he so terms him, as having been prepared by him for baptism; St. Aug.'s words lead rather to think that he baptized, and "so begat him in the Gospel."

3 "Which beginning of the holy Gospel, named after St. John, a certain Platonist, (as we were wont to hear from the aged saint, Simplician, who afterward presided as Bishop over the Church of Milan,) said, ought to be written in letters of gold, and put up in the most conspicuous places in all Churches. But that God was therefore disregarded as a teacher by the proud [philosophers] because 'the Word was made flesh and dwelt among us.'" Aug. de Civ. Dei, x. 29.

4 "Victorinus, by birth an African, taught rhetoric at Rome under Constantius, and in extreme old age, giving himself up to the Faith of Christ, wrote some books against Arius dialectically [and so] very obscure, which are not understood but by the learned, and a commentary on the Apostle" [Paul]. Jerome de Viris III. c. 101. It is of the same probably that Gennadius speaks (de Viris III. c. 60.) "that he commented in a

Christian and pious strain, but inasmuch as he was a man taken up with secular literature, and not trained in the divine Scriptures by any teacher, he produced what was comparatively of little weight." Comp. Jerome Præf. in Comm. in Gal. and see Tillemont l. c. p. 170 sqq. Some of his works are extant.

5 Æn. viii. 698–700. Trapp, I. 886.

6 The Apostles' Creed, which was delivered orally to the Catechumens to commit to memory, and by them "delivered back," i.e. publicly repeated before they were baptized. "The Symbol [Creed] bearing hallowed testimony, which ye have together received, and are this day severally to give back, are the words in which the faith of our mother the Church is solidly constructed on a stable foundation, which is Christ the Lord. 'For other foundation can no man lay,' &c. Ye have received then and given back what ye ought to retain in heart and mind, what ye should repeat in your beds, think on in the streets, and forget not in your meals, and while sleeping in body, in heart watch therein. For this is the faith, and the rule of salvation, that 'We believe in God, the Father Almighty, &c.'" (Aug. Serm. 215, in redditione Symboli.) "On the Sabbath-day [Saturday], when we shall keep a vigil through the mercy of God, ye will give back not the [Lord's] prayer, but the Creed." (Id. Serm. 58, sec. ult.) "What ye have briefly heard, ye ought not only to believe, but to commit to memory in so many words, and utter with your mouth." (Serm. 214, in tradit. Symb. 3. sec. 2.) "Nor, in order to retain the very words of the Creed, ought ye any wise to write it, but to learn it thoroughly by hearing, nor, when ye have learnt it, ought ye to write it, but always to keep and refresh it in your memories.—'This is My Covenant which I will make with them after those days,' saith the Lord, 'I will place My law in their minds, and in their heart will I write it.' To convey this, the Creed is learnt by hearing; and not written on tables or

any substance, but on the heart." (Serm. 212. sec. 2.) See the
Roman Liturgy, (Assem, Cod. Liturg. t. i. p. 11 sqq. 16.) and
the Gothic and Gallican. (p. 30 sqq. p. 38 sq. 40 sq. &c.)

7 Here be divers particulars of the primitive fashion, in this
story of Victorinus. First being converted, he was to take some
well-known Christian (who was to be his godfather) to go with
him to the Bishop: who upon notice of it, admitted him a
Catechumenus, and gave him those six points of Catechistical
Doctrine, mentioned Heb. 6, 1. 2. When the time of baptism
drew near, the young Christian came to give in his heathen
name, which was presently registered; submitting himself to
examination. On the eve, was he in a set form, first to renounce
the devil, and to pronounce, I confess to thee, O Christ;
repeating the Creed with it, in the form here recorded. The time
for giving in their names, must be within the two first weeks of
Lent: and the solemn day to renounce upon, was Maundy
Thursday. So bids the Council of Laodicea, Can. 45, 46. [Old Ed.]

8 See above, l. xii. sec. 12. l. xiii. sec. 11.

9 "As Scipio, after the conquest of Africa, took the name of
Africanus,—so Saul also, being sent to preach to the Gentiles,
brought back his trophy out of the first spoils won by the
Church, the Proconsul Sergius Paulus, and set up his banner,
in that for Saul he was called Paul." Jerome, Comm. in Ep. ad
Philem. init. Origen mentions the same opinion, (which is
indeed suggested by the relation in the Acts) but thinks that
the Apostle had originally two names, (Præf. in Comm. in Ep.
ad Rom.) which as a Roman may very well have been, and yet
that he made use of his Roman name Paul, first in connection
with the conversion of the Proconsul; Chrysostom says that it
was doubtless changed at the command of God, which is to be
supposed, but still may have been at this time.

10 "For it is the most just punishment of sin, that each should
lose what he would not use well; i.e. that he who knowing

what is right doth it not, should lose the knowledge what is right; and he who would not do well when he could, should lose the power when he would." Aug. de lib. arb. v. 18.

11 Illud placebat et vincebat, hoc libebat et vinciebat.

12 He was born A.D. 251. See his life in St. Athanasius, t. i. p. 793 sqq. Tillemont H. E. t. vii. p. 46 sqq. History of St. Antony in British Magazine, t. ix. p. 41, 158, 277. and the testimonies to the work of St. Athanas. prefixed by the Bened. p. 785 sqq. which shew incidentally how highly he was esteemed. Aug. speaks of him, "as a holy and perfect man, who is extolled as having, without any knowledge of letters, by hearing learnt the Divine Scriptures, and by thoughtful reflection understood them." De doctr. Christian. Prol. sec. 4.

13 See Athanas. Vita St. Anton. sec. 54, 56 sqq. Tillemont l. c. art. 7. Brit. Mag. l. c. p. 77 sqq.

14 "Egypt at that time was flourishing not only in men, learned in Christian philosophy, but in such also, as abiding in the vast wilderness, wrought, through the simplicity of their lives, and the sincerity of their heart, Apostolic signs and prodigies—so that the Apostle's saying was truly fulfilled, 'where sin abounded, grace did much more abound.'" Ruffin. H. E. ii. 8.—"Let them enquire how great a flock He there collecteth, what a numerous body of holy men and women He hath, who wholly despise the world. That flock has so much increased, that it hath banished superstitions even thence." Aug. Serm. 138. sec. 10.

15 Aug. (de morib. Eccl. Cath. c. 33.) calls it a diversorium. "I saw a lodging of holy men at Milan, not a few, over whom presided one presbyter, a most learned and excellent man."

16 Agentes in rebus. There was a society of them still about the court. Their militia or imployments were, to gather in the Emperor's tributes: to fetch in offenders: to do Palatina

obsequia, officers of court, provide corn, &c. ride of errands like messengers of the chamber, lie abroad as spies and intelligencers; they were often preferred to places of magistracy in the province: such were called principes or magistriani: St. Hierome upon Abdias cap. I. calls them messengers: they succeeded the frumentarii. Between which two, and the curiosi, and the speculatores, there was not much difference. [Old Ed.]

17 Whoso loves himself in his folly, will make no progress towards wisdom, nor will become such as he wishes to be, unless he hates himself such as he is. Aug. de Vera Relig. c. 48.

18 See above, b. iii. c. 4.

19 Manicheism.

20 For this is the punishment requited to the disobedient in himself, that he in turn should not be obeyed even by himself. Aug. c. advers. Leg. et Proph. l. i. c. 14.

21 The Manichees.

22 See above, b. iv. sec. 26.

23 See above, I. vii. sec. 5. note 3.

24 St. Paul.

25 Deterius inolitum, quam melius insolitum.

26 See Athanas. Vit. St. Antonii, sec. 2, 2. he was then 18, or, at most, 20.

BOOK IX

1 "To every one converted to God, his delights and pleasures are changed; for they are not withdrawn, but are changed." Aug. Præf. on Ps. 74. "For the love of things temporal would not be expelled, but by some sweetness of things eternal." Aug. de Musica, l. vi. c. 16.

2 In harvest and vintage-time had the lawyers their vacation. So Minutius Felix. Scholars, their *Non Terminus*, as here: yea, Divinity Lectures and Catechisings then ceased. So Cyprian, Ep. 2. The Law Terms gave way also to the great Festivals of the Church. Theodosius forbade any Process to go out from fifteen days before Easter till the Sunday after. For the four Terms, see Caroli Calvi Capitula, act. viii. p. 90. [Old Ed.]

3 Allusions to Ps. 130, in the old vers. rendered, "'what shall be given to thee for the subtile tongue,' *i.e.* says Aug. ad loc. 'whereby to defend thyself against it?' He answers his own question, 'sharp arrows,' &c. Sharp arrows of the mighty are the words of God. God knoweth how to shoot arrows into the very heart, and no one aimeth better at the heart than he who shooteth with the word. 'Destroying coals' are good examples; as if God should begin to urge on thee, 'Canst thou not this? Why can such an one? Why could such an one? Women have been able, shall men not? The rich and luxurious have been able, shall the poor not? See then why they have been named 'coals!' Because they who are converted to the Lord, are alive from the dead. But coals, before they are kindled, are dead. For coals not alight, are called dead, but those alight, live, coals. The examples then of many ungodly who have been converted to the Lord, are called coals. What follows? He puts aside 'the subtile tongue,' and ungodly lips, he goeth up the degree [steps], he begins to make progress."

4 It appears that the pain in the chest was of real use to him, and so, both grounds being true, Aug. mentions the one or the other as the cause of abandoning his profession, according to the character of the parties concerned. To the Milanese he names both; (inf. c. 5) to Romanianus (see above on l. vii. c. ult. note 36) only the pain of his chest. "These things [this world's goods] were in a way to hold me prisoner, though daily discoursing of the vanity of earthly things, unless a pain in the chest had compelled me to abandon my boastful profession, and to take refuge in the bosom of Wisdom;" (c. Acad. i. 3.) and to Theodorus de vita beatâ, sec. 4. "What then remained, but that while I was lingering amid idle things, the storm which was deemed contrary to me, came to my aid? So then so great a pain in the chest seized me, that, unable to support the toils of that profession, wherein I was spreading my sails for the Sirens' isle, I cast all over and moored, if but a shattered and gaping vessel, in the longed-for haven." To Zenobius he writes more plainly; (de Ord. i. sec. 5.) "For when the pain in my chest had compelled me to abandon the schools, already prepared, as you know, even without any such compulsion to betake myself to the study of wisdom [philosophia] &c." Elsewhere, (Epp.) he says, that he did this, induced rather by the desire of devoting all his leisure to God.

5 "What mountain should we understand, but the same Lord Christ, of whom another prophet says, 'The mountain of the Lord shall be revealed on the top of the mountains.' This is the 'mountain' said to 'yield milk,' (incaseatus, lit. 'abounding in curds,') on account of the little ones who are by grace to be nourished as by milk; the 'rich mountain' to strengthen and enrich them by the excellence of His gifts: for this same milk, whence curds are formed, wonderfully represents grace, in that it flows from the rich stores of the mother's inner self, and with a delighting pity, is poured freely into the little

ones." Aug. ad loc. The word וְרוּיִס in the E. V. "high," is rendered by the δ τετυρω μενοζ, by Synom, ευτρφιαζ, from a connected meaning of the root.

6 See above, l. vi. sec. 17. and note 13.

7 St. Aug. does not mean that he did not know what our Lord Intended by the title of "Abraham's bosom," but only that the nature of its peace and joys must be hidden from us, while in the flesh. He uniformly speaks of it in equivalent terms, as a hidden place of rest and joy: "bosom," because "detached and hidden." Serm. 14. c. 5. Ep. 164. sec. 7. de Gen. ad Lit. l. xii. sec. 63. c. Faust. xxxvii. as elsewhere, "that just men departed are at rest in the hidden abodes of the godly." (de Civ. Dei, c. 13.) The doubt refers to the character of the joys of the intermediate state, since "it is certain, that the souls of the faithful departed live in rest;" (de Civ. Dei, xiii. 19.) and yet the consummation of their joy is to be after the resurrection. In like way, St. Gregory of Naz. (Orat. Fun. in St. Cæsar.) said, "in Abraham's bosom, whatever it be, mayest thou rest."

8 Of this period, St. Aug. writes, that he had formed the habit of spending "the beginning or end, generally the half, of the night, in watching and seeking out truth," "nor do I allow myself, by the studies of the young men (his young friends whom he was instructing), to be taken away from myself." (de Ord. i. sec. 6.) He states immediately, that "he prayed God with almost daily weeping, that his wounds might be healed, but often upbraided himself as unworthy to be healed so soon as he wished." Ib. sec. 29.

9 These are, the three disputations against the Academics, the substance of the viva voce discussion of a few days, shortly after he had gone into the country. (c. Acad. i. sec. 4.) His book, de Vita Beata, begun on his birth-day, Nov. 15. (sec. 6.) and finished in three days' discussions, and the two books, "de Ordine," (Retract. i. 3.)

10 His Soliloquies, two books, in which, "being alone, he held a dialogue with himself, he and his reason, as though they were two." "In the first book, he investigated what sort of person he ought to be who would apprehend wisdom, and in the end is an argument, that things, which truly are, are immortal. In the second is a long discussion, in which he comes to no conclusion, on the immortality of the soul." (Retr. i. 4.) As a supplement to this, he wrote shortly after, at Milan, a book on the Immortality of the soul, (Opp. t. i. p. 387.) which got out against his will, and of whose obscurity himself complains. (Retr. i. l.)

11 Some, with the Epp. of Nebridius, are still extant. Ep. iii. xiv. ed. Ben.

12 Ver. 6. Who will shew us good things.

13 See ib. iii. 6.

14 While the fair changes of the seasons accomplish their order, the forms which men love, forsake them. Aug. de Vera Rel. c. 20. Space presents us things to love, time removes the things we love; and leaves in the soul crowds of phantoms, whereby longing is excited first to one, then to another. Thus the mind becomes disquieted and full of care, in vain striving to hold the things whereby it is held. Ib. c. 35.

15 Whose life is nothing else than to gaze, to strive, to eat, to drink, to sleep, and in their thoughts but to embrace phantastic images, which they derive from that life. Ib. c. 54.

16 For they who being famished, think that they abound, and being most empty, think they are full, are not converted. Aug. in Ps. 67.

17 For the multiformity of temporal things did by the senses distract fallen man from the Unity of God, and multiply his affections through an ever-changing variety. Thus there arose a toilsome abundance, or, so to speak, a copious want, while

he follows one thing after another, and none abides with him. Thus "from the time of his corn, wine, and oil, he was 'multiplied,' so as not to find the 'Self-Same,' i.e. that unchangeable and One Nature, which reaching after he would not err, and reaching to he would not grieve." Aug. de Vera Rel. c. 21. For "multiplying" does not always denote fulness, but rather, more often, poverty; since the soul when given up to temporal pleasures, is ever inflamed with desire, nor can be satisfied, but, distracted by manifold and toilsome thoughts, is not permitted to see the Simple Good, as it is said, "the earthly habitation presseth down the mind thinking on many things." (Wisd. 9.) Such a soul, by the coming and going of temporal goods, (i.e. "from the time of their corn, wine, and oil,") filled with numberless phantoms is so "multiplied" that it cannot do what is commanded, "in simplicity of heart seek Him." (Wisd. 1, 1.) For that multiplicity is strongly opposed to this simplicity. For we ought to stand alone and single, i.e. severed from the multitude and crowd of things born and decaying, lovers of eternity and of unity, if we desire to cleave to our One God and Lord. Aug. in Ps. 4.

18 It is not said, either "I have slept and taken my rest," or "I sleep and take my rest," but "I shall sleep and shall take my rest." Then "shall this corruptible be clothed with incorruption, and this mortal shall be clothed with immortality." "Then shall death be swallowed up in victory." Id. ib.

19 Bodily pain I only fear greatly, because it hinders me from investigation. For although in those days I was tormented with a very sharp pain in my teeth, which allowed me only to revolve in my mind things which I had already learnt, but disabled me wholly from learning, for which I required the whole energy of my mind; yet it seemed to me, as if, should

that effulgence of truth disclose itself to my mind, I should either not feel that pain, or bear it as nothing. Aug. Soliloq. i. sec. 21.

20 Isaiah, amid the reproof of sin and commands of righteousness and predictions of ill to the sinful people, also prophesied far more than the rest, of Christ and the Church, i.e. of the King and the city which He founded, so that by some he is called an Evangelist rather than a Prophet. Aug. de Civ. Dei, xviii. 29.

21 They were baptized at Easter, and gave up their names before the second Sunday in Lent: the rest of which, they were to spend in fasting, humility, prayer, and being examined in the scrutinies. Tertull. lib. de Bapt. cap. 20. Therefore went they to Milan, that the Bishop might see their preparation. Adjoining to the cathedrals, were there certain lower houses for them to lodge and be exercised in, till the day of baptism. Euseb. l. x. c. 4. [Old Ed.] See Bingham, 1. x. c. 2. sec. 6. "What else do they the whole time, that they hold the place and name of Catechumens, but hear what should be the faith and life of a Christian, that when they have "examined themselves, they may then eat of the table of the Lord and drink of His cup?" But what is done through the whole time, in which it has been wholesomely provided by the Church, that they who come to the Name of Christ should be received into the order of Catechumens, this is done much more diligently and earnestly in these days, during which they are called Competentes, after they have given in their names to receive Baptism." Aug. de fid. et op. sec. 9. Of himself, Aug. there says, "Do we so deny our own experience, as not to recollect how intent and anxious we ourselves were about the teaching of those who catechized us, when we were seeking the sacrament of that fountain, and were hence called Competentes (Seekers)?"

22 An answer of his is preserved in the de Vita Beata, sec. 18. "He is truly chaste (castus, see above,) who waits on God, and keeps himself to Him only." Aug. there says of him, "There was also with us, in age the youngest of all, but whose talents, if affection deceives me not, promise something great, my son Adeodatus." ib. sec. 6.

23 De Magistro, "in which it is disputed, and sought, and found, that there is no master, who teacheth man knowledge, but God, according to that also which is written in the Gospel, 'one is your Master, Christ.'" Retract. i. 12. It is extant, Opp. Aug. t. i.

24 Aug. was baptized by St. Ambrose himself. "Hear another excellent steward of God, whom I venerate as a father; for 'in Christ Jesus he begat me through the Gospel,' and through him, as the minister of Christ, I received 'the washing of regeneration;'—I mean the blessed Ambrose, whose graces, constancy, labours, perils for the Catholic faith, whether in words or works, I have both myself experienced, and the whole Roman world hesitates not to proclaim with me." Aug. c. Julian. Pelagian, i. sec. 10. cf. de Nuptiis et Concupise. see. ult. and Ep. 147. c. 23.

25 To induce him to give up to the Arians a Church, the Portian Basilica without the walls; afterwards she asked for the new Basilica within the walls, which was larger. See Ambrose, Epp. 20–22. Serm. c. Auxentium de Basilicis tradendis, pp. 852–880. ed. Bened. ep. Tillemont. Hist. Eccl. St. Ambrose Art. 44–48. p. 76–82. Valentinian was then at Milan. See below, note 29.

26 Ignatius, who lived An. Christ. 100, mentions singing in the Eastern Churches. Epist. ad Rom. 2. vid. Socr. Hist. vi. 8. Quiremen only were to sing in the Church. Anno 364. Concil. Laodic. Can. 15. [Old Ed.]

27 They were martyrs long before the time of St. Ambrose, since he speaks of "finding two men, of wondrous size, as was the case in old times." Ep. 22. sec. 2. Aug. says that "it is well known that they suffered long after the most blessed Stephen." (Serm. 318). "They lay hid under an unhonoured turf," (Ambr. ib.) "so that all walked over their bodies, who wished to go to the rails, whereby the tombs of the martyrs Sts. Nabor and Felix were protected from injury," (Paullin. Vit. St. Ambros. sec. 14.) until "they were made known in a dream to Ambrose and found by him." (Aug. de Civ. Dei, l. xxii. c. 8. sec. 2.) Afterwards, "old men recollected that they had formerly read their names and inscriptions." Ambrose, ib. Most suppose that they suffered under Nero. See Tillemont, H. E. t. ii. Art. St. Gervais and St. Protais, and notes, ib. They were Roman citizens, since their martyrdom was by the sword; "their head was separated from the shoulders." Ambrose, l. c.

28 The Arians did not deny this, but said that "that venerable man Ambrose bribed men to feign that they were vexed with unclean spirits." Paullinus (the notary of St. Ambrose), l. c. sec. 15.

29 Ambrose, in a sermon at this time before a large congregation, dwells at length on this miracle, l. c. sec. 17. "They [the Arians] deny that the blind man received sight, but he does not deny that he was cured. He says 'I have ceased to be blind,' and proves it by the fact. They deny the mercy, who cannot deny the fact. He is a well-known man; when well, was employed in public services, by name Severus, in office a butcher. He had laid aside his office when this hindrance happened. He calls to witness those, by whose benevolence he was before supported; he calls them as witnesses of his visitation, whom he had as witnesses of his blindness. He says aloud, that when he touched the hem of the garment of the

martyrs, wherewith the sacred remains are covered, his sight was restored. Is not this like what we read in the Gospel?— Their obstinacy is more detestable than that of the Jews. They, when they doubted, asked at least his parents: these enquire in secret, in public deny; shewing thereby that they disbelieve not the deed, but its Author." Aug. mentions the same miracle among those of his own days, which "could come to the knowledge of many, because the city is a large one, and the Emperor was then there, and it took place in the presence of an *immense* multitude, thronging to the bodies of the martyrs Protasius and Gervasius." (de Civ. Dei, l. xxii. c. 8. sec. 2.) "Of which so great glory of the martyrs, I also was a witness. I was there, was at Milan: I knew the miracles wrought, God bearing witness to 'the precious death of His saints,' so that through those miracles, that 'death was precious,' now not 'in the sight of the Lord' only, but in the sight of men. A blind man, very well known to the whole city, ran, caused himself to be led, returned without one to lead him. We have not heard of his death; perhaps he still lives. He made a vow that he would for his whole life serve in that basilica, where their bodies are. We rejoiced that he saw, we left him serving." (Serm. 286. sec. 4.) Paullinus, who relates the same, says, "To this very time he lives, as a religious, in the same basilica, which is called the Ambrosian, whither the bodies of the martyrs were removed." l. c. sec. 14.

30 See above on 1. viii. c. 15.

31 In this interval, before he returned to Africa, St. Aug. wrote the two books, de Moribus Ecclesia Catholicæ, and de Moribus Manichæorum, ("to repress the Manichæan boastfulness of a false and fallacious continence or abstinence, wherein, to deceive the unskilful, they set themselves above true Christians, to whom they are not to be compared;" Retr. i. 7.) and the "de animæ quantitate," to prove it incorporeal,

(ib. c. 8.) and the first of the three books, de libero arbitrio, to shew that evil had its origin no otherwise than in the free choice of the will. ib. c. 9.

32 Aug. thus addressed his mother, de vita beata, "You, through whose prayers I undoubtingly believe and affirm, that God gave me that mind that I should prefer nothing to the discovery of truth, wish, think of, love, nought besides. Nor do I fail to believe, that this so great good, which, through thee, I have come to desire, through thy prayers I shall attain;" and says of her, "chiefly my mother, to whom, I believe, I owe all which in me is life," and long after, (de dono persev. sec. 35.) "that to the faithful and daily tears of my mother, I was granted, that I should not perish."

33 Nec liberet, quod non liceret.

34 Many things are done by the wicked against the will of God; but He is of so great wisdom and power, that all things, even those which seem opposed to His will, tend to those results or ends which Himself foreknew to be good and just. Aug. de Civ. Dei, l. xxii. c. 2.

35 Our mother, whose endowments, and the fervour of her mind towards divine things, I had both before perceived through daily intercourse and careful observation, and in a discussion on a matter of no small moment, her mind had appeared to me of so high an order, that nothing could be more adapted to the study of true wisdom." de Ord. ii. sec. I. Aug. speaks there of her "ardent love of the divine Scriptures," and preserves an answer of hers as to what constituted happiness, "If a man desire what is good and has it, he is happy; if evil, though he have it, he is wretched." de Beata Vita, sec. 10.

36 See above, sec. 11.

37 What we cannot conceive, as it is, we know not [as we ought], but whatever occurs to our conceptions, we cast aside, reject, disown, we know it is not this we seek, though of what nature that is, we know not. Aug. Ep. 130. sec. 27. 9. v.

38 His name was Navigius. Aug. de Vita Beata, sec. 6.

39 I suppose they continued to the end of Psalm 102. This was the primitive fashion: Nazianzen says, that his speechless sister Gorgonia's lips muttered the fourth Psalm; *I will lie down in peace and sleep.* As St. Austen lay a dying, the company prayed. Possid. That they had prayers between the departure and the burial, see Tertull. de Anima. c. 51. They used to sing both at the departure and burial. Nazianzen, Orat. 10. says, The dead Cæsarius was carried from hymns to hymns. The priests were called to sing. Chrysost. Hom. 70. ad Antioch. They sung the 116th Psalm usually. See Chrys. Hom. 4. in c. 2. ad Hebræos. [Old Ed.] "The Psalms and readings of the divine promises are declaratory of those most blessed abodes of rest, whereto those who have had a godly end, shall eternally be received; and they are a holy greeting of him who has fallen asleep; and are an exhortation to those, who yet live, to a like end. Dionys, Eccl. Hier. c. 7.

40 Here my Popish translator says, that the sacrifice of the Mass was offered for the dead. That the ancients had communion with their burials, I confess. But for what? 1. To testify their dying in the communion of the Church. 2. To give thanks for their departure. 3. To pray God to give them place in His Paradise. 4. And a part in the first resurrec-tion:—but not as a propitiatory sacrifice to deliver them out of Purgatory, which the Mass is now only meant for. [Old Ed.] That the prayers for the dead in the ancient Church, so far from favouring, are opposed to the Romish doctrine of Purgatory, see Bp. Bull, Serm. 3. and "Corruptions of the

Church of Rome." Bingham, xv. 3. 16. xxiii. 3. 13. Collyer, Eccl. Hist. of G. Britain, part ii. b. 4. p. 257. Usher's Answer to a Jesuit. Field on the Church, p. 750, &c.

41 See above, sec. 17. and below, l. xiii. c. l. "When God crowns our merits, he does nothing else than crown his own gifts." Ep. 194. sec. 19. where is more on this. It appears even from this that "merits" has not in the Fathers any technical sense, but is equivalent to "good deeds."

42 "What is that righteousness whereby the Devil was conquered? What but the righteousness of Jesus Christ? And how was he conquered? Because when he 'found nothing worthy of death in Him,' he yet slew Him. And thus it is just, that the debtors whom he held should be set free, believing in Him Whom without debt he slew. This is it that we are said to be justified in the blood of Christ, for thus that innocent blood was poured out for the remission of our sins. Whence in the Psalms He calls Himself 'free among the dead;' for He was the only Dead free from the debt of Death." Aug. de Trin. xiii. 14.

BOOK X

1 Respirent, suspirent.

2 See above, l. vii. sec. 5. note 3. and viii. sec. 21. notes 3 and 20.

3 Against his Manichæan errors; see above, b. vii. sec. 3.

4 The earth's form of beauty is a sort of voice of the dumb earth. Thou observest and seest its beautiful form; thou seest, and by thy musing, as it were, askest it, and the very enquiring is a questioning. Aug. in Ps. 144. sec. 13.

5 Doth not, on considering the beauty of this universe, its very form answer thee, with one voice, "Not I made myself, but God?" Id. ib.

6 So also "mindful." "unmindful."

7 "I know what thou willest, thou sèekest happiness; if then thou wouldest be happy, be without spot. All will the first, few the last, without which the first, which all will, is not arrived at." Aug. in Ps. 118. sec. 1.

8 "For whoso enjoys what he loves, and loves the true and highest Good, who, but the most miserable would deny that he was blest?" Aug. de Civ. Dei, viii. 9.

9 See above, l. viii. sec. 10.

10 See above, c. 20.

11 "No wonder that miserable man obtains not what he longs for, *i.e.* a happy life; for that which accompanies it, and without which no one is worthy of it, no one attains it, namely, to live aright, he does not equally will." Aug. de lib. Arb. l. i. c. 14.

12 Ter. Andr. i. 1. 40.

13 See above, iv. c. 12. vii. c. 10.

14 See c. 17.

15 See l. iv. sec. 18. note 15.

16 Ib. note 16. note 19. and l. vii. c. 14. 20.

17 "These words of mine Pelagius at Rome, when they had been mentioned in his presence by a certain brother and fellow-Bishop of mine, could not endure, and contradicting somewhat excitedly, nearly quarrelled with him, who had mentioned them." Aug. de dono Persev. sec. 53.

18 "There are two labours enjoined in this life, to 'contain' and to 'sustain.' For we are enjoined to 'contain' ourselves

from those things which in this world are called goods, and to 'sustain' the evils, which in this world abound. The one is called 'continency,' the other 'sustenancy.' Two virtues, which cleanse the soul, and make it capable of receiving the Divine Nature. In restraining lusts, and checking pleasures, lest evil blandishments seduce, and so-called prosperity enervate us, we have need of 'continency,' not to trust to earthly happiness, and, to the end, to seek the happiness, which hath no end. But as it belongs to 'continency,' not to trust to the happiness of the world, so does it to 'sustenancy,' not to give way to the unhappiness of the world." Aug. Serm. 38. init.

19 "Not that the creature is not to be loved; but if that love be referred to the Creator, then it is not cupidity but love. For it is then cupidity, when the creature is loved for its own sake." Aug. de Trin. ix. sec. 13. "He who would be temperate in this sort of mortal and passing things, has a rule of life established by both Testaments, that he love none of them, think nothing to be desired for its own sake, but use them, as far as may suffice for the needs of this life and its duties, with the moderation of one who useth, not with the affection of one who loveth." Aug. de Mor. Eccl. Cath. sec. 39.

20 "These three sorts of vices, the pleasure of the flesh, and pride, and curiosity, comprise all sins. Which seem to me enumerated by the Apostle John. For curiosity chiefly prevails through the eyes and what the rest belong to, is plain. And that temptation of our Lord's human nature was threefold; by food, *i.e.* by the concupiscence of the flesh, when it is suggested, 'command these stones to become bread;' by vain boasting, when, placed on a mountain, all the kingdoms of this earth are shewn Him, and promised, if He will worship; by curiosity, when He is urged to cast Himself down from the pinnacle of the temple, to try, whether He would be supported by Angels. So then after the enemy could

prevail with Him by none of these temptations, it is said of him, 'After the devil had made an end of all temptations.'" Aug. in Ps. 8. v. fin.

21 "God then commandeth not impossibilities; but by enjoining, bids thee do what thou canst, and ask what thou canst not." Aug. de Nat. et Grat. c. 43.

22 Against the Manichees, who forbad to eat flesh.

23 According to the Manichees, the most impure food of all, as being insects.

24 "'Thine eyes have seen what is imperfect of Me, and in Thy book shall they all be written,' not the perfect only, but the imperfect also. Let not the imperfect fear; only let them hold on. Nor because I said 'Let them not fear,' let them love imperfection, and remain where they have been found. Let them hold on, as much as in them lies. Let them daily add, daily draw near; yet let them not draw back from the Body of the Lord; that compacted together in one body, and among these members, they may be accounted worthy to have those words pronounced of them, 'Thy eyes did see what was imperfect of Me, and in Thy book shall they all be written.'" Aug. in Ps. 138. sec. 21. "The Son Himself saith, 'Thy eyes saw what was imperfect of Me,' (lit. my imperfect). The imperfect, which is in My body, Thy eyes saw. And what then? Have they hope, who are imperfect? They have. Hear what follows, 'And in Thy book shall they all be written.'" Aug. Serm. 135. de verb. Ev. Joh. 9. c. 5.

25 "The hidden gifts of God in a man's self are not made known even to himself, except when proved by temptation." Aug. de Sancta Virgin c. 4.

26 The beginning of a hymn of St. Ambrose, which they were wont to sing at the commencement of night. The two first stanzas are quoted above, l. ix. sec. 32.

27 Assumunt eam, non absumuntur ab ea.

28 Sacrifico laudem Sacrificatori meo.

29 See above, l. xi. c. 5.

30 See above on c. 29. not.

31 "For, turning, as it were, their backs to Thee, they are fixed down upon the works of the flesh, as it were in their own shade, and yet what even there delights them, they still have from the encompassing radiance of Thy light. But the shade being loved, weakens the mind's eye, and makes it unequal to bear Thy countenance. Wherefore a man becomes more and more darkened, while he prefers to follow what, at each stage, is more bearable to his increasing weakness. Whence he begins to be unable to see that, which in the highest degree, IS." Aug. de lib. Arb. l. i. sec. 43.

32 "If the causes of the movements of bodies were to be known to us, none were of more importance to know than such as influence our health. But since, in ignorance of these, we seek physicians, who sees not how content we should be to be ignorant of the hidden mysteries of heaven and earth?" Aug. Enchir. c. 16.

33 "But now the faithful pray for themselves also, that they may persevere in what they have begun to be. For it is useful to all, or almost all, with a view to this humility, which is so healthful, that they should not be able to know, what they shall be hereafter. To this end it is said, 'Let him who thinketh he standeth take heed lest he fall.' For this beneficial fear, lest, having been regenerated and now beginning to live godly, we should, as being secure, think over-highly, there are mingled, by the permission and provision and disposition of God, with those who shall persevere, others who will not; alarmed at whose fall, we may walk on in the right path, 'with fear and trembling,' until, from this 'life on earth,

which is all trial,' we pass to another, where will be no pride to be repressed, and no strife against suggestions and temptations." Aug. Ep. 217. sec. 14.

34 "A man who makes progress amid prosperity, by adversity learns what progress he has made. For when he has an abundance of these passing goods, he trusts not in them; but when they are withdrawn, he recognizes whether they have not taken hold of him. For generally, when we have them, we think that we love them not; but when they begin to depart, then we discover what sort of persons we are. For on that we set not our heart, when present, which we part from without sorrow." Aug. de vera Relig. c. 47.

35 See above, c. 30. beg. and note 20.

36 "For the praise of man ought not to be desired by a well-doer, but to follow him, that they may profit who can imitate also what they praise, not that he should think that he had any advantage, whom they praise." Aug. de Serm. Dom. in Monte, l. ii. c. 2. "He knoweth, in Whose Presence I speak, yea, in Whose Presence I think, that I take not so much pleasure in popular praises, as I feel anxious and harassed how they live, who praise me. For to be praised by ill-livers, I mislike, abhor, detest; it is a grief to me, not a pleasure. But praise from well-livers, should I say, I mislike it, I lie; should I say, I like it, I fear lest I should be more desirous of unrealities than of reality. What shall I say then? I neither wholly like, nor wholly dislike it:—not wholly like, lest I be endangered by the praise of man; not wholly mislike, lest they to whom I preach should be ungrateful." Aug. Serm. 333 in die ordinat. suæ, sec. 1.

37 See above, c. 5.

38 "Whoso, with true piety, believes and hopes in God, Whom he loves, regards more those things in which he is

displeased with himself, than those, if there be such in him, which do not so much please him, as the Truth. And that, wherein he now is capable of pleasing, he ascribes to no other than His mercy Whom he feared to displease, giving thanks that the one has been healed, making supplication that the other may be healed." Aug. de Civ. Dei, l. v. c. 20.

39 "Long hast thou (O soul) lived absorbed, and lashed by various and discordant longings, thou bearest the marks of thy wounds, distracted amid many loves. Gather thee up to thyself; whatever from without pleases thee, seek whom it has for its Author." Aug. in Ps. 145. sec. 5. vid. sup. l. ix. sec. 10. et inf. l. xi. c. 29.

40 See above, c. 30. beg. and note 20.

41 See above, iii. c. 8. v. fin.

42 "That true and benevolent Mediator, shewed Himself to mortals in that mortal nature, which those malevolent and deceiving mediators, bore themselves the more proudly, for not having; and promised to miserable man a delusive aid, as if immortals to mortals." Aug. de Civ. Dei, x. 24.

43 "He who made man of the dust, and breathed life into him, and for that His creature gave His Only-Begotten to death, how much He loves us, who can speak, who can even worthily think?" Aug. Serm. 57. c. 13. "Moreover, man was to be persuaded how much God loved us, and as what, He loved us; how much, lest we should despair, as what, lest we should be proud." Id. de Trin. l. iv. c. 1.

44 "In these words especially, the person of the Lord appears. For who besides was 'free among the dead,' but He Who, 'in the likeness of sinful flesh,' among sinners was alone 'without sin?' He then was 'free among the dead,' Who had power to lay down His life, and to take it again, from 'Whom no one

took it, but He laid it down of Himself,' Who also could raise up His flesh, as the 'Temple, destroyed' by them; when He willed, Who, &c." Aug. in Ps. 87. sec. 5. See above, ix, b. note 42. on l. ix. sec. 36.

BOOK XI

1 St. Aug. says a little on his Ordination, to which he was brought against his will, in the Ep. 21. ad Valerium, and 126 ad Albinam, sec. 7. and on his Episcopate, Ep. 31. ad Paulinum et Therasiam: he speaks somewhat more fully as to what he did or what happened to him, in a sermon preached "lest his character be stained," on the "life and conversation of his Clergy." S. 355. sec. 2. "I, whom, by the grace of God, ye see as your Bishop, came as a young man to this city, as many of you know. I was looking for a place where to form a monastery, to live there with my brethren. For all worldly hopes I had abandoned, and what I might have been, I would not be; nor yet sought I to be what I am. 'I chose rather to be cast down in the house of my God, than to dwell in the tents of the ungodly,' I separated me from those who love the world, nor yet did I set myself with those, who are placed over the people. Nor in the Feast of my Lord did I 'choose the higher place,' but the 'lower' and abject one, and it pleased Him to say to me 'Go up higher.' But so exceedingly did I dread the Episcopate, that because my reputation had now begun to be of some account among the servants of God, I would not go to any place where I knew there was no Bishop. For I was ware of this, and did what I could, that in a low place I might be saved, lest in a high one I should be

perilled. But, as I said, the servant must not oppose his Master. I came to this city to see a friend, whom I thought I might gain to God, that he might live with us in the monastery; I came as being safe, the place having a Bishop already. I was laid hold of, made a presbyter, and by this step, came to the Episcopacy." He had sold and given to the poor what he calls "his petty little poverty," or his "few paternal acres," (Ep. 126. sec. 6.) to live on the common stock, "but our common, yea our large and all-sufficient support was to be God Himself," (ib.) "vehemently longing after that perfection whereof the Lord spake," Mat. 19, 21. and "having determined to be content with such food only as is necessary for the health of the body." (de Util. Cred. sec. 3.)

2 The hour-glasses of his time, which went by water. Old Ed.

3 See above b. vi. sec. 3. p. 112. sec. 15. p. 125. and note 9. and Actt. Eccles. St. Aug. Ep. 213. "Before mid-day and after mid-day am I involved in the business of men;" &c. and de op. Monach. sec. 37. "I call to witness on my soul the Lord Jesus, in Whose name I speak these things boldly, that as far as relates to my own advantage, I had much rather daily during certain hours (as far as is appointed in well-governed monasteries) work to a degree with my hands, and have the other hours free for reading and prayer, or composing something out of the Divine Scriptures, than be subject to those most disordered perplexities of others' differences in secular matters, either to be formally decided, or ended by mediation; to which toils that same Apostle has bound us, and that not by his own will, but by His, who spake by him. I pass by innumerable other ecclesiastical toils, which no one perhaps believes, who has not tried. We do not then 'bind heavy burdens, and lay them on your shoulders, which we touch not with a finger,' since if we might, consistently with

the nature of our office, (He seeth who trieth our hearts,) we had rather do this, which we exhort you to do, than those things, which ourselves are compelled to do."

4 "God has therefore in the Scriptures clothed his mysteries with clouds, that the love of truth in men might be kindled by the very difficulty of discovering them. For if they were such only as were very readily understood, truth would neither be earnestly sought after nor found with pleasure." Aug. de vera Relig. c. 17.

5 According to the Old Vers. "The voice of the Lord perfecting the harts." For the voice of the Lord first perfected those who subdue and repel the envenomed tongues [in allusion to the related enmity of harts to serpents]. "And will lay bare the forests." And then will He lay bare to them the dark depths of the Divine books and mysteries where they may feed freely. Aug. ad loc.

6 See on b. vi. c. 3.

7 See above b. vii. c. 11. p. 148. and note 16.

8 See b. x. sec. 53.

9 "For in the Eternal, speaking properly, there is neither any thing past, as though it had passed away, nor any thing future, as though it were not as yet, but whatsoever is, only is," Aug. lib. 83. quæst. qu. 19.

10 "He saith 'The Beginning, because also I speak unto you,' Believe me to be the Beginning, lest ye die in your sins. For as though in what they said, 'Who art Thou?' they had said no other than, 'What shall we believe Thee to be,' He answereth, 'The Beginning,' i.e. believe me to be the Beginning. For if the Beginning remained as He is, with the Father, not taking the form of a servant, or speaking, as man to man, how should they believe in Him, since feeble hearts could not hear the Intelligible Word without the intervention of a sensible voice.

'Therefore' He saith, 'believe me to be the Beginning, *because*
that ye may believe, I not only am, but also speak unto you.'"
Aug. ad loc.

11 "Whither should the mind return, to become good, but to
The Good, when it loves and desires and obtains It? Whence
if it turn away again, and become not good, thereby, that it
doth turn away from the Good, unless that Good, whence it
turns away abode in Itself, it would not have whither to turn,
if it would amend." Aug. de Trin. l. viii. c. 3. "Ἀρχή and
Principium, signifying "the first Principle" as well as
"Beginning" have a force, which cannot be expressed by our
corresponding Scriptural term.

12 See above b. vii. c. 15.

13 "For where the day neither commences with the end of
yesterday, nor is ended by the commencement of the morrow,
it is ever To-day." Aug. Enchir. 49.

14 "Before we arrive at the One, we need many things. Let the
One extend us on, lest the many distend us, and break us off
from the One" Aug. Serm. 255. c. 6. See above, b. xii. c. 16
and note.

15 "For if eternity and time are rightly distinguished, in that
time exists not without a varying changeableness, whereas in
eternity is no change, who seeth not that times could not have
been, had no creature come into existence, which should vary
something by some change?" Aug. de Civ. Dei, b. xi. c. 6. See
above, b. xii. c. 29, end.

16 "In God, all things are ordered and fixed; nor doth He any
thing, as by a sudden counsel, which He did not from
eternity foreknow that He should do; but in the movements
of the creature, which He wonderfully governeth, Himself not
moved in time, in time is said to have done, as by a sudden
will, what He disposed through the ordered causes of things

in the unchangeableness of His most hidden counsels, whereby each several thing, which in its appointed time comes to [our] knowledge, He both makes, when present, and, when future, had already made." Aug. in Ps. 105, 45. sec. 35.

BOOK XII

1 E. V. "The heaven, even the heavens," lit. "The heavens, heavens." The Targ. however, as well as the ó and Vulg. regard the words שׁמי שׁמים as equivalent to שׁמי השׁמים Ps. 148, 4. Deut. 10, 14. 1 Kings 8, 27. Neh. 9, 6, according to a construction which the Hebrew grammarians often apply; and so, I find. Obad. Sephorno and Ibn Yechaiah take it.

2 Tacitly opposed to the Manichees, as also much which follows, with whom darkness was a self-existent substance.

3 See b. iii. sec. 11.

4 See c. 8, end.

5 i.e. might one speak of a thing, floating between being and not being.

6 See above, l. ix. sec. 11.

7 Opposed to the Manichees, see b. iii. sec. 10. and b. iv. sec. 26.

8 Because at the first creation, it had no form nor thing in it. [Old Ed.]

9 Constat, et non constat. St. Aug. takes occasion of the word to say, that in its full sense it cannot belong to matter, which has no intrinsic consistency. Martin supposes the antithesis to be between its present and any future form which it may take, "consists and (as yet) consists not."

10 Moses.

11 The Manichees.

12 "Nor is it without reason said of Him, that 'He alone hath immortality;' for His immortality is truly immortality, in Whose nature there is 'no change.' The true eternity also is the unchangeable God, without beginning, without end; consequently also incorruptible." Aug. de Trin. l. xv. sec. 7.

13 "Ye say that evil is a sort of substance; we, that it is not a substance, but a declension from that which is, to that which less is." Aug. c. Secundin. Man. c. 12. "But the will turned away from the unchangeable and universal good, and turned to its own, or some outward or inferior good, sins. It turns to its own, when it would be in its own power; to an outward, when it strives to know what belongs to others, or not to itself; to an inferior, when it loves the pleasures of the body; and thus man, becoming proud, curious, fleshly, (see on b. x. sec. 41. note 20) passes over into another life, which, in comparison of the former, is death." Id. de lib. Arb. b. ii. sec. 53. See b. vii. c. 16.

14 See above, b. v. c. 2. and notes 2, 3, 4.

15 Above, b. xi. sec. 38. b. xii sec. 18.

16 See above on b. xiii. c. 35.

17 See above, c. 29, end, and note 25.

18 The Manichees, who rejected the Old Testament, wherefore he wishes that they should be smitten, to their healing, with the "two-edged sword" of the Old and New Testament. "The Word of God is the 'two-edged sword.' Whence 'two-edged?' It speaketh of things temporal, it speaketh of things eternal. In each it establisheth what it saith, and whom it striketh, it separateth from the world. Whatever is promised us in time, belongeth to one part of the sword; whatever to eternity,

belongeth to the other part of the sword. Our Lord came then, bearing a two-edged sword, promising things eternal, fulfilling those of time. For therefore also are they called the two Testaments.—Do the two Testaments belong to the 'two-edged sword?' The Old Testament promiseth things earthly, the New eternal. In both the word of God is found true as a two-edged sword." Aug. in Ps. 149, 6. cf. in Ps. 143, 17.

19 "For since God only is unchangeable, it must be confessed, that the angels also are by nature subject to change. But through that will, whereby they love God rather than themselves, they abide firm and stedfast in Him, and enjoy His Majesty, being most willingly subjected to Him only." Aug. de vera Relig. c. 13.

20 "But to His temple, which are all holy beings, both angels and men, God so imparteth His indwelling, that they should from Him have good of that sort, whereby they may be blessed, not He from them, a house of such sort, as without it, He should not be blessed." Aug. c. adv. Leg. et Proph. l. i. c. 2.

21 Pet. Lombard. lib. sent. 2. dist. 2. affirms, that by Wisdom, Eccl. I, 4. the Angels be understood, the whole spiritual and intellectual nature; namely, this highest Heaven, in which the Angels were created, and it by them instantly filled. [Old Ed.]

22 See on Joh. Tract. xiv. sec. 2. xxxv. sec. 3. and c. Ep. Parmen. l. ii. c. 14.

23 See above, b. ii. c. i. b. ix. sec. 10, and note. b. x. c. 29 and 40, and note. b. xi. c. 29.

24 See above, b. ix. sec. 24. end. above, b. xiii. c. 13.

25 Under the name "matter," with regard to "spiritual creatures," Aug. designates whatever, although incorporeal, still is not God, but the workmanship of God; *i.e.* as has been said, "The creature itself, such as it would be if not penetrated by a light eternal, and cleaving to God by that

pure and indefectible love, whereby its natural liability to change is restrained," (Dub. cp. sec. 9. 12. 15. 21. 25. and 33 end.) whence, to avoid ascribing to it a corporeal character, Aug. calls it elsewhere "a certain matter of its own peculiar nature," "a spiritual matter, if such there were, whence the soul was formed," a "quasi-matter." de Gen. ad Litt. I. vii. sec. 9. 10. "As flesh had a certain matter, *i.e.* earth, whence it was formed so as to be flesh, so perchance also might the soul— before that same nature was formed, which is called soul, and whose excellence is virtue, its deformity vice—have a certain spiritual matter of its own peculiar sort, as the earth out of which flesh was formed, was even then something, though not flesh."

26 "Inquiries on these subjects, and conjectures according to the ability of each, furnish no unprofitable practice to the mind, if they be carried on with lowliness, free from the error of opiniativeness, as if men knew certainly what they know not. For to what end, either to affirm or deny these or the like things, or with risk to pronounce upon them, when without risk we may be ignorant of them?" Aug. Enchir. c. 59.

27 See above, Book XI. note 10.

28 "Nor must God be supposed first to have made formless matter, and after an interval of time, formed what He had first made formless; but as intelligible sounds are made by a speaker, wherein the sound issues not formless at first, and afterwards receives a form, but is uttered already formed; so must God be understood to have made the world of formless matter, but contemporaneously to have created the world. Yet is it not without its use, first to relate, whereof a thing is made, afterward, what is made thereof, because though both could be made at once, both could not be at once related." Aug. c. advers. Leg. et Proph. l. i. c. 9. cf. de Gen. ad Lit. i. 14. v. 5. and above on c. 20. p. 294. note I.

29 "The course or time began with the motions of creation, wherefore it is idle to ask about time before creation, which were to ask for time before time. For were there no motion of any creature, spiritual or corporeal, whereby the future might through the present succeed to the past, there would be no time. But the creature could have no motion, unless it existed. Time, therefore, rather hath its commencement from the creation, than creation from time, but both from God." Aug. de Gen. ad Lit l. v. c. 5.

30 "When we read the divine books, amid such a multitude of true meanings, which are extracted from a few words, and are guarded by the soundness of the Catholic faith, let us by preference choose that, which it shall certainly appear that he meant, whom we read. If this is beyond us, at least that which the context (circumstantia) of Scripture prevents not, and which is in harmony with sound faith. But if the context of the Scripture also admit not of being handled and sifted, at least that only which sound faith prescribes. For it is one thing, not to distinguish what the writer chiefly meant, another to err from the rule of piety. If both be avoided, the reader obtains the full fruit. If both cannot be avoided, though we be uncertain about the mind of the writer, it is not without its use to have extracted a meaning agreeable with the holy faith." Aug. de Gen. ad Lit. l. i. fin.

BOOK XIII

1 See b. i. sec. 2.

2 "Nor had He need to make us, who needs us not, made." Aug. c. adv. leg. et proph. l. i. c. 4.

3 "For He needeth not our service, but we need His rule, that He may work in and keep us; and therefore is He the true and only Lord, because we serve Him not to His but to our benefit." Aug. de fin. ad Lit. l. viii. c. 16.

4 "Neque ut sic te colam, quasi terram, ut sis incultus, si non te colam." The French preserves better the strong irony of this play on the word, as if man's worship was any gain to God, "afin que vous ne soiez pas comme une terre *inculte*, si je manquais au *culte*, que je te dois." Mart.

5 "The creature, although spiritual and intellectual and rational, may have a life 'without form.' For turned away from the unchangeable Wisdom, it lives foolishly and miserably, which is its deformed estate. For it is formed, by being turned to the unchangeable light of Wisdom, which is the Word of God. For from Whom it hath existence, that it may be and live, to Him it is turned, that it may live wisely and blessedly." Aug. de Gen. ad Lit. l. i. c. 5.

6 "This being so, this nature having been created in so great excellence, that though in itself subject to change, yet by adhering to the unchangeable good, i.e. to the supreme God, it obtains its happiness, and is blessed only in the full satisfying of its cravings, and nought suffices to satisfy it, but God, it is truly a vitiated state of it not to 'hold fast to Him.'" Aug. de Civ. Dei, i. xii. c. I.

7 The "mountains" St. Aug. explains of the eminent saints of God, Apostles, &c. in Joann. Tract. i. &c. and in Ps. 35, 7. where (sec. 10.) he thus proceeds. "The 'Abyss' the Psalmist calls the depth of sin, whereat men come by despising God. As 'the mountains of God' are 'His righteousness,' who by His grace become great, so through His judgments come they into the 'deep,' who are sunk to the uttermost. Hereby then take pleasure in the mountains, hereby turn away from the deep and be turned to that which is said, 'my help is from the

Lord.' But whence? Because 'I have lift up my eyes to the mountains.' What is this? I will speak plainly; in the Church of Christ you will find a deep, you will find also mountains; you find there fewer good, for the mountains are few, the deep is large, i.e. many living ill through the wrath of God, because they so acted as to be given over to the desires of their heart, so as now to defend their sins, not confess them, but say, 'Why? What have I done? The one also has done this, the other that.' But thou art not yet a mountain, not yet an abyss; flee the abyss, look well to the mountains, but remain not even in the mountains. 'For thy help is from the Lord, who made heaven and earth.'"

8 "Thence is both the origin and formation and blessedness of the holy City, which is above, in the holy Angels. For if it be asked, whence it is, God founded it; if, whence it is wise, it is by God enlightened; if, whence it is happy, it enjoyeth God. Existing, it receives the mode of its existence; contemplating, it is enlightened; cleaving, it is made joyous; it is, sees, loves; in the eternity of God it liveth; in the truth of God, it shineth; in the goodness of God, it joyeth." Aug. de Civ. Dei, l. xi. c. 24.

9 "He who is blessed, not in another, but in Himself as His own good, therefore cannot be otherwise, because He cannot lose Himself." Id. l. xii. c. I.

10 "Under the name The Beginning, we understand the Son, who is a Beginning not to the Father, but to the creature— created by Himself." Aug. de Gen. ad Lit. l. i. sec. 12.

11 Aug. repeats this nearly in the same words. Ib. sec.13.

12 "The soul enjoys nothing with freedom (libertate), but what it enjoys with freedom from care (securitate). But no one can be without care as to those goods, which against its will it may lose." Aug. de lib. Arb. l. ii. sec. 37.

13 This sentence was generally in the Church Service and Communion. Nor is there scarce any one old Liturgy but hath it, *Sursum corda, Habemus ad Dominum*. [Old Ed.]

14 "Aqua sine substantia." Vulg. "What is that unsubstantial water, but the water of sins which have no substance. For sins have no substance; they have emptiness, not substance, poverty, not substance." Aug. ad loc. sec. 9.

15 "Its very sin being witness, it is convicted of having been created a good nature. For unless it also had been a great good, though not equal to the Creator, the desertion of God, as its light, could not have been its evil. For as blindness is the defect of the eye, and the same indicates that the eye was created to see light, and so that member which is capable of light is shewn even by its very defect to be more excellent, than the other members; so the nature, which enjoyed God, shews that it was formed good even by its very defect, in that it is therefore miserable because it enjoyeth not God." Aug. de Civ. Dei, l. xxii. c. 1.

16 "What place is this? He said not, Thou shalt hide them in Abraham's bosom. Poor be every thing unto you, which is beside God. He who protects us in the place of this life, be, after this life, Himself our place, as the Psalmist said to Him above, 'Be Thou my protecting God and my house of refuge.' We shall be hidden then in the countenance of God. What bosom is there in the face of God, look ye to hear of me? Purify the heart, that He may enlighten, and He, whom you call on may enter in. Be His house, and He will be Thy house; let Him dwell in Thee, and thou shalt dwell in Him. If in this world thou shalt receive Him in thy heart, He after this world will receive thee in His Countenance." Aug. ad Ps. 30, 21. Enarr. 4. sec. 8.

17 "Most rightly is the Holy Spirit, being Himself God, called also the Gift of God. By which gift, what else is properly to

be understood but Charity which leadeth up to God, and without which any other gift of God, leadeth not up to God?" Aug. de Trin. l. xv. c. 18.

18 "The body is borne by its weight, as the soul is borne by love, whithersoever it is borne." Aug. de Civ. Dei, l. xi. c. 28.

19 St. Aug. pursues this illustration elsewhere, not to explain the mystery of the Holy Trinity, but to shew that God "did not leave Himself without witness" in the human mind. "And we recognise in ourselves an image of God, that is, of the Supreme Trinity, not indeed equal, yea far and widely different, not coeternal, and (to express the whole more briefly) not of the same substance with God, yet that, than which, of all things made by Him, none is in nature nearer to God, which image is yet to be perfected by re-formation, that it may be nearest in likeness also. For we both are, and know that we are, and love to be this and to know it. In these three moreover which I have named, no falsehood resembling truth perplexes." Aug. de Civ. Dei, l. xi. c. 26. "As there are in a manner, two things, the mind and its love, when it loves itself; so there are two, in a manner, the mind, and its knowledge, when it knows itself. The mind itself, and its love, and its knowledge are, in a manner, three, and these three are one, and when perfect, are equal. For if its love to itself is inferior to its being, as, for instance, if the mind of man were to love itself, as much as man's body ought to be loved, being more than the body, its love offends, and is not perfect. So if its love to itself is greater than its being, as if it were to love itself as much as God is to be loved, being itself incomparably inferior to God, so also it sins too deeply, and hath not its love of itself perfect. Still more perversely and iniquitously does it sin, when it loves the body as God is to be loved. So knowledge, if it be less than that which is known, and yet may be fully known, is not perfect. But the

mind, when it knows itself, does not surpass itself by its knowledge; for it is it which knoweth, it which is known. When then it knows itself wholly, and nothing else with itself, its knowledge is equal to itself; because neither is its knowledge when it knows itself, of any other nature. And when it perceives itself wholly, and nothing more, it is neither greater nor less. Rightly therefore said we, these three when they are perfect, are consequently equal.—We are likewise given to understand, if we can in any measure see, that these things exist in the soul, and as being involved therein, are evolved so that they may be perceived, and numbered substantially, or, so to speak, essentially, not as colour or figure in a body, or any other quality or quantity. For whatever is of that sort, doth not go beyond the subject, wherein it is. For a certain colour or figure cannot belong to this body, and also to another. But the mind, with that love wherewith it loves itself, can love another thing beside itself. So again the mind does not know itself only, but many other things besides. Wherefore love and knowledge exist not in the mind, as in a subject, but they also exist substantially, just as the mind itself, because although they are spoken of relatively to each other, still they exist each in its own substance.—But in those three, when the mind knoweth and loveth itself, there remaineth a trinity, mind, love, knowledge, and it is not confounded by any intermixture, although each exists in itself, and all mutually in all, or each in the other two, or the other two in each. Therefore all in all. For the mind existeth in itself, since by itself it is called mind, although it is said to be knowing, or known, or knowable relatively to its knowledge; and again loving, or loved, or loveable relatively to the love, wherewith it loves itself. And although knowledge is referred to the mind, which knoweth or is known, yet in relation to itself also, it is spoken of as known or knowing; for that knowledge whereby the mind itself knows itself is not unknown to itself. And love, although it is referred to the mind, as loving, whose love it is, yet it existeth also by itself, so as to be also in itself; because the love is also loved, nor can it be loved by any other than by love, that is, by itself. So then these exist, each in themselves. But they are also each in the other, because in love, there is also a loving mind, and in the knowledge of that which loveth is love, and in the mind which knoweth, knowledge." Aug. de Trin. l. ix. c. 4, 5. St. Augustine pursues further this appeal to the mysterious structure of the human mind, as bearing testimony to, and being a sort of type of, its Maker, in Whose Image it was formed, and as an argument that it should not question about Him, until it understood itself. He sums up by an analogy bearing upon the very depth of that Mystery. "The mind itself, and its knowledge, and love, as the third, is a sort of image of the Trinity; and these three are one, and one substance. Nor is the offspring less (than the parent) since the mind knoweth itself just as much as it is; nor the love less, since it loveth itself, as much as it knoweth and as much as it is."

20 i.e. I conceive, "Each Person in the Blessed Trinity having the attributes of the Others, so that the distinction of Persons whereby They be, in some incomprehensible way, distinguished from Each Other, coalesces in the Unity of the Godhead." Mart. renders, "or whether it be both, so that the Three Persons after an ineffable and incomprehensible manner, blend (allient) infinitely, within themselves, simplicity and multiplicity, whereby the Sovereign Being is, and knows Itself, and suffices to Itself."

21 So that since under the name of "heaven and earth" the spiritual and carnal in the Church are often signified, he shews that the heavens belong to the serene intelligence of truth, saying, "who made the heavens in intelligence"

[wisdom] but "the earth" to the faith of the "little ones," simple but most surely founded on the prophetic and evangelic preaching, which is established by baptism, wherefore he subjoins, "He founded the earth above the water." Aug. de Gen. ad lit. l. ii. sec. 4. cp. Serm. 56. in Matt. vi. sec. 7. and 57. sec. 6.

22 His putting repentance and light together is, for that Baptism was anciently called illumination, as Heb. 6, 4. Psal. 42, 2. [Old Ed.]

23 "This is said on account of Christ Himself, Who in Scripture is continually called a mountain." Aug. de div. Quæst. 83. See b. ix. sec. 5, note 5.

24 What is that "deep which calleth upon deep?" If "deep" means depth, think we the heart of man is not a "deep." For what is deeper than this "deep." Men can speak, can see through the operation of the members, can be heard in discourse; but whose thoughts can be penetrated, whose heart looked into? What he beareth within, what he can within, what he doth within, what he ordereth within, what he willeth within, what he willeth not within, who shall comprehend? I think that man is not ill understood to be the "deep." "Deep calleth upon deep," man upon man. The holy preachers of the word of God "call upon the deep." Are they themselves also not a "deep?" What a depth of infirmity lurked in Peter, when he knew not what passed within him, and he rashly promised that he would die with the Lord, and for the Lord! What a deep he was! Which deep was yet naked to the eyes of God. Therefore every man, although holy, although just, although making proficiency in many things, is a "deep" and "calls upon deep," when he preaches to man, any thing of faith, any thing of truth, unto life eternal. But deep is then useful to the deep which is called upon, when it is done "in the voice of Thy waterspouts." Aug. ad Ps. 41, 8. sec. 13.

25 "He perceives that he sees not what he longs, and yet ceases not to hope. For hope which is seen is not hope. Yet he understandeth why he seeth not, because the night is not spent, i.e. the darkness which sin has described, "Thou," he says, "art not such, as can be seen by those from whose eyes the night of sin has not yet departed; when then the night of my errors is ended, and the darkness depart, which I have made for myself by my sins, Thou wilt hear my voice." Aug. in Ps. 5, 4.

26 See above, note 25. on b. vii. sec. 24.

27 "For we have the authority of the Divine Scriptures, whence our mind ought not to deviate, nor leaving the solid firmament of the Divine speech, be cast headlong down the precipices of its own conjectures, where neither the bodily senses guide them, nor the clear reason of Truth is self-apparent." Aug. de Trin. iii. 10. "God first placed this authority in His Church; then proceeded to execute the rest; for He placed the heaven, and 'stretched it out like a skin.'" Id. in Ps. 103. sec. 8.

28 "The sayings of dead men, because they were not theirs, but through them were His, who 'stretched out the heavens as a skin,' remain to our posterity. For after death the Prophets and Apostles were more widely known; for they were not so known, when they lived; Judæa alone possessed the Prophets when living; dead, all nations. For while they lived, the 'skin' was not yet stretched out, not as yet were the heavens stretched out to cover the whole world." Aug. ib. He variously illustrates this type whereby the "heavens" designate the "ministers of God," on this place, and Ps. 8, 4. sec. 7. Ps. 18, 1. Ps. 32, 6. sec. 4–7. Ps. 146, 8. sec. 15.

29 The Manichees, see above, b. iv. sec. 26.

30 "For the law is therefore read, because we have not yet

come to that Wisdom, which fills the hearts and minds of those who gaze thereon, and there will be no need that any thing should be read to us. For in what is read to us, syllables sound and pass away; that light of truth passes not by, but remaining fixed, inebriates the hearts of the beholders." Aug. in Ps. 93. sec. 6.

31 legunt, eligunt, et diligunt.

32 "God therefore above all things, who created all things, and ruleth all things, createth all things, being Good, ordereth all wills, being Just." Aug. de Gen. ad Lit. I. viii. c. 9. see above, b. 1. c. 10. and b. v. c. 2. notes 2, 3, 4.

33 "'Let the people praise Thee, O God, let all the people praise Thee; the earth brought forth her fruit.' What 'fruit?' 'Let the people praise Thee.' It was 'earth,' it was full of thorns; the uprooting hand approached, there approached the calling of His majesty and mercy, the earth began to 'confess,' then 'the earth gave her fruit.' Should it give its fruit, unless the rain first came down upon it? Should the earth give her fruit, unless the mercy of God came from above?—This then took place, the Lord raining through His words; there took place what we read of in the Gospel; and upon His raining by His clouds, sending the Apostles to preach the truth, the earth further gave her fruit, and that harvest has now filled the earth." Aug. ad Ps. 66, 6. sec. 8.

34 "If we distinguish the two Testaments, the Old and the New, there are not the same Sacraments, nor the same promises, but for most part the same commands. Not the same Sacraments; for Sacraments which impart salvation are different from Sacraments which promise a Saviour. The Sacraments of the New Testament impart salvation, the Sacraments of the Old Testament promised a Saviour. When then you already have the things promised, why seek you the things which promised, since you already have the

Saviour? The Sacraments are changed; they have been made easier, fewer, more healthful, more blessed." Aug. in Ps. 73. sec. 2.

35 "For there are none of these things, which are not necessary in the night of this world, which, when it shall pass away, they will be no longer necessary, therefore are they 'for the rule of the night.'" Aug. in Ps. 135. sec. 8.

36 He alludes to the primitive practice, which admitted not their Catechumenos or unbaptized, to hear the higher points of religion handled, till they were enlightened, that is, baptized; yet these he advised to rest contented with their Catechetical knowledge. [Old Ed.]

37 He alludes to the Sacrament of Baptism. [Old Ed.] The words of Is. 1, 16, are so explained in the ancient Liturgies, and the ancient commentators, and the Fathers generally.

38 "Because he wished to pass from one pleasure to another, and feared to abandon those wherein he took pleasure, he departed, grieved, to his earthly treasures." Aug. Serm. 38. c. 5.

39 "Our Lord God hath in sundry ways and divers manners diffused through the Holy Scriptures that faith whereby we live and whereof we live, varying the sacraments of the words, but inviting us to one faith. For one and the same thing is therefore expressed in different ways, that it may be varied in the form of expression, to obviate satiety, but may be retained the same to preserve harmony." Aug. in Ps. 46. init.

40 He alludes to Baptism in water, accompanied with the word of the Gospel; of the institution whereof, man's misery was the occasion. [Old Ed.]

41 "He means that Baptism, which is the Sacrament of initiation, was not so profitable without the Lord's Supper, which ancients called the Sacrament of perfection, or consummation." [Old Ed.]

42 "And because they abide with unshaken belief in the Baptism, which they have received, therefore it is said, 'He hath established the earth upon the waters.'" Aug. in Ps. 135. sec. 8.

43 "He means Christ; the first letters of whose Names did in Sybiles acrostic verses make up the word ιχθυζ, a fish. He was also resembled by Jonas drawn out of the fish and deep. And Himself was raised from the grave and hell. He is fed upon at the Communion. See also Luke 24, 36. [Old Ed.] "We little fish, are born in water according to our IXΘΥΣ (Ιησους Χριστος Θεου γιος Σωτηρ) Jesus Christ, nor are we safe otherwise than by remaining in the water." Tert. de Bapt. c. X. "This is that Fish, which in Baptism is by the invocation [of the Trinity] brought into the waters of the Font, so that what was water, is from Piscis called Piscina. The name of which, in Greek, comprises in one Name a host of holy Names through its several letters IXΘΥΣ, *i.e.* Jesus Christ, Son of God, Saviour." Optat. cont. Parmen. l. iii. p. 62.

44 See above, b. x. note 20.

45 "There is no life which is not of God, because God is the supreme life, and Himself the fountain of life.—Life, then, which, by a voluntary failure, falleth away from Him Who made it, and Whose Essence it enjoyed, and wishing against the law of God to enjoy things bodily, which God made subject to it, tends towards nothing. For if those things which die, died altogether, they would without doubt come to nothing; but they only die, so far as they partake less of the Essence." Aug. de vera Rel. c. 11.

46 "And what was said to them, 'Have dominion,' &c. (always retaining the plain meaning, that man by reason has dominion over all these animals,) is yet rightly understood also spiritu-ally, that we should keep in subjection all the affections and emotions of the mind, which we have, resembling those

animals, and have dominion over them through temperance and modesty. For when those emotions are not governed, they burst out and lead on to most foul habits, and hurry us along divers and destructive pleasures, and make us like all kinds of brute beasts. But when governed and kept subject, they become altogether tame, and live in harmony with us. For the emotions of our mind are not alien from ourselves. For, together with us, they are fed on the knowledge of grounds, and good moral action, and life eternal, as it were on seed-bearing herbs, and fruit-bearing trees, and green herbs. And this is the blessed and peaceful life of man, when all his emotions are in unison with reason and truth; and these are called joys, and holy, pure, and good loves. But if they are not in unison, (and not less when they are treated negligently,) they rend and dissipate the mind, and make life most miserable; and are called passions, and lusts, and evil concu-piscences. Which we are now enjoined, with all the exertion we can, to crucify in us, until 'death be swallowed up in victory.' For the Apostle saith, 'they who are Christ's, have crucified their flesh with its passions and lusts.'" Aug. de Gen. c. Manich. l. i. c. 20.

47 "That then is the full satiety of souls, that the blessed life, holily and perfectly to know, by Whom you are led into Truth, the Truth Whom thou enjoyest, by Whom thou art united to the highest Existence. Which then shew to those who understand, One God, and One Substance, excluding the vanities of various superstitions." Aug. de Vitâ Beata, sec. 25.

48 See above, sec. 29. not.

49 See above, sec. 21.

50 *Rationalem.* An old epithet to most of the holy things. So, *reasonable service,* Rom. 12, 1. λογικὴν γάλα, 1 Pet. 2, 2. *sincere* milk. Clem. Alex. calls Baptism so, Pedag. l. i. c. 6. And in Constitut. Apost. l. vi. c. 23, the Eucharist is styled, A

reasonable Sacrifice. The word was used to distinguish
Christian mysteries from Jewish. *Rationale ast spirituale.*
[Old Ed.]

51 "Any may suffer want, but to 'know to suffer want'
belongs to great souls. So, abound, who cannot? But to 'know
to abound' belongs only to those whom abundance does not
corrupt." Aug. de Bono Conjug. c. 21.

52 "That is not to be passed over lightly, which is said, 'and
God saw all things which He had made, that they were very
good.' For when He was speaking of individuals, he said
only, 'God saw that it was good;' but when all were spoken
of, it was too little to say 'good,' unless there were added
'very.' For if the several works of God, when they are
considered by thoughtful persons, are found, each within
itself and its kind, to have excellent proportions and
numbers and order, how much more altogether, *i.e.* the
universe itself, which is composed of these several things
collected into one. For all beauty, which consists of parts, is
much more commendable as a whole than in part; as in the
human body, if we commend the eyes only, or the several
other beautiful points, singly and alone, how much more the
whole body, to which all the members, being severally
beautiful, contribute their beauty! so that a beautiful hand,
which being in the body was praised even by itself, if it be
separated from the body, both itself loses its beauty, and the
other parts, without it, are deformed. So great is the force
and power of entireness and unity, that even a multitude of
things, in themselves good, please not until they meet and
harmonize in one universal [one whole]. And 'universal'
indeed hath its name from 'unity,' which, if the Manichees
would consider, they would praise God, the Author and
Maker of the universe; and whatever, being a result of our
mortal nature, does, in any part, offend them, they would

assign its place in the beauty of the whole, and see how God made all things, not only 'good,' but also 'very good.'" Aug. de Gen. c. Man. i. c. 21.

53 "We see these things, and if His Spirit be in us, they will please us in such wise that we shall praise their Maker, not so that turning to the works, we should turn away from the Maker; and setting our face in a manner to the things which He made, turn our backs on Him who made them." Aug. in Joann. Tract. 8. sec. I. See above, b. iv. sec. 18. note 15. and b. x. sec. 53. note 31.

54 "This was not said considerately enough; for the matter is hidden exceeding deep." Aug. Retr. ii. 6.

55 Cf. de Gen. c. Manich. ii. 15.

56 "Concipiendam," or the reading may be "concupiscendam," according to St. Aug.'s interpretation of Gen. 3, 16. in the de Gen. c. Manich. ii. sec. 15. "As an instance hereof was woman made, who is in the order of things made subject to the man; that what appears more evidently in two human beings, the man and the woman, may be contemplated in the one, man; viz. that the inward man, as it were manly reason, should have in subjection the appetite of the soul, whereby we act through the bodily members."

57 "Heavenly peace, which truly is in such wise peace, that it alone should be accounted or called the peace of the rational creature, being the fully ordered, and harmonious society, of enjoying God, and each other in God; whither, when we shall arrive, life will no longer be mortal, but merely and assuredly living; nor shall the body be mortal, which, when 'corrupted presseth down the soul,' but spiritual, without any thing lacking, wholly subdued to the will." Aug. de Civ. Dei, ix. 17.

58 "For as God is rightly said to do, whatsoever we do, He working in us, so is God rightly said to rest, when by His gift we rest." Aug. de Gen. ad Lit. iv. 9.